Isaac Butt, James Hewitt

The Irish People and the Irish Land

A Letter to Lord Lifford

Isaac Butt, James Hewitt

The Irish People and the Irish Land
A Letter to Lord Lifford

ISBN/EAN: 9783744689809

Printed in Europe, USA, Canada, Australia, Japan

Cover: Foto ©Thomas Meinert / pixelio.de

More available books at **www.hansebooks.com**

THE

IRISH PEOPLE

AND THE

IRISH LAND:

A LETTER TO LORD LIFFORD;

WITH COMMENTS ON THE PUBLICATIONS OF

LORD DUFFERIN AND LORD ROSSE.

BY

ISAAC BUTT,

FORMERLY PROFESSOR OF POLITICAL ECONOMY IN THE UNIVERSITY OF DUBLIN;

AND SOMETIME

MEMBER OF PARLIAMENT FOR THE BOROUGH OF HARWICH, IN ENGLAND.

"Whether an indifferent person who looks into all hands be not a better judge of the game than one who sees only his own?"

"Whether a single hint be sufficient to overcome a prejudice? and whether even obvious truths will not sometimes bear repeating?"—BISHOP BERKELEY.)

DUBLIN:
JOHN FALCONER, 53, UPPER SACKVILLE-STREET.
LONDON: W. RIDGWAY, PICCADILLY.

1867.

JOHN FALCONER, Printer, 53, Upper Sackville-street, Dublin.

THE LORD VISCOUNT LIFFORD.

MY LORD,

When your Lordship published the letter which you have done me the honour to address to me* I am sure that you wished for a full, a free, and a fair discussion of the important subject to which it refers. There is no question of deeper interest to every Irishman than that which relates to our system of land tenure. I believe that question capable of adjustment by free and unreserved interchange of thought between the parties interested in its settlement. Whatever, therefore, I may think of the opinions upon landlord right that have been put forward, I cannot but feel it a matter of satisfaction that persons in the position of yourself, Lord Dufferin, and Lord Rosse should come forward and boldly submit their views of their proprietary rights to the criticism and discussion of their countrymen. I gladly avail myself of the opportunity of discussing this question with one so well entitled to represent our best and most improving landlords as yourself.

If this were a question of the practical management of an estate I would feel myself under great disadvantages in a controversy with your Lordship. I might, perhaps, acquiesce in some of the criticisms which have gone so far as to assert that, "upon any question connected with the land question the opinion of a resident and improving proprietor, like Lord Lifford," is quite conclusive against anything that can be said by "a Dublin Nisi Prius Advocate." On the question with which we are now concerned I cannot so readily acquiesce in the argument which makes the landowner an absolute judge in his own cause. I am neither a landowner nor a tenant farmer. I may, perhaps, so far claim exemption from the prejudices of either class. I do not, therefore, admit that I am disqualified from forming an opinion on the relations between them—neither can I admit that my profession unfits me for doing so, although it does require me to know something of the laws which regulate these relations; not even were I also to concede that in my own

---

* *A Plea for Irish Landlords. A Letter to Isaac Butt, Esq., Q.C. By Lord Lifford.*

case I may have the additional disadvantage of having devoted some little industry to the obscure subject of Ireland's history, and of having given some attention to questions connected with economic science.

Indeed, my Lord, I am disposed to think that very often in courts of justice, especially in " Nisi Prius " trials, there is a great opportunity for learning something of what is really passing in the every-day life of all classes in the country. This is peculiarly the case in the political and social disputes which so frequently give rise to litigation before our Irish tribunals. Within the last two years I have taken part in inquiring, in courts of justice, into the management, not of one Irish estate, but of many. I have fought the battle on one side or the other, not of one but of many evictions; I have heard more than one evicted tenant depose to his own wrongs; and more than one landlord, or agent, give his evidence to justify the act. It sometimes happens that the state and condition of the country becomes an element in determining the rights of litigants. The disclosures which are thus incidentally made upon these subjects often afford information of the highest value.* Improperly used it may, of course, lead astray. Like all other

---

* In the Summer of 1865 a case was disposed of before the House of Lords on an appeal from the Irish Court of Chancery which involved, simply, the question, whether the representative of a deceased trustee should be charged with rents, on a county Cork estate, which, it was alleged, the trustee had lost by his negligence in the years immediately preceding, and following 1820. The litigation had been pending many years; it was finally disposed of by the Supreme Tribunal in 1865.

It was from the printed evidence in that case that I first realized to myself the enormous change in the circumstances of all Irish landed property which resulted from the cessation of war prices, and the resumption of cash payments. That evidence consisted largely of contemporary documents, and correspondence dealing with the circumstances of a Cork property about the period of the change.

I believe that if the parties in that case would consent to the publication of that evidence it would throw more light on the causes which led to the insurrectionary movements which disturbed the South of Ireland in 1822 than is supplied by any one publication to which my memory can refer.

I venture also to think, that in the report of the case of Clarke a. Knox, tried at the Tullamore Spring Assizes in March, 1865, an enquirer will gain more information as to the mode and acting of the working of the arbitrary power of eviction than he will in many pages of statistics however carefully and accurately prepared.

A writer in the *Saturday Review* complacently says, of the result of Lord Dufferin's statistics:—"This fact removes a disagreeable picture from the mind's eye; we need no longer dwell upon the smoking ruins of some Irish Auburn, from which the extirpated peasants are picking their melancholy way, in rags and destitution, with many a melancholy look behind."—*Saturday Review*, January 15th, 1867.

These sentences almost seem penned to meet the case of the evictions proved at that trial. I will presently have something to say of Lord Dufferin; but in spite of all his statistics, it is a fact proved in a court of justice, that, in January, 1865, an "Irish Auburn" was levelled by a landlord to the ground. The "smoking ruins" are wanting. The rags were absent, because the tenantry driven out were industrious—up to that eviction even comfortable; but thirteen houses were levelled, if they were not burned— a large force of military and police attended; and under their protection, as the sheriff turned out the inmates of each house, the landlord's servants proceeded to unroof each house, and pull down a portion of the walls, while the furniture of the tenants was flung out upon the road.

I heard these things proved by the tenant, and admitted by the landlord ; and the

information it requires some care and some intelligence to estimate its general effect. But I am sure that we will often find in the proceedings of courts of justice revelations of the minute details of social life, while we would look for it elsewhere in vain. Doubtless, it may often be of little things. But little things, in the aggregate, make up the whole of a people's life.

If it be seriously said, that no one but a landlord or a tenant farmer can take part in this discussion, I answer the objection, exactly as it was answered more than a century ago by Bishop Berkeley in his own case, by asking, in his words:—

" Whether an indifferent person who looks into all hands may not be a better judge of the game than one who sees only his own ? "

Perhaps there is no one to whom the expression—that "he looks into all hands "—may be more appropriately applied than to an advocate, whose professional duty may call him one day to uphold the extreme legal rights of property, and the next day to defend the privileges of the tenant against the encroachment of those rights. Perhaps, too, it may be thought that a disinterested man may have learned something of "all hands," if his inclinations and his position have given him the opportunity of unreserved intercourse with Irishmen of all classes and all creeds.

Without further preface, I come, at once, to the issue, which is raised in your Lordship's letter.

The question between us stands thus:—In a tract which I published a few months ago, I ventured to suggest a settlement of the Irish Land Question.* I proposed that the tenure of every Irish occupier chould be converted into a certain term of 63 years, at a rent to be fixed at the fair letting value of the land, and with covenants which would be effectual to secure all the just rights of the landlord.

tenant who proved them was able to produce his receipts for every gale of rent for the last twenty years, punctually paid within a few months after it fell due. He was able to tell of substantial improvements effected on his farm. He was a well dressed, respectable, and intelligent man. His manly nature gave way as he said that which every one in court knew well, that the eviction left him no alternative but beggary or emigration.

These tenants were evicted solely because the purchaser who bought the landlord's interest insisted on "a clearance," believing that he could more advantageously dispose of his purchase if the estate were "cleared" of human habitations and human beings.—*Report of the Trial of Clarke* a. *Knox, at Tullamore Spring Assizes*, 1865.— James Duffy, Dublin.

If the writer in the *Saturday Review* will read the details which were proved, without controversy, at that trial, the "disagreeable picture" of "the ruins of an Irish Auburn" will never be "removed from his mind's eye."

These are instances of the lessons which even "an advocate" may learn in the discharge of the duties of his profession.

* *Land Tenure in Ireland ; A Plea for the Celtic Race.* Falconer, Sackville-street, Dublin. Page 40. Third Edition.

That proposal you describe as "communistic," as

" Intended, or at least adapted, for the purpose of depriving the Protestant proprietors of all influence over the people—all management of their own estates," and of "all advantage of the increasing value of property arising from the development of the latent power of the land, in which the proprietor surely should be at least a partner with the tenant."

And in contrasting the proposal I have made with a suggestion thrown out by Mr. Bright, you say that—

"Irish contempt of law, and of the rights of property, are paramount in the proposal of the Irish lawyer, while the principle of fair dealing, and the respect of mutual rights, inherent to every Englishman, supersede the rancour of the Saxon man of business. Consequently, Mr. Bright's scheme is comparatively moderate, and is scouted by a Dublin audience. Mr. Butt's proposals are subversive of the rights of property, and no doubt are highly popular."

Before I proceed to examine how far my proposal is deserving of this condemnation, let me invite attention to one expression which I read with regret in any letter bearing your Lordship's name. The phrase, " Irish contempt of law," implies that this contempt is peculiarly the characteristic of the Irish people. No imputation could be more unjust. There does not exist upon earth a people whose instinct more quickly or more truly recognizes the great principles of natural equity, which are, or ought to be, the foundation of all law. Edmund Spencer was not their friend—yet he has left on record the testimony that " no people under the sun better loveth impartial justice." If laws are bad it may happen that, exactly as they respect or love that justice, they may despise or even hate the law. Once reconcile the law with justice, and there is no people that will more quickly appreciate or more readily obey it.

Expressions like that upon which I venture to comment are often used but to give point to a sentence. They are not the less eagerly seized on by those who hold everything connected with our country in contempt. They minister to the insolent prejudice which looks down upon your Lordship as an Irish landlord just as much as it does upon me as an " Irish lawyer," or upon one of your tenants as an Irish peasant.

Passing from this, I meet at once the statements contained in the sentences I have quoted. I deny that the proposal I have made exhibits any " contempt of law, or of the rights of property."

On the contrary, it scrupulously respects those rights.

I deny that I have proposed anything inconsistent with fair dealing, or shown any want of respect for mutual rights.

On the contrary, I propose to enforce fair dealing in matters in which the present law enables every landlord to do wrong, and I propose to make it possible for the Irish tenant to feel "respect for mutual rights" by the indispensable preliminary of securing to him some rights of his own.

And lastly, I deny that it is either intended or adapted to deprive the Protestant proprietors of all influence over the people.

On the contrary, it is intended and adapted to strengthen, or rather create, their legitimate influence, by removing the bitter sources of heart-burning, hatred, and discontent.

I admit that it is intended—it is a total failure if it be not adapted —to deprive a proprietary whom your Lordship correctly designates as Protestant, of a power of dominion and coercion. It is intended to deprive the landlord, whether Protestant or Catholic, of that dominion over his tenant which the odious power of arbitrary eviction enables him to enforce.

I suspect very much that this subject of "influence" or personal dominion over the people, lies at the very root of the question we are discussing, and that resistance to tenant right is far oftener a struggle to maintain a system of vassalage than an effort to preserve any right of property in land.

Your Lordship will be good enough to remember that I did not content myself with general suggestions. I drew up, and embodied in the form of a suggested legislative enactment, the provisions by which my proposal might be practically carried out.* These provisions were—

1st. That every occupier of an agricultural tenement in Ireland should hold for a term of 63 years.

2nd. That he should pay a rent not exceeding the fair letting value of the land.

3rd. That his landlord should have the most summary power of eviction if the tenant failed in paying his rent.

4th. That the tenant should be bound properly to cultivate his farm.

5th. I gave to the landlord the absolute right of prohibiting subdivision.

6th. I reserved to the landlord all royalties and manorial rights, even the objectionable one of entering on the lands in pursuit of game.

7th. And lastly, I conferred on the landlord the power of varying the rent when any accidental circumstances increased the value of the land.

I proposed to compel, by law, every landlord to adopt these rules of letting as binding him in the management of his estate.

---

* *Fixity of Tenure; Heads of a Suggested Legislative Enactment; with Introduction and Notes.* Falconer, Sackville-street, Dublin.

And lastly, I proposed that all these provisions should be merely
temporary—continuing in force for a period long enough to admit
of the creation of an independent class of tenantry, and then leaving
all future dealing in land unfettered by any legislative control.

In answer to the charge of being revolutionary, let me say,
first: that I do not propose by my plan to destroy the class of
estated gentlemen, and substitute for them a peasant proprietary.
This is the object of the plan which your Lordship eulogizes in
contrast with mine. I leave the " Protestant" proprietors in possession of their position and their estates. My plan, if carried out,
would not diminish by a single unit the number of existing proprietors. Whatever be the merits of the system of peasant proprietors, the destruction of the present class of landed gentry, either
in England or in Ireland, would be a revolution in our social and
political system.

Secondly, I pray you to observe that I propose to enforce a
system of management which surely is not unknown on Irish estates.
A lease for 63 years is not a thing utterly novel or unheard of.
We know of landlords having tenants holding by such leases, who
are very far from regarding themselves as entirely deprived of all
power or influence over their estates.   Such leases were common
in days when Irish landlords had far more influence than they have
now.   In settlements most strictly entailing property the power to
make these or similar leases is constantly reserved.   It never occurred
to any conveyancer that, in reserving to the first owner the power
of leasing the property at a fair rent, he was enabling that owner
to deprive all who were to follow him of all right of property over
the estate.

It may be right or wrong to make such leases for every landlord
by legislative enactment: but, most certainly, if we do so we would
be very far from depriving him of all control over his estate.

We would place the landlord, in fact, in the position of one
whose father had exercised this very power under a marriage settlement, and whose estate is therefore held by tenants holding by long
leases at a moderate rent.   We have a known and not unusual
condition of proprietorship, which we can compare with the present
position of a proprietor who has let his estate to tenants holding
from year to year, and we can see, by the comparison, of what powers
the latter would be deprived, by such a measure as I propose.
Only of the powers of exacting an exorbitant rent, of seizing on
his tenant's improvements, and of evicting that tenant whenever
he pleased !   We may, indeed, sum up all in one—we would take
from him the power of arbitrary eviction !

The circumstances of Ireland are such, that this power of arbitrary
eviction in the hands of the landlord gives him, over his tenant,
a dominion, compared with which the heaviest yoke of feudal vassalage was light.   To evict a tenant in Ireland is, in nine instances

out of ten, to reduce him to beggary—it is to deprive him of the means of living—to send him to the workhouse—or to drive him from his native land. The farm he holds is the only mode in which he can exercise his industry or work for his own or . his children's bread. The man who can deprive him of this at his will and pleasure is and must be his master by a law more absolute and exacting than that which gives the slave owner the mastery over his slave. If there were a man whose capricious order could shut me out from the exercise of my profession without giving any reason or being called to any account, that man would be my master. The power of eviction over the Irish tenant is far more coercive. Shut out from the exercise of his profession, the tilling of the soil, the tenant whom his landlord drives out has nothing else to which he can turn. Emigration, beggary, or the poorhouse, constitute the whole choice of the future to which he is to look. It is by no means unusual for him to make acquaintance with the bitterness of all three.

I may venture to ask your Lordship whether I have exaggerated the effect of the power of eviction? This is a point upon which the personal testimony of a resident proprietor might give us information upon a subject upon which he has a peculiar right to be heard. The statistics of emigration and eviction are just as open to me as to Lord Dufferin. Neither he nor your Lordship have the slightest advantage over me in tracing or in estimating the effects of past misgovernment and oppression. But if your Lordship were to assure me that I am quite mistaken in my judgment of the effect of an eviction—that it was something which the tenant regarded with no terror, and which left him just as happy and comfortable as before—if you were to tell me, according to the views of those who hold the doctrine of " commercial ownership," that whenever a landlord turned out a tenant, the evicted tenant would find two or three other landlords eagerly running after him, and offering " their wares for sale" in the shape of well furnished farms to let—if you were to bear your testimony that tenants in Donegal could change their farms with as little . inconvenience as a visitor to Dublin could migrate from one hotel or one lodging to another; then, indeed, I would say, that the testimony of a resident proprietor upon matters within his own peculiar knowledge had thrown a wholly new light upon the question, and I for one, upon such testimony, would re-examine—if that testimony were confirmed, I would modify, all the opinions I have formed.

We know that no resident proprietor ever will give such testimony as this. In the case of the great majority of Irish tenants, the man who holds over them the power of eviction holds their very life and existence in his hands. It is absurd to speak of commercial dealing, of mutual rights, of the laws of political economy, between men who stand to each other in such a relation as this.

It is a relation of pure serfdom without any of the mitigations with which old feudalism tempered the condition of the serf.

Upon this vital point of the question no Irish landlord who has written upon the land question has touched. What is the true position of the Irish tenant who holds his farm subject to be turned out at the will and pleasure of his landlord? Is that power of eviction a mere abstract right, really exercising no influence, because neither landlords or tenants ever think of its being enforced? or is it a terror constantly hanging over the occupier—ever present, at least in possibility, to his mind, paralyzing his exertions, and reducing him to complete dependence upon the absolute master of his fortune and his life? This is the great question of fact that lies at the very foundation of all discussion on land tenure, and upon this question every landlord advocate has been silent.

Is it not too notorious to be denied—is it not tacitly conceded and admitted, that the condition of the Irish tenant is now one of complete dependence upon his landlord? It is more than admitted by your Lordship. You justify it—and you complain of my proposal as intended to destroy the influence of the Protestant proprietors by depriving them of this personal dominion.

If the rights of property have been so exercised—if they are so exercised as to bring about between landlord and tenant this state of slavery and dominion—then we must ask of ourselves—is Ireland in such a state that the landed proprietor should possess this control and dominion over the people? and then it is that it becomes necessary to take into our account all the causes of antagonism which are still living and active principles in our social condition. No one can understand the Irish land question who will not trace the effects of our past history upon the present position of the landed proprietors of the country. It was, therefore, my Lord, that I ventured on that historical review, of which I do not understand your Lordship to dispute the substantial truth. I demonstrated, I am bold to say, in that review—I demonstrated, that to place in the hands of the landed proprietors of Ireland a personal dominion over the population is nothing more or less than to enforce against the people the most odious and extreme rights of conquest—" to keep," if I may repeat the expression, " the sword of Oliver Cromwell suspended over every peasant's door." That argument is certainly not answered until some better reply is given to it than to say, with Lord Dufferin, that I " antedate the responsibilities of the landlords." I say that no intelligent man can carefully read the history of Irish confiscations—can trace the effect of these confiscations upon all our social relations, and realize to his own mind the light in which proprietary rights are regarded by the mass of the people, and by the landlords, without coming to the conclusion that it is little short of insanity to expect peace or contentment in Ireland so long as the occupiers are kept in a position of serfdom to the owners of the soil. I repeat now that which I have already written, all references to past history are utterly valueless upon this question, unless as they throw light upon our present condition. But no man can understand that condition unless he has studied and taken into account the causes and the influences which have produced it.

The fact that the great mass of the people are serfs to proprietors whom they regard as aliens "in blood, in religion, and in race," lies at the very root of all the miseries of Ireland. It is necessary to alter our system of land tenure, because that system has created and is perpetuating that serfdom.

You have not, I venture to say, done justice to this argument, expanded as it is, in the *Plea for the Celtic Race*, when you represent me as attributing the necessity of such a change either to emigration or Fenianism. I distinctly disclaimed any such opinion. I regarded both emigration and Fenianism as proofs of the discontent of the Irish nation with our present land laws. I expressly said that they both " only revealed to us the importance which always belonged to the subject."* Emigration has actually relieved the misery which our land laws have occasioned. Fenianism has only manifested the power and depth of feelings which have always existed in the hearts of the people. The necessity for a change in our land laws lies in the circumstances which prevail in Ireland, and which surround Irish proprietary right. That necessity would be still greater if there were no emigration. The discontent of the people existed long before Fenianism was heard of. It preyed like a canker upon the prosperity of our country. It found its expression in all the secret societies, the real object of which was to control the arbitrary power of landlords by punishing their real or supposed tyranny by the penalties inflicted by agrarian crime.

Neither, my Lord, is it correct to say, that while I " stated broadly the sympathy of the whole population with those who would down with landlordism," I " omitted to state that there is equal sympathy with those who would down with the British Crown." Unhappily, my Lord, the latter assertion is true. But it is true just because the people identify British power with " landlordism "—I adopt the expression—which British power forces on the country. I certainly never meant to conceal the fact that the Irish people are disaffected to the British Crown. On the contrary, I used the existence of that disaffection as the strongest argument for the wisdom of conciliating their attachment by some measure that would protect them in the right to live upon their native soil.

In my view, the argument for the necessity of protection to the Irish tenant may be condensed into two or three short propositions. First.—The operation of our present system of land tenure acting

* *Land Tenure in Ireland.* Page 8, Third Edition.

on the peculiar circumstances of Ireland is to reduce the great mass of the Irish tenantry to a condition of dependence upon the landlord so complete as to be justly described as a state of serfdom.

Second.—The circumstances and condition of Ireland, of its landed proprietors and of its people, are such as to make this condition of serfdom in a large proportion of the people, one disastrous to the peace, the prosperity, and the improvement of the country.

Third.—There is no rational prospect of remedying this state of things except by some legislative interference for the protection of the tenant.

I will not now repeat the arguments by which I endeavoured to illustrate and support these propositions, or propositions to the same effect. I am sure that there is not any one who really knows the state of Ireland who will deny the first; no one who has intelligently studied the past and present history of the country will, I apprehend, entertain much doubt as to the other two.

Let me however observe that the argument against the present condition of things assumes a double form. It rests partly on political and social considerations, partly on economic grounds.

To the first I have already adverted. I believe that, considering the past history and present circumstances of Ireland, we must come to the conclusion that it is fatal to the peace and contentment of the country to permit the landed proprietors to exercise a personal dominion over the occupiers of the soil.

But I further believe that even were it abstractedly desirable that such dominion should exist, the process by which it is attained is one which is fatal to the improvement and most injurious to the wealth of the country.

That process is by retaining in the hands of the landlord the power of evicting the tenant whenever he pleases. The existence of this power involves insecurity of tenure on the part of the tenant. Insecurity of tenure makes improvement by the tenant hopeless. He never will expend his money or his toil upon improving his farm unless he has an assurance that he will enjoy the benefit of these improvements.

This is peculiarly mischievous in a country in which landlords do not let their farms in an improved state, but leave it to their tenants to supply even those permanent appliances which are absolutely necessary for the cultivation of the farm.

To complete the picture of the dependence of the Irish occupier we must regard him as placed, as not unfrequently happens, upon a farm upon which he has either partly or entirely to erect a dwelling-house—to construct some miserable sheds that cannot deserve the name of offices—it may be in addition to this to make some roadway to his house and erect or improve a fence to separate him from the high road or his neighbour, and to do all this almost as the condition of his living—without a tenure of the land which gives him the slightest security that the first time he offends his landlord he will not be turned out, or that he will not be compelled, as soon as his landlord thinks he is able to do it, to pay an increased rent.

The political and social, and the economic evils react upon each other. But speaking solely of the economic argument, I venture to say that there is not a maxim to be found, or a doctrine laid down in the writings of any political economist from Adam Smith to the present day which implies that such a state of things is not most injurious in its effects upon the national wealth of the country. All the established principles of the science lead necessarily to the conclusion that it is so.

If these things be so, we must then consider what are the effects of an arbitrary power of eviction in the hands of the Irish landlords—estimating these effects not by any abstract theories, but by the actual circumstances of the country?

They are these:—

The existence of this power reduces the Irish occupiers to a state of serfdom, placing them under the dominion of proprietors, between whom and the mass of the people there exists no sympathy of feeling.

The exercise of this dominion by such proprietors over such a population is the fruitful source of quarrels, ill feeling, and discontent.

This power of arbitrary eviction further places the tenant in such a position of insecurity as to take away from him all motive for the improvement of his farm.

The farms in Ireland are generally let in such a state that all improvement must be effected by the industry of the tenant.

The want of security that he will enjoy the fruits of his industry is calculated to take away from the occupier every incentive to prudence and to thrift—to deprive him of the opportunity of exercising the habit of devoting his energies to the production of remote results instead of present enjoyment—a habit which one of the most sagacious of political economists has well described as one of the great instruments in the creation of national wealth.* These are

---

* The common language of political economy describes the three instruments of production as land, capital, and labour. For capital Mr. Senior proposed to substitute the word "abstinence," using it as denoting that exercise of will and power by which each person performs the operation of devoting his command over resources to the purpose of remote results instead of immediate enjoyment.

Any one who has really considered all the fallacies and the confusion which have followed from propositions supposed to state truths or arguments of political economy, by the use of this most uncertain and deceitful word "capital," must feel that in this proposal Mr. Senior does a service to the cause of science which has never been sufficiently appreciated or perhaps understood.

I have read a very philosophic argument, in which it is said "There are three great instruments of the production of wealth—land, labour, and capital. Ireland has but two. The importation of English capital is therefore the only remedy for her present state."

I venture to say that the writer of this argument could not assign to the word

evils which follow from the very existence of the power. In its practical exercise it creates more.

It has enabled—it is constantly enabling—wicked or tyrannical, or even careless landlords, by driving out the people from their homes, to cause an amount of human misery and suffering—the extent of which in all its consequences it is not easy to estimate.

And it is every day enabling sordid or unprincipled landlords to seize on the property which the industry of his tenant has created— to do so, always in violation of natural justice, sometimes under circumstances of treachery and fraud.

If this be a correct representation of the state of things which actually exists, is it too much to say that our system of land tenure is largely responsible for the disaffection of the people? for the hostility between classes? for the neglected state of our resources? for our national misery, poverty, and discontent?

To adduce all the instances by which these things can be proved would be to fill many volumes. It would need to photograph every Irish peasant's home. In the tract on land tenure I have cited some few instances chiefly because they were within my own personal knowledge. Even from that source I could add to them many more. To one who, like your Lordship, is a resident in the county of Donegal, within a morning's drive of the romantic solitudes of Glenveagh, I want no instance to prove that under our law a landlord has, and sometimes at least exercises, the power of exterminating at his own will and pleasure, a whole community—of levelling a whole hamlet, and leaving a whole country side desolate of all human inhabitants except his game-keepers and the attendants on his sheep. Try and sum up in your own mind the miseries which that one clearance caused—bring before you the naked and starving children that shivered as, in the depths of winter, they were turned out upon the road—the homes that were desolated—the agonies that wrung the hearts of those simple mountaineers as they saw the roof-tree of the dwelling of their fathers tumbled down! I forbear to pursue the picture or to follow the miserable groups of human beings who wandered out homeless and hopeless from that

---

"capital" any clear or distinct meaning, so as to give to his proposition any accuracy of statement, such as to make it a fit subject for really scientific discussion.

Its fallacy is exposed at once if we adopt Mr. Senior's phraseology—Ireland has abundance of land, or rather, to use Mr. Senior's words, "natural agents" in the un-developed fertility of her soil, and she has abundance of the second instrument of production in the labour of her hardy population. The third instrument of production is an appropriation of the resources at our command to permanent or remote results. This instrument of production is in the hands of every farmer who devotes, or is willing to devote, his industry to draining a piece of wet land upon his farm. It is more than "capital"—it is the creation of capital. Like all our sources of wealth— like our land and our labour, it continues unproductive because our system of land tenure will not permit the staple industry of the country to be exercised with any assurance that "remote results" will be enjoyed by the man whose industry creates them.

once happy glen. Bring these things to your mind! multiply these miseries by all the evictions of the last twenty years! and then with your kind and generous heart defend our present system of land tenure if you can!

Believe me, my Lord, that if ever there be written a history of the Irish evictions of the last twenty years—and that history will be written if men will insist on upholding the power which caused them—there will be disclosed to the indignation of mankind scenes of human misery and of the cruelty of man to his fellow, which will kindle up feelings in the excitement of which even proprietors like your Lordship must share the hatred which will be visited on all proprietary rights.

I know—I feel how unjust this would be; and it was exactly because I knew and felt how unjust it would be, that in the tract on land tenure I abstained, as far as possible, from writing one line which was calculated to excite popular feeling against Irish proprietors as a class. I almost weakened my argument to avoid this. If I had not so tempered and measured my language I might have won from the passionate and the unthinking that popularity which your Lordship supposes I have gained. I wrote not to excite or exasperate popular feeling, but to win over the judgment of rational and moderate men.

It was enough for me then—it is enough for me now—to say, that the power of arbitrary eviction has been exercised, and is exercised under circumstances of cruelty or injustice, frequently enough to make that power the source of misery and discontent; frequently enough to make every Irish tenant feel and know that he has no reliable security that it will not, one day or other, be employed against himself.

If this be the condition of the relations connected with our land tenure, the next question is—Is THAT CONDITION TO BE PERMANENT? When this question is answered I will ask again—has any man ever pointed out, can any man point out, a hope of its being altered in the present course of things, unless by a process which numbers as one of its essential conditions the extermination of the greater portion of the present occupiers of the soil?

I am not bringing a charge against any man—I am calmly examining, as a matter of fact, the prospects of improvement which are held out to us. So far as I have read the publications which present to us these prospects, they, one and all, contemplate a large additional emigration of the people. This is the question between those who oppose legislation by presenting to us such prospects, and those who argue that by legislation we may find the means of keeping the people at home. The question, no doubt, is a large one—it involves many that come home to the heart and the conscience of every man. Foremost among them is one of justice. Is our duty fulfilled to the people that have been reared upon our soil

when we drive them from their native land? The law of England
claims these people wherever they go as the subjects of the
Queen. It would visit with the penalties of treason any one of
them who engaged in the service of the country that protects
him if that country were at war with England. Are we, the
educated classes of this country, prepared to tell the Irish people
that Ireland is no place for them to live in? Are you, the
landlords of Ireland, ready to make to the people this avowal? Is
the English Government ready to venture on this declaration, one
without precedent in the history of governments? Another question
still remains—is it to be expected that the Irish people, "the
Celtic race," * will tamely submit to a law which dooms them to
extermination from their native land? Will impartial history
hereafter say that they ought?

I do not believe that the proposal will be seriously maintained
that we are to wait for the prosperity of Ireland until the Irish
nation is driven out. I may, at least, presume that men like
your Lordship—men of kind heart and liberal views—will desire to
see the rights of property reconciled with the right of the people
to live in their native land.

Then, my Lord, I ask you—if it be intolerable to think that our
present condition should continue perpetually unchanged—if we
shrink from the statement which tells us that it will be remedied
when it has driven out the present occupiers of the soil; what
remains but some legislative interference which may arrest our
present course, and turn us, if I may use the expression, into a
different groove?

I have no difficulty in discovering the historic causes which
make this interference absolutely necessary. I give no weight to
theoretic arguments which tell me that all things are best regulated
by the operation of natural laws. The truth is, that the condition
of land tenure in Ireland has not, for the last two centuries, been in
a "natural" state. It is not so now. A country, of which the
landed property was tossed as a prey to be scrambled for by
"adventurers" and "soldiers who claimed arrears of pay," had its
whole system of land tenure violently disturbed from its natural
course. That disturbance has never yet settled down. There
has not been the opportunity. The provisions of "the settlement" intended to prevent the very state of things which has
arisen, were wholly neglected and set at nought. Other causes
have perpetuated to the present day the disturbing influences of
confiscation and conquest. Want of means on the part of the new
possessors prevented them from putting their estates into order.

---

* I have been taken to task for speaking of the occupiers as constituting the Celtic
race. They do so—mingled as they are in blood with the Saxon—the great mass of
the Irish population still represent in religion, in feeling, in habits, and in race, the
old inhabitants of the land.

The degradation of the old population enabled them to use that population as slaves. Their successors were all brought up to disregard the obligations on the faith of which they held their estates. Seven generations of these proprietors have passed away without effecting any improvement on their estates. All that has been done in the way of improvement has been done by the industry and labour of the occupiers of the soil. The instances in which this is not the case have been so few as to constitute no appreciable exception to the rule. The worst of all is, that the evils of the state following on conquest and confiscation, have become chronic. A serfdom has grown up which, if we do not interfere with it, will for ever perpetuate itself. To get rid of it we must go back to the beginning and undo, if necessary with a strong hand, the neglects and the errors which attended the original settlement of a new proprietary in the country. I will show you presently that it is only necessary to enforce against the representatives of these proprietors a *bona fide* observance of the conditions of their grants.

But this review of our history is not necessary for the particular argument upon which I am now engaged. I cannot too often repeat that the transactions of past days would have nothing to do with this question if they did not enter as living, and moving, and actually present elements into our existing social state. I return to the statement that, except when the people are exterminated, there is no prospect that without some legislative interference the present miserable condition of our land tenure can come to an end.

This much at least almost all men now concur in admitting, that there must be some legislation on the Irish land question. Your Lordship proposes a change in the law which would give the tenant compensation for improvements when made with the landlord's consent. Lord Rosse would extend to Ireland the Scotch statute known as "The Montgomery Act." The late ministers had a measure of tenant right, not going so far as Lord Derby's measure of 1852, to which even Lord Dufferin, under certain terms, is willing to assent. The present ministers are about to legislate on the subject.* Suggestions innumerable have been offered in letters, in articles, and the press. One Irish landlord, objecting strongly to fixity of tenure, is willing to concede, as a substitute, that no tenant should be evicted except after a six years' notice to quit.† Conviction has been forced upon the minds of all men that there must be some legislative interference with the system of land tenure in Ireland.‡

---

* These sentences had been printed before Lord Naas introduced the promised measure of the Cabinet of Lord Derby. In the closing pages of this letter will be found a few observations both on this measure and on that proposed by Mr. Fortescue last year.

† Letter of "An Irish Landlord" in the *Irish Times* of January 21st.

‡ Among the measures already submitted to Parliament is a bill brought in during

I had been perfectly convinced of this long before I ventured to offer a definite proposal to the public. In considering the question I came to three conclusions, in which I may hope your Lordship will agree with me.

First.—A measure should be passed which would finally settle the question by effectually remedying the evils which now exist.

Second.—That it should interfere as little as possible with our existing system of landed property.

Third.—That it should not, without the clearest necessity, take from the landlord any right which he now possesses.

There is, indeed, another consideration which must be present to the mind of every person dealing with this question. No measure ought to be proposed unless it places the occupiers in as good a position as that held by the Ulster tenant in districts where the custom of tenant right is observed. In the first place, if you fall short of this you do not do equal justice to all. In the next place you run a great risk of depriving the northern tenant of the custom, and reducing him to the privileges, which you establish by law. Such a law would supply a plausible pretext for the destruction

last session, and introduced in the present session by Sir Colman O'Loghlen and Mr. Gregory. This bill provided that whenever a tenancy was created without a written agreement it should operate in law as a tenancy for 21 years.

I am very far from saying that objections might not be urged against the adoption of such a measure. In my view it would be far, very far, from even touching the evils of our present system. But the very proposal of such a measure by the men who have made it shows how deeply the necessity of security of tenure has impressed itself upon thoughtful and intelligent minds.

I recognize in this attempt the old, and, as I believe, the fruitless effort to steal in the principle of security of tenure without trenching on the landlord's absolute dominion. I am quite sure that all such attempts are vain. I do not, therefore, the less respect those who make them.

I have not noticed among the measures intended for the settlement of the Irish land question the proposal of Mr. Bright for the purchase of the estates of some Irish absentee proprietors, regranting them in lots to the occupying tenants.

It would be doing the greatest injustice to that proposal to treat it as one intended for the general settlement of the Irish land question. It is one dealing with a political question as to the advisability of introducing into the country a class of peasant proprietors. If adopted it could only have, of course, a limited operation, and would leave the great mass of the Irish tenantry exactly in the condition in which they now are.

That proposal was plainly never meant as a substitute for general legislation between landlord and tenant, but as a partial and cautious attempt to break down the system of great landed estates by trying the experiment of a peasant proprietary upon a small scale.

Whatever opinion may be formed of that proposal, it is obviously one which leaves the question discussed in this letter and in the tract on Land Tenure perfectly untouched. Its adoption would not in the slightest degree supersede the necessity of a general measure such as I suggest. The passing of such a general measure would not interfere with the carrying into effect of the proposal of Mr. Bright. The two proposals are distinct in their object, and the adoption of either could neither interfere with or supersede the other.

The same observation may be applied to another proposal, which has found many advocates, that of giving the tenant a compulsory power of purchasing the fee-simple of his farm.

of a custom which, in too many instances, is already stealthily undermined.

It did occur to me that all these conditions would be fulfilled by an enactment compelling every landlord to regard each existing tenant as holding under a lease for 63 years at a fair rent—a tenure perfectly well known in the management of estates—a tenure under which some tenants in Ireland still actually hold—a tenure not exceeding that which tenants-for-life have constantly the power of creating so as to bind their successors.

Of course I do not mean to say that this is not an interference with the present rights of the owner of property—that is, with the absolute right which he now exercises, of dealing with his land exactly as he pleases, subject only to the engagements into which his predecessors in the proprietorship have entered. The admission of the necessity of any legislation presupposes that there is to be some such interference. The question is no longer one of principle, but one of degree. I believe that the very first requisite of any interference is that it should be effectual. Nothing can be more mischievous than abortive legislation; the passing of measures which will still leave evils unremedied, and grievances unredressed. It will but inflame the difficulties of the subject to adopt legislation which will excite hopes only to disappoint them. The landlords are deeply interested that if any remedy be applied it should be one that will be effectual and complete.

I confess, my Lord, I cannot see how we can really redress the evils arising from the serfdom of the occupier, and the insecurity of his tenure, unless we place him in the position of a tenant, holding by a long lease and at a rent which it is not in the landlord's power to fix. To enact that every landlord must let his lands on lease, but to leave it in his power to insert in that lease a rent as exorbitant as he chose, would appear to me to give him the power of making the whole measure absolutely nugatory. If it be once conceded that we ought to compel the landlord to give his tenant a secure tenure, it follows, of necessity, that we must also oblige him to give it at a rent which the tenant can pay. An ejectment for non-payment of rent is just as effectual a disturbance of tenure as an ejectment upon notice to quit. The man is equally a serf who holds his land upon a condition which he cannot perform, as he who holds it directly at his landlord's pleasure. Indeed, the tenant who is bound by lease to an exorbitant rent, is practically in a worse position than a tenant-at-will.

Now, my Lord, bearing these principles in mind, I will ask of your Lordship to take up the bill which I have sketched, and waiving objections to details which may be, and which probably are imperfect and even faulty, and considering only the purport of its provisions, I ask of you, is it possible effectually to remove the evils of insecurity of tenure with less interference with the landlord's

rights, or in a manner more consistent with the territorial arrangements of our social system?

I propose to bind the estate of every landlord by the very
engagements by which, under many of the most strict entails, his
father, although only owning the estate for life, might have bound
that estate if he pleased.

I take away from the landlord the power of arbitrary eviction.
I consequently take away from him the power of extorting an
exorbitant rent, and the power of confiscating the improvements
effected by the industry of the tenant.

I admit, also, that I take away from him the "influence," or, as
I say, the dominion and coercion, which is or are attendant on a
power of eviction in a country in which eviction is in most instances
a sentence consigning the evicted to beggary and ruin.

Throwing aside for a moment the question whether the State
ought to tolerate the use of proprietary rights for the purpose of
holding the people in a state of personal serfdom, let us deal with
the question of property.

For what honest purpose of property can the power of eviction
be used which is not fully provided for in the measure I propose?

I am sure your Lordship would indignantly disclaim the intention of ever using it for the purpose of exacting an extortionate
rent, or of seizing on the improvements effected by the hard toil of
the tenant.

For what legitimate purpose of property is it then required?

Is it to enforce the obligation to pay the rent? I give you
remedies more stringent than any you now possess.

Is it to enforce the due cultivation of the farm? My measure
leaves it with you for this purpose unimpaired.

Is it to discharge that which your Lordship considers "one of
the first duties of property"—"to take care that his farms are not
so subdivided as to be unable to support a family?"

For this purpose I leave it with you.

Is it even to secure to the landlord "a partnership with the
tenant" in "the advantage by the increasing value of property
arising from the development of the latent powers of the land?"

I have aimed at securing even this, by providing for a periodical
revision of the rent.

If all objects connected with the rights and legitimate purposes
of property be provided for, the struggle must be to keep the
power of eviction in order to retain in the landlord that more than
feudal dominion which is enforced by the exercise of that power.
To this dominion I do not believe the Irish people ever will tamely
submit. There never will be peace in Ireland while it exists. The
old feud never will be forgotten while the people are made to feel
that their right to live in their own country is held at the mercy of
those who represent the rights of confiscation and conquest. There

never will be improvement or prosperity in Ireland so long as the occupiers of the soil are serfs.

I feel how difficult it is to reason with a person in your Lordship's position upon such a question as this. I assume that you now have over the tenantry on your estate the dominion which the power of eviction gives. I ask you to lay it down.

It is difficult so to reason exactly in proportion to the merit which belongs to your Lordship for "having made the improvement of your tenantry the laborious object of your life." If I could charge your Lordship with having used your dominion for purposes of oppression or wrong; if I could accuse you of ever having seized on the property of your tenant's industry; or if I could even say that you have contented yourself with exacting your rents heedless of the duties which those who have station, and property, and education, owe to their dependents—then I would have comparatively little difficulty in proving to you that you ought not to have this power.

In your case assertions like these would be not only untrue, but the direct contrary of the truth. Many years have separated me from the district in which you have become a resident, but I have sufficient interest in it to learn something of what is passing, and I know that your presence has been a great good. You have yourself reclaimed and cultivated the mountain wilds, and you have taught—I do not believe you ever had occasion to coerce—your tenantry to do the same. Honestly and laboriously you have devoted yourself to the improvement of the people among whom you live. Nay, more, my Lord, I may admit that the very dominion I assail has been in your hands the instrument of good, which possibly, in some rare instances, you could not have effected without it, or at least effected only at the cost of great additional labour and trouble. The more honestly and successfully you use your power over your tenants the stronger is the temptation to persuade yourself that it ought to be left with your class.

Believing as I do that free government is the greatest boon that can be conferred upon a nation, I have sometimes speculated why there is no instance in history of an absolute sovereign voluntarily conferring it upon his people. The very best and wisest of such sovereigns has too easily persuaded himself that to part with his absolute dominion would only be to deprive himself of the power of carrying out wise and enlightened legislation. Perhaps there is no man among us who has really wished to benefit his country, who has not some time or other wished he were a dictator. I can well understand that your Lordship desires to retain the power which you are conscious you use only in the effort to do good.

And yet, even if the question were one wholly between landlords like your Lordship and their tenants, I still would desire to see the tenants independent. Believe me if they were so we would lose nothing of all that can be effected by your influence for good. I have confidence in the power of intelligence, in the influence of example, in the authority of station. There is no people so easily swayed by such influences as the Irish. Ancient lineage and high position have over them a power which to those who are not fortunate enough to possess these advantages appears to be undue. When combined with high character and benevolence and kindliness of disposition, the power of these things is immeasurably increased. Were all your tenantry independent your real influence would not be less, even though you advised where you can now direct, and persuaded where now you command.

And even in such instances may I not suggest that after all the personal character of his landlord is but a poor security for the tenant. The best of men are not exempt from the influences of passion, of caprice, and of mistake. It is not certain that the good landlord may not part with his estate. It is certain that, one day or other, he must die. Who is to answer for the character of the purchaser or successor? The cruellest cases of evictions which I have known were upon estates on which the tenantry had lived happily under the old proprietor, but a purchaser ruthlessly expelled them from their homes. I have known instances of oppression where " the good old Irish gentleman" was gathered to his fathers, and a distant relative succeeded to the estate. The best of landlords, who leaves his tenants in a state of serfdom, has no security that the homesteads which have risen under his fostering care may not one day be desolated by the exterminator. Of one thing, too, I am sure, that while a landlord keeps his tenantry in subservience and subjection, whatever else he may teach them, he cannot teach them the great lesson of independence, he cannot train them in the qualities of manliness, and self-reliance, which are the springs of industry and enterprise. He cannot teach them the best lesson of all, that of being able to do without his aid.

Let me add to what I have said that many, very many, of the instances in which the property created by the industry or capital of the tenant has been seized, have occurred where tenants have made these improvements upon the faith of their landlord's character; but on the death of that landlord the next successor to the estate has considered himself at liberty to disregard all the engagements, implied or expressed, of his predecessor.

But, my Lord, unhappily the question is not between landlords like your Lordship, and their tenants. It is a question generally between the Irish proprietors and the Irish occupiers of the soil. I am not, as your Lordship has done me the justice to observe, the assailant of the Irish landlords. There are among them many, very many, high-minded and humane men. I am also sure that there are among them many who are sordid, or cruel, or tyrannical, or unjust. There are many, perhaps the most numerous class, who do not deserve any of these characters, but who yield themselves almost as involuntary agents to the influences by which their position surrounds them. I regard the Irish landlords as neither better nor worse than other people. I take them just as all our knowledge of human nature might lead us to expect to find them.

But, my Lord, our experience of human nature tells us that in all the relations of life the characters and the conduct of men are moulded and formed by the circumstances in which they are placed. There is in the Irish gentry an hereditary distrust of the Irish people. They are taught from their youth up to believe in "Irish contempt of law, and of the rights of property." The people reciprocate the hostile feelings of the gentry. I have already described, and traced to its cause, this miserable estrangement of classes. I have no wish to dwell upon the picture. It is enough to say that this mutual estrangement and distrust exist. They exist with a universality and intensity which it requires a close observation of what is passing in Irish society to understand.* Judging by the feelings with which they regard each other, I believe the Irish proprietors to be altogether unfitted—if, indeed, any men could be fit—to exercise the dominion of vassalage over the Irish people.

All things of this nature must be judged with reference to the habits, the feelings, and even the passions and prejudices that prevail in any country. You cannot deal with human beings as machines that are to move as you think they ought to move. So long as the Irish peasant feels himself in the absolute power of an alien proprietor he never will think that the oppression of the

* I may, perhaps, be forgiven for mentioning one of those "little things" which yet make up a very large portion of the daily life of Irish Society.

Not very long ago a deputation from a tenantry of an estate waited on me for the purpose of being advised whether they could resist certain conditions which their land-lord was enforcing under the penalty of the dreaded notice to quit.

I was obliged to tell them that they had no alternative but to "go out" or to submit. I well remember the emphatic bitterness with which a fine respectable looking old man among them exclaimed—"And all the time, sir, he will come out and say to us, I know you are all a pack of d—d Fenians, and, smooth as you speak, there is not one of you that would not cut my throat."

"I never heard," I replied, "that Fenianism made its way into your district."

"We never heard of it in the whole county," was the answer of the old man.

I am quite certain that in both respects the old man told the truth. He was corroborated by all the other tenants who were present. I am equally certain that this incident gives no exaggerated indication of the feeling which too generally prevails.

It was but the other day that I heard a gentleman of kind heart and even of liberal views, express, before a large party, his opinion of the peasantry of a whole district, by saying that they would be perfectly ready to shoot the gentry, but they were too great cowards—they would run from a gentleman with a pistol in his hand. The district of which he spoke is one in which, for nearly fifty years, an agrarian or insurrectionary crime was unknown.

Alas! alas! how often does language like this grieve the spirit of every man who really desires, as I do, to see the old feud of classes reconciled, and the Irish gentry and the Irish people live together in peace.

policy of conquest is past. He feels every day the iron entering
into his soul. The feelings which are cherished, ay, and deeply
cherished, in the hearts of both the proprietors and occupiers, make
it hopeless to expect peace so long as you grant the one dominion
over the other. Irish society must always, while this dominion
continues, represent, either on a great or on a small scale, the
passions and the crimes of a servile war.

   This, I am satisfied, is the true view of this question. Is it
right, or just, or expedient, that the representatives of the titles of
confiscation and conquest should be absolute masters of the Irish
people? The attempt to make them so lies at the root of all our
distraction and discontent. There never will be, there never can be,
peace in Ireland until we sever from the right of property in land
the right to hold in a state of serfdom the occupiers of that land.

   Do not understand me as saying that the grievance is not a real
actual grievance, pressing on the people. In a thousand ways,
which it would be vain to recount, the Irish peasant is made every
day bitterly to feel that his lord and master regards him as of an
inferior race. This is not measured by the number of evictions.
The tyranny may be the most oppressive when the penalty never
is enforced. I am not one of those who believe that grievances
which may be called "sentimental," are therefore no grievances at
all. The deepest wrongs to human nature are those which wound
the keen susceptibilities of the soul. The Great Being who has
implanted in us those susceptibilities intended us for something
better than the mere transmission of an animal existence or the
enjoyment of material good. Neither in nations or in individuals
can you disregard either sentiments or susceptibilities. But I deny
that the grievance of subjection to the dominion of a landlord whom
he regards as an alien, is to the Irish tenant a mere grievance of
sentiment. In every instance it is slavery. There are many cases
in which that slavery may be mild. I am not sure that there are
any in which it is not galling. Slavery disguised as it may be is
slavery still. The peasant who holds his livelihood by the tenure
of subservience to the will of his landlord is a slave. The result is
that which always must follow. The condition of his servitude is
as variable as the character of the lord he serves. Where power is
given to a class some bad men must enjoy it. Where bad men
possess it it will be badly used. The modes in which it will be so
used will be as various as the evil passions of the human heart.
There is no conceivable object of ambition, of fanaticism, or of
passion, for which the dominion of the landlord has not been used.
From the coercion of a vote at an election down to purposes the
basest and the most unholy, there is nothing within the range of
the follies, the lusts, or the evil passions of power, in respect to
which some Irish tenant has not felt the iron hand of tyranny press
heavily upon him.

When I speak of the absolute dominion of the landlord—of the complete serfdom of the tenant, no one, I suppose, will imagine that I mean to represent the power of the landlord as altogether uncontrolled. In a country possessing a free press and free judicial institutions it could not be so. What I do mean to assert is that, legally, the landlord has a power which amounts to absolute coercion over his tenants. All the restraining influences which may act upon him are, in many instances, insufficient to control the exercise of that power. In no instance are they sufficient to assure the tenant that it will not be put forth to accomplish his destruction. Very likely there are many cases in which the tenant yields, in which, if he resisted, the landlord would not venture to enforce the penalty; very many in which the landlord hesitates to risk his power by issuing the mandate which might bring matters to a decisive issue. Perhaps this is, of all others, the most unsatisfactory condition in which such relations could be placed. Where serfdom is acknowledged and acquiesced in, there is at least peace. The constant struggle between the claims of vassalage and the principles of freedom involves in Ireland a perpetual state of petty and vexatious war.

Unhappily, the sword has not always slumbered in its sheath. We have had experience of actual evictions! I will write more fully of these when I come to the letters of Lord Dufferin, to which you have referred me. But is there a man in Ireland who does not know how they have been used? Have they been used ruthlessly to sweep away the population which was likely to become a burden by swelling the poor rates on an estate? Have they been used to drive out the honest and industrious tenant, at the call of his landlord's interest or caprice? In how many instances have they been used, and are they used, to rob the widow and orphan of the little property which the husband and the father had created in improvements on his farm? If your Lordship, or any truthful man, will tell me that these things are not done, then I will believe that I have exaggerated the evils of the power of eviction; but then I will also believe that while imagining I was observing what was passing, I might say before my own eyes, I have really been living in a dream.

And, let me ask—is it possible for men placed in the position of the Irish farmer to be industrious? How many tenant farmers in Ireland can walk out this day into their fields and dig the trench that is to drain the morass, or turn up the soil of the uncultivated hill side, and feel that they are toiling for themselves. The result of insecurity of tenure is that our fields are half cultivated, and our lands unimproved. This is no light matter in a country like Ireland, where so much is yet to be done in the way of improvement, and where, as a general rule, the landlord does nothing. In such a country the man who has the occupation of the soil must be the improver; and therefore,

if you have improvements at all, you must give to that occupier
such a tenure as will enable him to improve.

Your Lordship, indeed, admits this, for you propose a change in
the law by which the tenant is to be " repaid all outlay on permanent improvements which had been made with the consent of the
landlord."

" With the consent of the landlord!" How hard is it for the
best of men to bring themselves to give up arbitrary power!

I do not know that any law is necessary to enable a landlord to
make such an agreement with his tenant, unless it may be to confer
upon the owner of a " limited estate" the power of binding the in-·
heritance. If this power be not already conferred upon such an
owner our past legislation has been a miserable blunder. But why
with the consent of the landlord? You admit that the things done
are improvements, that they have added to the value of the farm, and
so increased the wealth of the country, as well as added to the
property of the landlord. Why claim for the proprietor the power
of preventing this? What right has any territorial proprietor to
prohibit improvement? It is a dangerous thing to assert for Irish
proprietors the odious prerogative of putting a veto upon the
increase of national wealth, upon the development of those powers
by which the earth giveth her increase—powers surely intended
by a beneficent Creator for the common benefit of all.

In fact, my Lord, the issue is brought to this: Are the landlords
of Ireland to have in their hands the power of prohibiting permanent improvements, of putting a veto upon national progress,
and of blighting every indication of prosperity that may appear?

But surely a very little reflection will satisfy us that any measure
that would require the assent of the landlord to be given as " a
precedent condition" to improvements would, in the great majority
of cases, be perfectly prohibitory of all improvements.

There are cases, no doubt, to which such a permission might be
applicable. If an Irish tenant farmer were prepared to drain some
lake—if he were ready to embank some tidal river—if he were, on
an humbler scale, anxious to build a new farm-house, or even to
erect substantial offices—if he were prepared to submit the plans of
his engineer and his architect—then, indeed, I can understand permanent improvements effected with his landlord's consent.

But such arrangements belong to a state of things entirely remote
from that with which, in Ireland, we have to deal. These are not
the improvements which Ireland wants, or which Irish tenant
farmers are capable of effecting. The industry of the tenant can
gradually carry cultivation to the hill-top—it can, by slow and
imperceptible degrees, reduce the watery bottom to the rich and
luxuriant meadow—it can, by constant and unflagging attention,
turn the waste ground, bit by bit, into a potato ridge, until, in the
process of years, the whole becomes a corn field. These changes,

and changes like these, are the improvements by which, gradually and in almost unnoticed steps, the industry of the occupier, might convert all Ireland into a garden. To forbid changes like these unless they are mapped out and planned for the specific and special assent of the landlord beforehand, is simply to prohibit them.

The man to whose occupation any portion of the Irish soil is entrusted ought, with its occupation, to receive a licence to improve. He ought to be permitted to expend his industry or his "capital" when and where he thinks best; to go out on his fields at every spare hour, and do the best he can to raise the productive powers of the soil; to struggle inch by inch with its natural sterility; to do manful battle, day by day, with the thorns and briars of the primæval curse; to watch his opportunities of winning, rood by rood and perch by perch, the waste ground to the purposes of human food. The occupier who cannot do all this, and do it with the certainty that if he does do it, he himself and not another shall reap where he has sowed, is debarred by the wickedness and the folly of human law from making the most of God's earth for the benefit of all the creatures of God. There may be countries— I am not sure that there are—in which agriculture is in such a condition that there is no room for improvements of the character I have just described. Farms may be let in such a high state of cultivation that the industry of the tenant can only be applied in maintaining that cultivation paying himself by its annual proceeds. No one will tell me that this is the condition of the great majority of Irish farms.

If over the greatest extent of the Irish soil there be room and need for such improvements, then I ask again—Will your Lordship, or any thoughtful person, tell me that insecurity of tenure does not discourage, ay, and prohibit, improvements like these. Upon how many Irish estates would you advise an occupier to make them, and tell him that he had even a reasonable chance of being permitted to enjoy them?

Let me pause here, and reiterate that which I have, perhaps, too often repeated, that the whole argument resolves itself, in its most important element, into a question of fact—the question, what is the real position of the occupier of the Irish soil?—a question not to be answered, by any abstract theories of proprietary right, but to be resolved by the actual state of things practically and in real life existing.

I venture, therefore, to ask of your Lordship—let me ask of Lord Dufferin, or of Lord Rosse, of any fair-minded man who has deluded himself into the belief that there can be either peace or prosperity in the country while the present system of land tenure continues—

FIRST.—Is it true that, as a general rule, Irish proprietors have retained in their hands the power of arbitrary eviction?

SECONDLY.—Is it true that, as a general rule applicable to the great mass of the Irish tenantry, eviction involves the consequences of beggary and ruin?

If these two questions be answered, as they must be, in the affirmative, then I ask—

THIRDLY.—Am I right in saying that the Irish proprietors are retaining in their hands a power of coercion which, if pushed to the extreme, amounts to absolute dominion over the tillers of the soil? And—

FOURTHLY.—Does this absolute dominion, depending, as it does, on the power of arbitrary eviction, involve the destruction of all certainty of tenure on the part of the tenant, creating an insecurity for his holding, which, where it is experienced, amounts to an absolute prohibition of the improvement of the soil?

If no truthful man can answer these four questions otherwise than affirmatively, is not the whole mystery of Ireland's discontent and wretchedness explained?

This is my argument for the measure I have suggested. I have not seen any answer to it even attempted.

But, though your Lordship does not answer that argument, you meet it by the assertion that my proposal is "communistic" and "subversive of the rights of property," and must therefore be rejected. But if the premises be conceded—if the facts upon which I reason are not denied, the statement amounts simply to this— that it is the right of Irish landlords to keep the Irish people in serfdom, and the Irish nation in a state of wretchedness and dis- content. Beware of this argument, my Lord. It leads rationally to but one conclusion. There are intellects even in Ireland acute enough to follow it out. The rights of property which are destruc- tive of national welfare cannot be maintained.

I have not said this. I have argued the contrary. I have, I think, shown that it is possible to respect every true right of pro- perty in the Irish landowners—to maintain in the land a class of "Protestant proprietors," exercising every just influence over the people, and yet to reconcile their proprietary rights with the national welfare, and with the prior and higher right of the Irish people to live upon their native soil.

He is the true Conservative who reconciles these things. He is the revolutionist and the anarchist who insists that they shall clash.

Let us be clear and explicit upon this point—to what future for Ireland are we to look? I place before you four possible results—

1st. Is the present state of things to last for ever? Are successive generations of Irishmen to waste and wear away their lives, as we have done the best part of ours, amid the distractions and miseries of an impoverished country—impoverished because its energies are preyed on by the slow fever of a servile war? Have we no better inheritance to leave to our children?

2nd. Are the people to leave the country to the landlords?

3rd. Are the landlords to leave it to the people?

Or,4th. Are we,by some bold and fearless measure, to reconcile the people to proprietary rights by making proprietary rights consistent with their living in freedom and happiness in their native land?

Either the second or the third of these results might ultimately make the Irish soil as useful to mankind as it ought to be. Neither of them, not even the last, could be realized without an amount of injustice, and misery, and probably bloodshed from which every right-minded man must shrink.

The first result, I think, necessarily follows from the proposal of those who, like your Lordship, advise that matters should be let alone.

The second is really involved in the argument of those who say that emigration is the only remedy for the condition of Ireland.

The third was the rough and ready remedy of the Fenians.

The fourth is that which is proposed by myself and others who believe it possible to preserve proprietary rights, and yet prevent the extermination of the people.

I cannot help saying, my Lord, that if the only choice were between the second and the third—if we were driven to the alternative that either the people should abandon the country to the landlords or the landlords give it up to the people—the " Fenian" view of the question, appears to me of the two the more reasonable and just.

I may be told that I am omitting another possible contingency. It may be said that Ireland is just beginning to enter on a path of progress and improvement—that if we only wait, discontent and misery will pass away, and the natural progress of events, and (of course) the laws of political economy, will very soon remedy all the evils of which we complain. I have already pointed out that all the arguments of this nature assume that emigration is to drain away a large proportion—I believe about two millions more of our people. This is in truth to propose that the people are to leave the country to the landlords. But, independently of this, is there any man, woman, or child in Ireland who is fool enough to believe in these promises of the advent of Irish prosperity?

I have heard and read this as long as I recollect; I presume that in days before my recollection, this poor island was, as it has always been within it, on the very commencement of an era of prosperity and peace. There is not a country gentleman, for the last thirty years, who has written on any Irish subject without the confident prediction that time was bringing the remedy for all our misfortunes.

> " Rusticus expectat dum defluat amnis, at ille
> Labitur et labetur."

I believe that there is no rational hope for Ireland of things righting themselves; they have been too violently wrenched from their natural course; they are kept in the wrong direction by the force of English power. I agree with your Lordship—in a different sense, perhaps, from that in which you have used the phrase—that "the vicious circle must be cut." Whether it shall be "cut" by peaceful legislation, or one day or other by violence, depends greatly on the Irish landlords themselves.

I cannot help thinking that in this remarkable passage you admit all that I have urged. You describe the vicious circle as one in which "chronic civil war excludes capital; want of capital prevents employment."

"WANT OF EMPLOYMENT PLACES THOSE WHO DO NOT EMIGRATE ENTIRELY IN THE POWER OF THE LANDLORD AND LANDOWNERS *to make what terms the latter pleases as the conditions of a bare subsistence.*"

"THE OCCASIONAL MISUSE OF THAT POWER AND THE KNOWLEDGE OF THE TENANT THAT IT EXISTS (coupled with false notions of Irish social history, and continual tamperings in Parliament with the rights of property) perpetuate chronic civil war." *

What more than this have I said in *The Plea for the Celtic Race?*

I have asserted that in Ireland there exists "a chronic state of civil war."

Your Lordship says the same.

I have asserted that the peasantry who remain in the country must submit to a state of serfdom.

That rent is regulated solely by the disposition of the landlord to extort and the ability of the tenant to pay.

Your Lordship says that the condition of the country places those who do not emigrate entirely in the power of the landowner; that it is "in the power of the landowner to make WHAT TERMS HE PLEASES AS THE CONDITION OF A BARE EXISTENCE."

Is not this serfdom?

You say further that there is "occasional misuse of that power."

That "the knowledge of the tenant that it exists" exercises an injurious influence on his mind.

And that "notions of Irish history" which you consider "false," with "occasional tampering with the rights of property or Parliament," combine all these causes to "perpetuate the chronic civil war."

These are exactly the grounds upon which I have urged the absolute necessity of a legal enactment which would give security of tenure to the Irish occupier of the soil.

Your Lordship agrees with me that this miserable state of things must be met by legislation, but rejecting my proposal for a sixty-three years' lease, you say:—

---

* Lord Lifford's letter to Mr. Butt, page 14.

"I believe it can be met by a measure perfectly legitimate. I would give every man his rights. I would allow the landlord, according to the laws of every civilized country, to do as he would with his own, but the property of the tenant invested in the soil with the knowledge and consent of the landowner, I would secure to the tenant by a law which I believe to be so founded on the abstract principle of right, justice, and of political economy, that though it be only imperatively needed in Ireland, it ought to be extended to England and Scotland. I therefore, would support a bill for a law by which the tenant may register the cost of all buildings, drains, fences, &c., made with the knowledge and consent of the landlord, or his agent, to be repaid his outlay, if evicted. Such is my first remedy."

The fatal words "with the consent of the landlord" would make such a measure nugatory. In the case where a landlord is disposed to encourage his tenant's improvements, it is unnecessary; in a case where he is not, it would be ineffectual.

I have already pointed out that there is nothing utterly destructive of the rights of property in the granting of a sixty-three years' lease. The many proprietors who have granted it have not denuded themselves of their proprietary rights. Marriage settlements are framed with the very object of preserving to the unborn inheritor the estate unimpaired by any act of the tenant for life; yet in most of such settlements a power is reserved to the tenant for life of creating a tenure equivalent to this. Why? Because the power of creating such a tenure, so far from being a thing inconsistent with the transmission of the property, is one essential to the due management of the estate.

All property, especially all property in land, is the creation of the State. The monopoly of the surface of the earth which confers the power on any proprietor of shutting me out from walking over the mountain or the moor rests upon no natural right. It is an arrangement of society, which is justified because such an appropriation is necessary to enable the land to be most profitably used for the benefit of all. But there is no proprietary right in land which excludes the right of the whole community to have the land of the country made useful to the national wealth. No wise statesman, indeed, would venture to legislate so as to prevent every possible case of misuse or abuse of proprietary right. I admit that there are limits, within which, in civilized society, every landowner should be permitted to do what he likes with his own, even although he may like to do that which is very wrong. There is, however, a case in which the necessity and the right of legislation are patent—whenever the abuse of proprietary right is such or so general as to become a public mischief and wrong. The very first principles of the social compact teach us that for the purpose of preventing this the State ought to interpose to regulate and control.

Now this is just what has occurred in the case of Irish land.

Insecurity of tenure has become nearly universal. The power of arbitrary eviction has become a public mischief and wrong. Therefore the supreme Government ought to interfere and prohibit the proprietors from letting the lands at extortionate rents or on uncertain and insecure tenures. If the necessity be made out, there is nothing plainer than the right of legislation to regulate to this extent the exercise of proprietary rights in land.

I am within this principle when I propose to enact that no proprietor shall be permitted to let his land at a rent higher than the fair letting value, or for a tenure shorter than sixty-three years. I believe in the perfect right of the State to impose these conditions upon all owners of landed property, if the necessity for imposing them be made out.

In the case of the Irish proprietors I do not need to resort to these general principles. The very conditions which I think may reasonably be insisted on by legislation are already incorporated with the titles to many, if not most, of their estates. The original grants contain stipulations intended for the express purpose of preventing the state of things which has now arisen—stipulations by which the landowners are bound never to place on their estates a tenantry holding by a short and precarious tenure.

I have in my former tract endeavoured to show that all Irish proprietors held their estates in such a manner as to create an implied trust to use their proprietary rights in a manner with which their present system is entirely inconsistent.* In this respect the condition of the Irish proprietor differs from that of the proprietors of every country with the history of which I am acquainted. We can positively say of almost all the grants of land which have been made in Ireland since the accession of James I., that they were made for the express purpose, and upon the express condition, of placing on the estate so granted a loyal, and a peaceful, and a contented population. The proprietors have in scarcely any instance carried out the purpose or fulfilled the condition. That, which can be positively shown of the grants of James the First and of Cromwell, may with almost equal certainty be stated of the earlier grants of Elizabeth. But even those which have been made since the beginning of the seventeenth century cover almost the entire of the island. These circumstances distinguish property in Irish land from similar property in all other countries. In other countries, as was the case in England, wide and fair domains have been granted as the reward of adherence to the partisans of a conquering side. But the lands so granted were settled and reclaimed. In getting the grant of his castle, his manor, or his lordship, the soldier entered into his rest; the conditions upon which he held it were those of settled and civilized life.

* Land Tenure in Ireland, &c. Third Edition, p. 73.

In the case of these Irish grants the case was wholly different. The grantee received his estates for the purpose of reclaiming hostile or unsettled districts to the service of the English sovereign. Even in his ownership he was the servant and trustee of that sovereign. He was expressly told that the lands he was receiving were wild and uncivilized wastes, and that no man must take them for the purposes only of his private profit, but for the good of the commonwealth. He was to civilize and subdue his possessions before he could enjoy them. He was sent there not for the purpose of enjoying a pleasant and indolent proprietorship, but for the purpose of doing active service to the State. Such a condition of proprietorship is wholly unlike that of other countries. No one dealing with the land question in this country ought to overlook the fact that almost all Irish estates have been granted for purposes which are public ones, which involve in fact public trusts, trusts which affect the interests, the peace, and the well-being of the whole community, both of Ireland and England—and that up to this time these trusts have not been carried out, and these purposes have not been fulfilled.

I do not rest even on the general trust which I think attached to all these grants. Unless I am wholly mistaken I believe I can show that Irish estates over at least a great portion of the island were granted upon distinct and specific conditions, very often recited on the face of the patents, which if enforced would remedy many of the evils of which we complain; and that these conditions are not dead and obsolete stipulations, but are now binding on the present proprietors, while they are systematically and openly violated. Possibly, I will surprise many persons when I say that even my measure, which has been denounced as " revolutionary" and " communistic," amounts to nothing more than enforcing conditions binding upon the owners of all Irish estates—conditions, for the violation of which it is not at all clear that the Crown might not, by legal process, have long since resumed possession of many of these estates—conditions which certainly would now justify, in an equitable adjustment, the imposition of terms more stringent than any which I propose.

The assertion may seem a bold one. The subject is of such importance that I may devote some space to the endeavour to make it clear.

There are few portions of Irish history upon which we possess information as clear or as accurate as that which throws light upon the plantation of Ulster by the first King James. Papers are in existence said to be drawn up by the King's own hand, containing the project of this plantation. In a paper printed in the year 1608, after a recital,

" That the greatest part of six counties, in the Province of Ulster, within the realm of Ireland, named Armagh, Coleraine, Donegal,

Fermanagh, and Cavan" had "eschcated and come to the Crown, and latterly been surveyed, and the survey presented to his Majesty."

It is declared that " his Majesty"—

"Not regarding his own profit but the public peace and welfare of this Kingdom by a civil plantation of these unreformed and waste countries, is graciously pleased to distribute the said lands to such of his subjects, as well of Great Britain as of Ireland, as being of merit and ability, shall seek the same with a mind not only to benefit them-selves, *but to do service to the Crown and commonwealth.*" *

The paper then proceeds to complain of—

"Importunate suitors for greater portions than they are able to plant, intending *their private profit only, and not the advancement of the public service.*"

King James would scarcely have recognized in one of his patentees a right " to do what he liked with his own," " intending his own private profit only, and not the advancement of the public service." But the matter was not left to any general recital. Very strin-gent terms were imposed upon the grantees. The lands were divided in certain proportions between English and Scotch under-takers, Irish servitors, or servants of the Crown, and Irish natives.

"The persons of the undertakers shall be of three sorts :—
"First.—English or Scotch, as well servitors as others, who are to plant their portions with English, or inland Scotch, inhabitants.
" Second.—Servitors in the kingdom of Ireland, who may take mere Irish, English, or inland Scottish, tenants, at their choice.
"Third.—Natives of Ireland, who are to be made freeholders."

It is very singular that from the two first classes these regulations required the taking the oath of supremacy, and " to be conformable in religion." In the case of the Irish natives these conditions were omitted—the only conditions of a political nature imposed upon them being

" A proviso for the forfeiture of their estates if they entered into actual rebellion."

But it is to this that I desire to call attention—that in every paper ever published, from the earliest inception of the project, upon every class of grantees one condition was invariably imposed.

---

* "Orders and Conditions to be Observed by the Undertakers upon the Distribution and Plantation of the Escheated Lands in Ulster." From a copy printed in the year 1608. *Harris's Hibernica*, page 123. See also the same document in *A Concise View of the Origin, Constitution, and Proceedings of the Irish Society*, printed by order of the Court. London. 1822.

Of the English and Scotch undertakers it is declared—

"The said undertakers shall not demise any part of their lands at will only, but shall make certain estates for years, for life, in tail, or in fee-simple.".

Of the Irish servitors—grantees who had been in the service of the Crown—

"They shall make certain estates to their tenants, and at certain rents, and forbear Irish exactions."

Of the Irish natives—

"They shall make certain estates for lives or years to their under-tenant, and shall take no Irish exactions."

I do not intend to follow out the history of the Ulster plantation. In a work of high authority, the introduction to Carte's *Life of Ormonde*, the final conditions of the plantation are thus accurately summed up. After describing the several classes of grantees—

"The King granted estates to all, to be held by them and their heirs; the undertakers of two thousand acres held of him *in capite;* those of one thousand five hundred by knight's service as of the Castle of Dublin; and those of one thousand, in common soccage. The first were, in four years, obliged to build a castle and bawn; the second in two years, a strong stone or brick house and bawn; and the last, a bawn; timber for that purpose, as well as for their tenants' houses, being assigned them out of the King's woods. The first were obliged to plant on their lands, within three years, forty-eight able men, eighteen years old or upwards, born in England or the inland parts of Scotland, to be reduced to twenty families, to keep a demesne of six hundred acres in their hands, to have four fee-farmers on a hundred and twenty acres each, six leaseholders on a hundred acres each, and on the rest eight families of husbandmen, artificers, and cottagers: the others were under the like obligations proportionably; and they were all, within five years, to reside in person on some part of the premises, and to have store of arms in their houses. *They were not to alienate* any of their lands without a royal license, NOR SET THEM AT UNCERTAIN RENTS, OR FOR A LESS TERM THAN FOR TWENTY-ONE YEARS, OR THREE LIVES; and their tenants were to live in houses, not in cabins, and to build their houses together in towns and villages. They had power to erect manors, to hold courts baron, to create tenures, with liberty of exporting and importing timber, and other privileges; which were likewise extended to the natives, whose estates were granted them in fee-simple and held in soccage, but with no obligation on any to erect castles or build strong houses. These were not thought proper for the residence of persons who might well be deemed willing to arrogate to themselves all the power that had been formerly usurped and exercised by the Irish chiefs: to guard against which, they were restrained from having tenants at will; they were enjoined to set their lands at rents certain for the like terms as the undertakers, and were to take no chief rents, cuttings, and other Irish exactions, from their under-tenants, who were obliged to leave their creating (or running up and down the country with their cattle, from place to place for pasture), and to dwell in towns, and use the English manner of tillage and husbandry. In this manner and under these regulations were the escheated lands in Ulster disposed of to a hundred and four English and Scotch undertakers, fifty-six servitors, and two hundred and eighty-six natives, *all which gave bond to the government for performance of covenants; for the better assurance whereof, the King required a regular account to be sent him from the state, of the progress made by each undertaker in the plantation.*" *

Just the same statements are repeated by Leland and by every Irish historian.

It appears by the printed conditions that every bond expressly secured the fulfilment of the stipulations as to conferring "fixity of tenure" on the tenants. The King, it will be seen, reserved to himself the right of personal supervision over each estate. We shall presently see in what manner, and with what results, he exercised that right.

For what purpose, or with what object were these restrictions imposed upon the grantees? Why were they prohibited from letting their lands to tenants-at-will? why were they bound to create independent interests under them, the least of which was to be a term for twenty-one years or three lives? Exactly to prevent their holding their tenantry in a state of serfdom. The sagacity of King James, or of his councillors, foresaw the danger that proprietors who held their estates in a country where conquest had broken the spirit of the natives might fall into the evil habit of placing wretched serfs upon the soil. This mischief was expressly guarded against—and guarded against in the only possible way. Security or fixity of tenure in the tenant was made the express condition of proprietorship in all the grants of King James I.

Is it "revolutionary," or "communistic," or a violation of the rights of property to insist on the fulfilment of the conditions upon which the estates were granted, and on which they are now held?

So far as lands are held under these grants there is not a tenant upon one of these estates who has not a right to insist upon fixity of tenure. His ancestor, very probably, came over to this country on the faith of these conditions being observed. The Sovereign and Parliament of England have a right and a duty, by the most peremptory measures, to enforce them. And every Irishman whose lot is cast in a country that will never be a happy country to live in while the occupiers of the soil are serfs—has, in the sight of Heaven and his country, a right to demand of our rulers the enforcement of these conditions. The descendants of these grantees, or the purchasers of these grants, do not hold their estates "for their own private profit only," but in order, by "the civil plantation of these wild and unreformed and waste countries, to promote the public peace and welfare of the Kingdom of Ireland;" and they are bound, expressly bound, as the first condition of a "civil plantation," to let their lands upon terms which will give their tenants security of tenure at certain rents.

The late Mr. Sharman Crawford pointed out that the custom of the Ulster tenant right was originally permitted by the grantees of the Ulster plantation in lieu of the fixed and settled tenures which they were bound by their patents to give to their tenantry, but the granting of which they had evaded.

This opinion is confirmed by a reference to all the records which describe the dealings of the undertakers with their estates.

It was scarcely to be expected that all these undertakers, once settled in remote districts of Ireland, would either very scrupulously observe the conditions of the plantation, when they found them inconvenient, or be actuated solely by a desire to "serve the King and Commonwealth," without any regard to their own gain and profit. It was probably impossible for the Government to insist in every case upon a strict compliance with the conditions, even if the Castle of Dublin had been as free from the influences of favouritism as it is now. Difficulties there were, no doubt, in the way of that compliance which supplied an excuse to the indolence of the undertakers for not observing, and to the Irish Government for not enforcing, the conditions of the grant. Even the personal enterference of King James was unsuccessful in completely carrying out the conditions of the plantation; and commissioners whom he sent from time to time, to report to himself the progress he had made, were only able to tell him of the partial accomplishment of his scheme.* Many of the undertakers failed altogether in bringing over the English or Scotch settlers, and retained the native Irish as serfs upon their lands. Even when the settlers were brought over the granting of land to them was, in many instances, evaded or postponed. Some of them returned to their own country. Others of them remained, constantly appealing to their landlord to fulfil the obligation, and occasionally bringing their complaints before the King's Commissioner when he visited the estate.† It was in such

* There are, I doubt not, extant, in some of the archives in which the most valuable documents of Irish history are buried, many papers containing the reports from each Irish estate, which King James required to be furnished to himself.

† In *Harris's Hibernica* there is preserved a very curious document, known as *Pynnar's Survey*, in which very considerable light is thrown upon the manner in which the conditions of the plantation were carried out. In November, 1618, a Royal Commission was issued to Nicholas Pynnar, directing him to visit the plantation, and report on the progress made on the several estates. This document contains the result of the visitation.

The general result is that while upon many of the grants the conditions of giving

a state of things that the Ulster custom of tenant right had its
origin. These tenants held under terms which bound the landlords to give them fixity, in some instances perpetuity, of tenure.
The landlord, while he was evading this obligation, could not

estates to the tenants had been, at least partially, complied with, upon a very large
number they had been evaded. The English settlers had, in many instances, been
brought over, but were not given the covenanted estates. In many instances they left
the land. In several they obtained access to the King's Commissioner, and complained
of the violation of the conditions on which they had come to Ireland. The pretexts
under which the leases were delayed or refused were various. Some of the short entries
in the "Survey" go far to reveal what was passing in the country. I select them almost
at random, from the pages of "Harris." Each item is applicable to a different estate :—
    "I find upon this, proportion of British tenants, ten ; but I find no estates except
by promise."—P. 158.
    "These hold their land but by promise."—*Ibid.*
    "Not one freeholder, but many Irish."—P. 159.
    "There are twelve others whose estates I saw not, and therefore can say nothing of
them, for many of them do dwell in another country."
    Sir Hugh Worrall "hath no freeholder, nor leaseholder, and but three poor men on
the land, which have no estates ; for all the land at this time is inhabited with Irish."—
P. 162.
    "The rest of the tenants have no estates, but promises."—P. 177.
    "I find planted on this estate a good number of men, but they have no estates but
by promises from one year to another."—P. 172.
    "They who are upon the land have no estates, but mynnets " (minutes).—P. 174.
    "These held their land but by promise. I saw but very few of them, for they dwelt
far asunder, and had not time to come to me."
    These are specimens of the entries that meet us at every page. It would seem
that in some instances the custom had begun of introducing unreasonable covenants
in leases. The tenants of Lord Castlehaven complained that :—
    "They do dwell dispersedly upon their own land, and cannot dwell together in a
village, because they are bound every one to dwell upon their own land, which, if
they do not, the lease is void."—P. 198.
    On another estate of the same nobleman "the agent for the earl showed me the rent
roll of all the tenants that are on these proportions, but their estates are so weak and
uncertain that they are leaving the land."—*Ibid.*
    From many of the entries it is quite plain that Nicholas Pynnar believed that the
owners of the estates were evading his inquiries as to the tenures they had granted
to their tenants. In some instances, he says, "I came suddenly upon them ; " in
others he complains that under one excuse or another he did not see the tenants
themselves ; in others he relates, with manifest suspicion, that he had seen the "rent
roll" of "estated tenants," but had not been shown any counterparts, or, as he calls
them, "counterpaines of leases."
    Of Sir John Stewart, in the County of Donegal, he writes :—
    "What estates they have I know not, *neither would he call the tenants together*,
but shewed me the counterpaine of one lease and said the rest of the tenants had the
like."—P. 188.
    Of Mr. Pringle in Tyrone, who was "dwelling on the land in a poor cabin":—
    "What tenants he hath I know not, for he refused to shew them unto me, but he
brought after me a list of just twenty tenants ; but I know not whether they have any
estates, for the list doth not make any mention which they held."
    He is even ungallant enough to hint his suspicions of the conduct of a Lady
Drummond. "There are many tenants on the land ; insomuch that, knowing I
was in the country, they came and complained unto me, and said that for many years
they could never get anything from him but promises, *and therefore the most part are
leaving the land.* I desired the lady to show me their counterpaines, but her answer
was that her Knight was in Scotland, and she could not come at them." Again,
in Armagh, on Mr. Acheson's estate:—"I find a great many tenants on this land,
but not that they have any estates but by promise. They petitioned unto me
that they might have their leases." These petitions of the tenants for leases are

venture, even if he were disposed, to interfere with their possession. They were somewhat in the condition of persons holding lands under what are termed accepted proposals, without a legal title, but with a claim in equity strong enough to prevent them from being disturbed. Matters continued in this unsettled state for years. In the troubles which soon after agitated Ulster as well as the rest of the kingdom, arising from the war which has been called " the great rebellion "—it was scarcely to be expected that there should be any authoritative adjustment of these claims. During these troubles it was not probable that landlords would interfere with the tenants, upon whose fidelity they relied; and at the end of the great rebellion, the tenants claim for security for their holdings resulted in the establishment, in the case of the Protestant tenantry, with an acquiescence on the part of the landlords, of that virtual fixity of tenure which has puzzled us in modern days under the name of the " Ulster tenant right."

The obligation of conferring fixity of tenure in the grants of King James extended equally to the mere Irish, or Catholic proprietors. They, as well as the English " undertakers," were bound to give fixity of tenure to the tenants whom they were to place on their estates. So were the servitors of the Crown, who were to choose, at their own discretion, the tenants whom they were to select, either from the old inhabitants of the country, or from Englishmen or " inland" Scotchmen. In this scheme of plantation both Catholic landlords and Catholic tenants were permitted upon the largest portion of the escheated land. But in every case, whether both landlord and tenant were to be Irish and Catholic, or whether Protestant landlords were to have Catholic tenants, or Protestant and English landlords were bound to settle on their estates imported tenants of their own religion and race—to each and every case the prohibition against the lettings which are now the universal rule in Ireland strictly applies. In the early part of the 17th century the spirit of religious ascendancy trampled down the native population. The strife of

frequent. The report of such cases is generally accompanied by the significant addition that for want of leases " the tenants are going away."

The excuses for not granting leases are very singular. One gentleman refused to give them because he had some reason to suspect that " the land he had been granted was glebe." Another cannot give them for " that the children were still under age." And one of the " Irish gentlemen " assigns the same excuse, which I have read in some of the " letters of Irish landlords," within the last six months :—

" He hath made no estates, for his tenants will have no longer time but from year to year."

In this very curious and instructive document, we frequently meet with the expressive phrase, " estated" tenants, as applied to the neglect or fulfilment of the condition of the grant.

Thus early begins the struggle of the new proprietors to evade the obligations on which they hold their estates.

This survey records probably the first contest between the desire of the landlords to keep in their own hands " the management of their estates," and the interest of " the King and the Commonwealth ;" that they should observe their covenant, to give fixity of tenure to the occupiers of the soil.

"the great rebellion" completed the subjugation, and the Catholic "estated tenantry" disappeared with the 285 native Irish, who were to fill the place of "estated gentlemen" in the original scheme of the plantation of King James.

It is impossible to write an incidental treatise on Irish history in a discussion like that upon which I am engaged, yet I think we shall see that in other parts of Ireland there was an equal, if not as explicit an obligation to give "fixity of tenure" to the occupiers of the soil. This is, indeed, the leading principle of every plan for the plantation or settlement of the country. The fulfilment of that obligation has been forced upon the landlords in Ulster, because they had to deal with a tenantry belonging to the dominant class. It was neglected in other parts of Ireland, because the old population were crushed down by civil war and penal laws. Even in Ulster the prevalence of tenant right and of Protestantism will be found to be very nearly identical in the several districts.

At all events the existence of the Ulster custom of tenant right is in reality a provisional arrangement during the pendency of the claim which every Ulster tenant has to the fixity of tenure provided for him in the conditions of "the plantation" under which his landlord holds his estate. If this be a true description of the state of things the moment an interference is attempted with the Ulster tenant right the Ulster tenant has a right to demand from Parliament the protection of law.

But independently of this "perpetual claim," by the assertion of tenant right, it cannot be said that these conditions are obsolete stipulations now only matters of historical and antiquarian interest. Those who hold their properties by a title of a great and general confiscation, cannot ignore the objects for which that confiscation was carried into effect. The objects and conditions of these great settlements of property are a portion of the history of the country, and as such have become a part, as it were, of the common law of the land. In equity and justice, and according to all the higher principles of jurisprudence, a right of visitation over these estates remains in the supreme power as completely as the right exists in the Sovereign to visit a charity which holds estates under grants from the Plantagenets. If it needs the authority of the Queen in Parliament to enforce that visitation, then Parliament ought to give its aid to the Sovereign to interfere. While the great purposes of these grants are unfulfilled the conditions never can become obsolete. They are not so regarded in our courts of law. In two instances, in modern times, they have been discussed before judicial tribunals.

One was that of a suit instituted in the English Court of Chancery by one of the London Companies against the Irish Society, in reference to the distribution of the rents of their estates. The printed copy of the conditions from which I have quoted was one of the documents principally relied on. This suit was finally disposed of in the House of Lords in the year 1843. The decision rested, no doubt, in a great degree, upon the charter of the Irish Society. But Lord Lyndhurst, who then was Lord Chancellor, in a masterly review of the objects of the Ulster plantation, distinctly recognized the "printed conditions" as declaring trusts which were public and permanent, in the fulfilment of which the nation has an interest, and which are binding as long as the property to which they are attached is held under the grant.*

This, no doubt, was the case of a corporation incorporated under a special charter for the purpose of carrying out the objects of the plantation. The conditions of the grants to private individuals became very recently the subject of investigation before the late Master of the Rolls in Ireland. The purchaser of an estate in the county of Donegal actually objected to complete the purchase because some of these very conditions were inserted in the patent under which it had been originally held. The objection was overruled, not because the conditions had become obsolete or ceased to be binding, but because the circumstances were such as, in the opinion of the Court, to show that when he purchased the estate he ought to be held as having notice that it was held on these conditions,† one of the principal foundations of this decision being that these patents were confirmed by a public statute of Charles I.

So far as these Ulster estates are concerned, it scarcely seems a violation of the rights of property to propose that the tenants should be secured by a lease for sixty-three years. It would be an average between the fee-farm estates and the leases for lives or twenty-one years which the original grants provided. The adoption of such an average would be greatly in favour of the landlord. It would leave him far more "dominion" over his estate than the original grant intended he should have.

It would be a great mistake to suppose that the grants of King James were confined to the province of Ulster. They were made largely in Longford, in Westmeath, in Kildare, and in Wicklow. In all these counties the conditions corresponded with those of the Ulster plantation. According to the unexceptionable authority of Sir John Davis the estates in Munster are held on the same condition of giving fixity of tenure to the tenants.

I cannot pass from this subject without observing, that, with respect to the plantation of Ulster, a very great injustice has been done to the memory of King James. We must carefully distinguish, in tracing Irish history, between the intentions of the English

---

* "The Skinners' Company a. The Irish Society."—*Clarke and Finnelly's House of Lords Reports*, Vol. xii., p. 476.
† Decision in the case of "Stewart against the Marquis of Conyngham."—*Irish Chancery Reports*, Vol. i., p. 545.

Sovereign and the mode in which the orders of the sovereign
were carried out by the rapacity or venality of those to whom the
execution of the plans was entrusted. The imagination of Curran
discerned a great truth, when, in poetic imagery, he described the
twilight of viceregal government as offering opportunities for
schemes of spoliation which would never have been carried out in
the noon-day light of a royal presence—a twilight better for the
robber than even the darkness of night. I am now speaking of the
original project of King James. It never was a part of his
plan to exterminate the native population. Ulster had been
thinned of its population by long-continued wars. Independently
of this, they were days when certainly over-population was not the
crying evil of the country. The scheme of the plantation, was
founded on the assumption that the condition of the province left
room for a large immigration. Of the forfeited lands in Ulster, a large
proportion was expressly reserved for the Irish, to be granted to
them on conditions not very dissimilar to these upon which the new
settlers obtained theirs. There were, as we have seen, three classes
of proprietors. The new settlers, or English undertakers—the Irish
servitors, that is, persons who had been previously engaged in the
Irish service of the crown, and lastly, native Irish proprietors.
The new settlers were bound to bring over Englishmen and
Scotchmen, an obligation from which both the Irish servitors and
the Irish proprietors were exempt;* and so far was the King from
desiring to make the plantation scheme one of compulsory
proselytism, that the Irish proprietors were exempt from taking the
oath which recognized the royal supremacy. Neither their tenants,
nor those of the Irish servitors, were required to be " conformable in
religion."†
I mention this particularly because your Lordship has fallen into
the common error of supposing that " the confiscated estates were
granted to the ancestors of the present proprietors, on the condition

---

* "The persons among whom were distributed the royal grants were distinguished as
now undertakers, servitors, and old natives. The first were natives of Britain, and
permitted to take only such for their tenants. The second, men who had sometimes
served in Ireland, in stations military or civil, were allowed to choose any tenants,
with exception only of recusants. The third were under no restrictions as to the
religion or birthplace of their tenantry, and were tacitly exempted from the oath of
supremacy by which the two former were bound."—*Gordon's History of Ireland*,
Vol. i., p. 321.

† Bacon, in recommending the scheme of the Ulster plantation, had strongly urged
the necessity of religious toleration. Among many excellent arguments was one
intended probably for the prejudices of his royal master. He urged that it would not
be for the credit of Protestantism to make that religion responsible for the scandalous
lives which were led by the Irish natives.

In other words, he said:—Let Protestantism be introduced on the vacant lands in
Ulster, and let each religion he judged by the Christian influences it exercises on the
conduct of its adherents.

In whatever language it was couched the advice had high authority for its
principle.—" By their fruits ye shall know them."

of the removal of Irish Roman Catholics and the introduction of Protestant tenants." There was no such condition. There was the condition imposed upon one and only one class of the grantees, to bring over a certain number of English and Scotch settlers,* but it was because there was abundance of vacant land in which they had room. Any Irish occupiers who might be displaced were provided for on the portion which was left in the hands of proprietors of their own race and creed. Nay more, as Carte, quoting from high and unquestioned authority, tells us, the escheated lands of Ulster were apportioned to

104 English and Scotch adventurers,
 56 Servitors,
286 Natives!!

Upon the lands of the first alone was there a condition to plant English and Scotch immigrants.

Let us be just to the English sovereign. The extermination of the native people was then as now not the act of the English government, but the act of those whom unfortunately and unwisely the English government protected as the instruments and upholders of its power. I quote from the history of Ireland, written by Mr. Gordon.† Upon this point it differs in nothing from the statements of the more partizan Leland. Speaking of the commissioners who carried the plantations into effect, he says:—

"Abuses were practised, cruelly unjust and oppressive; too various for a circumstantial detail. With a scandalous breach of trust the commissioners appointed to distribute lands, deprived the natives by fraud and violence of possessions reserved to them by command of the King; sometimes leaving them a pittance—sometimes in fact no means of subsistence at all. In the words of Leland 'the resentment of the sufferers was in some instances exasperated by finding their leases transferred to hungry adventurers who had no services to plead, and sometimes even to those who had been rebels or traitors. Neither the actors nor the objects of such grievances were confined to one religion. The most zealous in the service of Government and the most peaceable conformists were numbered in the ravages of avarice and rapine, without any distinction of principles or profession."

This was the case in Ulster. In other places the provision for the old inhabitants was still more liberal. Of confiscations in Longford more than one-half was appropriated by the king to the old proprietors. The reservations

---

* In the case before the late Master of the Rolls he decided that since the Union the condition would be satisfied by settling Irish born natives on the estate.

† This history of Ireland was published in 1805, as the title page informs us, by a pluralist of the Protestant Church—"By the Rev. James Gordon, Rector of Killegney, in the Diocese of Ferns, and of Cannaway, in the Diocese of Cork."

in favour of the latter were almost everywhere defeated by the fraud or the violence of the Irish officials. In Wicklow, when everything else had failed, when the English sovereign had thrice overruled the injustice of his subordinates in the Irish government, the Irish owner was sent to prison on a false accusation of murder, and tried by a jury expressly packed by the sheriff for the purpose of convicting him.

If we are to credit Sir John Davis, even in Munster especial care was taken by King James to secure " fixity of tenure" to the occupiers of the soil. Describing the trouble which was taken to obtain the surrenders of the estates from the " Irish and degenerate English and the regranting estates unto them according to the course of the common law," he claims for his royal master the credit of having changed the old forms of inquisitions. He tells us that since the accession of the king the inquisitions had always separately found the lands which were occupied by the lord himself as demesne lands, and those which were in the hands of tenants. As to the latter, a money value was set upon all the different customs or duties which the lord had been in the habit of exacting, and in the regrant the interests of the tenant were preserved, subject to an annual rent equivalent to the value of these customs and duties. Subject to this rent the occupying tenant was fixed in the possession of his farm:—

" The lands which are found to be in possession of the tenants are left with them respectively, charged with the certain rents in lieu of all uncertain Irish exactions."

But this was not all. This policy was not confined to the estates surrendered by " Irish, or degenerate English." Whenever there was a regrant to cure a doubtful or defective title—fixity of tenure was secured to the occupier.

" In like manner, upon all grants which have passed by virtue of the commission for defective titles, the commissioners have taken especial caution to preserve the estate of the particular tenants."

The effects of securing fixity of tenure to the occupier, Sir John Davis thus describes:—*

" And thus we see how the greatest part of the possessions (as well of the Irish as of the English) in Leinster, Conaght, and Munster are settled and secured since his Majestie came to the crowne ; whereby the hearts of the people are settled not only to live in peace, but raised and incouraged to builde, to plant, to give better education to their children, and to improve the commodities of their lands, whereby the yearly value thereofe is already increased double of that it was within these few years, and is like daily to rise higher till it amounts to the price of our lande in England."

Sir John Davis was not the friend or advocate of the Celtic

* Tracts by Sir John Davis—page 709.

race.   Yet he took a view of the best mode of effecting the
improvement of the country, rather more favourable to them than
that which is taken either by Lord Lifford, Lord Dufferin, or Lord
Rosse.   He did not think it necessary to drive them from the
land.   He did not even deem it an indispensable condition of
Irish prosperity that there should be over them the absolute
dominion of the landowner, or, to borrow the expressive phrase of
Lord Rosse, that " the landlord's hands should be untied."   On
the contrary, he prided himself on the fact that whenever in
Munster it was found that the lands had been in the occupation
of tenants, fixity of tenure had been granted to the tenants, and
as a consequence " the hearts of the people were not only settled
to live in peace, but raised and encouraged to build, to plant, to
give better education to their children, and to improve the commodities of the lands."

" Whereby "—I pray your Lordship's attention to this—" the
yearly value thereof is already increased double of that it was within
these few years."

Would it be a great calamity to Ireland if Sir John Davis had
continued Irish Attorney-General to this day?   What would have
been his reply to a proposal to adopt, in the case of the regranted
estates of Munster, a measure as little favourable to the tenants as
that which I propose?

In our days, as in those of King James, there are " Irish exactions" from tenants which need to be converted into fixed and
certain rents.   There are Irish holdings for uncertain and precarious
tenures, which need to be converted into certain terms of years.   If
I am right in saying that there is scarcely an Irish estate upon
which the terms of the original grant are observed, or the purposes
of the original grant fulfilled, a commission of defective titles might
not improperly regrant all Irish estates, " taking especial care to
preserve the estates of the occupying tenants,"

It would be impossible for me, with the space or time, or, I may
add, with the resources at my command, to trace out the historic
documents which throw light upon the grants of Elizabeth and
Cromwell.   The grants of Cromwell were admittedly framed on
the model of the Ulster plantation of King James.   An attempted
and indeed partial plantation of Ulster by Queen Elizabeth had
preceded its settlement by James.   I have no doubt that a careful
enquiry into the documents which illustrate the Elizabethan grants,
would establish with equal clearness that they were made on
conditions intended to secure the settlement on the estates of an
independent and contented tenantry.

It is not necessary for my argument to go back to these.   The testimony of Lord Clare, which I quoted in the *Plea for the Celtic
Race*," refers only to the confiscations which took place after the
accession of King James.   Since that period the greater extent of

the island has been the subject of confiscation—some of it has been subjected to the process several times. And without drawing in aid the regrants upon surrenders, or on the commission of defective titles, which Sir John Davis describes, we may safely assert that almost the entire island is now held under grants of which the avowed policy was to compel the proprietors to give up all arbitrary exactions, to renounce all lettings upon precarious tenures, and to place independent and—to use the expressive words of Pynnar's survey—"ESTATED" occupiers upon the soil.

The grants of Cromwell were recognized after the restoration. A Parliament, called that of Ireland, but in reality a provincial assembly of the delegates of the new proprietors, took especial care not to cumber the title of the new masters of Ireland by any inconvenient reference to the conditions upon which Cromwell had given them the properties of the ancient proprietors of the soil.* Cromwell's "usurpations" had been ignored for all purposes except the robbery of the Irish nation. English judges had directed in opposition to the settled principles of law, that adherence to the *de facto* government of the Commonwealth was treason, because Charles the Second was a king "*de facto*" as well as "*de jure*," while "the usurper" was exercising supreme authority in England, and the sovereign *de facto* was a fugitive in France. The acts of the "usurping" government were only held legal when they robbed the Irish nation. And while the bones of Cromwell were dragged from his grave to the gibbet, and acts of Parliament canonized the martyred king, in Ireland every trooper who had acquired property as a reward for fighting against the sainted martyr was confirmed in his grant. By an act, which it is not too much to call one of treachery, the "innocent Papists," that is the men who had been robbed by Cromwell for their adherence to the cause of their sovereign, were actually despoiled of their ancestral estates, and the compensation "in Connaught" which was awarded to them was postponed to the pay due to the soldiers of the general who had brought the "blessed martyr" to the block.

* There is something almost ludicrous in the solemn burlesque in which the Irish Parliament in the preamble of the Act of Settlement described the robberies of Cromwell's troopers and Cromwell's grants, confirming them as absolutely acts of loyalty to the exiled king. After describing the "horrid" rebellion of the confederated Irish Roman Catholics, this document proceeds:—
"Whereas several of your majesty's subjects, by whom, as instruments, the rebels were totally subdued, did, in the time of your majesty's absence beyond the seas, and to prevent the further desolation of this, your majesty's, kingdom, inquire inio the authors, abettors, and contrivers of the said rebellion and war; and after much deliberation among themselves, and advice from others had thereupon, did dispossess such of the said Popish rebels of their land tenements and hereditaments, as were guilty of, and found to have been engaged in the said rebellion and war, and did withhal distribute, and set out the said lands to be possessed by sundry persons, their agents and tenants, who by advancing of their money or goods, or by hazarding of their lives, had contributed to the said conquest, or been otherwise useful in the suppressing the said rebellion and war."

All, however, that concerns my present purpose is to point out that even the troopers who parcelled out Ireland in the "acts of settlement and explanation" did not escape—it was not possible to escape—the recognition of Cromwell's grants, and with those grants of the conditions on which the grants were made.

Where are now the subverters of the rights of property? Where are the violators of ancient right? Are they those who insist on the fulfilment of the conditions on which estates are held; or those who, in order to convert the proprietors into the tyrants and despots of the nation, would disregard every obligation by which, in Ireland, the very origin of proprietary right was bound, and trample on all the principles of the policy upon which that right depends? How often does it happen that men denounce as "revolutionary" proposals which, in reality, are a return to the most ancient and sacred principles of the law.*

I ask of those who are accustomed to boast of the plantation of Ulster as the one wise act of the English Government of Ireland if the policy of that plantation was to place the new proprietors as lords over a discontented tenantry of serfs? But I confine my attention to the one stipulation I have quoted—the stipulation that rents should be certain and tenures secure. I am not, as

---

* A very curious passage occurs in that introduction to Carte's *Life of Ormonde*, from which I have already made an extract. Speaking of the Ulster plantation he says :—"It was thought proper to avoid a mistake committed in the plantation of Munster, where the Irish were mixed among the English in order to learn civility and good husbandry from them ; but experience showed that they only learned to envy the fortunes of the English, and to long for the lands improved by their industry ; and that they made use of the freedom of access which they had to their houses, and of conversation with their persons, only to steal their goods and plot against their lives. It was therefore deemed advisable to lessen this intercourse between the two people, and to plant them separately in different quarters ; the Irish in some one place of the plainest ground of their own country, and the British by themselves in places of the best strength and command."

In every project for the " plantation" of any part of Ireland some provision was made for the "meer Irish." In the Elizabethan plantation of Munster they were freely mixed with the English settlers.

In King James' plantation of Ulster they were relegated to separate districts, or at least to separate estates.

In "the Cromwellian settlement" it was proposed to banish them to a province, almost exclusively awarded them.

Every provision for them was thwarted by the rapacity of those who practically administered Irish affairs ; and the old Irish Catholic people, contrary to the terms of every settlement, were kept as serfs upon the lands which had been allotted to Protestant proprietors upon the express terms of planting them with independent settlers.

The old proprietors were for ever deprived of the portions of land which were reserved to them by the policy of James. Even Cromwell's provision of Connaught was not left to the miserable victims of wrong. In the acts of settlement and explanation, many of the "innocent Papists," that is Roman Catholics who had adhered to King Charles, were cheated out of the lands in Connaught which had been allotted to them in compensation for the estates which they had lost by their loyalty to the King.

The credit of the idea of sending the Irish to Connaught is due to the Irish Privy Council, who first made up a project for carrying out the Ulster plantation, to be submitted to King James. This part of the project was omitted in the plan which received the final sanction of the King.

Lord Dufferin accuses me, "antedating responsibilities." The Irish proprietors hold their estates under a title which requires as a condition that they should not let their lands in the very way they are doing; that they should not create the very mischief which they are creating. The object of the prohibition was to prevent their peopling their estates with dependent serfs.

This is, indeed, but a strong illustration of the truth I have attempted to enforce, that all Irish estates were really granted on conditions which attached to them a trust. It was a trust to train up an orderly and loyal people. There was a positive and express trust not to suffer those estates to be overrun by a population destitute of any fixity of tenure, and subject, at the will of the landlord, to an arbitrary variation of the rent.

I may be told that in referring to these old conditions and ancient transactions I am attempting to apply to a long-settled and peaceful order of things the principles which were intended only for the days of unsettled relations—that I am falling into the error of insisting, in the management of reclaimed and settled "countries," on the terms which were designed only for the process of reclamation and settlement; that when a few years had passed over, and the objects of the plantation been once attained, the owners of the planted estates then held their properties free from the restrictions of the early years. The argument would be this:—The right of Government to control has ceased with the circumstances which made that control necessary. Irish landed property is now in the same condition as that of England, liable indeed to the general power of interference which the State possesses, but bound by no special responsibilities, and subject to no peculiar right of visitation by Parliament or the Crown. Such a commission and survey as that of Pynnar may have been very proper in the days of James I. But no sovereign has now a right to inquire whether it suits the pleasure or the convenience of any proprietor to place an "estated" tenantry on his lands. Ireland has now reached that condition of "civilized countries" in which, as your Lordship tells us, every proprietor is allowed, and ought to be allowed, "to do what he likes with his own."

In the first place, any one studying the conditions of the Ulster plantation must see, with Lord Lyndhurst, that they were intended to create permanent trusts, and impose lasting conditions on the ownership of Irish estates. To go no further than one: every grantee of 2,000 acres was bound to create four "fee-farms," each consisting of 120 acres. A fee-farm grant is not a thing temporary in its nature. The object and intention plainly was that there should always be a class of higher and independent yeomanry upon each estate. The provisions against letting for short tenures and at uncertain tenures were equally intended to secure a lower but still independent class of cultivators of the soil.

But in the next place the conditions of the grants have never been really fulfilled. In Ulster they have been partially complied with; yet even in that province the fulfilment has been generally evaded by substituting the mere customary security known as tenant right for the legal fixity of tenure specified in the grant. In the rest of Ireland the properties are but few upon which an estated tenantry were at any time placed to occupy the soil. The leases for lives renewable for ever to middlemen may have been the result—they were not the fulfilment of these conditions. No time can really run against the nation's right to have these essential conditions of national tranquillity and prosperity enforced. The bargain was made that, as the price of these estates, the landowner should place an independent class of occupiers upon the soil If I may use a professional illustration—as long as this purchase money is unpaid the State has a lien for it on the lands. Until they have given us that class of proprietors we have a right to insist on any measure that is necessary to create them.

The truth is, Ireland has never yet got through that "transition state" which of necessity intervenes between the imposition on the country of an alien class of proprietors and the adjustment of their new proprietary rights to settled and peaceful relations with the occupiers of the soil. We have never passed over the state of things for which these very conditions were intended. After the lapse of two centuries we are still face to face with the "unreformed" and unsettled state of society which was the necessary result of conquest and confiscation. Queen Victoria has just the same interest as the first James in preventing the grantees of the "escheated lands" from extorting "Irish exactions," and from letting on insecure tenures and at uncertain rents.

It is vain to tell me that many of the present owners are the representatives of those who purchased these "escheated lands." They could not buy the lands without accepting the responsibilities of those from whom they bought. No principle is better established in law than that which recognizes covenants that "run with the land;" and the great compact which was entered into between the British Crown, and those who accepted grants of Irish property from that Crown binds every owner who claims Irish property by virtue of any of these grants.

If it be conceded, as it must be, that in the early days of these grants—those who held them were amenable to the visitation and control of the British Crown in respect to the tenure they created on these lands—surely it cannot be said that this right of visitation and control is gone as long as the landowner depends upon the British Crown for force to protect him in his right. It never can be forgotten, it cannot be too often repeated, that all proprietary rights in Ireland are upheld solely by the military power of England. It is vain for those whose rights are thus upheld to claim

D

the extreme privileges which may or not belong to landed property
in countries where that property is held by a tenure depending
upon the influences existing in the country itself. Ireland is the
only country in Europe in which proprietary rights in land are
upheld by foreign bayonets. While this is the case, Irish landowners can never say that the relations connected with land tenure
in Ireland have assumed their settled and normal condition. For
all practical purposes we are still dealing with the "unreformed
and unsettled countries" which were the objects of anxiety to the
councillors of Queen Elizabeth and King James.

The more this subject is reflected on the more apparent will be
the right and duty of the British Government to take up, even after
so long an interval, the work of settlement and plantation, which
was interrupted in the troubles of "the great Rebellion" and in
the case of the land included in Cromwell's grants, disturbed even
by the Restoration of Charles. It is not an unfair test of the continuance of the original trusts and conditions upon which Irish
property was granted, to ask whether England is for ever to bear
the odium and the expense of maintaining the present system of
"landlordism" in Ireland. Let me say, once for all, my Lord, that
in using this phrase "landlordism" I meant no disrespect to the
owners of land. I am happy that your Lordship has adopted it,
because it appears more expressively than any word I know of to
designate that system of dominion over the people which too many
people in Ireland confound with the just claims of proprietary right.
A phrase for which I have your sanction may, I hope, be used
without offending any prejudices of your Lordship's order.

"Landlordism" in Ireland has been maintained, and is maintained,
at a positive money cost to the British Crown, of which it is not easy
to reckon the sum. The troops that have been recently hurried
to Ireland and Canada have been sent to uphold it. The gunboats
that have been despatched in hot haste to the western coast of
Ireland are gone upon the same mission. Since the restoration of
Charles II. the defence of landlordism in Ireland has drained the
English Exchequer of millions of money. It is now draining it of
hundreds of thousands—if I add the loss of revenue from Ireland,
it is draining it of millions—every year. It is lowering and
weakening England in both hemispheres of the globe. It is vain
to disguise it, Ireland is the weakness of England, and foreign
nations know it as well as we do ourselves. Irish "landlordism" is
hanging like a millstone round the neck of England, and dragging
her down from her once proud position in the commonwealth of
Europe.

I forbear to pursue this subject. But if it be true that proprietary
rights are upheld in Ireland at this enormous cost to England, would
it be unreasonable for English statesmen to say that all the burden
must not fall upon the State; that Irish landlords must even share

the losses of this ruinous partnership; and that if the losses can be put an end to by a sacrifice, on the part of the landowners, of their extreme rights of property, which give them dominion over the people, that sacrifice must and shall be made?

These conclusions follow inevitably from the circumstances under which Irish property was granted—from the circumstances in which it is now placed. The time is come when the Legislature must call on those who were and are but stewards of the "escheated lands" for an account of their stewardship. England, in self defence, must cease to connive at the violation of all the conditions on which Irish property is held, and enforce upon Irish landowners an observance of these stipulations, originally made to ensure the peace and prosperity of the country, over the people of which those proprietors were placed, and are kept, by the force of English arms.

I venture to say, my Lord, that no proposition is more clearly demonstrated than that which asserts the present right and duty of the British Government to regulate the letting of land upon every Irish estate, so far at least as to secure that there be no precarious tenures, and no exaction of uncertain rents.

I rest my proposal, so to regulate these lettings, upon clear and distinct principles:—

First.—Upon the principle that the State has a right, by the supreme law of the social compact, to regulate the enjoyment and use of all property whenever the safety of the whole community requires that this should be done.

Secondly.—Upon the condition of all landed property held under the law of England, a law which vests all that property in the Crown, and treats every owner as only enjoying its use.

Thirdly.—And lastly, and above all, I rest it on the peculiar conditions and circumstances under which all Irish land is held—conditions and circumstances which actually impose upon every Irish landowner the most clear and distinct obligation of giving to all occupiers under him that security of tenure which I call on the Legislature to enforce.

If the measure I propose can really be sustained by such principles, it is surely neither "revolutionary" nor "communistic."

I have still a few words to say in reply to some other portions of your Lordship's letter. Before I do so I must claim your Lordship's permission to offer some observations upon the letters of Lord Dufferin. You refer me to the second letter of that nobleman to *The Times*, "the unanswerable reasoning of which" seems to your Lordship to "set the question of the culpability of Irish landlords as regards the exodus at rest." So far as I am

concerned, that letter does not touch one single argument, or
question one fact which I adduced. It is only in a third letter that
Lord Dufferin incidentally notices the *Plea for the Celtic Race*.
Before noticing the second letter I claim your Lordship's permission
to offer some observations on the third. I cannot say that, in this
letter, Lord Dufferin has even made an attempt to answer me. I
gather, indeed, from the way in which he alludes to it that his
Lordship had not then condescended to read the tract upon which
he commented.* In his third letter he observes that—

" It has been objected I have mistaken the nature of the accusations
directed against the landlord class in Ireland, who, *I am informed*, have
been ruthlessly gibbeted, not exactly on account of their own acts, but as
representatives of those bygone generations to whose vicious mismanagement of their estates the present misfortunes of the country are to be
attributed.

" The writer who thus proposes to antedate our responsibilities seems
satisfied that he has arrived at the fountain-head of Ireland's calamities
when he points his finger at the Irish proprietary of former days. Nor
does he ever dream of enquiring whether the landlord of 100 years ago
may not himself have been the creature of circumstances involved in the
complications of a system of which he was as much the victim as his
tenants."

As in a subsequent part of the letter Lord Dufferin does me the
honour of mentioning me by name, I presume that I am " the
writer" referred to in this passage, and that this is intended as a
criticism on the *Plea for the Celtic Race*. The very language of
the reference, " I am informed," implies that Lord Dufferin had
formed his opinion of the tract upon the opinion of others. I did
not need, indeed, that reference to assure me that this was so. It
was, I believe, impossible, if he had read it, for a writer as intelligent and able as Lord Dufferin so completely to misunderstand—
equally impossible for one of his station and character so entirely
to misrepresent.

If, as I have reason to believe from his subsequent letter, Lord
Dufferin has since read the *Plea for the Celtic Race*, I am sure he will
admit that it would not be fair to describe me as having "ruthlessly
gibbetted" Irish landlords or " gibbetted" them at all. My whole
argument was that " the landlord of 100 years ago" was, as Lord
Dufferin describes him, the creature of circumstances. I never once
alluded to any management, vicious or otherwise, of the estates of a
century ago. I did point to some specific instances of the management of estates, but they were every one of the present day.
Looking at Irish landlordism, from the days of confiscation to

---

* It is needless to say that this was written before the publication of Lord Dufferin's
letter in *The Times* of January 31st. I have preferred leaving the text, with some
trifling alterations, as it originally stood. In subsequent pages I deal with that letter.

the present, I believed the Irish landlord, in his character of landowner, to be the vicious creation of the most vicious set of circumstances that ever degraded a nation, or lowered the character of a gentry. This is an opinion from which I do not know that Lord Dufferin very much dissents.

But no one understands the Irish land question who does not take into account the causes which created that feud between proprietor and occupier which is perpetuated to our own day, and which is now the Irish difficulty. The man who looks at that question without considering the inheritance of enmity and strife which has been bequeathed to us can literally know nothing of the subject. The writer who would use the events of our past history for any other purpose than that of laying bare our present social condition would pervert them. The occurrences—the wrongs—the oppressions of former days—have nothing to do with the question except as they enter as elements into our present life. That they do so enter is notorious. To ignore them is merely childish. To attempt to discuss the question of land tenure without reference to them is but trifling. It is by understanding their influence that most of the anomalies of our social condition are explained. It is only by making allowance for the feelings they have created that we can estimate the nature of the difficulties with which we have to deal. You might better think to understand the Polish question while you had never heard of the partition of Poland, or form a judgment of the condition and feelings of the Venetians without taking into account the memories that are attached to the history of the Doges. The existing relations of the owners and occupiers of the Irish soil are the result of a long series of causes, commencing in conquest and confiscation, and running down, through dismal years of oppression, to the present serfdom. No man who has written or spoken on Ireland, with a mind above that of a land agent's clerk, has failed to see this. Sir George Lewis glanced at it in a few sentences, in which, as in all his sentences, much wisdom is condensed. I endeavoured to trace out the operations of these miserable elements to their present and actual result. I may have been successful, or I may not; but Lord Dufferin himself, in the very arguments he uses, admits that a writer could have no real apprehension of the subject who would "dream" that he could dispose of it by speaking of "antedating the responsibilities of landlords."

I am justified in saying so because in this very same letter Lord Dufferin, notwithstanding his somewhat slighting allusion to my reference to the origin and history of Irish proprietary rights, proceeds himself to discuss the Irish land question by a review of the injuries inflicted on Ireland in the last century by the commercial jealousy of England. I believe these very injuries have something to do with our present position, but little, immeasurably little, compared to the blight which has been cast upon us by the never-ceasing oppression inflicted on the occupiers of the soil. Although a century has very nearly passed since the restrictions upon our trade and our manufactures have ceased, I am far from saying that even in estimating our present system of land tenure we may not reasonably take the effect of these restrictions into account. But surely if we may, it is of far more consequence that we should consider the influence of the laws and circumstances which have ground down and degraded the occupiers of the soil.

After tracing the effects of English commercial injustice, his lordship thus proceeds:—

"Feeling that our best chance of dealing with the difficulties of Ireland is to arrive at a correct appreciation of their origin, I have done my best to detail the facts, which prove that it is unjust to refer them to the influence of owners of property in Ireland, while I have detailed a succession of circumstances amply sufficient to account for them."

" Our best chance of dealing with the difficulties of Ireland is to arrive at a correct appreciation of their origin." To endeavour to trace them to their origin was the whole aim and purpose of the essay for which I am visited with his Lordship's contemptuous rebuke. I should be sorry to suppose that my crime is, that I traced them a little too clearly to an origin that does not quite suit the views of high proprietary right.

Lord Dufferin is far too intelligent not to see that some cause must be assigned for the present condition of our country. He admits, in most remarkable words—

"Some human agency or other must be accountable for the perennial desolation of a lovely and fertile island, watered by the fairest streams, caressed by a clement atmosphere, held in the embrace of a sea whose affluence fills the richest harbours of the world, and inhabited by a race valiant, tender, generous, gifted beyond measure with the power of physical endurance, and graced with the liveliest intelligence."

Lord Dufferin's description, glowing as it is, is not more glowing than that of Lord Bacon:—

"For this island it is endowed with so many dowries of Nature, considering the fruitfulness of the soil, the ports, the rivers, the fishings, the quarries, the woods, and other materials, and especially the race and generation of men—valiant, hard, and active, as it is not easy, no, not upon the Continent, to find such confluence of commodities, if the hand of men did join with the hand of Nature." *

There is a startling similarity in the complaints of Lord Dufferin

* Bacon's Works, Vol. iii., 321.

and Lord Bacon, although an interval of two centuries and a half divide them—an interval in which the " perennial desolation" of the country has remained unchanged.

Is it possible to imagine words that more perfectly describe all the elements of national happiness and greatness.   If " natural economic laws" had their free operation in Ireland, Ireland must be prosperous and great.   Some human and malignant agency has disturbed them.   What is it?   This is the Irish question.   The very same question—immortal as the miseries of our country—which Bishop Berkeley asked more than 120 years ago, and which, if matters go on as they are, may be the subject of controversy between our great grandchildren 120 years hence.

" What hindereth us Irishmen from exerting ourselves, using our hands and brains, doing something or other, man, woman, or child, like all the other inhabitants of God's earth?"

Lord Dufferin says it is because, in the reign of Elizabeth, England prohibited the importation of Irish cattle; because, from the reign of Charles II. to 1782, England did her best to destroy and suppress the woollen manufacture of Ireland; because a century ago England prohibited Ireland from trading freely with the colonies and foreign nations; and because (I will do full justice to the argument) the effect of this English policy was to drive the whole population upon the soil for their support; to cause an un-natural competition for land, and so to create all the evils of a redundant population and exorbitant rents.

Lord Dufferin has one great advantage in preferring an indictment against England.   The argument is one that would be dexterously framed if it were intended to divert the attention of the Irish people from the practical object before them; as bulls have been turned from the men they have been pursuing by flaunting before them a piece of scarlet cloth.   Any argument that throws blame upon England is popular with the Irish people.   Something would be gained for Irish " landlordism " if an appeal to the patriotic hatred of English rule could be used to turn that people away from the consideration of that great question of land tenure, in which their very existence in their own country is now involved.

I do not deny that the matters to which Lord Dufferin refers are important as the subject of historical study.   They suggest questions of the greatest moment to the mind of every thinking Irishman; but these questions relate not to the practical remedy which is to redress the evils of our land tenure, but to the opinion which asserts the absolute necessity of self-government for this country.   In this way the events which Lord Dufferin describes have been used, and fairly used.   All that Lord Dufferin has told us of the past misconduct of England will be found far more fully, and I think more accurately, narrated in the publications of the Repeal Association. If Lord Dufferin means to insist on the right of Ireland to self-government he will find many, very many, of us perfectly ready to leave the settlement of the land question to an Irish Parliament, as soon as he shows us the prospect of obtaining one.

But if Lord Dufferin does not draw or intend to draw this practical inference, this " ruthless gibbetting" (is not this the proper phrase?) of the past generation of English statesmen and English commercial men can help us but little to solve the problem we have in hand. Lord Dufferin admits that we have to deal with this question—a country with advantages—if Lord Dufferin's description be true—with advantages unrivalled by any country in Europe; and yet the most miserable, poor, and discontented in Christendom. We want to know can nothing be done to remedy this? to permit a people possessing all the noble qualities Lord Dufferin has attributed to them to use and enjoy the advantages of their native land? Lord Dufferin tells us that England prohibited the importation of our cattle into England, destroyed our woollen manufacture, and deprived us of the benefit of a free trade.

If any stranger unacquainted with Irish history were to read this, he would say at once—the remedy is plain; let England give up her unjust commercial policy; let her freely admit Irish cattle to her markets; let her remove all restrictions on the Irish woollen trade; and let her freely share with Ireland her trade with the colonies and the world. With what astonishment would he learn that all these remedies have been applied! that for sixty-seven years, indeed for eighty-five years, all vexatious restrictions have been removed, and that the condition of Ireland is every day getting worse and worse. I am disposed to say that the stranger, upon hearing this, would say that however much Lord Dufferin's speculations might be interesting as an historical inquiry, they do not offer us much help in providing a practical remedy for the evil condition of our affairs.

And, accordingly, Lord Dufferin proposes none.* Describing Ireland as he has done, he offers no advice as to the means by which the curse and blight that is upon her—a curse and blight created by some malignant human agency—may be removed. The only approach to a suggestion on the subject is a hint very plainly thrown out that it is essential to the prosperity of Ulster that the ruinous custom of tenant right should be destroyed.

But even though Lord Dufferin may decline to propose a remedy for our national distresses, he may, I admit, contribute usefully to the discussion, if he helps us to trace out the cause. I have, I think, fairly stated the substance of Lord Dufferin's reply to

---

* In his letter of the 31st of January Lord Dufferin does suggest a mode of dealing with the land question, of which in subsequent pages I say a few words.

Bishop Berkeley's question. Let me now endeavour to restate my own.

I say that our condition is to be traced to this:—Wars which were treated as rebellions eventuated in parcelling out the greater portion of the island among a "motley crew of English adventurers,"* to make room for whom the old inhabitants were deprived of their estates. The whole, or nearly the whole, property of the island was held by a title of confiscation. The new proprietors treated the old population as serfs. The relations between owners and occupiers have been embittered and exasperated by long and angry struggles, social, political, and religious, between the representatives of the conquerors and the conquered; and at this hour a "hostile population brooding over their discontent in sullen indignation,"† are held by the descendants of those proprietors in a state of the most abject thraldom and servitude, by the expedient of keeping them without any tenure of the land, and, therefore, without any means of livelihood except at the good will and pleasure of their lord.

Will any one deny that if this be true it is a sufficient answer to the question? "The human agency" that is "accountable for the perennial desolation" of our whole country is, to use an expressive, even if it be an incorrect, phrase, "landlordism." I do not say landlords—I believe many, nay most, of the Irish landlords are "the victims of these complexities" just as much as their tenants; but I say that the hindrances to "Irishmen doing something for themselves like all the other inhabitants of God's earth" are—the state of serfdom in which they have been and are kept—the utter discouragement to their industry which is involved in the insecurity of tenure by which that serfdom is maintained.

It is a mere trifling with this question to talk of "culpability" or "responsibility" of landlords past, present, or to come. We are dealing with a great political and social question, which cannot be frittered away in miserable quibbles about words. Lord Dufferin seems to think that he is defending Irish landlords against an indictment, and that he is successful if he can pick holes in it. His second letter is nothing more than a special demurrer to some phrases in that which he calls the accusation of Mr. Maguire and Mr. Bright. It matters not who is culpable or who is responsible. We are not administering criminal justice, but searching for the principles of remedial legislation. There is the state of things in Ireland creating by "human agency" the "perennial desolation" of the country. Is that state of things, however it originated, perpetuated and aggravated by the present system of land tenure? If it be, that system must be changed. After all the information we can derive from historical inquiry, it is with the existing state

* Lord Clare's Speech on the Union.—*Land Tenure in Ireland*, p. 25.
† Lord Clare.

of things—with the present condition of land tenure—that we are concerned. No matter what produces it, it is there. To trace it to its causes is important only as it may help us thoroughly to understand it, or may guide us in the suggestion of a remedy.

I believe it of great importance to understand the relations that have existed between owners and occupiers from the days of Oliver Cromwell to the present day. But I do so because they are still subsisting, and because their character in the present day is impressed with the history of the past. It is a very different thing to inquire into the operation of causes that have long since passed away. I admit this inquiry fairly occupies a place in the discussion, but the place of that inquiry is very secondary and subordinate to an investigation which traces out the result of elements which, though existing for two centuries, are still actually present in, and actually influencing our existing social condition. If that which I have stated of the present relations of landlord and tenant be true the remedies I have suggested would not be the less necessary or applicable, even though Lord Dufferin should succeed in proving that these relations would never have assumed their present miserable form if England had given free scope to our manufacturing industry at the time of the Revolution.

It is of such immense importance that the real question should be understood—that we should get rid of all false issues, and be distracted by no irrelevant inquiries, that I venture, even at the risk of being tedious, to repeat the propositions which I attempted to support in the tract on Land Tenure; propositions which, at all events, are clear, intelligible, and distinct. They were these:—

"I.

"The position of the occupiers of the soil of Ireland is at present generally that of serfs, without any security either for their tenure or the fruits of their industry. They are dependent for their very means, of existence on the will of their landlord, while the amount of that which is called rent is regulated, not by any economic law, but by the disposition of the landlord to extort, and their own ability to pay.

"II.

"This state of things has originated remotely, perhaps not very remotely, in the fact that English power confiscated the whole property of our island, and placed over the inhabitants alien and hostile proprietors without making any sufficient provision to secure or protect the right of the old inhabitants to live upon the soil.*

"III.

"The evil effects of the original injustice were increased by the in-

---

* Some provision was made for this purpose in the settlements of King James; even in those of Oliver Cromwell there was a pretence at making it. Inadequate, as these provisions were, especially in the latter case, they were defeated by the venality and the rapacity of those to whom the administration of Irish affairs was entrusted.

fluence of the laws, which for a long period after the confiscations, reduced a great proportion of those occupying the soil to the condition of slaves in the religious and political disabilities to which they were subjected.

"IV.

"They have been up to the present hour aggravated and continued by the antagonism of religion, of habits, and of race, which exists between the class that constitutes the owner, and that which supplies the tillers of the soil.

"V.

"The events of the last fifty years have brought these evils to a climax, which is now rapidly completing the extermination of the old Irish race."

These five propositions resolve themselves into, matters of fact, or very nearly so. From these matters of fact I deduced a sixth proposition, which, of course, rests on inference and opinions. It was this:—

"VI.

"The only remedy that can be applied to this lamentable and miserable state of things is to elevate the occupier from his position of serfdom, by giving him an interest in the soil; to do so at any price—to do so by giving him that without which every other remedy is but a miserable palliative—by giving him FIXITY OF TENURE—while we leave to the owner of the soil every right and every power, except those which he cannot continue to exercise without the waste and destruction of human life, and without bringing ruin both on himself and the entire community."

Has Lord Dufferin in all his letters written one single line to disprove the first proposition? He has written much to confirm it. If that proposition be admitted, the admission is fatal to the system of land tenure. Are we, in the year 1867, seriously to argue the question of serfdom? I have sometimes felt in discussing land tenure in Ireland as if I were only repeating the arguments of the slave question. I have felt, indeed, as if I were throwing away labour in proving that while the mass of the population are in a practical condition of serfdom we cannot expect the blight of our " perennial desolation" to be removed.

I am bold to say that in the *Plea for the Celtic Race* I have conclusively established every one of the five propositions which I have stated as matters of fact. I have indeed seen no attempt at their disproof, or even their contradiction.

Lord Dufferin's argument might perfectly consist with mine. It might even strengthen it. If it were true that the destruction of our woollen manufacture and the other commercial wrongs of the last century had the effect of driving upon the soil a population which would otherwise have found employment in manufactures, this might have facilitated the exaction of exorbitant rents, and—in increasing the number of serfs have aggravated and extended the powers of serfdom. I am quite sure that political and religious disabilities had that effect; so, in some degree, had everything which discouraged the industry of any class. But all this would only amount to saying that there were causes which made it more difficult for the Irish occupier to emancipate himself from the state of servitude, in which, by virtue of his land tenure, he was held. If it be true that these things aggravated the case, it is only the more necessary that a remedy should be applied.

Lord Dufferin, as I understand him, goes the full length of saying that the evil condition of our present land tenure is to be traced solely to the commercial injustice of past days which he points out—that if England had not discouraged our industry and our commerce there never would have existed unsatisfactory relations between landlord and tenant. He says that it " is unjust to refer to the difficulties " that beset our land tenure " to the influence of the owners of property in Ireland." All must be laid at the door of England's jealousy and injustice. Let us examine the proposition in which Lord Dufferin thus states his views:—

" It will be sufficient for me to record my own profound conviction— a conviction shared by many of your readers—that had Ireland only been permitted to develop the other innumerable resources at her command, as she has developed the single industry in which she was permitted to embark, the equilibrium between the land and the population dependent upon the land would never have been disturbed, nor would the relations of landlord and tenant have become a subject of anxiety."

" Relations between landlord and tenants BECAME a subject of anxiety ! "

" The equilibrium between land and the population dependent on it DISTURBED ! "

Who that reads this would not suppose that in the days which followed the revolution—in the days of Swift and Primate Boulter— the relations between the Irish owner and the Irish occupier were long settled and peaceful relations rudely disturbed by the discouragement of the Irish woollen trade? So that to gain " a correct appreciation of the source of Ireland's difficulties" we are to assume that in the days of William and Anne there were " relations" and " equilibriums" which would never have been a cause of anxiety if they had not been rudely disturbed. We are to ignore the wicked confiscations which had just parcelled out two-thirds of the island among Cromwell's soldiers, the policy of conquest and confiscation which protected the new titles by reducing the old inhabitants to be slaves, the penal laws that crushed down the native tillers of the soil into slavery, the laws of exclusion which shut out Roman Catholics from admission to the manufacturing guilds of our cities and our towns, the bigotry which in many instances debarred them even from residence within their walls; and we are to mourn over the disturbance of those happy relations of owners and occupiers which would never have given cause for anxiety if it had not been for England's suppression of our woollen trade.

Between the new proprietors and the mass of the people there never existed any relations to which Lord Dufferin's language could be applied. In the history of Ireland's miseries I really do not know what is meant by the disturbance " of the equilibrium between the land and the population dependent upon it." It is, I repeat, impossible to epitomize Irish history in a letter. Let us briefly glance at the social condition of the people during the existence of these restrictions, and from their cessation in 1782* to the present time.

In the period between the Revolution and the era of Irish independence the population of Ireland was certainly not in excess of that which might easily find employment and maintenance on her soil.

In 1712 it barely exceeded two millions.†

In 1782 it had not risen to three.‡

Can it possibly be said that three millions of people could not have been supported on the Irish soil?

The mere statement of the numbers of the population is sufficient to displace the theory that the suppression of the woollen trade, or any commercial injustice, disturbed an "equilibrium" previously subsisting "between the land and the population dependent on the land." When the restrictions were abolished, the population had not yet reached the number actually required for the due cultivation of the soil.

The wars of the great rebellion had depopulated Ireland. Her grievance was not an excessive but a deficient population. Lord Clarendon tells us that in his day the great want of Ireland was men. So far, during this period, were Irish landlords from finding an excessive agricultural population in the country that many of them imported and planted German Protestants on their estates.

Where in this period are we to date the fatal "disturbance of the equilibrium between land and the population dependent upon land?"

It can scarcely be said that a population of two millions, which in the days of Dean Swift was the entire population of Ireland, could have created any extraordinary competition for land. We shall see presently how he describes the condition of the "serfs" of his day.

---

* "Some relaxation of the system," said Mr. Pitt, speaking in 1785 of the commercial injustice to Ireland, "took place at an early period of the present century. Somewhat more of the restrictive laws were abolished in the reign of George the Second, but it was not until a time nearer our own day, and indeed within the last seven years, that the system had been completely reversed."—*Pitt's Parliamentary Speeches.*

† *Sadler on Ireland,* p. 5.　　　　‡ *Ibid.*

I have now before me a volume, the opening pages of which I wish earnestly could be read by every one who has to deal with the condition of Ireland. I mean the work on the Evils of Ireland, by Michael Thomas Sadler. I quote from one of his notes a striking collection of testimonies, covering a long period, as to the condition of the Irish occupiers of the soil. Where in the midst of these shall we place the date at which the relations of landlord and tenant *became* matter of anxiety?

EDMOND SPENCER.—" The landlords there most shamefully rack their tenants."

DEAN SWIFT.—" Rents squeezed out of the blood, and vitals, and clothes, and dwellings of the tenants, who live worse than English beggars."

ARCHBISHOP BOULTER.—" Here the tenant, I fear, has hardly ever more than one-third for his share; too often but a fourth or a fifth part."

ARTHUR DOBBS.—" What was it induced so many of the commonalty lately to go to America but high rents? These kept them poor and low, that they had scarcely sufficient means to procure necessaries or till the ground."

LORD CLARE (when Attorney-General, 1787).—" The peasantry are ground down to powder by enormous rents."

" Exorbitant rent."—*Gordon's History of Ireland.*

" Exorbitant rents."—*Newenham's Inquiry.*

" Exorbitant rents."—*Bishop Woodward's Argument for the Support of the Poor.*

" Exorbitant rents."—*Curwen on the State of Ireland.**

The passage from Swift thus described the relation of landlord and tenant within the early years of the new state of things.

" A stranger would be apt to think himself travelling in Lapland or Iceland rather than in a country so favoured as ours, both for fruitfulness of soil and temperature of climate. The miserable dress, and diet, and dwelling of the people; the general desolation in most parts of the kingdom ; *the old seats of the nobility and gentry all in ruins,* and no new ones in their stead ; the families of farmers, WHO PAY GREAT RENTS, living in filth and nastiness upon buttermilk and potatoes, without a shoe or a stocking to their feet, or a house so convenient as an English pig stye to receive them. These, indeed, may be comfortable sights to an English spectator, who comes for a short time only to learn the language, and returns back to his own country, whither he finds all our wealth transmitted.

" ' Nostrâ miseriâ tu magnus es.'

" *The rise of our rents is squeezed out of the very blood, and vitals, and clothes, and dwellings of the tenants, who live worse than English beggars.* The lowness of interest, in all other countries a sign of wealth, in ours is a

* *Ireland and its Evil.* By Michael Thomas Sadler, M.P. for Newark. London. 1829.

proof of misery; there being no trade to employ any borrower. Hence alone comes the dearness of land, since the savers have no other way to lay out their money. Hence the dearness of the necessaries of life; because the tenants cannot afford to pay such extravagant rents for land, which they must take or go a begging, without raising the price of cattle and of corn, although they should live upon chaff."*

This description of the state of Ireland was written in 1727. The generation who had been confirmed, by a second conquest, in the possession of the rapine of Cromwell had scarcely passed away. Down to the day of Ireland's independence that description is verified by the testimony of all who write of, or who even incidentally allude to, the condition of the people. Through successive years we trace the dismal sameness of a testimony that never varies in its story of desolation and exorbitant rents. Archbishop Boulter, Bishop Berkeley, Arthur Young, Arthur Dobbs, Bishop Woodward, Lord Clare, and even Archdeacon Paley,† are among the witnesses who bear an unbroken and continuous testimony to the wretchedness of the people. almost from the very hour when the dominant caste were established as conquerors over the land.

Never, perhaps, was the physical misery of a country more directly connected, by clear and overwhelming evidence, with its national prostration and its political degradation—with its trampling down by the iron hoof of conquest, and the subjugation of its people to religious and social slavery.

The mere statement of events in the consecutive order of their occurrence is sufficient to carry conviction as to their relation as cause and effect. We find the confiscations and the penal code immediately followed by such a state of things as Swift describes. The property of the country was partitioned among men actuated by the passions of fanaticism, of conquest, and of fear. The soldiers of Cromwell had been suddenly made masters of the Irish people. They implicitly believed that the very security of their title depended on keeping that people as slaves. A penal code was enacted which crushed to the earth all the professors of the religion to which the mass of the population adhered. That code excluded them from every civil privilege—from the meanest office. The very exercise of their religion was tolerated by connivance, while down to that of the village constable all authority was exclusively vested in the adherents and partisans of the new masters of the country. Immediately following on this we find that old population

---

* *State of Ireland.* Swift's Works.

† There is something strange, to an Irishman humiliating in the singular variety of quarters in which we meet with incidental testimony as to the degradation of our people. We would scarcely look for it in the pages of the novelist and the theologian. Paley, *who had been in Ireland*, selects the Irish peasant for one of his illustrations :— "The lowest class of the Irish afford a proof in point. They are poor, and in point of situation in a state of slavery."—*Paley's Memoirs.* By Meadly. 2nd edition, p. 379.

on the estates of the masters set over them by confiscation, we
find them in poverty and wretchedness, submitting to exactions not
always in the shape of rent, which left them a bare and miserable
existence for themselves.   Is it possible to conceive any connexion
of events more clearly established than that which is thus shown
to exist between the confiscations and the consequent policy of
conquest and the depressed condition and serfdom of the people.
     From that serfdom the occupiers of the soil of Ireland have
never yet been raised.   I know of no historic deduction more clear
than that which traces almost year by year the perpetuation of its
evil influences to the present day.   The calm and philosophic
judgment of the late Sir George Lewis thus described the state of
the Irish occupiers of the soil.
     In his work on Irish Disturbances and the Irish Church Ques-
tion, after pointing out the evils produced by grants to an absentee,
who was represented either by an agent or "middleman," he
proceeds:—

     "The landlord, if resident and an Irishman, was almost invariably a
Protestant, as Catholics were incapacitated from holding land; and, as
in the three southern provinces nearly all the tenants were Catholic, the
landlord exercised over his tenant not only that influence which a creditor
necessarily exercises over his debtor, but also that power which the law
gave to the Protestant over the Catholic, to the magistrate and grand
juror over the suspected rebel.   In these two ways all friendly connexion
between the landlord and the tenant of the soil was broken; either the
landlord was . . . represented by an oppressive, grasping middleman,
or . . . he was the member of a dominant and privileged caste,
who was as much bound by his official duties as he was prompted by
the opinion of his order, by the love of power, and by the feeling of
irresponsibility to oppress, degrade, and trample upon his Catholic
tenants." . . .

     Under this system the occupiers of the soil bore, of necessity, the
relation to their masters, not of tenants in any sense in which
tenancy is understood in England, but that of miserable, oppressed,
and discontented serfs.   Sir George Lewis goes on to describe
the Irish peasants:—

     "Deprived of all self-respect by the operation of the penal statutes,
prevented from rising in the world or from bettering their condition by
legal disabilities and the legalized oppression of their landlords; without
education, excluded from a public participation in the rites of their own
religion,* they endured all and more than the evils which belonged to the

---

* Although this statement as to the exclusion of Roman Catholics from a public
participation in the rites of their religion is in one sense true, I have already pointed out
in the Tract on Land Tenure (p. 30, 31), that the penal laws were never executed in
their full and relentless rigour, partly owing to the good feeling, more perhaps to the
self-interest, of the Protestant settlers in the country.   This statement is exactly

lot of a serf without looking forward to the interested protection and relief which a master would afford to his bondman."

Sir George Lewis refers to the testimony of Arthur Young. Half a century after Swift had written, that careful and accurate observer found the people in this condition:—

" 'It must,' he writes in 1776, 'it must be very apparent to every traveller through that country, that the labouring poor are treated with harshness, and are in all respects so little considered that their want of importance seems a perfect contrast to their situation in England. . . . . . The age has improved so much in humanity that even the poor Irish have experienced its influence, and are every day treated better and better; but still the remnant of the old manners, the abominable distinction of religion, united with the oppressive conduct of the little country gentlemen, or rather vermin of the kingdom, who never were out of it, altogether still bear very heavy on the poor people, and subject them to situations more mortifying than we ever behold in England. *The landlord of an Irish estate inhabited by Roman Catholics is a sort of despot, who yields obedience in whatever concerns the poor to no law but that of his will.'* "

Sir George Lewis stopped in his quotation from Arthur Young. I shall presently have occasion to refer to the authority of that writer.* I am anticipating a little in completing that extract. If it seems like a " ruthless gibbetting" of the Irish landlords of other days—it was written by a man who had been the inmate of the houses of the aristocracy and gentry—who, in his tour through Ireland, was the honoured guest of many of the first men of the kingdom, and whose writings are, let me say it, in many respects, manifestly tinged by the tone of thought prevalent among his entertainers. If such things be revived it is not my act, it is that of those who expect us to ignore all history, and acquiesce in the statement that it is " unjust to refer the difficulties of the Irish land question to the influence of the owners of property," and that the serfdom of the Irish people originated in the refusal of England to allow us to export our cloth.

confirmed by a report given us by Arthur Young of a conversation which he had with Lord Chief Baron Foster at his residence at Collon.
" In conversation upon the Popery laws, I expressed my surprise at their severity : he said they were severe in the letter, but were never executed. It is rarely or never (he knew no instance) that a Protestant discoverer gets a lease by proving the lands let under two-thirds of their value to a Papist. There are severe penalties on carrying arms or reading Mass ; but the first is never executed, except for poaching (which I have heard), and as to the other, mass-houses are to be seen every where : there is one in his own town. His lordship did justice to the merits of the Roman Catholics, by observing that they were in general a very sober, honest, and industrious people. This account of the laws against them brought to my mind an admirable expression of Mr. Burke's in the English House of Commons, CONNIVANCE IS THE RELAXATION OF SLAVERY, NOT THE DEFINITION OF LIBERTY."—*Young's Tour in Ireland*, Vol. ii., p. 151.
* Post.

"A long series of oppressions, aided by many very ill judged laws, have brought landlords into a habit of exerting a very lofty superiority, and their vassals into that of an almost unlimited submission; speaking a language that is despised, professing a religion that is abhorred, and being disarmed, the poor find themselves in many cases slaves even in the bosom of *written* liberty. Landlords that have resided much abroad are usually humane in their ideas, but the habit of tyranny naturally contracts the mind, so that even in this polished age there are instances of a severe carriage towards the poor, which is quite unknown in England.

"A landlord in Ireland can scarcely invent an order which a servant, labourer, or cottar dares to refuse to execute. Nothing satisfies him but unlimited submission. Disrespect or anything tending towards sauciness he may punish with his cane or his horsewhip with the most perfect security, a poor man would have his bones broke if he offered to lift his hand in his own defence. Knocking down is spoken of in the country in a manner that makes an Englishman stare. Landlords of consequence have assured me that many of their cottars would think themselves honoured by having their wives and daughters sent for to the bed of their masters;* a mark of slavery that proves the oppression under which such people must live. Nay, I have heard anecdotes of the lives of people being made free with without any apprehension of the justice of a jury. But let it not be imagined that this is common; formerly it happened every day, but law gains ground. It must strike the most careless traveller to see whole strings of cars whipt into a ditch by a gentleman's footman to make way for his carriage; if they are overturned or broken in pieces, no matter, it is taken in patience; were they to complain they would perhaps be horsewhipped. The execution of the laws lies very much in the hands of justices of the peace, many of whom are drawn from the most illiberal class in the kingdom. If a poor man lodges a complaint against a gentleman, or any animal that chuses to call himself a gentlemen, and the justice issues out a summons for his appearance, it is a fixed affront, and he will infallibly be *called out*. Where MANNERS are in conspiracy against LAW, to whom are the oppressed people to have recourse? It is a fact that a poor man having a contest with a gentleman must—but I am talking nonsense, they know their situation too well to think of it; they can have no defence but by means of protection from

* I am sure that this representation if applied to the manners of the people generally was untrue. This does not affect the testimony of Arthur Young. It was the statement to him "OF LANDLORDS OF CONSEQUENCE." The more mistaken they were the more fearful is the testimony to the terrible vassalage in which "their cottars" were held. Even in our own day we have seen the terrors of serfdom almost as cruelly crush down the feelings, upon the existence of which in our peasantry we take most pride. No one will deny this who will read the dismal story of the murder of the poor outcast boy. Narrative in a subsequent page.

After all, while human nature is what it is, to give absolute power is to insure its abuse.

Not two years ago I was present when those who filled a crowded court listened with admiration to language even of vehement indignation, in which, from the judgment seat, and in a charge to a jury, an Irish judge denounced a trafficking in landlord influence for purposes as base as any that could justify the statements of Arthur Young. Those who heard the almost impassioned charge of Judge Keogh, to which I refer, have not, I am sure, forgotten, and will not easily forget it.

one gentleman against another, who probably protects his vassal as he would the sheep he intends to eat.

"The colours of this picture are not charged. To assert that all these cases are common, would be an exaggeration; but to say that an unfeeling landlord will do all this with impunity is to keep strictly to truth : and what is liberty but a farce, and a jest if its blessings are received as the favour of kindness and humanity, instead of being the inheritance of RIGHT?"*

Subjects such as these were among those with which "I dealt gently, very gently,"† in the *Plea for the Celtic Race*, and on which I was content to "assume that every Irishman was at least moderately acquainted with the history of his country."‡

When we speak of the agricultural population of Ireland during that period between the revolution and 1782, which might, in one sense, be called the dark age of Ireland, it is absolutely necessary to distinguish between very different classes of persons connected with the land.

There were, first, the owners of the soil, supposed by law to be always Protestants, and who, almost universally, were so. Many of these owners resided on their own estates, and dealt directly with their tenantry. Many of them were absentees, whose agents were, in truth, the lords of the soil. Some of these latter, and some even of the resident gentry, let their lands to a class of persons known as middlemen, who, holding considerable portions of lands re-let them at a considerable increase of rent. These middlemen were very often mere rent farmers, taking land already occupied by tenants for the very purpose of making profit by the collection of the rents. In many instances they were persons who had acquired leasehold interests when the value of Irish property was not understood, and who, in the course of some years, found that their leasehold interest while it lasted was, in fact, equivalent to a very valuable estate in the land. They preferred being landed proprietors to being farmers; and they relet their lands very often in small portions. In very many cases the grants were for so a long period, and the rents reserved so small, that these persons were the proprietors; the owner in fee a mere rent charger on the estate. Many even of the gentry—the "county families" of Ireland—held their properties on a tenure peculiar to this country, that of leases for lives, with a covenant for perpetual renewal, an ingenious contrivance to give to the grantee a perpetual interest in the land, while the chief lord still retained the feudal remedies and powers which the law then conferred only on an owner who retained a reversion in his hands.

I shall presently have occasion to refer again to these interests which were so often interposed between the chief lord and the

---

* *Young's Tour in Ireland.* Vol. ii., part ii., p. 51.   † *Land Tenure in Ireland,* p. 95.
‡ *Land Tenure in Ireland,* p. 7.

occupiers of the soil. But upon the soil itself were located three classes of persons in a very different position from each other.

There were, first, the Protestant freeholders, holding farms often of very considerable size and at a very moderate rent, cultivating these farms themselves, almost universally holding leases for three lives, generally with the addition of thirty-one years, either concurrent or in reversion. These persons formed a body of rich independent and substantial farmers; and with the Protestant gentry and with the Protestant traders and artizans they constituted that which in the history of the last century is known as the Irish nation. Upon this tenantry no oppression ever was—none ever could be practised. The English tenantry did not hold their lands upon terms as independent or as easy, and so far as they were concerned the relation of landlord and tenant was in a state, perhaps, more satisfactory than in any country in Europe.

Protestant tenants in many parts of Ireland could not be found numerous enough to occupy all the land. We know in the history of landed property in Ireland of more than one instance in which the attempt was made to supply the deficiency by importing German and other foreign settlers. If land was to be cultivated at all it must be cultivated by heretic hands, "Popish spade and scythe" must dig and cut the soil and the crops of the "Sassenach" proprietor. From this necessity arose the indulgence in the penal laws, that Papists might have leases not exceeding thirty-one years and at not less than two-thirds of the letting value. To the very same necessity we may trace the universal non-enforcement of the worst atrocities of these laws. Accordingly a considerable number of Roman Catholic farmers were put in possession of large farms, which they cultivated themselves, holding by leases for the thirty-one years which the law allowed. They also held their lands at moderate rents, sometimes below the legal limit of two-thirds of the full value, and were often independent and substantial cultivators of the soil.

Their position was not, and it could not be, as good as that of the Protestant of the same class. The very law which admitted them to tenure declared that their tenure must not be as beneficial as that of their Protestant neighbours. It must not exceed a certain term, and it must not be below a certain rent. The rent of the Catholic farmer was higher than that of the Protestant; and this absurd and mischievous distinction was actually the creation of the law. This was not all. The Catholic could only exercise his religion by sufferance and connivance. Mass houses and priests were common, but it was felony by law for a priest to say mass. For the non-execution of the law the Catholic was indebted to the forbearance of his Protestant landlord and neighbours. It is an entire mistake in Irish history to suppose that the laws which actually prohibited the exercise of the Catholic religion were enforced. They were—as the power of eviction is now—the sword suspended over the serf, the lash kept hanging up to terrify the slave. It would be even a mistake to say that between Catholics and Protestants a very large amount of good feeling and good fellow-ship did not exist. Yet the Catholic farmer, even the gentleman farmer, belonged to a degraded caste. He was generally the object of distrust and suspicion. He was excluded from the common rights of citizenship by the denial of the elective franchise, perhaps even more so by the law which prohibited him from serving on juries. His children could not aspire to any of the learned profes-sions, nor even enter into trade upon terms as advantageous as their Protestant neighbours. Roman Catholics, even of the better class, were prohibited from bearing arms, and the legal prohibition was sometimes enforced when the jealousy of a Protestant sportsman was excited by seeing a Papist carrying a fowling piece in pursuit of game. Their tenure of thirty-one years was shorter than that which Protestants generally enjoyed. It was denounced by every one—by statesman and practical agriculturist, by Edmund Burke, and Arthur Young—as one utterly inadequate to give a real interest in the improvement of the soil. Yet after all they held an interest in their lands which gave them a certain amount of independence. They accumulated wealth even by the industry which they could venture to expend on a thirty-one years' lease ; and they have been mainly the creators of that great Roman Catholic community which has at last vindicated its place in the Irish nation.

Below these two classes lay the great mass of the Irish people. Beside, or even on, these large farms of prosperous tenants, that people were living, an inferior and degraded caste. Driven out from their land by the Cromwellian or Williamite persecutions, in some instances they actually "fled to the mountains," and settled in miserable colonies of their own. Of course the landlord followed them and exacted not a rent but a tribute. From these mountain regions they could be seen at seed time or harvest, descending to the towns—shaggy and ill-clad savages, exhibiting themselves on Sundays at the market-cross, carrying their mattock or their reaping hook, and waiting to be hired of any farmer who wanted extra labour on his farm.

Some few of them were admitted as cottier labourers upon the large farms, giving their labour for a house, a potato garden, and a few pence a day. Some were clustered as cottier tenants in miserable assemblies of cabins called towns or villages, paying for a few fields exorbitant rents, "squeezed out of their very blood and vitals." More of them obtained small holdings, frequently on the lands of middlemen, generally with leases, but always at exorbitant rents and on slavish conditions.* These rents were throughout

---

* Mr. Wakefield, who wrote his *View of Ireland* in 1812, points out that the leases of these miserable tenants were in fact instruments by which the lessees were legally bound as serfs and "bondsmen" to their lords.

three-fourths of Ireland invariably exacted, whether by landlords
or middlemen, upon the cottier lettings, and upon those of
the smaller farms. Then as now the people who wanted them
were ready to promise any rent. Then as now they had to
get the bit of ground or go a-begging. There was an interval
so complete between them and the men who could hold or
cultivate large farms that they did not interfere with each
other. There were many parts of Ireland on which, although the
vast majority of the occupiers of the soil were serfs, the larger
portion of the surface of the soil was occupied by independent
men. The anxiety, indeed, of the landlords in some parts of the
country appears to have been then as now to get rid of such a
tenantry. In Tipperary, and, I suspect, in other parts of the
country, they were unquestionably driven out of their little holdings
to make room for vast sheep farms; and there is the strongest
reason for believing that the anxiety of the landowners for the
freedom of the woollen trade originated in the feeling that it would
enable them to carry out this object without loss, or even with
profit to themselves.

But, whatever may have been the condition of the upper tenantry;
in whatever proportion, in any district, the land may have been
apportioned to them, beyond all question the mass of the people
were settled on the soil in a miserable state of serfdom and
degradation; and Ireland presented a state of things without parallel
in any nation. There were prosperous and independent tenants,
long leases, and moderate rents. There were occupiers of the soil
ground down by oppression, with uncertain tenures, and paying
rents that scarcely left them enough to sustain a miserable existence.
The latter was the condition of the great mass of the people. It
was actually made more miserable by the presence of the free and
independent occupier under whom, or beside whom, they worked
on in their hopeless misery and degradation.

It was not possible for such a state of things to last for
ever. Those, who were ready to give exhorbitant rents, were in
the end almost sure to get the land. The slave labour was
preferred to the free.* The class of independent occupiers gradually
disappeared. It was of course the trade of the " middleman "
to accept the tenant from whom he could extract the highest rent.
It was the business of the agent of the absentee to swell, by
any means, the remittance, the amount of which was in the eyes of his
principal the only measure of his good or bad management of the
estate. The Protestant freeholders who held large farms were
gradually tempted to underlet them at exhorbitant rents. The
chief landlords, as leases fell in, did the same. The serfs who had

* Arthur Young mentions that even when he wrote the most wretched of cottier
tenants were ready and anxious to get more land.

been originally scattered throughout the country, gradually overran it. Among the causes which led to this result there is one that must not be forgotten. The habit of dealing with wretched dependents made the landed proprietors unfit to deal with those who would not submit to the same usage. Men whose spirit was not broken by persecution and a sense of inferiority, would not brook the treatment of serfs. The habits of imperious command overcame the sympathies of caste and of religious creed. There is abundant evidence that tenants of the dominant caste have given up their farms and been replaced by others, sometimes because they would not undertake a higher rent, frequently because their independence did not suit a landlord or an agent who had learned to enjoy the mean luxury of trampling upon slaves.

In the presence of serfdom an occupation by freemen could scarcely last. In many districts of the country the prosperous Protestant freeholders or Catholic leaseholders were displaced by tenants of an inferior grade, holding indeed by leases, but in lesser portions, at far higher rents. There is scarcely any part of Munster in which you cannot find in the large and ruined farm mansion—it was more than a farm house—in the broken gates and tumbled down out offices, the traces of this process. This is the subdivision of farms which is so much complained of. It was the inevitable result of keeping an enslaved population upon the soil. It was impossible permanently to combine the degradation of the great mass of the people with the continuance of a higher and better class of occupiers on the land. This is a subject upon which a volume might easily be written. The process may have been accelerated by the premium in the shape of political importance which the enfranchisement of the Catholics offered to the proprietors, who wished to multiply small freeholds on his estate. But after all it was slower than is generally supposed. An independent tenantry lingered for some time. It was not until some years after the Union that the degradation of the Irish occupier was complete.

It is only by bearing in mind the peculiarities of the social condition of Ireland that we can intelligently estimate any accounts that have come down to us of Ireland's condition. We must remember that accounts either of prosperity or misery which are perfectly true as applied to one class of the people or of the tenantry, would be perfectly untrue as applied to another. Even Arthur Young, whose description of the miserable state of the degradation of the Irish peasantry I have quoted, had been, throughout the records of his tour, giving descriptions in every part of Ireland, except Ulster, of prosperous and well-to-do tenants holding by long leases and at moderate rents.

Whatever was the position of the upper portion of the tenantry, there is abundant evidence of the miserable condition to which the great mass of the people were reduced. Let us take the period from the Revolution to the period when Young wrote, just on the eve of Irish independence.

I have pointed out that it cannot be said that during this period an excessive population created an undue competition for land. Throughout the greater portions of that period the population of Ireland was little more than half what it is now. In the days of Swift it was little more than one-third. We shall presently see that with the prosperity or depression of the manufacturing industry of the country, this miserable peasantry had only one connexion—their poverty effectually debarred them from being consumers of manufactured goods. It is impossible to read ever so carelessly the records of the 18th century and not see that the wretchedness of the Irish people is wholly and solely to be traced to the state of serfdom in which the great mass of the occupiers of the soil were held.

Although it be correct to say that, during that century, the complaints were generally of exorbitant rents, rather than of evictions, yet the latter were, even then, the source of misery and even outrage. About the period of the accession of George III. " The Levellers" disturbed the peace of Tipperary. At a later period " The Hearts of Oak," and " The Hearts of Steel," convulsed some of the northern counties. Still later, the Whiteboys, or Right Boys, threw Munster into a state of open insurrection. The complaints everywhere were the same. It can scarcely be forgotten that it was with reference to the same period that Goldsmith described his Irish " Deserted Village," and pointed out, in lines so often quoted, the ills of the State in which

> " Wealth accumulates and men decay."

Unhappily, it is in the history of crime and criminal conspiracies that the grievances of the Irish people are most clearly to be read. Leaving aside for a moment the effect of the penal laws, not only in crushing down the native population as occupiers of the soil, but also in excluding them from manufacturing industry, let me very briefly state throughout the eighteenth century the history of Irish agrarian crime.

In the century which elapsed between the Revolution and the Union, Ireland was agitated by local insurrections, some of them of a formidable character. They, every one, originated in oppressions practised on the occupiers of lands. The first of these disturbances which has attracted the attention of those who have written on Irish history—at present I can deal with none other— was that created in Tipperary by persons calling themselves " Levellers," about the period of the accession of George III. The grievances of which they complained were, the turning of arable land into sheep walks, " and the consequent expulsion of great numbers of labouring peasants;" " while those who remained unexpelled had no means of paying exorbitant rents." By these expulsions were formed the monster farms in that county, the gigantic dimensions of which excited the wonder and admiration of Arthur Young. The misery of the poor people was brought to a climax by the illegal enclosure of the commons, upon which the right of commonage had been granted them with their holdings, for which they paid exorbitant rents. Their fury was first directed against the fences which bounded the fields of the enclosed commons; and their violent destruction of these fences gave them the name of " Levellers."

The atrocities of these insurgents are said to have been great. They probably were so. The truculence of every servile insurrection is proportioned to the cruelties with which the slaves have been treated. But at the same time we must remember that we have only the accounts of the upper classes, and a very little experience must lead any one to distrust the picture drawn of Irish rebels by the frights and the passions of these classes. The fury of religious and political fanaticism was directed against the levellers, by tales implicitly believed, which represented their movement as the creation of a plot of Jesuits and Jacobites, the undoubted work of the Pope and the Pretender. The judges who were sent down to try the peasants accused of participation in these outrages, had to interfere between the blind fury of partizan juries and the accused; and Chief Justice Aston, who presided at the special commission at Clonmel, was met, as he left the town, by crowds, who knelt on the road, praying blessings on him for his impartiality.

Previous to this period we find in Irish histories no notice of agrarian outrages. It may be that they existed, but were not of magnitude enough to attract notice. The spirit of the oppressed people may have only then begun to rise in a reaction against the cruelty of the penal laws; or possibly when the last hope of political relief appeared to expire with the downfall of the cause of the Stuarts, the despair of the peasantry prompted the wildness of these desultory attempts.

The rising of the Levellers was, beyond all question, caused by the oppression of the landowners; and from that year to the present the very same cause has produced all the peasant insurrections which, under many a fantastic name and symbol, have perpetuated in Ireland the chronic condition of suppressed civil war.

In Munster " The Levellers" were followed, at no distant interval, by " The Whiteboys," insurgents whose fantastic designation has become a household word in the legal history of Irish crime. They had the questionable honour of giving their name to laws of Draconian severity, still in force in Ireland, known as the Whiteboy acts. Their name was originally derived from the white shirts which they placed over their dress when they went upon their nightly expeditions of vengeance or marauding. These insurgents spread widely through Leinster. They extended into Carlow, Kilkenny, Queen's

County, and even to Wexford. Dr. Troy, then Catholic Bishop of Ossory, in vain delivered a pastoral, in which he denied the rites of the Church to any one engaged in the illegal association. It is stated that this pastoral threatened that no service of the church should ever be performed for any of them after their death. The terrors of this world were brought to bear on them as well as those of the next. The severities which had been visited on the Levellers were of course resorted to again, and Special Commissions and gibbets vindicated against the crimes of the oppressed people the supremacy of the law.

In 1786 an armed association, starting with the name of " Right Boys," disturbed the counties of Kerry and Cork. Originally they assailed the tithe exactions of the clergy, and while they did so the gentry were suspected of, at least, conniving at their movements. They very soon began to regulate the wages of labour, and to fix a limit to the rent of land.

Mr. Fitzgibbon, who was then Attorney-General, declared, in his place in the House of Commons, that this insurrection was owing solely to the cruelty of the landlords, and that " the peasantry of Munster, bound to pay six pounds an acre in rent, and to work for their landlords at five pence a day, could no longer exist under the wretchedness they endured."

In a debate upon the bill for the suppression of these disturbances he used these remarkable words :—

" I am well acquainted with the province of Munster, and I know that it is impossible for human wretchedness to exceed that of the miserable peasantry of that province. I know that the unhappy tenantry are ground to powder by relentless landlords. I know that far from being able to give the clergy their just dues, they had not food or raiment for themselves ; the landlord grasps the whole. And sorry I am to add, that not satisfied with present extortion, some landlords have been so base as to instigate the insurgents to rob the clergy, not in order to alleviate the distresses of the tenantry, but that they might add the clergy's share to the cruel rack rents already paid. . . The poor people of Munster live in a more abject state of poverty than human nature can be supposed able to bear ; their miseries are intolerable." *

This statement, it will be remembered, was made under the responsibility which attaches to official station. It was the deliberate assertion of the Irish Attorney-General, made in the Irish House of Commons, an assembly almost exclusively composed of the Irish gentry, in the presence of the representatives of the very persons whose oppression of their tenantry he described.

Fully to understand these references we must remember two incidents connected with the tenure of Irish land.

In many, indeed most, districts of Ireland an instrument of small

* *Irish Parliamentary Debates*—Speech of Mr. Fitzgibbon, Attorney-General, 1787.

but yet very galling oppression was found in a reservation almost universal in Irish leases, of " duty days." Each tenant, in addition to his rent, was bound by his lease to work for the landlord a certain number of days in the year. In the larger farms the obligation extended to supplying horses. The result naturally was, that the landlord demanded this labour exactly at the time when it was most wanted—that is, at the very time when it was most required on the tenant's own farm. But the evil did not end even there. Those who were bound to this duty work were often compelled to exceed the stipulated number of days. Some miserably low remuneration, more in the nature of a gratuity than of wages, was given them for this extended labour. In many instances their leases bound them to work at some low rate whenever they were called on. It was to this Lord Clare alluded when he stated, as one of the grievances of the Munster Whiteboys, that the peasantry were compelled to work for fivepence a day.*

It must be remembered that throughout all this period the miserable peasantry were subject to another exaction, less, indeed, in its amount, but far more harassing, or at least vexatious, in its attendant circumstances than that of rent. The Protestant clergy-man was entitled by law to the tenth of the produce, and this throughout the south of Ireland, was claimed not only from sub-stantial farmers, but from wretched cottiers struggling for the means of life. The tithe of potatoes, not levied in the north, was enforced from the potato garden attached to the hovel of the ill-fed labourer in the South; and those who had not fuel to supply the wants of the Winter were compelled to compound with the parson for every tenth creel of the turf which they cut and dried on the

---

* Arthur Young thus described the system which prevailed in Kerry in 1776 :—
"The state of the poor in the whole county of Kerry represented as exceedingly miserable, and, owing to the conduct of men of property, who are apt to lay the blame on what they call land pirates, or men who offer the highest rent, and who, in order to pay this rent, must, and do re-let all the cabbin lands at an extravagant rise, which is assigning over all the cabbins to be devoured by one farmer. The cottars on a farm cannot go from one to another, in order to find a good master as in England: for all the country is in the same system, and no redress to be found. Such being the case, the farmers are enabled to charge the price of labour as low as they please, and rate the land as *high* as they like. This is an evil which oppresses them cruelly, and certainly has its origin in its landlords, when they set their farms, setting all the cabbins with them instead of keeping them tenants to themselves. The oppression is, the farmer valuing the labour of the poor at 4d. or 5d. a day, and paying that in land rated much above its value. Owing to this, the poor are depressed ; they live upon potatoes and sour milk, and the poorest of them only salt and water to them, with now and then a herring. Their milk is bought ; for very few keep cows, scarce any pigs, but a few poultry. Their circumstances are incomparably worse than they were 20 years ago ; for they had all cows, but then they wore no linen : all now have a little flax. To these evils have been owing emigrations, which have been cosiderable."—*Young's Tour*, Vol. ii.
We shall see presently that this extortion was carried far beyond anything stated by Young. In many leases the tenants were bound to work for the landlord whenever called on at a miserably low rate, and this has been continued down to recent times.

bog, the right of turbary over which, together with their potato
garden, very often constituted their whole possessions upon earth.*
The system that required the husbandman to set aside the tenth
sheaf as an offering to pious purposes was never intended for such a
state of things as this. The exaction had become more intolerable
since the landowners of Ireland had determined, by a vote in the
House of Commons, that no tithe should be paid for pasture lands,
and enforced this decree by resolving that any person who took
part, even professionally, in enforcing that claim in a court of
justice, should be committed to prison for a breach of the privilege
of the House of Commons.

The exemption of the pasture lands of the rich threw the clergy-
man more for his living upon the potato gardens of the poor. It
may have been true, as stated by Lord Clare, that the actual
receipts of the clergy fell short, very far short, of their legal rights.
But this leniency was chiefly manifested in compositions with the
more opulent of the cultivators of the soil. Upon the poor the
system pressed with very disproportionate severity. There were
middlemen of tithes as well as of rents. And tithe farmers, tithe
"viewers," tithe bailiffs, and tithe proctors, constituted a goodly
array of ecclesiastical oppressors, who frequently led the way to the
miseries of a suit in the Bishops' Court for " the subtraction of
tithes."

This exaction occupied, it may well be thought, a place in the list
of grievances which all these disturbances attempted to redress.
A local tithe oppression gave the first occasion for the Munster
outbreak in 1786.† It was even said that the landowners of the
district connived at, if they did not actually encourage, the movement against the clergy, whom they regarded as taking away some
of the earnings of the peasants which they would otherwise have

---

* At a period nearly thirty years later Wakefield tells us, with just indignation, of
clergymen who exacted tithes from gleaners; for whom the superstition or the religion
of the Irish cultivators of all creeds was wont to leave, after the example of Boaz, and
in accordance with Scripture precept, some stray ears of corn scattered on the field.
I cannot but hope that this is a mistake.

† There was something very "unsectarian" in the mode in which many of the insurgents dealt with ecclesiastical affairs. The Right Boys in Kerry claimed the
nomination of Protestant curates and Protestant parish clerks. The "Threshers" in
Roscommon claimed the right of regulating the amount both "of tithes and of priests'
dues." In some instances they regulated the morals of the Protestant clergy in cases
in which the Bishops' Court would seem sadly to have neglected that duty.
Mr. Curran said, in the Irish House of Commons, when opposing the Right Boy Bill,
"I will mention a cirumstance of disturbance in that very diocese from which the
publication so much reprobated issued, in a parish worth 800 or 900 pounds a year,
which would make the House blush. It was a rising to banish a seraglio kept by a
rector who received near a thousand pounds a year from the Church, and to reinstate
the unoffending mother and innocent children in their mansion."—*Irish Parliamentary
Debates.* February 27th, 1787.
Among many strange objects which have been contemplated by the lawless societies
of more recent times, they have iu some instances undertaken to regulate the moral
conduct of the gentry.—Mortimer O'Sullivan—*Byeways of Irish History.*

seized on themselves. The tithe owners and the landlords were rival claimants for the privilege of fleecing the people. Both rent and tithe were the imposts of confiscation levied without mercy upon a conquered race. And no serfdom in any European nation brought men down to the wretchedness of the Munster occupier of the soil, paying to the landlord the utmost rack rent which that landlord thought he could squeeze " out of his blood and vitals," obliged to hand over to the tithe proctor a portion of the little that was left—and carried off from his own miserable industry to do " duty work" for his landlord, frequently without any payment, in the most favourable cases for the wretched pittance of fivepence a day.

Predial disturbances were not confined to the Catholic peasantry of Munster. The most formidable occurred among the Protestant population of the North. At the same time that the Levellers and Whiteboys disturbed Tipperary, the Hearts of Oak, in 1763, occupied, in tumultuous bodies, first the county of Armagh, and afterwards the counties of Tyrone, Fermanagh, and Derry. They insisted on regulating the amount of tithe, and of rent, especially the rent of turf bogs. Their chief grievance was an oppressive impost connected with that extraordinary system of local taxation administered under laws known as the Grand Jury Laws—a system by which an inquest, selected by the sheriff for the purposes of aiding in the administration of criminal justice, imposed an indefinite amount of taxation, for the repair of roads, and other fiscal purposes, upon the occupiers of land.

" The Hearts of Oak" were Protestant. They wore the English emblem, the oak leaf, in their hats, and swore men to be true " to the King and the Hearts of Oak." They were followed, a few years later, by " The Hearts of Steel." This insurrection assumed far more formidable dimensions. It originated in an attempt to enforce exorbitant renewal fines on the dropping of leases, on the estate of the Marquis of Donegall. It began in the county of Antrim, but a large proportion of the population of all Ulster joined in the revolt. Thousands of armed men marched into Belfast, and forced, without bloodshed, from the military commander, the surrender of one of their confederates, who had been committed to the gaol. A large military force was sent into the disturbed districts; the ringleaders were seized and put on their trial for high treason. Northern juries, unlike those of Tipperary, sympathized with the insurgents, and refused to bring in verdicts of conviction. A statute was passed authorizing the trial in other counties of persons accused of the insurrectionary movements. Trials in Dublin were attended with the same result as in Antrim. Protestant juries everywhere sympathized with Protestant insurgents. Popular feeling forced the repeal of the law, changing the venue when it had been not two years in force. It was passed in the month of March, 1772, and repealed in December, 1773. When these things happened in the case of a Protestant agrarian insurrection, we can, perhaps, understand how the tenant right of Ulster has been preserved.*

* The spirit of "The Hearts of Steel" is not yet extinct in Ulster, at least it was not twenty years ago. From the Report of the Committee of the Repeal Association on Tenant Right, I borrow some extracts from the evidence taken before the Devon Commission in 1845 :—
" 82. Do you consider, that if the tenant right was abolished in the district with which you are acquainted, that it would lead to outrage ?—[*Mr. Orr.*]—I have not the least doubt of it, not the slightest."

"JOHN ANDREWS, ESQ., *Agent to Lord Londonderry.*

" 39. With regard to Lord Londonderry's estate, can you state the usual amount of the purchase of the tenant right ?—Yes, I can. I would give as the average £10 the English acre ; the tenant right will sell for that with or without a lease.
"40. Is there much difference ?—Very little ; I would say almost none.
"42. Do you think that curtailment of the tenant right can be carried out without danger to the peace of the country ?—I am sure it cannot. You would have a Tipperary in Down, if it was attempted to be carried out."

"REV. JOHN LYNCH, *Co. Antrim.*

"14. You spoke of the landlords beginning to question the tenant right ; do you think if landlords were to attempt to abolish the tenant right, that it would lead to any disturbance in the country ?—I have not the least doubt of it.

"REV. JAMES PORTER, *Presbyterian Minister, County Down.*

" 33. What effect has the holding without lease on the condition of the tenants, the improvement of the farms, or the rent ?—On those estates where what is called tenant right amongst us is yet allowed, the want of a lease does us little injury ; but where that is beginning to be altered, it has paralyzed real improvements every where.
" 34. Are there many estates upon which the tenant right is not allowed ?—There is no property where it is entirely denied. There were just three instances in which there were agrarian outrages committed since I settled in this country, and these originated in the total denial of the tenant right ; that was a denial on the part of the landlord of the tenant right. It is right to say those were aggressions of Protestants. The landlords yielded the claim of tenant right, to the popular feelings in those three cases.
" 37. In those cases where the tenant right was disallowed, was it an attempt on the part of the landlord to put the purchase-money into his own pocket, or to charge an additional rent ?—An attempt was made to dispossess the owner, without allowing him to sell, which has been invariably the practice throughout our own country, and we were greatly scandalized by it. In fact, armies were brought in, and honest men were involved, and surprised at the violence and murderous dispositions manifested, when parties were excited about it ; for I ought to state, perhaps, that every particle of improvement, every stone upon my farm, and every slate, was put together by myself, and every drain was made, and every tree planted out of my own pocket, and I did it with great confidence ; because, when I purchased, I paid a very high value for what I got, and I considered that I was to have the same right to remuneration."

"ROBERT SMITH, ESQ., *Clerk of Peace, Co. Monaghan.*

"81. Where the tenant is ejected for non-payment of rent by his landlord, is he allowed to sell his tenant right ?—I am not aware that any such right of sale is recognized by the landlord ; but it is generally known throughout the country that an agrarian law exists, such as to intimidate any of the lower class of farmers from taking land from which a tenant has been ejected for any cause without the person coming in making compensation to the party turned out.
" 82. That applies to the tenant going out, under all circumstances ?—I think so."

JOHN LINDSAY, ESQ., *Banbridge, Co. Down.*

" 39. Is the tenant right, or sale of good-will, prevalent in the district; and to whom is the purchase-money paid ?—It prevails in the district; the tenants who have held the

On the repeal of the law convictions were obtained in the northern counties. Some of the leaders of the revolt were executed. The Marquis of Donegall renewed the leases without the fines, and no Ulster landlord ventured to attempt a similar exaction. The oppressive road tax was abolished. "The insurrection was quelled, but its baneful effects long remained. So great and wide was the discontent, that *many thousands of Protestants emigrated from these parts of Ulster to the American settlements, where they appeared in arms against the British Government, and contributed powerfully, by their zeal and valour, to the separation of the American Colonies from the Empire of Great Britain.*" *

England has already felt the mischief of raising up, even on the other side of the Atlantic, a hostile community of exiled Irishmen. With the suppression, or the success, of the Hearts of Steel ceased all Protestant disturbances in Ulster directed against

land think they have a right to dispose of the land when they are going to leave it; he thinks always he has a right to do so; and very reasonably, I think.

"40. Is it generally recognized by the landlords?—Some recognize it, and some do not; but where they do not recognize it, and set their face against it, they are very generally defeated, and have been obliged to do it, after risking life, in some instances, in my neighbourhood.

"41. Is it done behind their backs, without their knowing it?—No; they have even ejected the tenantry. I have known some of them to do it in the parish I live in; one of them put a man out of his farm, and there is no person will take it; he sent down a person to cultivate the farm, and he was sent home again. The people gathered that night and desired him to go home and not come there again; and the man got leave to sell his tenant right afterwards.

"42. How long ago is that?—About three years ago. Something similar happened to a man about two or three miles from my place, last Winter was a year."

"MR. HANDCOCK, *Lord Lurgan's Agent, Down, Antrim, and Armagh.*

"38. The landlords are compelled to recognize tenant right, as, in several instances in this neighbourhood, where they have refused to allow tenant right, the in-coming tenant's house has been burned, his cattle houghed, or his crops trodden down by night. The disallowance of tenant right, so far as I know, is always attended with outrage. A landlord cannot even resume possession to himself without paying it. In fact, it is one of the sacred rights of the country, which cannot be touched with impunity ; *and if systematic efforts were made amongst the proprietors of Ulster to invade tenant right, I do not believe there is a force at the disposal of the Horse Guards sufficient to keep the peace of the province :* and when we consider that all the improvements have been effected at the expense of the tenant, it is perfectly right that this tenant right should exist; his money has been laid out on the faith of compensation in that shape."

A very distinguished gentleman—one subsequently connected in a professional capacity with the Irish Government—one well acquainted with Ulster—did not hesitate to use this language in a paper read before the Statistical Society of Ireland, in May, 1864. I quote from a paper of Mr. Heron's:—"If another Vico were to prophesy on the future of Ireland, he would say :—' No insurrection in Ireland will occur until the progress of the destruction of the rights of the peasantry the tenant right of Ulster shall cease to be recognized. The tenant right of Ulster is worth twenty-four millions of money. If some political seer, gifted with political insight into the future of nations, was to prophesy as to Ireland, he would, in all probability say, the last Irish insurrection will be made by the peasantry of Down and Armagh, upon their tenant right being finally taken away from them.' "—*Transactions of the Irish Statistical Society.* Paper read by Denis Caulfield Heron, Esq., Q.C. May 18th, 1864.

* *Gordon's History of Ireland*, Vol. ii., p. 249.

grievances in land.   The Peep of Day Boys, who disturbed
Armagh in 1795, were a band of Protestant zealots; and their
outrages were directed entirely against the Catholic inhabitants.
    In Munster, the insurrection of Catholic serfs was attended with
different results.   Landlord oppression continued, and the combination of the people continued too.   A criminal association, known
as that of the "Defenders," professing to be formed to resist the
Peep of Day Boys, spread from the border counties of Ulster into
the south.   It contemplated treasonable objects; some of its leaders
suffered the penalties of high treason; and it finally merged in the
attempt at insurrection in the year 1798.   Since the Union, the mo-
notony of the long roll of criminal confederations is varied only by
the strange selection of new names.   The Threshers, in the western
counties, in 1807.   The Whitefeet and Blackfeet, in the
Leinster counties, in 1832.   The Terry-Alts, in Clare, in 1830.
Captain Rock, throughout Munster, in 1822.   Captains Starlight
and Moonlight, in some obscure localities.   The Shanavests and
Caravats, in Kilkenny and Tipperary, in 1810.   The Ribbonmen,
in all places and at all times.   These, and "whatever other, were
the vagrant names by which tumult delighted to describe itself,"[*]
were all but varying forms of the many-headed but indestructible
civil war in which the Irish people have now for a century and
seven years maintained their bloody protest against the iniquity of
the land tenure by which they were trampled down.
    That which is instructive in this dismal catalogue is, that under
many forms and many names, there is everywhere and always one
feeling, everywhere abiding and everywhere active—hatred of the
oppressions which were practised in connexion with the land.
Through the blood-stained records of a century, we trace with a
wearying and dreary sameness the working of the one miserable
cause of Ireland's misery and crime.   In 1822, Lord Glenelg, then
Mr. Grant, pointed the attention of the House of Commons to the
unvarying character of Irish insurrectionary crime.   He traced the
unbroken chain which bound together the "Levellers" of 1760
with the "Rockites" who were disturbing Munster when he
spoke.   Nearly another half century has passed, and the links of the
same dismal chain are still dragging slowly on.   In this remarkable
speech, Mr. Grant was dealing with an insurrectionary state of
things, to suppress which Parliament had just armed the Government
with the extraordinary powers of the Insurrection Act.   They were
days when it was not a matter of course to suspend the constitution,
and the assent to this Act was followed by a motion for a redress of
grievances.   In his speech on that motion, Mr. Grant referred to the
earlier disturbances.   Describing the insurrection of the Hearts of
Steel, as resembling in its origin the then existing troubles, he said:—

* Grattan.

" A disturbance which, in its origin, so far resembles the present (the insurrectionary movement of 1822), that its exciting cause was the resentment produced in the minds of a body of tenantry by what they deemed the oppressive conduct of the agent of a great landed proprietor. The evil was, as usual, suppressed by force.

" With respect to the latter, it is notorious, as I have already intimated that they originated in the discontent and resentment excited in the minds of the tenants of a very extensive property by the proceedings of the agent under whose management that property was placed. This was the proximate cause ; and without reference to any other circumstances, it is obvious how widely the peace of a county would be affected when a body of tenantry, amounting to 20,000 persons, were thrown into a state of furious agitation.   .   .   .   .

" Such, sir, has been the series of commotions which for the last sixty years have tormented and desolated Ireland. It is remarkable how nearly they resemble each other in their principal features, though varying unquestionably in the shades of atrocity. It would be easy to quote, with regard to each of them, passages of speeches pronounced in Parliament, or of publications written at the time, which, with slight alterations, would describe them all. The complaints respecting the causes of these calamities are, through this long period, nearly echoes of each other. In truth they all spring immediately from local oppressions, and were diffused and propagated by the operation of the same peculiar circumstances in the character and condition of the people of Ireland. They were all, in succession, quelled ; but as yet no effort has been made by the Legislature to effect a permanent and satisfactory cure. This very fact, however—I mean the continued recurrence of such events—is itself a proof that there must be something diseased in the system. In every country local oppression may take place, and local commotions may follow. But the question that naturally suggests itself with respect to Ireland is this :—How does it happen that a local commotion becomes so rapidly a general disturbance ? How does it happen that the spirit which at first discovers itself in a small district spreads almost instantaneously over a large territory, and throws, in a very short time, nearly half a province into the most frightful convulsions ? This is the peculiarity of the subject. What is the state of society that admits of such an evil ? Are there no laws—no guards and preservatives of civil order—no barriers to resist encroachments on the public tranquillity ?" *

In tracing out this strange descent and pedigree of Irish crime—making out, so to speak, the genealogical tree of our turbulence—let me recall attention to that great characteristic which has marked all the varying forms in which the resistance of the people to the oppression connected with land tenure has assumed.

All of them in which the Roman Catholic peasantry have been engaged, have been more or less identified with general projects of revolt. It is quite true "that those who have cried 'down with landlordism,' have been equally ready to cry 'down with the British

---

* Speech of Mr. Grant on Sir John Newport's motion, April 10th, 1822.

Crown.'"* This fact has long since been pointed out and strongly relied on by the ablest of those who have advocated towards Irish discontent, a policy, not of concession, but of coercion. Whatever may be the inference to be drawn from it, the fact is certain. In the minds of the Irish peasantry, a resistance to landlord oppression is associated with revolt against the British Crown. Rebellion against that Crown is regarded as a movement against the grievances which are connected with the tenure of land. There seems an instinct or a memory in the breasts of the people which unites in an inseparable connexion the rule of England in their country with the oppressions that have been inflicted on them in their occupation of their native soil. This is equally apparent in the annals of every insurrectionary movement, and in the story of every agrarian crime. Conspiracies of a general agrarian character, like the ribbon society, have invariably included among the objects specified in their oath and in their constitution the subversion of the government. This is not all; even in the case of those isolated disturbances in which local discontent attempted to suppress local grievances, or avenge local oppression, a general purpose very soon became engrafted on the particular object,† and "lodges" that were formed for the purpose of preventing an ejectment, or shooting a landlord, soon bound their members by an oath to resist national oppression, and be ready to aid in subverting the authority of the Sovereign. The open insurrections in which this latter object has been avowed, so far as the Southern peasantry took part in them, engaged that peasantry by the promise that the success of an insurrection would rid them of the local miseries and exactions under which they groaned.

In Ulster this was not the case. If "Hearts of Oak" were executed for high treason it was not because they conspired to subvert the King's crown, but because, by construction of law, they made war upon the Sovereign by attempting a general redress of grievances by armed force. The Ulster Protestant had no

* Lord Lifford.

† "It was one of the great peculiarities of these agrarian crimes that they scarcely ever existed without becoming associated with objects of a more general character. The illegal combination which was formed to protect the tenantry of a particular locality, or to avenge their wrongs, very soon included in its objects a conspiracy hostile to all English power and law. One who knew Ireland well, the late Major Warburton, thus describes the course of secret societies in the country:—

"'The propagators of the Ribbon system avail themselves of any local disturbances for the purpose of introducing their own principles; and it is invariably found that where disturbances are of long continuance, they lose their desultory character and are methodized into political organization.'"—Tract on Land Tenure, p. 97. Third Edition.

In the tract on Land Tenure I collected the evidences which appear to place these peculiarities of Irish agrarian disturbance beyond all doubt. They are all but acts of the civil war in which to this hour the mass of the Irish people believe themselves to be engaged. Lord Clare, Mr. Bright, Mr. Poulett Scrope, Mortimer O'Sullivan, and Charles Boyton were among the witnesses whose testimony, agreeing with a marvellous coincidence, even of expression, I cited to establish this.

traditions of confiscation or presence of a penal law to remind him of the fact that it was the iron hoof of conquest which had trampled him down.

Throughout the other three provinces the case was as I have stated. To the Irish occupier of the soil English authority was known in the oppression of " Sassenach" landlords ; and from the days of Oliver Cromwell to the present, the whole life of that people has been a revolt—often crushed and often broken—but a never-abandoned revolt against the proprietary rights, in which they see nothing but their own oppression by the hand of English power. In the minds of the peasantry the discontents and the resentments of the conquered still live. Unhappily, in those of their masters the passions and prejudices of the conqueror are not extinct. Unhappy—most unhappy, for all parties—has been the identification of land-lordism with the authority of the British Crown.

In this review of our social history I have only glanced at the condition of Ireland between the Union and the great famine of 1846. Throughout the earlier part of this century all the political and social oppression to which Arthur Young bears testimony still existed uncontrolled. In many respects it was aggravated by the unsuccessful attempts at revolt of 1798 and 1803. I am happy that I am not called on even to advert to the history of the former of these years. It is enough to say that, whatever were the origin or designs of the United Irishmen in the North—in the South that rebellion assumed the invariable form of all Irish insurrectionary movements. It was the rising of an aggrieved peasantry against oppressions connected with the tenure of the land.

It is scarcely necessary for me to adduce evidence of the miserable state of the Irish peasant in the years which followed the Union. Nobody, I believe, will deny it. In 1835 the inquiries of the Poor Law Commission disclosed an amount of misery and wretchedness for which no parallel can be found in any country or in any age. In 1845 the inquiries of the Devon Land Commission could add nothing to these disclosures, but they confirmed them. I am spared the necessity of dwelling on the miseries of the later period, that which comes down to the days of this generation, when at last, before our own eyes, " centuries of horrors, for which history has no parallel, appear to be closing in the expatriation of the people." *

And yet to complete the miserable chain of testimony which identifies, in an unbroken series of causation, the present condition of Ireland with the miseries and oppressions of by-gone days—let me dismiss this part of the subject by a reference to an authority which describes the state of the people ten years after the Union, completely verifying the contemporaneous statement of the Knight

* Godwin Smith.

of Kerry, in the House of Commons, that "the condition of the
Irish peasant was not superior to that of the negro." *

In the year 1809 Ireland was travelled over by Mr. Edward
Wakefield, a gentleman who came to the country for the purpose of
informing himself, and writing on its state. His review of its condition is written in imitation of the tour of Arthur Young. Far
inferior to Arthur Young in breadth of view and sagacity, he had,
perhaps, one advantage over him—his mind was not wholly occupied
with the views of an agriculturalist, and he had, at all events, escaped
the passion of his predecessor for the consolidation of farms. His
work supplies a curious comparison with the account which Arthur
Young gives of the country only thirty years before. The large
farms were disappearing—the process by which the serfs overran
the country had made way. In other respects there is a dismal
sameness in the description of the degradation of the people.† On
some matters Mr. Wakefield's inquiries give us details with a
minuteness which we do not find in the pages of Young.‡

At this period the exaction of work from the tenant at a low rate
of wages appears to have been almost universal.§ Throughout a

---

* *Cobbett's Parliamentary Register*, May, 1810.

† It is needless to repeat those statements. In one respect, that relating to the last
badge of the degradation of the serf, he goes far to confirm the testimony of Arthur
Young.

These statements throw some light on the strange fact already mentioned, that the
ribbon societies have included among their objects the regulation of morals.

‡ Mr. Wakefield adduces many instances of magisterial oppression, authenticated
from the Records of the Courts of Justice.

He also narrates incidents of personal chastisement, inflicted by gentlemen upon
persons not belonging to their own class, such as would not have been endured in any
other country.

Young states such matters generally—Wakefield mentions the details.

Both agree in a picture of serfdom, on the part of the people, as complete as it is
possible to conceive existing in any civilized country.

§ I extract one out of many passages of this volume, one in which Wakefield gives
an account of an interview which he had with an English gentleman who had
experience in the employment of agricultural labour in several counties in Ireland.
" He complained of not being able to get labourers to go on with his work. I shall never
forget," says Wakefield, "the account which he gave me on this occasion. It is impossible to repeat it without pity and indignation. 'These poor people,' said he,
'are glad to get a holiday in order that they may enjoy a little relaxation at a pattern
or a fair.' On inquiring the reason, his answer was—'Because they are paid only
sixpence a day for their labour, and seldom obtain a settlement in less than six months.
By the terms of their lease they are obliged to work as many days as will pay their
rent, and when they have accomplished this it is difficult to get them at all; for if they
worked at home their landlords would see them, and order them to their demesnes, so
that they must remain idle or work for their landlords for the paltry sum of sixpence a
day.' Is this generally the case?—'Throughout all the West of Ireland you may
rely upon it.'"— *Wakefield's Account of Ireland*, Vol. i., page 510.

I cannot tell to what extent this practice prevails in modern times. But this I do
know, that in one of the cases in which my advice has been sought by tenants on an
estate—not in the West of Ireland—one great grievance of the tenants was, that their
landlord compelled them to work for him, and give him the use of their horses and
carts at wages far below the general rate. The new agreements which were tendered
to them for signature, on pain of instant eviction, contained a clause binding them to
supply work, when called on, at this inferior rate.

great portion of Ireland the leases bound the tenant to work for the landlord whenever he called on him, frequently at less than half remuneration. The oppression he describes as connected with this practice prove more forcibly than any general account the serfdom of the people.

Not only were duty days exacted in addition to the rent, but conditions which made the landlord almost the pilferer of the cottier's small store of poultry were rigidly enforced.* The lease always reserved a high penal rent if these petty robberies were not submitted to.† "In consequence of the service required by this clause being neglected, I have seen," writes Wakefield, "a poor man's cattle taken from his door, and driven away, without the least expression of feeling or regret."‡ But the exactions were not confined to those which were authorized by an instrument, miscalled a lease, in reality the covenant by which the bondsman sold himself to his landlord.§ Agents and landlords insisted on the tenant working for them for nothing, and vengeance followed those who disobeyed the hint that such gratuitous labour would be acceptable to their lord.‖ In other respects a system of fleecing the tenantry was pursued, in comparison with which the oppressions and exactions of the Turkish tax gatherer upon the Christian subjects of the Porte are not very tyrannical.¶ The whole secret was, the tenant was a serf, and his master extorted from him all he could. The tenant resorted to the usual device of those who are thus oppressed. Like serfs in all countries, he hid his money by burying it in the

---

* "The beggarly system of extorting duties from tenants is so shamefully reprehensible in this enlightened age, that it is surprising to see such claims still insisted on in leases. It is not on such paltry considerations that men of rank and fortune should hold their superiority."—*Coote's Survey of Monaghan.*

" A poor man who enjoys these ' conveniences,' as they are called, would be thought a rebel did he not abandon his own crop to gather in that of his master ; and if to this be added the duty fowl, the duty turf, and, in short, the duty in general, which is but another term for personal service, it will be seen to what a great extent this kind of slavery is carried in Ireland."—*Wakefield*, Vol. i., 599.

† " A still more grievous oppression was resorted to in connexion with these penal rents. The 'duties' were not demanded. The receipts were passed for the ordinary rents, without mentioning the duties ; and the penal rents were afterwards enforced."— *Sir Charles Coote's Survey of Monaghan.*

‡ Vol. i., p. 245.

§ These covenants in leases were by no means confined to leases granted by landlords of an inferior class.
" The leases granted by Lord Belmore oblige his tenants to work with their horses and cars a certain number of days in the year, especially at the season of cutting turf."—*Wakefield*, Vol. i., p. 259.

‖ "The landlord, to get in his crop, cart his turf, thrash his oats, or accomplish any other work, obliges his tenant to neglect his own occupation in order that he may perform his labour at a fixed rate of payment, which is always less than that which he pays to a person who does not reside under him."—*Wakefield*, Vol. i., p. 507.

¶ In a subsequent page will be read his account of the exactions practised on the people by the agents of the absentees.

ground.   The actual burying of guineas was common among the
Irish peasantry ; * it has not altogether ceased.   Well might Wakefield contrast the condition of the Irish peasant with that of the
Russian boor to the disadvantage of the former.   Well might he
say that tenants so circumstanced must be considered as slaves—
" that, as between the bondsman and his master, to call the former
tenant would be a perversion of terms, to name the latter landlord a
prostitution of language."†

This was the state of the peasant in many districts of Ireland in
1810.   Is it really unjust to refer the difficulties of the landowners
to the influence of the owners of property ?   It is vain to distinguish
between the acts of owners in fee, and their agents, or their middlemen.   For the acts of the agent the landlord was strictly responsible ;
but all the oppressions that were practised upon the occupiers by
any class were only possible from the miserable slavery to which the
people were crushed down.

Fully to examine the whole character of the change which had
passed over Ireland between the visit of Arthur Young and that of
Wakefield would be far beyond the object of this letter.   These
are things which can only be fully understood by patient and
laborious investigation of a number of small facts to be collected
from many quarters.   It is not always easy to gather the information
which enables us to trace the progress of a nation, not in the great
events that are supposed to make up its history, but in the

---

* Mr. Wakefield describes the practice of burying money as one common in his time,
and quotes from several writers to show that it was so.—Vol. i., p. 593.
He adverts to the singular fact that it " was the child of latter times."   Such a
practice, if prevalent at the time of Arthur Young's visit, could not, he thinks, have
escaped the notice of so acute an observer, and there is not a trace of it to be found in
the tour of Young.
This is one of the many points of comparison between the accounts of the two
visitors which suggest some strange reflections.
In the interim that great change had taken place which I have attempted to
describe as the process of overrunning the country by the serfs.
Those who read the history of that process, as sketched in the next pages, will
probably think that if guineas were not hid in the days of Arthur Young it was
because the serfs had no guineas to hide.
They acquired them as soon as they were permitted to occupy the soil.

† *View of Ireland.*   Vol. i., p. 518.
I dismiss for the present Mr. Wakefield's volumes by citing one most singular,
but most instructive, passage, which will show how far economic laws regulated the
rent exacted from the occupiers of the soil :—
" October 20th, 1809, Woodlawn.—Mr. Trench says that if the occupying tenants
be desired to state how much they will give for their land, *they are so frightened that
they never make an offer,* but rather remain silent, and afterwards consent to any terms
the middleman may choose to impose.   *He knows no instance of their quitting the land
rather than accede to the proposed conditions.*   This information agrees with an instance
which I witnessed in the county of Waterford, where 900 acres were re-let at an
advance of 15s. an acre, by a gentleman, in the course of a week after he had obtained
a lease of them, though the tenants had refused an offer of the land at the same rent
at which he had taken it."—Vol. i., p. 260.
Strange as it may seem he confirms this by other instances.

changes of the everyday life and habits of the people, which are unrecorded, and almost unnoticed, by the generation over whom they pass. There is yet no part of our history in which so many changes of importance to Ireland have taken place—none into which a minute investigation would throw more light upon many of the anomalies of our present position. The labour would be well repaid which would be devoted to that investigation; which would gather up the details which are to be found in obscure chronicles of rural affairs—the incidental revelations which are met with in records written or prepared for very different purposes—and would mould all the facts that could thus be ascertained into a review of the change of the state of Ireland from the condition in which it was found by Arthur Young to that in which it was when George IV. came to the throne, the period at which Mr. Grant made the speech to which I have referred.

Within that time large farms had been generally broken up into small ones, and at the period of Wakefield's visit the process was nearing its completion. Strange to say, it commenced after the period upon which all injurious restrictions on our manufacturing industry had been removed; during their existence the reverse process had been going on. Up to 1783 the subdivision of farms had only taken place in the province in which a free manufacturing industry prevailed. In the interim between 1783 and 1810 it had become almost universal.*

Without any attempt to go fully into the history of that change, there are considerations so obvious that they must not be overlooked. I have pointed out that, under any circumstances, it was the inevitable result of the serfdom of the mass of the people that the class of independent occupiers should disappear, and the soil be overrun by those who were willing to till it as slaves. But there are many other circumstances which we must not forget. The change was not only one from large farms to small, but from pasture land to tillage. While the process was going on Ireland had been converted from a grain-importing to a grain-exporting country. When Arthur Young visited Ireland, Dublin was supplied with bread partly by an importation from England, partly by grain sent to the metropolis under the stimulus of a bounty which more than paid the average expense of its inland carriage. In 1810 Ireland

---

* The subdivision of large farms among an inferior class of tenants commenced immediately after 1782. Arthur Young saw Ireland just on the eve of the transition.

In a speech against the bill giving the elective franchise to Roman Catholics, delivered in the Irish House of Commons, on the 18th of February, 1793, Sir Laurence Parsons described the change which even then had taken place:—

"Consider the state of the country; first, the great increase of tillage. Those large farms which a few years ago were all in pasture ground, each occupied by a single Protestant farmer, are now broken into several patches, tenanted for the most part by Catholic husbandmen, so that seven or eight Catholics hold the ground at present which one Protestant held formerly." "Consider this also, land within five or six years has risen one-fourth of its value."—*Irish Parliamentary Debates*, 1793.

exported to England 800,000 quarters of grain. The unparalleled advance of the English manufacturing system, at the close of the last century, created a demand for corn which gave a stimulus to the agriculture of the whole United Kingdom, from which Ireland could not be exempt. The effect was increased by the long revolutionary war. Pasture land was turned into corn fields. The trade in provisions declined.* The export of wool was given up, because tillage presented a more profitable occupation to the farmer.† In the ten years preceding the visit of Arthur Young the average price of wheat was 45s. the quarter; in the ten years preceding that of Wakefield it was 82s. In the first decennial period it had never risen above 53s.; in the second its maximum was 110s. In 1774 it was 52s.; in 1810 it was 106s.‡ In estimating the latter price some allowance must be made for the depreciation of the currency caused by the suspension of cash payments at the Bank of England. Still the rise of price was really enormous, and its natural effects followed—not only were pasture fields turned into tillage, but cultivation was carried to soils which before it had never reached.

It is not difficult to estimate how such a process resulted in a country circumstanced as Ireland was. If the landowners had been ready to spend the eighty-eight millions which Arthur Young calculated was the expenditure necessary to put the Irish land in the same condition as that in which English farms were let—if there had been Irish farmers possessed of the capital necessary to cultivate them in the most profitable manner—possibly the system of large farms might have been at least partially maintained. But when tillage became profitable the cheapest and the readiest way of making the profit was to give the land to those who were ready to take it at any price that was demanded. The population who were then located on the land, in many instances, were even unacquainted with the language of their masters—law had doomed them to be uneducated; oppression had crushed them down into slavery, without any spirit of independence or manly feeling. They took the land upon any terms upon which it was offered to them—in any state in which they could get it—they bound themselves by the conditions of bondsmen, and paid, or endeavoured to pay, any rent which they were asked. They were placed on the land to till it, unprovided with a house, and unsupplied with the conveniences without which no English tenant would have taken a farm. Everything that was

---

* "There has been, since the Union, a decrease of the more valuable export provisions, and an increase in the less valuable, viz., the live animals."—*John O'Connell's Argument for Ireland.*

† "Ireland exported no unmanufactured wool; it worked up all it had; and there was little reason to suppose the quantity would be enlarged, as the great increase of agriculture, and of the linen manufacture, gave a better profit in the land than sheep afforded."—Speech of Mr. Foster, Irish House of Commons, 1799.

‡ *Porter's Progress of the Nation. M'Culloch's Commercial Dictionary.*

requisite they had to do for themselves, while the rent was fixed at the very utmost limit which it was thought the produce of the land could yield. They grew the corn not for themselves but for the landlord, and his bailiff often went with it to the merchant's store, and received the price in payment of the rent. The few guineas which they were able to gather together untouched by the exactions of the landlord, the middlemen, the tithe proctor, or the agent, they hid by burying in the ground. This is the state of things described by all who, during this transition period, give us a view of the condition of the people; and every sentence of this sketch can be corroborated by abundant testimonies derived from all the sources I have indicated as those in which information is to be found.

I express no opinion upon the effect which this process had upon the real welfare of the country. To the observers who viewed the country as Young and Wakefield did, it would have seemed disastrous. Great and thriving farms were broken into small and, to all appearance, miserable tenements. A great population of serfs displaced a few free occupiers of the land. But the serfs had been there before, although at the earlier period they were permitted only partially to occupy the land. The hungry cattle had overleaped the bounds, as the old proverb tells us hungry cattle always will. Wretched as the results were in all that we are accustomed to regard as the indications of national prosperity, I am very far from being sure that the breaking up of the large farms, the "placing six or seven" Catholic occupiers where before there had been one Protestant,* was not in reality a boon to the miserable population which had previously been dwelling on the outskirts of these farms. If the hungry cattle trampled down the fences and spoiled the pastures, they had, at least, the more to eat themselves.

To many classes in Ireland the result was to give a prosperity which, in one sense, may be called fictitious, but which for the time at least was real. The rental of Ireland—meaning by the rental the sum actually paid, whether to landlord or middlemen, by those who tilled the soil, for the privilege of tilling it— was, in the southern and western districts, multiplied three-fold. There were, no doubt, many persons besides the landlords who profited by this state of things. A great milling trade grew up in the country. Corn merchants throve in many of the seaport towns. As far as the owners of land were concerned a grievous reaction came with the cessation of war prices, and the return to a currency measured, not by the value of a paper obligation, but in gold. It is utterly impossible to describe the depression which fell upon the agricultural interest in the south of Ireland between 1815 and 1826. Leases had been granted to the occupiers, partly in compliance with ancient and universal custom, partly to secure the political influence attached to the tenant's vote.

* Speech of Sir Laurence Parsons. Note to page 87.

But the rents at which farms were let in 1816 were mere rents on paper. In 1821 the attempt was made still to extract them from the wretched occupiers of the soil. Hence arose, in the first instance, the insurrectionary movements which disturbed Munster at the time when Mr. Grant spoke. Hence, too, arose to the landowners themselves the unnumbered evils of fictitious rentals, of incumbrances proportioned not to the real value of the land, but to the rents which pauper tenants had covenanted to pay. Habits of extravagance contracted upon false notions of their income—debts incurred ·upon the same exaggerated estimate—family charges placed upon the inheritor out of all proportion to the true value of the estate— all conspired to make Irish landed property, in too many instances, a delusion and a cheat. Pauper tenants and bankrupt proprietors were the natural result of such a state of things. Chancery receivers and the Incumbered Estates Commission were, as directly as Captain Rock and Captain Starlight, the creations of the system by which a tenantry of serfs were placed upon the lands, without capital, without intelligence, and without anything supplied to them, yet bound by an instrument, called in mockery a lease, to pay the uttermost farthing which an unnatural demand at any time enabled them to realize for the corn which they grew, not for themselves, but for their lords.

It was during this process, or in this process, that the subdivision of farms took place which is now so often the subject of complaint with the advocates of "landlordism," as if it was something done against the will of landlords, and which landlords would have prevented their immediate tenants doing if they could. That subdivision was the inevitable result of the circumstances of the country—the working of an economic law which neither landlords nor even legislators could control. It is very easy to blame subdivision of farms for the wretchedness of the beings who occupied small plots of ground. But there is behind this the inquiry—what would have been the condition of these very persons if they had not had their small plots of ground to occupy?

In Ulster subdivision had been carried to an extent which it has never yet reached in Munster. In Ulster it has given us a loyal, a contented, and even a prosperous population. In Munster and in Connaught it has been the multiplication of misery, simply because in these provinces the people were miserable, and every new habitation, and every new family, and every new patch of potato garden, made an addition to the sum of wretchedness that festered and fretted on the soil.

These observations must be borne in mind when I come in future pages to discuss the subject of middlemen, and the subdivision of farms—a subdivision, in the circumstances of the country, which could no more be controlled than could the instinct which bade even the Irish peasant to multiply and increase, and which, like that instinct, propagated prosperity or misery exactly according to the circumstances of the people among whom it acted. I have thought it more convenient, in this part of my argument, even partially to complete the view of the condition of the country down to the period of the insurrection which was the subject of the speech of Mr. Grant.

From the date of that speech to the great famine it will be found in the statements of the Poor Law Commission, in 1835, and those of the Devon Land Commission, ten years later.

Is it possible to conceive more accumulative or more decisive testimony to this one great truth, a truth never to be overlooked in our enquiries into Ireland's social state. There is, and there must be, one cause always existing and always unchanged, which is always creating misery and discontent. What is it? What is that something which existed in 1727 and which exists in 1867?—which blighted Ireland in the days of Swift as it is blighting Ireland now?—which armed the Levellers of 1760 as it has armed the Fenians of the present day? Through how many changes has Ireland passed? How many political disabilities have been removed? Yet there is one discontent and one misery " in all the changes and chances" of our national existence unremoved and unchanged. There must be some unchanging cause. It was not excessive agricultural population that created the evil in the days of Swift. The misery was then as it is now. All restrictions upon the woollen trade have been removed for nearly a century. It cannot be these restrictions which create it. Among all the varying grievances of Ireland— in all the changing complaints of political, and social, and commercial injustice—there is one constant evil that meets us always, unchanged and unchangeable—the " perennial" cause of a " perennial" desolation. The perpetual origin of misery and degradation has been the fact that the great mass of the people have been treated as belonging to a conquered race. All legislative and administrative efforts have been directed to secure the position of the landowners, to protect them against the people, and to enable them to raise as much as they can from the serfs that were located on their estates. No effort has been made to elevate or improve the condition of the occupiers. In a country of which the dominant caste consists of those who hold their properties by a title of confiscation, it is not, perhaps, surprising that the rights of property have been religiously, or rather irreligiously, upheld— the rights of industry and labour slighted, and no account taken of the first and most sacred of all rights—the right of the Irish people to live in their native land. I have adverted to this account to bring down the description of Irish serfdom to the time bordering on our own. When Wakefield visited Ireland our manufacturing industry and our trade had been free for thirty years. I return to the period of the restrictions, and pass from this view of our social condition to the question whether it be possible to suppose this miserable state of things to have been either caused or aggravated by that restriction on our woollen trade which finally expired in 1783.

All measures that affect the industry or the progress of a nation must be judged of by the state of society in the nation whose welfare they are supposed to affect. We must remember what Ireland was when we consider the influence of the commercial or economic injuries which England inflicted on her in the hour of her dependence. These injuries and wrongs may have affected, nay, did, no doubt, affect the upper and the dominant caste of the country. They exercised no perceptible influence upon the misery and degradation of those who were reduced to a state of serfdom.

From the battle of the Boyne to the year 1792, the Roman Catholic population did not in truth constitute any part of the Irish nation with which in history we are concerned; they were excluded from admission to any trading guilds in cities or towns, and no man could follow a handicraft in a city or town who was not free of a guild. The provisions of the law may have been evaded, but by law manufacturing industry was confined to Protestants. In point of fact, even to a comparatively recent period, the effect of these laws continued. Within the memory of living men, the majority of artisans were Protestant. It is very hard for us now to realize the condition of society in which no Roman Catholic could pursue the practice of medicine, except under terms of degrading inferiority—or could, on any terms, be admitted to practise as a barrister or an attorney. Yet I myself have conversed with many men who remembered such a state of things.

In everything which we read of the condition or the claims of the Irish nation during this period we must remember that the Irish nation was then represented by the Protestant colony that was planted in the country. There was a population of slaves outside the pale of that nation of whom no account was taken, except as far as it suited the purposes of their masters. The suppression of the woollen trade injured the Protestant artisans; it had no effect upon the Catholic serfs who were excluded by persecuting laws from the industry of towns. I have already stated my belief that if it were worth while to pursue the inquiry we would find that the suppression of the woollen trade of Ireland, so far from being an injury, was a boon to the old occupiers of the soil. There are many of the queries of Bishop Berkeley which point clearly to the conclusion that the success of the woollen manufacture would only have led to the extermination of the peasantry by making it the interest of the proprietors to turn their estates into sheep walks. The grievances of " The Levellers" are plainly pointed in the same direction. The " Irish nation" complained of the injustice of England, because the " Irish nation" consisted wholly of the Protestant proprietors and farmers, the Protestant professional classes, and the Protestant traders and artisans. It does appear that some at least of the landed proprietors of Munster desired a woollen manufacture because it would have enabled them to get rid of their " Popish tenantry" by making sheep walks of their estates. Whatever loss that suppression may have occasioned to the Protestant landlords or the Protestant artisans, I am disposed to think that the discouragement of the woollen trade was, if anything, an advantage to the mass of the people.

The effect of the encouragement of the growth of Irish wool would have been to offer a premium for the turning of tillage land into sheep walks—that is, it would have been a premium on the extermination of the people.

It is scarcely necessary to say that this was not and could not be the effect of encouraging the linen manufacture. The culture and management of a field of flax requires absolutely more hands than are employed upon a field of corn. The manufacture of flax into yarn, and of yarn into linen was, as I have pointed out, then wholly a domestic one. The growth of the linen manufacture encouraged small holdings just as much as the growth of a woollen manufacture would have destroyed them. The flax, in all its processes, from the sowing of the seed to the weaving of the web in the loom, gave profitable employment to many inmates of the peasant's home   The conversion of estates into vast sheep walks would have driven many peasants from their homes.

May not these considerations throw a gloomy light upon that strange fact in Irish social history, that the cultivation of flax was not, as a general rule, encouraged in any districts of Ireland except those in which the occupiers were attached to the dominant caste? If a Tipperary landlord had taken the advice of Bishop Berkeley,* and

* I do not think it is any undue regard for an illustrious name which induces me so often to refer to the authority of Berkeley. Very many of his queries plainly point to the strange neglect of the southern gentry to introduce the growth of flax and the linen manufacture among their tenantry. When we read the history of the time, there is no mistaking the meaning of such questions as the following :—

" Whether it would not be more prudent to try and secure ourselves in permitted branches of industry, than to fold our arms and repine that we are not allowed the woollen ?"

" Whether, if all the idle hands in this kingdom were employed on hemp and flax, we might not find sufficient vent for these manufactures ?"

" If all the land was tilled, that is fit for tillage, and all that sowed with hemp and flax, that is fit for raising them, whether we would have any sheep-walks, beyond what was necessary to supply the necessities of the kingdom ?"

" Whether it is not a sure sign of a country's thriving to see it well cultivated and full of inhabitants, and if so, whether a great quantity of sheep-walks be not ruinous to a country, rendering it waste and thinly inhabited ?"

" Whether the employing so much land under sheep be not, in truth, an Irish blunder ?"

" Whether the county of Tipperary be not much better land than the county of Armagh, and yet whether the latter be not much better improved and inhabited than the former ?"

" Whether every landlord in the kingdom doth not know the cause of this, and yet how few there are the better of the knowledge ?"

" Whether large farms under few hands, or small ones under many, are likely to be made most of, and whether flax and tillage does not naturally multiply hands and divide lands into small holdings, and well improved ?"

" Whether a scheme for the welfare of this nation should not take in all the

taught his tenants to cultivate flax instead of "patriotically" demanding a woollen manufacture, the Popish serfs upon his estate must
have shared in the prosperity which a linen manufacture would have
created. Encouragement for the growth of wool would have
enabled him to get rid of them without loss.

While the penal laws were in force whatever commercial wrongs
were inflicted by England on Ireland were really inflicted on the
Protestant population. They could scarcely reach the depths of
the misery to which the old people had been thrust down. The
traders in wool were Protestants; even the wool combers must
have been Protestants; and so were the landowners, who could
have made profit by replacing human beings over the surface of
their estates with sheep. The Catholic people would have known
the prosperity of the woollen trade only as it led to their extermination. During the period in which the penal code was in force
the manufacturing prosperity of Ireland would have but little
enriched the miserable occupiers of the soil. Lord Dufferin has
probably heard of the inscription over the gates of Bandon. The
most prosperous woollen factory within those gates would have done
little for the peasantry of the district outside the walls of that
" ancient and loyal " town.

But it is a mistake to suppose that before the Union Ireland had
no manufacturing industry, except that of linen. Surely Lord
Dufferin has heard of our silks and our tabinets. In the city of
Dublin this manufacture gave employment to thousands of operatives; it laid the foundation of many noble fortunes. The desert
by-ways of the Liberty were once the busy haunts of industry.
There were Irish hosiery manufacturers known in the great marts
of commerce. Who has not heard of Limerick gloves and Limerick
lace? of twenty other industries, in some of which we even
excelled? The startling fact is that all these manufactures have
both flourished and declined since the period at which all restrictions were removed. Whatever be the reason of their fall it
cannot be traced to these restrictions.

It would be impossible in these pages to collect the evidence
which shows that immediately before the Union Ireland enjoyed a
great manufacturing industry which is now gone. I would have
thought this one of the facts of Irish history which might have
been assumed. I can only refer to one or two testimonies which
occur to me as the most striking.

In a very remarkable speech delivered by Mr. Boyton, at the
Irish Conservative Society, on the 23rd of February, 1833, he

---

inhabitants, and whether it be not a vain attempt to protect the flourishing of our
Protestant gentry exclusive of the bulk of the natives?"

These and many others of his questions pack up in small parcels strong arguments
against the depopulation schemes of his day—the encouragement of the woollen
trade, and the consolidation of farms into sheep-walks.

pointed to the proofs of the existence of great manufacturing industries in Ireland, and traced the falling away of those industries. From this masterly essay on the decline of Ireland I extract one sentence as to the woollen trade:—

" Formerly we spun all our own woollen and worsted yarn. We imported, in 1790, only 2,294 lbs.; in 1800, 1,180 lbs.; in 1826, 662,750 lbs.—an enormous increase. There were, I understand, upwards of thirty persons engaged in the woollen trade in Dublin, who have become bankrupts since 1821."

Let me ask attention, upon this very subject of the woollen trade, to some startling facts collected by the tradesmen of Dublin in the year 1841. I add some few notes of the present day:—

In 1800 there were, in the city of Dublin, engaged in the woollen manufacture, 91 master manufacturers.

In 1840 there were but 12.

In 1864 there were 8.

In 1800 the hands employed were, - - - 4,038

In 1841, - - - - - - 682

In 1800 there were in the town of Roscrea, in Tipperary, 900 persons supported by the woollen manufacture.

At present there is not one.

In the year 1800 the manufacture of flannel employed 1,000 looms in the county of Wicklow.

At present, in all that county, there is not one.

In 1800 there were 30 master wool combers in Dublin. In 1834 they were reduced to 5.

In Kilkenny, in 1800, a blanket manufacture existed which gave constant employment to 3,000 operatives. In 1841 they were reduced to 925. I am not able to say the number that there are now.

In 1800 there were 1,491 persons employed in the city of Dublin in stuff serge manufacture. In 1834 there were 131.

In 1800, 720 operatives were employed in the carpet manufacture, under 13 masters. In 1841 there was but one carpet maker.

If the inquiry were extended to other branches of industry, the result would be still more striking. Dublin, at the time of the Union, had 2,500 broad looms in the silk manufacture; in 1840, just one-tenth of the number.

When Arthur Young visited Ireland, just as the restrictions upon Irish trade were drawing to their close, he found the manufacturing industry of Ireland very far from being destroyed. It is a great although a common mistake to suppose that before the Union the linen trade was confined to Ulster. It flourished wherever the landlords encouraged it. I confine myself to the reports given us by Young. In the neighbourhood of Slane, under the fostering care of Lord Conyngham, "there was a loom in almost every cabin." In Mayo there was an extensive linen market in many of the towns. At Westport, he found a weekly market in which £10,000 a-year was expended in the purchase of linen webs. Under the care of Lord Altamont, "the progress," he writes, "of this manufacture is prodigious. Three hundred pieces of linen were sold in Castlebar every week, and in the town and neighbourhood 200 looms were employed." "Spinning of yarns was universal throughout Leitrim and Longford"—"all Connaught was full of weaving." Even in the extreme South Mr. Longfield, animated very probably by the precepts of Berkeley, had established a linen manufacture in the neighbourhood of Cloyne.

Of other manufactures he found numbers, if not very flourishing, yet certainly far from being in decay. In Wicklow "all the wool of the county was wrought up by the inhabitants, spun, combed, and wove into flannel and frieze;" and to such an extent, "that numbers paid half their rents by this manufacture." Cork gave employment to a vast number of wool combers—"half the wool in Ireland was combed in Cork." Bandon had a large manufacture of stuff and camlet exchanged for one of brown linen. Carrick-on-Suir had its great manufactories of rattans and serge. There were few, very few parts of Ireland in which some species of manufacturing industry did not prevail. But this industry was, in all its higher branches, in the hands of Protestants. Arthur Young thus sums up the general result:—

"The only considerable manufacture in Ireland which carries in all its parts the appearance of industry is the linen, and it ought never be forgotten that this is wholly confined to the Protestant parts of the kingdom. The poor Catholics in the South of Ireland spin wool very generally, but the purchasers of their labour, and the whole worsted trade, is in the hands of the Quakers of Clonmel, Carrick, Bandon, &c."

Of the strange connexion between the linen manufacture and Protestantism we shall presently see some explanation.

Such was the condition of Irish manufactures at the very time when all restrictions upon them were finally removed. All reliable evidence assures us, that between that period and the Union those manufactures had advanced with a rapidity not surpassed in any country in the world. Surely I have cited sufficient to show that even as regards the working of woollen fabrics, the displacement of our people from that manufacturing industry is not attributable to the restrictions of days that have long since passed away.

But again it is implied in Lord Dufferin's argument that the effect of the linen trade was to diminish the number of agricultural holdings—to prevent "the disturbance of the equilibrium between land and the population dependent on the land." Its effect was directly the reverse. Up to a comparatively recent period the linen manufacture was a domestic one; the yarn was spun by women at the spinning wheel which always stood beside the cottage fireside. The farmer on a wet day or of an evening worked in his own farmhouse, at his own loom. Spinning in mills and weaving in manufactories were unknown. The result was that which is now happening in Belgium—the cottier tenant could by the aid of this domestic industry live comfortably on a few acres of land. Small holdings multiplied. The County Down has been always justly looked on as the model county of Ireland. In that county, in 1841, there were, in proportion to its extent, more holdings under fifteen acres than there were in any three of the southern or western counties in Ireland.

This mistake of Lord Dufferin's is the more unaccountable because all the objections which are now made against tenant right and small farms were in former days urged against the linen manufacture. It caused, it was said, the endless subdivision of farms.

"Farms," says Arthur Young, in recording his visit to Shane's Castle, "farms, as in all the linen counties, are very small. They rise from five acres to one hundred, but they are in general from five to thirty. Scarce any of them but are weavers or the employers of weavers, but they have such a custom of splitting their farms among their children that one of six acres will be divided."

In Derry, again, he complains of "the weavers' patches of four and five acres," of "farms lessened to seven or ten acres by the farmers dividing them among their children." In Armagh farms were "constantly getting less and less." In this county "there were no flax farmers, scarcely any flax but what was raised on patches by the cottiers." It was true that many weaving families had tea for breakfast; but even this—for the poor man at that time a very unusual luxury—could not reconcile the great agriculturalist to small farms and the unscientific husbandry of men who knew nothing of the rotation of green crops. Of the effect of the linen trade upon the size of farms, he says:—

"The variety of these is very great in Ireland. In the North, where the linen manufacture has spread, the farms are so small, that ten acres in the occupation of one person is a large one, five or six will be found a good farm, and all the agriculture of the country so entirely subservient to the manufacture, that they no more deserve the name of farmers than the occupiers of mere cabbage garden. In Limerick, Tipperary, Clare, Meath, and Waterford, there are to be found the greatest graziers and cow-keepers perhaps in the world, some who rent and occupy from £3,000 to £10,000 a year: these of course are men of property, and are the only occupiers in the kingdom who have any considerable substance." *

The landlords hated the linen manufacture because they supposed

* *Tour in Ireland.* Part ii., p. 21.

G

it reduced their rents.* Scientific agriculturalists hated it because it gave the land to small farmers, who grew flax on "weavers'" patches; and actually went out hunting hares,† in some instances, having actually clubbed to keep a pack of hounds—who gave their families tea for breakfast, and yet only grew "a few beggarly oats on a variety of the most fertile soils." "A whole province peopled by weavers." "The lands infinitely subdivided." "Ten acres are not an uncommon quantity to be in one man's occupation; four, five, or six are the common extent." "The whole region is the disgrace of the Kingdom." "The crops are contemptible." "There is not a farmer within a hundred miles of the linen country in Ireland." Such is the language in which the advocate, in his day, of the con- solidation of farms describes the effects of the manufacture which the leniency of England left to Ireland to withdraw the people from the soil. At last, repeating the statement of Lord Tyrone, as to the worst of its evils, that of lowering the rents, he winds up, in a climax of disgust and indignation, by saying:—

"I am so convinced of this, that if I had an estate in the South of Ireland, I would as soon introduce pestilence and famine as the linen manufacture upon it, carried on as it is at present."‡

Ulster violated all the laws of political economy, of scientific agriculture, and of landlord social science—and Ulster prospered. Possibly there could be no better rebuke to such theories than to read these very passages of Young, and then remember what Ulster is now.

They will, perhaps, be sufficient to satisfy Lord Dufferin that the preservation of the linen trade had not the effect of diminishing the agricultural population on the soil. They may go some way to prove that even the excessive subdivision and re-subdivision of farms are not in themselves sufficient to account for the misery and

* "Lord Tyrone is clear that if his estate in Londonderry was in Waterford, *or that all the inhabitants of it were to emigrate from it, so as to leave him to new model it,* he would be able to get full one-third more for it than he can do at present; rents in the North depending not on quality, but on price of linen."—*Young's Tour,* Vol. ii., p. 178.

† It is strange, in many cases, to trace in the diary of Arthur Young, the same prejudices among the upper classes which still prevail in our own day. Mr. O'Neill, of Shane's Castle, complained, with some reason, that the linen trade and the sub- division of farms, in some years, when the linen trade was bad, deprived him of his rents. At the Palace, in Armagh, Young was taught to believe that the weaving trade was injurious to the morals of the weavers, who were guilty of the enormity of wasting their time in coursing, and even keeping hounds of their own. He was told by others that the linen manufacture was identified with turbulence, and that it was the unruly temper of these republican weavers that caused the rebellion of the Hearts of Oak. One gentleman informed him that the emigration which had been complained of had done the country a great deal of good, it carried away "the vicious and idle," and had certainly not been caused by Lord Donegall's high rents. And another was firmly convinced that the great mischief to Ireland was the leniency of the Government in pardoning some of the Hearts of Oak. The country would have been all right if they had hanged all the rebels whom they caught.

‡ *Young's Tour.* Part ii., p. 163.

wretchedness of the Irish people. With testimonies such as these before us, and there are many of them, and with the admitted prosperity of Ulster, we must seek in something that lies deeper than subdivision of farms, or cottier patches, or even the want of a trade in woollen fabrics, for the " perennial" cause of our " perennial desolation."

I think we can understand why the linen manufacture was almost coterminous with the Protestantism of the tenantry. It was the home industry of the farmer. The web was woven by a man who had leisure hours to himself. It could not be the industry of serfs. Neither did it find favour in the eyes of the landlord : it produced bad oats, and it did not raise the rent. Under an exorbitant rent for the " weaver's patch," and duty work at five pence a day, the weaver's shuttle would soon have ceased to ply, even if one of such wretched serfs could ever have been the owner of a loom. The industry that gave extra hours to the plying of that shuttle was that of men who knew that the fruits of their labour would be their own.

Can any other reason be given to account for the marvellous fact, that manufacturing industry has long since been extinguished in every other part of Ireland, and has prospered only in some districts of Ulster? and those districts precisely those in which the sturdy spirit of Protestant independence asserted a practical security of tenure by forcing on the landlords the custom of tenant right. Why was the linen manufacture a failure out of Ulster? Surely, to all this there is and can be but one answer. In every other part of Ireland the occupiers of the soil were ground down to slavery; in Ulster they were Protestants, belonging to the conquering race—they extorted security of tenure, and therefore Ulster is the land of linen, bleach-greens and tenant right.

There are matters of Irish history which it is impossible fully to discuss, or even to state in a letter like this, and upon which, therefore, it is absolutely necessary to appeal to the knowledge and the candour of those with whom we reason. But surely, I may assume, that during the period which passed between the Revolution and 1782 the cultivation of the soil was open to the Irish nation. The discouragement of the woollen trade did not prohibit the application of industry to that soil. The Irish Parliament actually were giving bounties on the inland conveyance of corn to try and stimulate agricultural industry. There were then other manufactures besides that of linen. England was freely taking from us our provisions. She was, to some extent, especially in the article of woollen fabrics, enforcing against us the system of protection, which was then believed to be the wise rule. But throughout the South and West of Ireland the people were, to use the language of Bishop Berkeley, starving in the midst of plenty. Landlord oppressions were producing misery, and even provoking insurrectionary movements

and prædial or agrarian crimes. Population certainly was not
unduly pressing on the powers of the soil. Why were the rural
peasantry thus miserable and wretched? We are driven to account
for it, as we do now, by the miserable state of serfdom in which
they were held. It matters not whether they were so held by the
superior landlord or by " the middleman." For all purposes with
which we have to deal the middleman was the landlord. He was
the man who to the occupier had the giving of the soil.

Is it possible for any one who reads ever so carelessly the records
of that period, to say that the misery and wretchedness of that
period proceeded from an excessive agricultural population, being
driven by the suppression of manufactures upon the resources of
the soil?

But more than this—for nearly a century the causes to which
Lord Dufferin attributes the miserable condition of our land tenure
have ceased to exist. Why has that condition not improved? As
to insecurity of tenure, it is worse, absolutely worse now than it
was in 1782. Nay, more, it is since such restrictions were removed
that manufacturing industry has wholly disappeared, except that
which is still preserved in the districts of tenant right.

The answer is obvious—they are the vainest of " dreamers"
who imagine that manufacturing industry can flourish, or even
exist, where the great mass of the people are impoverished and
slaves. The south of Ireland has lost her manufactories exactly
because " landlordism" has kept the people serfs. Belfast is great,
and Derry is prosperous, not because the " clemency of England"
spared the linen manufacture, but because the freedom of the people
won from the landlords fixity of tenure—and the habits of manly
independence and industry trained a people to enterprise, energy,
and thrift.

The growth of flax, and its manufacture, have been as open for the
last century to the people of Munster as to those of Ulster. Why are
they not as prosperous? More than a century ago, Bishop
Berkeley pressed that industry upon the miserable people among
whom he lived. There was wanting the very first element of all
national prosperity, a free and independent people.

With these things before us it is impossible to regard the suppression of the woollen trade as accounting for all the wretchedness
of the Irish people. English power, it will be remembered, never
ventured to interfere with the right of the Irish nation to manufacture
woollens for themselves. It prohibited their export to England and
foreign countries. Ireland was deprived of nothing but the foreign
trade in her woollen fabrics—and we are seriously told that this is
to account for the misery and wretchedness to which the people of
Ireland were reduced; that because they could not supply foreign
countries with those fabrics a population of three millions could not
find sustenance and comfort on the Irish soil! If there had been an

independent and comfortable population on the soil, a respectable woollen manufacture could have been maintained in Ireland by the home demand. The wretchedness of the people prevented the existence of a domestic market, and therefore our manufacture fell. The history of industry abundantly teaches us that it is from the encouragement of home consumption that all manufactures take their rise. It is from the gatherings of home industry that manufacturing capital is created. It was not by prohibiting our export of broadcloth, but by defending and protecting the landlords who " ground the people to powder," that England prohibited the first rise of all prosperity and all " capital" among the Irish people. The blight and the blast of all Irish industry was at home. The " east wind" may have brought the locusts, but the locusts ate up and devoured on the Irish ground. If English power had left the people their own soil; if it had not planted over that people a horde of extortioners, who, by themselves or their deputies, wrung from the wretched natives all that could be raised from the soil by the blood and toil of slaves—if it had not upheld the extreme rights of proprietors while it crushed the occupiers to the earth—if the soil of Ireland had been occupied by freemen and not by serfs, all the laws by which England could have repressed our woollen manufacture might have injured our wealth, but they could not have kept down the industry and the enterprise of a free people.

In confirmation of the views which I have expressed I am fortunately able to quote an authority which at least has the merit of being perfectly independent. In the year 1840, a commission of enquiry as to the condition of the hand-loom weavers was issued. The report of Mr. Cæsar Otway, one of the commissioners appointed to conduct that enquiry, and who conducted its Irish department, contains, perhaps, the clearest view of the causes of the position, during the eighteenth century, of Irish manufacturing industry which has ever in the same space, been given to the public. I certainly take no credit to myself for the omission—in saying that, when I wrote the *Plea for the Celtic Race*, I had not read this most remarkable and instructive document. I do take credit to myself when I say that by a perfectly independent train of thought and enquiry I have arrived at conclusions almost identical with those so clearly and ably expressed by the author of this report.

Mr. Otway thus traces the causes which blighted the prosperity of Irish manufactures.:—

" One great and fatal error in the system of colonization to which I have adverted was, that it became a fixed principle of policy to exclude the native Irish from the benefits of all the improved arts introduced by the new settlers. It had been found, that the Anglo-Norman lords who had obtained estates from the Plantagenets, became, in the course of time, alienated from English allegiance and usages; to use the phrase of

the day, they were '*Hibernis ipsis Hiberniores*.'   To prevent such a result
from the new settlement was perversely regarded as an object of greater
importance than the settlement itself; it was said to be essentially necessary 'to preserve and maintain an English interest in Ireland.'   But for
the unhappy difference of religion between the settlers and the natives
this exclusive system would not have been long maintained; the Irish
and English would gradually have amalgamated, like the Normans and
the Saxons; but the distinction of religion gave strength and permanence
to the distinction of race, and rendered the line of demarcation scarcely
less broad than if it had been perpetuated by difference of colour and
physical organization.

  "*The hand-loom weavers, the wool-combers, the clothiers, the dyers, the white-
smiths, and even the mariners, in the south of Ireland, were so exclusively
Protestant that they would not allow a Roman Catholic apprentice to be received
in any of their trades.*   The only branch of manufactures permitted to 'the
meer Irish' was that of brogues or common shoes; and even this trade
was not permitted to be carried on within the precincts of walled towns.
Hence, these manufactures were, and continued to be, exotics; they
struck no root in the soil.

  "The early settlers were long a flourishing and numerous body.   In
1689, William and Mary were proclaimed in several small towns in
Munster; and the Protestant artizans raised a respectable army to resist
James.   At an earlier period the desertion of the Royal cause by the
Munster Protestants, under Lord Broghill and Inchiquin, was the principal cause of the easy conquest by Cromwell.   It may be added, that
James II., in his letters, ascribes his failures in Ireland to the fact that
the Protestants alone understood the art of making and mending gun-
locks, and that in consequence he never was able to keep his partisans
supplied with serviceable arms.

  "During the reigns of William and Anne this exclusion of the Irish
from all manufactures was rigorously continued; but to compensate for
this, great encouragement was given to the immigration of foreign Protestants, especially the Huguenots, who had fled from France on the
revocation of the edict of Nantes.   The bigotry of Louis the XIV. upset
the magnificent schemes of his minister, Colbert, by the expulsion of his
Huguenot subjects; and numbers of these men brought their arts, their
industry, their capital, and their faith into Ireland—they established
several branches of trade in various parts of the country—the woollen
manufacture in the South—linens and cambrics in the Counties of Down
and Armagh, and the silk manufacture in Dublin.   In support of these
refugees, and the arts they carried with them, the Irish landed proprietors
were very active—a subscription was raised, as appears from Primate
Boulter's letters, for establishing the cambric manufacture in the town
of Dundalk, amounting to £30,000, and a Monsieur De Joncourt was
appointed to collect French operatives, and conduct the establishment.
But the Huguenots adopted the baneful system of exclusion, and exerted
themselves to prevent the Irish from learning their arts or profiting by
their industry.   *The Duke of Ormond, following the example of the Earl of
Cork, also prohibited the instruction of Roman Catholic apprentices, as did the
principal landholders, who encouraged foreigners to settle on their estates.*

  "Now this exclusive system at once destroyed the basis of all manufacturing prosperity—the home market. The fabrics introduced by the English and French settlers were of a superior quality, for which the native Irish could only gradually acquire a want, as they were raised in the scale of civilization. But instead of thus raising them, the foreign manufacturers, aided by the legislature, employed every possible means to depress them, and thus blindly drove from their market a whole nation of customers, and confined them to the use of the rude and cheap fabrics which were woven amongst themselves. The manufacturers were thus forced to rely on their foreign trade ; but here they came into competition with the English merchants, and aroused the spirit of commercial jealousy. .   .

"*The act of William, prohibiting the export of Irish wool and woollens, destroyed the Irish woollen manufactures, simply because they depended almost solely on foreign sale for their support. There was no independent peasantry or respectable and wealthy middle class, for them to supply.*

"It may be asked why the manufacture of the North did not share the same fate of those of the South ; but the question is easily solved by a glance at the state of the population in the province of Ulster. The settlement in Ulster was more complete and extensive than that in any other part of Ireland. The natives had been either wholly exterminated or driven into mountainous and remote districts. The landlords and tenants in the manufacturing districts of the North thus belong to one class ; they did not regard each other as hereditary enemies ; there was no legacy of oppression on one side, and revenge on the other. *The Ulster tenant felt (and feels) he had a property in his farm—something on earth he could call his own ;* and the fruits of his industry would be allowed to accumulate into a small capital, and in point of fact, such an accumulation did take place ; for *the greater part of the capital in the linen manufactures of Ulster was derived from the savings of agricultural industry,* and hence arose the numerous class who were each at the same time a farmer, a weaver, and a linen-dealer (jobber). In the south of Ireland the title to property was unsettled ; for more than a century confiscation and re-confiscation followed each other, until the Acts of Settlement and Explanation secured the followers of Cromwell in their estates ; there was no community of feeling or interest between the proprietor and the occupants brought about by these acts. The great object was to establish an English interest in Ireland ; and to accomplish this hereditary policy, the two last Stuarts, while they patronised Roman Catholics in their own courts, rigorously maintained the new Protestant proprietary in the south of Ireland. It was not until James II. was driven from England, that he would allow even of an enquiry into the Act of Settlement, and it is doubtful whether he would have consented, even in Dublin, to its repeal, if a large portion of the re-confiscations had not reverted to the Crown. The repeal of the Irish Act of Settlement, by the Parliament of James the 2nd, gave the Protestant proprietors a fright from which they have not perfectly recovered even to this day ; since that time they have been persuaded that every change of policy, or isolated disturbance, threatens their titles ; they deem that they only garrison their estates, and therefore they look upon the native occupants (I cannot call them tenants) as persons ready to eject them upon a favourable opportunity. Hence, the Munster landlord was afraid to give the persons who occupied his ground a permanent hold upon the land, or a beneficial interest in its occupancy.

" The old struggle of title, in natural course, produced the new contest of tenure; and Captain Rock and Lady Clare were as legitimately descended from the Catholic lords of the pale, as Jack Straw and Wat Tyler were from the Saxon thanes, who fought at Hastings. *There is, and until the relation between landlord and occupant are altered, there can be no accumulation of savings in the South of Ireland from agricultural industry*— and hence there was not and can be no spontaneous growth of manufactures from small capitals."

This report, it will be remembered, was made in the year 1840 when no agitation existed on the subject of tenant right. No political object could be served by the expression of such views. There was no social or party discussion then going on which could exercise the slightest influence over the mind of the clear-sighted and able writer whose enquiry into the condition of Irish manufacturing industry led him to these results.

I say, then, that Lord Dufferin's solution of the causes of our misery is utterly inadequate to account for it. It fails, because for nearly a century the causes which he assigns have absolutely ceased to exist—it fails, because it does not touch, throughout an entire century, the question of the miserable condition of the occupiers of our land—it fails, because it assigns no reason for the superiority of one province over the rest of Ireland—it fails, because it is utterly insufficient to account for the degradation of a people such as he eulogizes, placed in a country such as he describes. It fails, lastly, because, if the Irish tenantry had been independent, the home demand would have sustained a woollen manufacture to supply the wants of the tenantry itself. Whatever we may think of the commercial policy of England as to our wool, we must go deeper, far deeper, to find the causes of the " perennial desolation" of our land.

I am still unwilling to part with Lord Dufferin's third letter without noticing two passages of no little significance; one, in which he avows himself the apologist of exorbitant rents; the other, in which I think he acknowledges his enmity to Ulster tenant right. The first passage to which I ask attention runs thus:—

" Whether even the middleman is deserving of all the abuse which is heaped upon him may be a question. It has always seemed to me that the moral responsibility of accepting a competition rent is pretty much the same as that of profiting by the market rate of wages. If the first is frequently exorbitant, the latter is as often inadequate; and inadequate wages are as fatal to efficiency as a rack-rent is to production; though each be the result of voluntary adjustment, it is the same abject misery and absence of an alternative which rule the rate of both.'

This is but a plain and, I must say, a consistent following out of the principles of those who tell us that all things connected with the tilling of land are to be left to voluntary adjustment, and the natural laws which regulate prices. The value of everything is just what it will bring. Upon this principle competition rent and competition wages are the value of the land or the work, and he who takes less than he can get for the one, or gives more for the other than that for which he can get it, is taking less or giving more than the value, and is making a gift of the difference to his tenant or his workman.

There are, after all, great principles implanted in our conscience, which tell us that the man does not do his duty by his neighbour when he avails himself of his distress to exact from him his toil for some miserable pittance. There are laws of God as well as of political economy, and some, at least, of the former, are written in our hearts.

I cannot stop to argue the question upon the grounds at which, in the *Plea for the Celtic Race*, I have already glanced. There is an instinct in human nature which revolts at the idea that no moral responsibility attaches to the Irish landlord, who would squeeze from the miserable peasant the last penny he could extort from his dire need of a bit of land. This is to make the landlord a usurer (I admit usury is become respectable), but a usurer who is neither respectable or honest; a usurer who remorselessly trades upon the necessities of his victims.

I notice the passage for the sake of a fallacy which pervades a great deal that is written on this subject. There is no process of competition in the raising of Irish rents. As a general rule a landlord does not raise his rent because some other person has offered more for the land than the existing tenant pays, but because he thinks that he is entitled to or can exact the additional amount. When an unscrupulous proprietor thinks that the circumstances of the tenant will bear the exaction of an increased rent he simply sends the land bailiff to tell him that his rent will be raised. If the tenant does not sign the new agreement the refusal is followed by notice to quit. In the immense majority of cases the tenant has no choice but to submit. The increased rent very probably will beggar him as soon as the little hoard of savings upon which his conscientious landlord speculated is gone. To speak of rents being fixed in Ireland by "competition" is to speak of something utterly foreign to the great majority of instances with which we have to deal. A very little reflection will make it plain that whatever be the case in any other country, in Ireland at least the letting rent of land is not fixed by the same laws as that which in open market regulate generally the price of commodities.

The process by which the price of every commodity is fixed, in ordinary cases, is familiar to every one who has studied even the elements of political economy. A knowledge of it is in truth the foundation of all the reasonings of the science. It is fixed on the one hand by the competition of buyers anxious to obtain the article, and by the competition of sellers anxious to get rid of the articles which they have to sell. In any case in which these two things do not freely act, political economy teaches us distinctly that we cannot apply the rules which determine, in ordinary cases, price. Neither of the elements of adjustment act freely in fixing the price of Irish land. The landlord has his tenant, in most cases, so completely in his power, that he is not driven to regulate his land even by the principle of competition among buyers. If he were even compelled to the alternative of leaving his land waste, he knows he can insist on the tenant paying him exactly the rent which he chooses to fix, and he fixes it not by any consideration of the probability of obtaining another tenant, but by his own view of what the tenant ought to pay.

The second element, that of competition among sellers, exercises an influence so feeble and insignificant that it may be said to be wholly absent. The man who would seriously say that there is a competition among Irish landlords to undersell each other in the letting of land, may then appeal to the laws of political economy and the process which regulates the natural price. Scientific reasonings will only lead us astray, if these reasonings are based on the assumption that an Irish landlord is generally influenced in the fixing of his rent by the fear that another landlord will attract away his tenants by offering his farms at a cheaper rate.

In denying, then, that the rent of land in Ireland is fixed by the operation of the mercantile laws of price, I am not impugning, but actually upholding and applying the principles of the science of political economy. One of the very objects of that science is to fix and determine the cases in which price is regulated by the process of competition. Its investigations have determined that where certain conditions exist price will be regulated by certain rules. But they have equally determined that where these conditions do not exist these rules do not prevail The conditions do not exist in the case of either the letting or taking of Irish land.

I might as well be told that the ransom which the brigand demands for his captive is a matter within the ordinary rules of commercial demand and supply—or to use, perhaps a more appropriate illustration, that those rules adjust the price which could be extorted for a night's lodging from a traveller benighted on a solitary road. In all instances of this nature the sum that is paid depends upon the conscience or the cunning of the one party, and on the ability to pay possessed, or presumed to be possessed, by the other. Political economy warns us not to apply to such cases the calculations which ascertain for us the "market overt" price. So to apply them is simply a blunder in science, and an outrage upon common sense.

The other passage in Lord Dufferin's letter which demands notice is one which seems to be a very clear and distinct warning to the Ulster tenant-farmers that unless they make common cause with those of the rest of Ireland, and force a legislative recognition of fixity of tenure, their own provincial custom of tenant right is doomed.*

* I am not sure that there is any where to be found as full and accurate information on the subject of the Ulster tenant as that which is contained in a report, to which the name of the late Mr. O'Connell is attached, and which was presented to the Repeal Association in April, 1845, the same from which I have already taken the evidence bearing on tenant right.

To this report are appended very well selected and most valuable extracts from the evidence taken before the Committee of the House of Commons on townland valuations in 1844, and before the Devon Commission, which made its report in 1845.

The general result is thus accurately summed up in the report :—

"That it also appears from the Report and Evidence of the said Commissioners, and of the Committee on the Townland Valuation of Ireland, that throughout the greater part of Ulster the practice of Tenant-right prevails, and that along with it are found industry, comfort, and peace.

"That according to the practice of this right, no person can get into the occupation of a farm without paying the previous occupier the price of his right of occupation or good-will, whether the land be held by lease or at will.

"*That on the ejectment of any occupying tenant, he receives the full selling value of his Tenant-right, less by any arrears due to the landlord ;* but this does not extend to middlemen.

"That the same custom, unrecognized as it is by law, prevents the landlord who has bought the tenant-right, or otherwise got into possession of a farm, *from setting it at such an increase of rent as to displace Tenant-right.* Thus, middlemen are almost unknown, and *the effect of competition for land is principally to increase the value of the Tenant-right, not the amount of the rent.*

"That *Tenant-right exists even in unimproved land, and that five years' purchase is an ordinary payment for the Tenant-right of such land,* while 15 or 20 years' purchase is often given for the Tenant-right of highly improved farms."

The report then proceeds in words of warning and suggestion, more applicable now than they were when they were written :—

"That, nevertheless, this right is regarded by many of the present landlords of Ulster with jealousy and dislike ; that several of them have endeavoured to shackle and reduce this right ; that some of them on the borders of the customary counties, have tried, with success, to abolish it, and that ' it is in danger ' (in the words of The Northern Whig) ' of being frittered away in course of years, and no equivalent provided in its stead.'

"That the said Commissioners appear to have studiously endeavoured in their examination of witnesses, to disparage the character of this Tenant right, which the present farmers of Ulster bought with their money, or inherited from their fathers—a right, of which one witness (the agent of Lord Lurgan) said, that were it disallowed, there was ' no force at the disposal of the Horse-guards which could keep the peace of the province.'

"*That the Commissioners* (not daring openly to attack such a right so defended) *have insidiously reported that any 'hasty or general disallowance' of the right would be inexpedient—purporting thereby that its gradual and cunning disallowance would be expedient,' and proposing many schemes for this purpose.*

"That portions of the said Report and Evidence, presented herewith, fully bear out the preceding propositions on the tenant-right.

"That, under these circumstances, *it is desirable that a law should be passed recognizing tenant right in the customary districts of Ulster,* and giving process from a tribunal of arbiters, with an appeal to the Assistant Barrister's Court, for the adjustment of disputes as to this right."—*Report of Parliamentary Committee of Repeal Association of Ireland,* Vol. ii., p. 298.

"In Ulster," says Lord Dufferin, "though under a more subtle guise, rack rents and the middlemen are as rampant as they are in Connaught."

In a note this is explained:—

"The tenant right, or good-will of the tenant is disposable; the incoming tenant pays the purchase, almost invariably made with money borrowed at a high rate of interest. This interest is, of course, a second or rack rent paid to the lender of the purchase money, and the recipient who walks off with it is neither more nor less than a kind of bastard middleman, who takes a fine in lieu of an annual payment for a non-existing value. As a consequence, the new tenant commences his enterprize burdened with debt and destitute of capital. Hence low farming, inadequate profits, uneducated children, and, too frequently, the ruin and emigration of the Ulster tenant, in spite of indulgent landlords and a secure tenure."*

The right of sale is essential to the very existence of the custom of tenant right. Lord Dufferin himself so defined tenant right before the Land Tenure Committee of 1865:—

"The custom may, I think, be thus defined:—Tenant right is a custom under which the tenant farmers of the North of Ireland, or, at all events, in those districts where the custom prevails, expect, when they have occasion to give up possession of their farms, that their landlords will allow them to obtain from the incoming tenant such a sum as shall remunerate them for their improvements upon the farms."—(Lord Dufferin, Question 966.)

The definition, as Lord Dufferin intimates in another part of the same answer, is inadequate. It is put in the cautious and guarded language of one unfavourable to the custom, but it describes that custom as consisting entirely in the practice of the sale of the outgoing tenant of an interest in the farm. I do not admit this to be anything like an adequate account of the custom of tenant right. It is that which would be given by a person anxious to find a plausible excuse for destroying it. Tenant right is the insufficient substitute for the old right of every occupier on the

---

* I cannot take much credit to myself for sagacity in having, months before Lord Dufferin wrote these sentences, predicted this. In July last I urged the necessity of a legal enactment to preserve the Ulster tenant right.

"Of the necessity of some such legal enactment there is unhappily too much proof. In those which may be termed the border districts of tenant right, the sacredness of the custom is gradually encroached upon. There are estates from which, as opportunity offers, it is excluded. The right which it confers is, in other instances, frittered away; and one after another the debateable points are ruled by the landlord in favour of himself. *Political economy and public policy are always at hand to supply excellent reasons for the extinction of a custom which requires an incoming tenant to expend what is called his capital before he enters on his farm. It cannot be very difficult to prove to the satisfaction of a landlord that his capital could be better expended in improvements upon the soil, while the want of the tenant right was represented by an addition to the rent."*—Land Tenure in Ireland, p. 61, Third Edition.

Ulster plantation to be an "estated tenant" on his farm. It had its origin in the days when Lady Drummond pretended to the King's Commissioner that her knight was gone to Scotland, and that having lost the key of his paper desk, she could not produce the counterpanes of the leases which the tenants complained they had not got. If Lord Dufferin's description be accurate, this custom robs the landlord of a rack rent, which is paid to a usurer who is the owner of money, not of land. The custom which leads to "low farming, inadequate profits, uneducated children! and, too frequently, the ruin and emigration of the Ulster tenant," cannot too soon be abolished.

This is certainly not the light in which, in other parts of Ireland, we have been accustomed to regard either Ulster tenants or Ulster tenant right. Wise men have spoken of it in terms of admiration as the glory of the province. Men as well acquainted as his Lordship is with Ulster have described the maintenance of tenant right as the sole guarantee for its prosperity and peace.

When a nobleman of Lord Dufferin's character and station palliates the exaction of exorbitant rents, and classes the custom of Ulster tenant right with the system of rack-renting middlemen, it is high time for the Ulster tenantry to look out for themselves.

And yet Lord Dufferin has the strange boldness to say that arguments derived from the confiscations and the settlement consequent on them point to the extermination of the Protestant population of Ulster. It is scarcely possible to conceive a more singular or more complete misrepresentation of the whole effect of such arguments. The advocates of fixity of tenure invariably point to Ulster as the illustration of its value—to its effects upon the inhabitants of that province as the conclusive proof of the wisdom of perpetuating it by law where it exists, and establishing it where it does not. Can this strange statement be a miserable and unmanly appeal to the religious passions of the Protestants of Ulster to prevent them joining in the demands for justice to all Irish occupiers of the soil? I am very unwilling to impute this to Lord Dufferin, yet I hardly know what else this marvellous allusion to the extermination of Protestants means. I do not know that in immediate connexion with this singular argument he named me; if he did so, it is scarcely worth my while to say my whole argument was that the Protestant population of Ulster were to be taken as a model for the rest of Ireland, exactly because their freedom and independence had won for them tenant right. I stated that whenever that custom was broken down, the prosperity and the peace of Ulster would be destroyed—that in the Protestant population of that province were to be found the qualities of industry, of manly independence, and of self-relying energy and thrift. I argued that the tenant right which had made them what they are ought—just because it had made them so—to be extended to the rest of Ireland.

There is indeed a policy which would tend to the extermination of that people—it is the policy of "landlordism" which drove many of the Ulster Protestants into exile just a century ago*—the policy which would make way for landlords' improvements by getting rid of "small holdings" and of the obnoxious custom of tenant right! I would do Lord Dufferin injustice if I described him as the advocate of the extermination of the Protestant population of the County of Down, yet there would be surely some excuse for so designating arguments which tell us that Ulster tenant right is only a form of the worst class of rack rent middlemen, and assume, as an axiom, that no farmer who holds less than fifteen acres can continue with advantage to occupy his farm.

I cannot avoid adding that if Lord Dufferin's proposal to graft on a land bill provisions enabling landlords to borrow public money *to buy up their tenants' improvements*—in other words, *to purchase out their tenant right*—should ever unhappily be adopted, a very large extermination of the Protestant population of Ulster will be the result. Except to facilitate the removal of many of them from their farms, I can see no object in the proposal.

Let us argue out this question fairly, but let us have no evasions of the real issue on either side.

---

* In a previous page I have adverted to the singular fact of a large emigration from Ulster of the Protestant population in the beginning of the last century. It was very considerable at the time of the suppression of the rebellion of the Hearts of Oak. Arthur Young, who visited Ulster some years later, was assured that this latter emigration was confined to "the dissenters," "the idle," and "the worthless." It must be remembered that his reports on the state of Ireland were generally derived, so far as they were not the result of personal observation, from the aristocracy and high gentry. His tour in Ireland was a succession of visits to the houses of noblemen, bishops, and great landed proprietors. Occasionally the answers to his inquiries disclosed a very different result. Primate Boulter, in his lettings, gives a totally different representation of the earlier Protestant emigration. He draws a very melancholy picture of the distress which, upon his visit to Derry, he found prevailing among the people, even in the Protestant districts of the North.

The subject is well worth a careful inquiry. Some materials for it must certainly exist. I am very much disposed to believe that the emigration was caused, like our present emigration, by landlord oppression. That the last expatriation was of those who went in despair, upon the suppression of the insurrection of the Hearts of Oak—the last struggle to vindicate tenant right. They went before they knew that the struggle had been really successful in its object. With that insurrection ceased all attempts at interference with the Ulster tenant right.

An inquirer who would follow out the matter "too curiously," might fall into a strain of reflections on the different results of the "risings" in Ulster and Munster. He could hardly overlook the fact that the Protestant rebels of Ulster were tried by sympathising juries, who brought in repeated verdicts of acquittal under circumstances which were thought to justify the legislature in passing the extreme and unconstitutional measure of enacting that the trials should be in Dublin. In Dublin the prosecutions equally failed, and the unpopular statute was obliged to be repealed.

In Munster the "Popish" rebels were tried by juries, the fury of whose partizanship against the prisoners the judges were compelled to moderate and restrain.

The Ulster people obtained their fixity of tenure. The Munster serfs were left to the landlords, the Whiteboys, and Captain Rock.

There are many passages in English history—there are very few in Irish—which tell us how trial by jury has really vindicated popular liberty and right.

I must do Lord Dufferin the justice to say that his views upon
these questions are only legitimate—indeed necessary deductions
from the theories of the absolute right of property in the landlord,
and from the economic argument which is employed against any
interference with contracts relating to land. If these arguments be
valid against fixity of tenure, they are equally valid against the
Ulster tenant right. If land is to be dealt with in its letting, as a
grocer sells his tea and his sugar, and if landlords be mere traders
in the article, they are not to be blamed for exacting the
market price, and the market price is the utmost which any one
will give. I have endeavoured to show that these principles are
not applicable to the letting of Irish farms. I believe that any
theories founded on them must be delusive, but I give Lord Dufferin
full credit for the boldness and the clearness with which he has followed out those principles to their logical and inevitable conclusion. If land is really in the market an article of free trade, then
rack rents are but the healthy development of natural and inevitable
laws, and rack-renting middlemen were as useful as " regraters and
forestallers." They were the retailers to the small customer of the
article of land purchasing at the wholesale price, and making the
profit on the retail. They bought in the cheapest, and sold in the
dearest market, and were only the useful agents in carrying out the
great object of bringing land to the consumer at its true market
value; and the profits they made upon their share in the transaction
would not have been paid if they had not rendered services to all
parties equivalent to the commission which they charged.

There are, no doubt, persons who will think that as long as the
argumentum ad absurdum is recognized as a legitimate mode of
reasoning, it is one of the most conclusive arguments against the
application of those principles to land tenure in Ireland that they
lead by an inexorable logic to these results. But unquestionably
Lord Dufferin has done nothing more than follow them out to their
inevitable conclusion.

Upon this subject of "middlemen" I must say that the observations of Lord Dufferin, much as I dissent from them, like all the
mistakes of able men, are far from being destitute of some foundation.* I cannot agree in his defence of the middlemen whom he
describes. I believe the exaction of extortionate rents to be both
an evil and a crime, whether the rents be wrung from the people
by a middleman or an owner in fee. But it is an absurdity to say
that the existence of middlemen was the cause of the miseries of
the people. At the very worst they were the administrators of a

* *The Edinburgh Review*, in one of its early numbers, justified the existence of
middlemen upon grounds not very unlike those upon which Lord Dufferin defends
them. If rent in Ireland be regulated by the same economic laws as those which fix
generally the price of commodities, it is impossible to maintain the argument against
middlemen.

vicious system of land tenure—not its creators. They may have preyed upon the miseries of the people, but they did not make them. The fact that a man paid rent himself gave him no power over the occupiers which the chief landlord did not personally possess. A system of extortion was possible, because the occupiers of the soil were crushed down by oppressive laws, and the worst effect of interposing an intermediate agent between the owner in fee and that occupier was to place the power of extortion and oppression in the hands of a class of persons who may be supposed more likely to be remorseless in its use. In the circumstances of Ireland this was injurious. It placed over the tenantry a landlord of lower rank, and therefore one more likely to oppress the people. It deprived the people on the estate on which the owner was resident of the benefit of whatever humanising influence high rank, and superior education, and great possessions, might be supposed to exercise upon the disposition of their landlord. Injurious as all this may have been, it is not possible to carry the argument against middlemen farther than this. It is plain that whatever the middleman did the chief landlord might do, and if the power of extortion and oppression did not exist in that chief landlord it was not possible for him to delegate it to another. The middleman was obnoxious because wherever he did exist he was the instrument of oppression who came in contact with the people; and it was the natural tendency both of the people and the aristocracy to throw all the blame of every oppression upon him.

In the first place we must remember that many of the holders of these intermediate interests were in reality the owners of the estate. Large tracts of land in Ireland are held under fee farm grants, or leases in perpetuity, paying an inconsiderable rent. I am acquainted with a district in the South of Ireland thickly studded with gentry, in which, a few years ago, there was just one man, and he was not of the higher rank of gentry, living on his own fee simple estate. The ancestral mansion of one of the proudest families among the landowners of Ireland was built upon a tract of land held under a neighbouring nobleman, at an almost nominal rent, for 999 years. A title in the family has become extinct; but that mansion in modern times was the residence of a peer more influential than the nobleman from whom he rented his estate.* To speak of persons of this class as middlemen would be an entire misapplication of the word. They were, and are, to all intents and purposes, the real owners of the soil.

The frequency of grants of this nature forms a singular feature in the history of landed property in Ireland. In many instances they were the result of unsettled times, when little value was set

---

* Sales have recently taken place in the Landed Estates' Court in which the trifling head rent has been bought up ; and the representative of Lord Longueville can now say that he lives upon his own fee-simple estate.

THE IRISH MIDDLEMEN. 113

upon property in many districts of Ireland, and men were ready to give it for almost anything they could get. Many of the new proprietors parted with their estates in perpetuity, because they had not the means of meeting the expenditure which appeared absolutely necessary to make them productive at all. Others granted these long tenures because, while they claimed the rank and the dignity of landed proprietors, they did not choose to have the trouble and annoyance of managing property in a country to which they were strangers, and with the people of which they had no community of habit or of feeling. They were made very frequently by grantees who desired to draw a certain revenue from their Irish estates without either risk or trouble to themselves. In many instances these long leases were the result partly of this feeling, and partly of the proverbial recklessness with which men part with ill-gotten possessions. *Facile parta, facile dilabuntur.* The history of Irish titles abounds with instances that seem the mixed result of prodigal generosity and ignorance, the feeling which makes the soldier sell for a trifle the articles he has seized in his pillage.*

There were, no doubt, many persons who ought to have been farmers holding long leases of large quantities of land, who, instead of occupying it, let the land to under tenants; and there were instances in which those under-tenants were grievously oppressed. But it would be the greatest of all mistakes to suppose that all such persons were peculiarly extortionate, or still greater to imagine that oppression and extortion were confined to estates which were so let.

On the contrary, the agent of the absentee proprietor was generally, if not always, a more grievous oppressor than even the worst of the middlemen;† and the resident landowner, having just

* Every one acquainted with Irish titles or Irish estates must remember many such instances. Occasionally they were like the acquisition of property in the early days of the Incumbered Estates Commission; bargains made at a time when the state of the country made Irish property of little value.

Arthur Young tells us that the great Munster estates of Lord Lansdowne had a narrow escape of such an alienation.

"The present Earl of Kerry's grandfather, Thomas, agreed to lease the whole estate for £1,500, a year, to a Mr. Collis, *for ever*, but the bargain went off upon a dispute, whether the money should be paid at Corke or Dublin. Those very lands are now let at £20,000 a year."

If Mr. Collis had been fortunate enough to close the bargain his descendant could scarcely be called a middleman.

Wakefield gives a later instance. Writing in 1809, he tells us:—

"Lord Donerail's father let an estate *for ever* at £2,000 a year, and lived to see it re-let at a profit rent of £18,000."

† Mr. Wakefield, in 1812, gives us a vivid picture of the extortions practised even by men of high character, the agents of absentee estates. The forcing of unpaid work from the tenants was really the least of these. Tenants holding even by leases were the slaves of the agent, and literally bound to submit to whatever he ordered. Agents' fees were an impost levied at the discretion of the receiver, and "gratuities" in one form or another attended every step taken on the estate. "Lease money" was invariably exacted on the renewal of a lease. Wakefield mentions an instance which came to his knowledge, in which new leases were granted on an estate of £10,000

H

the same opportunity for oppression, used it just as often. The "tornybeg," as the people designated the middleman, may have been, from his position, more insolent and more rapacious; but insolence and rapacity were certainly not confined to those landlords who happened themselves to pay rent for their estates. The fact that the oppressor was himself but a tenant gave a bitterness to the popular feeling, and a sting to the popular reproach; but that fact affected the condition of the occupier not much more than did the payment by the chief landlord of a quit rent to the Crown.

All the grievous instances of oppression which have become historical by provoking serious insurrections were upon estates in which the occupiers held direct from the chief lord. The exactions of an agent of Lord Donegall excited all Ulster to the rebellion of the Hearts of Oak. The Munster insurrection of 1821 was distinctly traceable to the oppressions directly practised upon one great estate. Both middlemen and chief landlords had the power of persecution in their hands. It is an absurdity as well as an untruth to say that all of one class used it, and that none of the other did.

Of middlemen, properly so called, there were two classes; there were men who originally took their leases for the very purpose of collecting the rents from the occupying tenants. There were others, who having originally farmed their own property, gradually parted with the possession to a large number of tenants occupying small portions. As to the first, they were really mere farmers of rents. Their occupation existed because there were owners of estates who desired to draw a certain and secure income from them without any trouble and without the necessity of personal contact with the misery and poverty from which this income was wrung. That occupation would have no place if there had not been such landowners, aliens in every sense to the country, and a miserable tenantry. Both these elements must have been in existence to give any opportunity for the rent farmer's trade.

But we would suppose, from some of the arguments that are now used, that long leases were used only for the purpose of subletting.

a year. The agent demanded and received from each tenant one year's rent, pocketing the sum of £10,000. On single transactions the per centage was much larger.

These payments, or presents, or exactions, were received by men of "unblemished character"—men selected, as Wakefield tells us, "for their probity and independence." It was the custom of the country. More than this—these extortions were connived at, or even sanctioned by the landlord, who, so long as his agent secured his rent, had no objection to his doing a bit of plunder on his own account.

Wakefield tells us of a nobleman of the highest character and rank, who, "upon the appointment of a new agent, borrowed of him £20,000. The agent, who was a man of character, being desirous to have it understood whether he was to follow the usual custom and receive presents from the tenants, asked his employer in what manner he should act. The reply was, ' Get all you can.' "—*View of Ireland*, Vol. i., p. 299.

How is all this to be accounted for except by believing that—in that class opinion which after all upon such matters determined class morals—the Irish occupier was regarded as a being made and existing only for the purpose of being fleeced.

I will take the period of 1777, because it is one as to which the curious record preserved to us in the publication of Arthur Young, supplies us with something like authentic information.* In the

* The book of Arthur Young, to which I have so often referred as an authority, contains a most valuable and instructive account of the state of agriculture in the several districts of Ireland in the three or four years preceding 1780.

Arthur Young came to Ireland in the Summer of 1776. He spent nearly two years in residing at the seats of the principal nobility and gentry in Ireland, principally engaged in enquiries into the agricultural condition of each neighbourhood. After this he spent some time at Mitchellstown, with Lord Kingsborough, as an agricultural manager of his estate. He published, in two volumes, in a species of diary the result of his observations in each district, together with a summary of his general views of the country. The former is given us with some minuteness of detail. We can learn how Mr. Jeffreys, of Blarney Castle, then farmed his estate—what rotations of green crops Lord Courtown adopted on his admirably farmed demesne—how Mr. French, of Monivea, grew his hops—the care and taste with which Lady Clanwilliam planted her shrubberies—how many acres of turnips Lord Mornington grew at Dangan—the food Lord Doneraile gave his hogs—how Mr. Herbert at Mucruss persisted in planting his potatoes in the "lazy bed" fashion, and maintained against all his visitors' arguments that it was the best—how Lord Shannon made his bullocks draw by the horns, and supported the practice by authorities from the most recent travels in the East—and even the weight of the farm carts which were used at Shane's Castle, by Mr. O'Neill. This singular detail of the mode of husbandry adopted, by each of nearly a hundred Irish proprietors, a century ago, has a deep interest even for those who might take none in its purely agricultural details. Combined with observations upon the condition of the surrounding farms—and with descriptions more or less full of the condition of the peasantry and the labouring class—it supplies us with almost a photograph of the actual state of many rural districts in Ireland at the time.

In this lies its value. Young came to Ireland as an agriculturist. He exhibits in every page of his diary his ruling passion for large farms. Of the state of political feeling in the country he says nothing; of its social condition very little; and the little that he does say is coloured by the tone of society in which he moved. An intelligent and travelled Englishman could scarcely fail to be struck by the degradation and slavery of the Irish peasant; and he has recorded in the strongest terms his protest against the folly and iniquity of the penal laws.

His observations upon the country are, however, those of "the mere agriculturist." In the heart of the country which had been just agitated by the treason of the Hearts of Oak he devotes more pages to his morning rides with Primate Robinson to visit his improvements than he does lines to that remarkable insurrection. Strange to say, in all his enquiries into the condition of Ulster he never once mentions the custom of tenant right. Possibly, he was so indignant at the existence of the linen manufacture, and the consequent multiplication of small farms, that he turned from the province in disgust. It is still more singular that it is only in an incidental allusion that he notices the most striking difference between the rural economy of England and Ireland, the absence in the latter country of any legal provision for the poor. On the eve of the great struggle for Irish independence he incidentally mentions that, "since Mr. Flood has been silenced with the vice-treasurership of Ireland, Mr. Daly, Mr. Grattan, Sir Wm. Osborne, and the Prime Sergeant Burgh, are reckoned high among the Irish orators." In his proper place Sir William Osborne is honoured with several pages as the intelligent and humane improver of his estate.

Taking the book for what it is, it is not possible to overrate its value as a dry matter-of-fact record, made by a most intelligent and accurate observer of many of the most important points connected with the rural economy of Ireland at the time.

Possibly, to the minds of many, a careful perusal of it will suggest the same dismal reflection that it has done to me. Ireland, in the year 1777, was in a far better condition than it is now. The promises of improvement even in the breeding of sheep, the feeding of bullocks, and the growing of turnips, were far brighter than they are now. An Arthur Young, who would now travel round Ireland, from the Primate's at Armagh to his resting place at Mitchellstown, could record no such signs of present improvement, nor such hopeful prospects of future advancement as are told in the graphic, although homely, pages of the diary of this tour.

North of Ireland farms were at that time small, as they are now, generally below the magic fifteen acres. As we have seen they provoked Young—who was an enthusiast for " husbandry" and an advocate for large farms and great capital applied to agriculture—to say that the linen manufacture was "the pest and ruin of any country in which it prevailed." It enabled persons to live upon small patches of land. But in the South and West, and even in the midland counties of Ireland, the farms were generally of considerable size, often containing 200 or 300 acres, in some districts as many thousands. Young tells us in perfect ecstasy of one farm in Tipperary containing 10,000 acres farmed by one man. In the same county another farmer occupied 13,800 (!!!) acres in his own hands. In Waterford and Limerick farms were often of the size of 2,000 or 3,000 acres.* At this period certainly the evil of Southern Ireland was not the absence of large farms.

I have already offered some observations on the process by which a country like this was converted, in a great degree, into one of small holdings.† The owners in fee had just as much to do with it as " the middlemen." The creation of forty-shilling freeholders was carried to an almost incredible extent upon some estates, many of which were expressively called " warrens of freeholders," but, in addition to all this, subdivision was profitable—letting in small portions for tillage became, for the reasons I have adverted to,

* " Farms are generally large, commonly 3,000 or 4,000 acres, and rise up to 10,000, of which quantity there is one farm, this is Mr. M'Carthy's, of Spring House, near Tipperary, and is, I suppose, the most considerable one in the world."—*Young's Tour*, Vol. ii., p. 457.

Even this appears to have been exceeded by another farm in the same county—in a subsequent page he writes :—

"I had heard much of the late Mr. Keating's farm of Garrahland, as the largest that ever was. His son gave me the following particulars :—

"£10,000 a year rent ; 13,800 Irish acres ; 3,000 head of black cattle ; 16,300 sheep ; 300 horses ; 500 couple of ducks ; 300 turkies ; 70 hogsheads of cider a year."

"This county (Waterford) is divided into large farms."

Kerry.—"The best part of the county is under dairies ; great farmers have vast quantities of land."—*Ibid*, 122.

Cork.—" Castle Oliver—Farms of all sizes, but the occupying tenants have from 15 to 100 acres, some 300."

Limerick.—"The farms are of all sizes ; the bullock farms rises to 600 acres."—*Ibid*, 144.

Wexford.—" Farms are large, few less than 500 or 600 acres."

Kildare.—" Farms generally about 100 acres."

Kilkenny.—"About Kilfaine the farms generally rise from 100 to 200 acres, among many very small ones."

Granard.—" The farms are in general large, many about 200 acres."

Leitrim.—" The size of farms rises commonly to 500 or 600 acres, but the general size is about 100 acres, with many small ones."

Strokestown.—" The farms rise to 3,000 acres, few under 400 or 500."

Elphin.—" Farms in general from 100 to 1,500 acres."

These descriptions are taken from his account of districts in various parts of Ireland. In many places he speaks of farms from 15 to 20 acres. But out of Ulster large farms were generally met with. It is only where the linen manufacture prevailed that the land was almost everywhere portioned out in plots under 15 acres.

† *Ante*, pages 84, 85.

the mode of using the land which appeared to offer the largest and the easiest profit to the need or the rapacity of its owner. Those who held the land by long leases were, of course, the only persons, as to lands so let, who could take advantage of this turn of affairs, and therefore middlemen are blamed for the subdivision. But we have not the slightest reason to believe that if these lands had been in their own hands the owners in fee would not have done the same as they did in point of fact do in the cases in which they were so; * and while they complained that middlemen were violating covenants against alienation, they acquiesced. Mr. Wakefield tells us that this was the case in 1810. " A landlord if he sees his tenant making money by dividing his farm looks forward with anxious hope to the expiration of the lease, when he expects to enjoy the benefit of alienation, mud cabins, and tillage, instead of grass lands; he therefore favours, rather than opposes, the custom."† If this be so, as far as the subdivision of farms is concerned, the only crime of the middleman would appear to be, that he happened to be, for practical purposes, the owner of the lands at the time when motives of avarice tempted the owner, whoever he was, to give it in small parcels into the possession of the serfs.

But again I say all descriptions of Ireland lead us astray if we do not bear in mind that on the surface of the country there were in fact two nations settled. Two castes as distinct in their feelings, their habits, and even in their interests, as if seas and mountains had separated their habitations. There were the Protestants and upper class—well treated by the landowners—holding large farms by long leases and at moderate rents, and there were the conquered and the plundered class—ground to the earth by penal laws and local oppression. The latter, unfortunately, were the great majority of the people. These constituted the cottier class and the " small farmers," who were everywhere miserable and oppressed. They were treated as an inferior race.‡ In some few instances kind and

---

* Sir L. Parson's speech, *ante*, p. 92.
† *Wakefield's View of Ireland*, Vol. i., p. 284.
‡ After what I have written I will not be understood as asserting that all the Roman Catholic tenantry of Ireland were crushed down to the rank of cottiers, but the mass of the people were. Roman Catholic farmers had, as I have elsewhere said, more security of tenure than they have now. They held very generally the statutory leases for 31 years—the tenure against which Burke directed his invective, as a tenure so short as to destroy all rational hope of improvment of the country. But still even Roman Catholic tenants of this class were in every respect treated differently from those of the favoured caste. From that marvellous collection of photographs of Irish rural life which Arthur Young has left us, I take one instance of an improving " Popish " tenant :—
" July 4th,—Lord Longford carried me to a Mr. Marly's, an improver in the neighbourhood, who had done great things, and without the benefit of such leases as Protestants in Ireland commonly have."
He then proceeds to describe this gentleman as renting 1,000 acres of wild mountain land ; he recounts his expensive and laborous improvements by which the mountain land was improved, the raising of his rent after his improvements from 20 pence an

considerate masters did something to ameliorate their condition. These instances, as we might expect, were more frequent where men of high rank and large possessions were residing personally on their estates, but whether in the case of resident landlords or the agents of absentees, or the middleman, who represented either a resident or an absentee, the " meer" Irishman was trampled on. It was almost the religion—it certainly formed the politics of the upper classes— to keep him down. He was a rebel, and the enemy of the " Protestant interest ;" and with the dominant caste the " Protestant interest" meant their ascendancy and their estates.

But to say that the misery of the people resulted from the fact that they often took their small tenements from the Protestant freeholder, instead of obtaining them direct from the Protestant owner in fee, is simply to pander to the prejudices of a landed aristocracy, who are always anxious to blame for the miseries of the country any one but themselves. Middlemen and chief lords were both oppressive, because conquest, and confiscation, and penal laws had kept an outcast population upon the soil; a population who would only be admitted as serfs, to be the tillers of the ground, and whom poverty and oppression made ready to be the serfs of any one whether landlord or middleman, who would give them a morsel of land.

In whatever varying forms the malignant " human agency " may disguise itself, in whatever changing shape it may attempt to elude the chains which wisdom and liberality would throw around its powers of mischief, we have but fearlessly to follow every disguise, and after all it must appear in its true form.* We grasp the one old monster grievance of the Irish race—the " landlordism" which embodies the policy and the passions of territorial conquest—a policy which has for two centuries trampled on that race—passions which are at this moment driving them from their homes.

It is very reasonable to contend that either the system of

acre to £850 a year; and, after some fastidious criticisms on his mode of fallowing, he thus concludes :—
" It was with regret I heard that the rent of a man who had been so spirited an improver should be raised so exceedingly. He merited for his life the returns of his industry. But the cruel laws against the Roman Catholics of this country remain the marks of illiberal barbarism. Why should not the industrious man have a spur to his industry, whatever be his religion ?   .   .   .   It is impossible that the industry of a nation should have its material progress where four-fifths of the people are cut off from these advantages which are heaped upon the dominering aristocracy of the remainder."—Vol. i., p. 66.

* " Verùm ubi correptum manibus vinclisque tenebis,
   Tum variæ illudent species atque ora ferarum.

   Sed, quanto ille magis formas se vertet in omnes,
   Tanto, nate, magis contende tenacia vincla :
   Donec talis erit, mutato corpore, qualem
   Videris, incepto tegeret cùm lumina somno.—
                                                    Georgics, iv. 405.

middlemen or the commercial injustice of England has aggravated the evils of our land tenure. It is unreasonable to say that they have caused them.

It is always of some consequence upon social questions connected with past history, as far as possible to ascertain the exact truth. Yet, for the purpose of our present enquiry, I am not sure that it would make any, even the slightest difference whether the present evils, which require present remedies, are to be traced to the dealings with the people, of middlemen, or of the owners in fee. I have devoted so much space to the subject because it has been made one of some importance in the discussion of the proposal I have made.

———

I now turn to the second letter of Lord Dufferin, in which he is supposed to have completely vindicated the landlords of Ireland from the charge of having caused the emigration of the people.

His first argument is that drawn from the proof that those who emigrate are not actually evicted persons. This argument evades the real issue, which is this:—Has insecurity of tenure the effect of driving the people from their native land? That it has this effect has been established by a clearness of evidence very rarely attained upon any social question. The assertion is not that the emigrants consist of tenants who have been actually evicted. The assertion is that in consequence of the insecurity of tenure, and all the evils that follow in its train, the occupiers are leaving a country in which they have no opportunity of exercising their industry—that the farm labourers are emigrating because they cannot get employment on the farms—that the country towns are ruined because the farming classes are destroyed, and that ruined shopkeepers and unemployed and educated young men all are compelled to leave a country in which they cannot find a means of living. In this melancholy bead roll of emigrants the actually evicted tenants present but a very inconsiderable portion of the array.

It does not follow that the landlords, or rather the present conditions of land tenure, have not caused the emigration, because the persons who emigrate are not all driven out by actual evictions from their farms. I do not know that any one ever asserted that they were. For myself, I was so far from making such a statement that I thought it essential to one point of my argument to state directly the reverse. My statement was this:—

" That the emigration is caused by the deep-rooted discontent of the people with the existing arrangements connected with land tenure, no one who studies it attentively will doubt. It would be a mistake to represent it as the aggregate of a number of isolated movements of individuals, or as resulting from the pressure of individual distress. In many instances no doubt it has been so. A great deal of emigration was that of persons actually evicted under the operation of the present land laws. Thousands of Irishmen have left the country from personal inability to find the means of supporting themselves at home. But in addition to these there are other causes now acting. A passion for emigration appears to have seized upon a whole class. Those who are comparatively well to do in the world are often the most anxious to go. This general desire to leave the country originates in the conviction in the minds of the people, that under the present system of land tenure they have not fair play at home. The emigration of the people in masses is not the proof or result of individual suffering, but of general discontent. They believe that as a class they have not fair play under the present land laws, and they are at last beginning to despair of a change."*

On turning to the evidence given before the Land Tenure Committee of 1864, I find exactly the same statement made by those witnesses who represented the cause of tenant right. Dr. Keane, the Roman Catholic Bishop of Cloyne, in answer to the question whether he attributed emigration to the eviction of small farmers, said:—

" Yes, to a certain extent I do ; but I attribute emigration principally *to the want of employment.*"—(Question 3403.)

Again—

" A man who has only 10 or 12 acres, and who is only a tenant-at-will, finding that the land requires improvement, he is afraid to waste it, and he goes away. *I see many of these poor people in Queenstown every day.*" (Question 3612.)

Those who really desire to understand the connexion between emigration and the present system of land tenure will do well to read the whole of the evidence of this distinguished prelate. It is not evidence of opinion, but evidence of matter of fact. *He had conversed with the emigrants.* He had ascertained from themselves the reasons of their emigration. He found it was in the case of the labouring classes want of employment, in the case of the tenant farmers the same cause in another form. They were farmers willing and anxious to improve, but they had no security that the improvements, if they effected them, would be their own. They had waited patiently to see if any of the promises of the Legislature would be fulfilled. Disappointed and despairing, they at last made up their minds to give up their holdings and abandon their native land.

Strange to say—the admission is not to my credit—I had not read this evidence when I wrote the sentences which I have ventured to reprint.

---

* *Land Tenure in Ireland,* Third Edition, p. 9.

The evidence of Bishop Keane is full of instruction. I have given a very imperfect condensation even of its general result. But there are statements so striking, so vitally important, that I must endeavour to extract the passages in which they are contained:—

" I HAVE MADE INQUIRIES OVER AND OVER AGAIN, IN QUEENSTOWN AND ELSEWHERE, AND I NEVER YET HEARD THAT A SINGLE FARMER EMIGRATED AND LEFT THE COUNTRY WHO HAD A LEASE."—(Question 3401).

"Those who go attribute their being compelled to go to the want of good legislation. Their disappointment is made more bitter in consequence of all that has been done, or rather in consequence of all that has been discussed, within the last twenty years or more."—(Question 3408.)

And after referring to the measure of Lord Derby, in 1844, and especially to Mr. Napier's clause for retrospective compensation, in 1852, the Bishop continues:—

"The cup of hope is presented to them over and over again, and it is dashed from them at the time they least expect it; and the disappointment they feel on that account is doubly bitter.—(Question 3408.)

"I do not think I could overrate the amount of discontent which is in the very depths of their soul.—(Question 3409.)

"Many persons give up their farms because they are in such a position with regard to the law that they cannot establish a claim to compensation, which they would willingly establish if they were certain that the fruits of their industry would be their own."—(Question 3423.)

"Is it," he is asked, "within your own knowledge that many persons do give up their farms on that ground?"
The answer is—" SEVERAL."
And, lastly, the Bishop describes the emigrants as consisting in a great proportion of those who have thus thrown up their farms for want of security for their improvements; " but besides, in that mass, there are the labourers, the tradesmen, and the broken down shopkeepers."

"I never knew," he repeats, "I never knew of a single tenant, though I made several inquiries, who left who had a lease."—(Question 3425.)

I say again that this evidence is not a statement of speculative opinion. It is evidence as to matter of fact. Here we have a Roman Catholic Bishop, residing at the port from which the greatest number of emigrants depart, conversing with the emigrants as they leave the shores of their native land, making inquiries of all who can throw light upon the strange spectacle which is going on before his eyes. It is impossible for any one to read a page of this prelate's evidence without seeing that these inquiries were directed by a mind vigorous and large enough to grasp the whole question of Irish land tenure. Is it possible to conceive evidence more important or more decisive in enabling us to understand the real causes and motives which are driving our people from the land ?

I quote it not only for the value of the testimony but to show that it is a mere evasion of the real issue which has been raised to inquire whether the emigrants consist of those who have been actually evicted. That was never the argument of those who trace the emigration to our system of land tenure. If emigration were really confined to those who are actually driven out it would not bear the same testimony as it now does to the discontent of the people. The worst feature of that emigration is—that it is the voluntary departure of a whole people—a flight from oppressive laws which leave them no hope of ever living in comfort in their native land.

I turn from the evidence of Bishop Keane to that of Mr. M'Carthy Downing. This gentleman, as well acquainted as any man living with the practical condition of land tenure, distinctly describes the emigration of late years as voluntary, and the evictions as comparatively rare. He describes the emigration as that of men of superior intelligence:—

" Who leave their country with pain and sorrow, and who would re-main in that country if they thought they could live in it.—(Q. 3141.)
" It is the strong man, and the man that has capital, that go. We are left with the old and feeble.—(Question 3142.)
" They go because they find that no matter how they may work and slave in their own country they do not reap the fruits of it."—(Q. 3143.)
" That is your view," he is asked by an adverse questioner. His emphatic answer is—" I KNOW IT."—(Question 3144.)

This was the case, and the only case, that was made as to emigration before the Land Tenure Committee. It was not that tenants were driven out by the landlords. It was that tenants were throwing up their farms of their own accord, and flying from the operation of the land laws. That they were doing so because insecurity of tenure left them no opportunity of exercising their industry, or raising their position in their native land. That the ban which is thus put upon all national progress has driven out the labourer, who can no longer find employment. That as the small farmer sinks, or departs, the country towns decay, and bankrupt shopkeepers and broken tradesmen swell the miserable train of exiles who " leave their country with pain and sorrow," victims to that evil system which leaves the soil of Ireland untilled, and dooms to beggary and serfdom the Irish peasant who lingers behind his fellows in his native land.

This was the case made against our land laws, founded on the emigration which is carrying away the Irish people. I believe no proposition was ever more incontestibly proved than that which asserts that it is insecurity of tenure, and discontent with the system of land tenure, which is driving the Irish race from their home. The very evidence I have quoted proves it beyond doubt. But this is a fair subject of inquiry. It may be that insecurity of tenure has nothing to do with it—that the people are really flying from the unjust restrictions of the last century on our woollen manufacture, or from the commercial restrictions against which the volunteers so energetically and so successfully protested in 1782. But let the real question be discussed—that is, whether the Irish people are voluntarily leaving their country in hatred of the present system of land tenure—not whether the emigrants are the actual victims of arbitrary eviction.

I am afraid the melancholy truth is, that of those actually evicted in the earlier period of the last twenty years a large number were not fortunate enough to find shelter in emigration.

In 1849 Lord Derby complained that a neighbouring proprietor had evicted no less than 349 persons, who came and settled on his Lordship's estate. There is scarcely a town or city in Ireland that is not at this moment burdened with heavy poor rates to support paupers who have been driven from the rural districts by evictions, on estates, an element which has formed no inconsiderable item in the aggregate account of the injury inflicted by these evictions on our country towns.*

Unhappily indeed, unhappily for the character of Irish landlords, some years ago the population were driven from the soil by a general process of extermination unparalleled in modern history. The statement quoted in the note will show that these evictions by

---

* See the Pamphlet report of an admirable speech delivered in the House of Commons on Union Rating, by Sergeant Barry, the Member for Dungarvan. In that speech Sergeant Barry quoted a most remarkable statement on this subject, made at a public meeting in Tralee, by Mr. James O'Connell.

"What," says he, "did this law of electoral division rating do? It gave a premium and encouragement, even before the famine, for depopulation on every estate. When the famine came, and we had staring us in the face rates from eight shillings to fourteen shillings in the pound, landlords and farmers had a fearful dread of the labourers coming into or near their farms. If they came into their farms they were looked upon as if they were wild beasts. They were hunted out, and we know too much of the fatal results that followed. . . . I say with as much solemnity as if I were giving testimony in a court of justice that it would be impossible for me to describe the odious acts of oppression that were then perpetrated, consequent on this electoral division rating. The poor were driven into the town, estates were cleared, and notices to quit were served. If that did not answer, the houses were levelled. Perhaps fifty families were cleared for every three or four kept. The only refuge of those poor creatures then was to go into the town. The young and healthy, and those who could afford it, left the country for England or Scotland; for emigration to America was not as easy then as it is now. The old, the indigent, and infirm, came into the towns, went into those dens that Mr. Downing described, and dragged out a miserable existence, at most for a few years, and then became chargeable on the town electoral division."

no means proportionately swelled the emigration. *The evicted tenants had not the means of emigrating.* Enough to say, that in 1848 the Legislature found it necessary to pass a law prohibiting the execution of eviction decrees on Good Friday or Christmas Day! The same Act made it a misdemeanour to pull the roof off a house before the inmates had left it; and it also contained a provision that before any landlord executed an ejectment he must give notice to the relieving officer of the poor law union, that some provision might be made for the wretched beings he was about to turn out.*

This statute speaks volumes as to the character of the evictions with which the Legislature had to deal.

Upon Lord Dufferin's estimate of the number of evictions, I have only one remark to make. Lord Dufferin states that those upon which he relies have been ascertained by "the indefatigable industry of Mr. Handcock." Upon turning to Mr. Handcock's essay I find them stated by that gentleman to have been "ascertained by the police." Mr. Handcock does not inform us how, or when, or by what authority the police collected these statistics. Lord Dufferin, in a subsequent letter, offers an apology for not having used the parliamentary returns of Lord Belmore which, it seems, vary from those obtained by "the indefatigable industry of Mr. Handcock." Lord Belmore's return goes back only to 1860—covering the period within which, all parties agree, that evictions have been less frequent. If the statistics of eviction for the last twenty years were of any value in determining the question we are discussing, we have no full and reliable information on the subject.

But of this I am quite sure, that the most reliable information we can have of the number of evictions for the last six years cannot throw the least light upon the enquiry whether the effect of our present system of land tenure be to drive the Irish people from their native land. I am very much disposed to think that within the last few years some of the landlords have been more anxious for the present to retain the people than to drive them away. The process of emigration is going on in some districts too fast for that of "consolidation." The people are as far-seeing as the landlords, and will not remain while the system of land tenure remains as it is now. There are tenants who are stupid enough not to appreciate the boon of the Cyclops, and will not wait with thankfulness in the expectation of being devoured the last.

Lord Dufferin then points attention to the fact that a greater number of emigrants go from Ulster than from any other of the three provinces of Ireland. Therefore, he argues that as tenant

---

* For reference to this statute, I am indebted to the same speech of Sergeant Barry, to which I have acknowledged my obligations in the last note.

right prevails in Ulster it is not insecurity of tenure that is driving the people away.

In the first place, and even admitting the representation to be correct, a great fallacy pervades this argument, in supposing that the " Ulster" which is included in the emigration returns is coextensive with the " Ulster" in which tenant right is observed.

Within the nine counties which constitute the province of Ulster there are large districts in which it does not even nominally exist. The two strongest illustrations of the evils of insecurity, which I cited in the tract on Land Tenure, both occurred on Ulster property. Glenveagh is in the county of Donegal. The Shirley estate, the other with regard to which I mentioned instances of its management, proved in a court of justice, is situated in Monaghan. Upon the latter estate, one of £30,000 a year, the landlord stated on his oath that he never thought of permitting the claim of tenant right. No mistake could be greater than to suppose that every tenant within the magic limit of the province called Ulster enjoys the protection of the custom of tenant right.*

But more than this; it is unhappily true, that in very many even of the tenant right districts of Ulster the integrity of the custom has been gradually broken down. No one can carefully read the Ulster newspapers without seeing constantly accounts of instances in which that custom is violated. There are large estates in Ulster upon which the right has been of late years reduced to a mere name. There are many upon which it no longer exists. The prediction of O'Connell, made more than twenty years ago, is realized; and that custom, which has been the glory and the pride of the province, is now gradually broken in upon and undermined.

It is easy for any man to look wise in quoting figures—but it often happens that exactly as he looks wise he is really foolish.

It will scarcely be credited that Lord Dufferin makes out his representation BY LEAVING OUT OF ACCOUNT THE RELATIVE PROPORTION OF THE POPULATION OF ULSTER TO THAT OF THE REST OF IRELAND.

---

* There is great difficulty in fixing the precise limits of the tenant right districts of Ulster.

When Judge Longfield was asked to do so by the Irish Land Committee of 1864, he could only answer that tenant right was strongest in Down, Antrim, and Armagh, and extended into part of Tyrone."

This is certainly not an accurate, or at least a full answer, but its very vagueness shows the difficulty of fixing the limits.

At all events, in his opinion, the custom of tenant right is far from extending over Ulster.

His evidence contains a still more important statement on the subject. He tells us that where estates on which tenant right prevails are set up for sale in the Landed Estates Court, unscrupulous purchasers often give a higher price for them with the very intention of destroying tenant right.

He proposed, that when such estates were sold the Court should have the power, before selling the estate, to protect the tenant's interest by granting him a lease.

It is not necessary to use more words than those which are requisite to make this clear.

By the census of 1861 the population of the whole of Ireland was, in round numbers, 5,700,000; that of Ulster was 1,900,000; about a third of the entire. The total emigration from Ireland in the year 1864 was 114,908 persons, in round numbers, 115,000. Of these, Ulster ought, in proportion to its population, to have supplied 38,500. The number of emigrants for that year from Ulster was 19,815. Leinster, with a smaller population, supplied the same number. The population of Connaught is not one half that of Ulster, yet the number of its emigrants was very nearly the same.

Let us compare the population and the emigration from Ulster and Munster in the years 1864 and 1865. These figures are few and simple, they can be understood by every one. By the census of 1861 the population of the two provinces was as follows:—

Ulster,   -   -   1,900,000
Munster,   -   -   1,500,000

If, therefore, emigration were in proportion to population, the emigrants from Ulster would have exceeded those from Munster in a proportion of 19 to 15, that is, by a little more than one-fourth.

How stand the facts as to the last two years. The emigration of these two provinces was as follows:—

	1864.	1865.	Two years.
Munster,	- 48,387	37,426	85,813
Ulster,	- 19,853	22,302	41,635

So that the actual emigration from Ulster, with a population of 1,900,000, was not one-half of that from Munster, with a population of 1,500,000. In proportion to the population, the emigration from Ulster was 41 out of 1,900, or little more than two per cent., in Munster it was 85 out of 1,500, or very nearly 6 per cent.

It cannot be said that the last two years are exceptional. For the statistics of emigration, as for most of the information of this nature which we possess on the state of Ireland, we are indebted to the exertions of Mr. Donnelly.* In each year he gives us a

---

* The services which this gentleman has unostentatiously and disinterestedly rendered to the cause of social science in Ireland have never been sufficiently acknowledged. The agricultural statistics, which he has now brought to a reasonable perfection, he began to compile under every difficulty and discouragement. While Irishmen are constantly accused of deficiency in methodical administrative ability, an Irish official has devised and almost brought to perfection a system of collecting information which, in the sister country, English ministers and the English Parliament were for years vainly attempting to obtain.

These emigration statistics have been furnished by the personal enquiries of the police at every port, from the emigrants themselves, and at the offices at which they take their passages.

Carefully as these enquiries are conducted and analysed, I am far from saying that after all they can present a perfect account of the places from which the several emigrants come who embark in each port; but they unquestionably present an account

summary of the returns which, since the year 1851, he has, with marvellous skill and industry, obtained; in the fifteen years ending with the year 1865, the emigration from these two provinces was as follows:—

Munster,   -   -   626,968
Ulster,   -   -   436,000

In proportion to the population the emigrants from Ulster do not number one-half of those from Munster.

And yet from these very figures Lord Dufferin rushed recklessly by the conclusion that want of security of tenure could not be the cause of emigration, because it was as great from Ulster, where tenant right prevails, as from the other provinces of Ireland.   And more strange still, this wild statement, disproved by a reference to the figures on which he relied, was accepted as " proof from Holy Writ," by many of the most influential—I cannot add best informed guides of public opinion.   " Lord Dufferin has proved," in the language in which this burlesque upon all statistical argument was, and is still cited by the defenders of the present system of Irish land tenure, at the English and even at the Irish press.   There never was such an instance of the credulity with which the rash assertions of a man of rank are accepted by some portions of the public as proof.

This extraordinary fallacy—respect for Lord Dufferin prevents me from saying blunder—was detected and exposed by Mr. Dalton, the gentleman who, under the name of "Philocelt," has written so ably in the columns of the *Daily News*.   Every one seemed to acquiesce in the imposing array of Lord Dufferin's figures, until the publication of Mr. Dalton pointed out the palpable error upon which *the* argument was based.*

sufficiently accurate for all practical purposes of general enquiry; at all events they give the information upon which Lord Dufferin relied.   The errors, which in such a process are unavoidable, may be safely supposed to compensate each other, and it adds to the confidence with which these returns of the enumerator may be regarded, to find that they class many of the emigrants—leaving a proportion of about two per cent. to the entire—as persons whose locality has not been ascertained.

* "I come now to Lord Dufferin's third point, pronounced to be unanswerable by *The Times*, that if, as Mr. Maguire states, insecurity of tenure produces emigration, there ought to be hardly any emigration from Ulster, where a custom of tenant-right gives that security ; whereas the emigration from Ulster is in excess of that from Connaught and Leinster, and as 23 to 27 when compared with all Ireland.

"I turn to the statistics again, and I find (page x.) that the total number of farms above one acre decreased, between 1841 and 1864, by 15·1 per cent. in Leinster, 29·9 per cent. in Munster, 22·6 per cent. in Connaught, and only by 14·2 per cent. in Ulster.   So that, other things being equal, though there is little difference between Leinster and Ulster, the emigration of occupiers from Munster was about two to one, from Connaught as three to two, compared with Ulster.

"But other things are not equal. `It is not fair to take Leinster into consideration at all, for there, owing to the general nature of the soil, better adapted for grazing than tillage, a good deal in the way of consolidation had been effected before the potato famine.   It should be remembered that if the smallness of the holdings were the sole cause of the emigration of the occupiers, it ought to have been nearly twice as great from Ulster as from the other provinces, as the following figures taken from the

But this is not all. Lord Dufferin virtually tells us that no tenant of a holding under fifteen acres can, with any advantage, retain possession of his farm. He tells us in words that this is the smallest farm upon which any farmer can live comfortably. We might suppose, therefore, that emigration from each district would be in proportion to the number of such farms. How stands the fact as to Ulster. We must take our information from Mr. Donnelly's statistics. In the year 1864, the last year for which, on this subject, they have been made up, there were in Ireland, in round numbers, 150,000 holdings between five and fifteen acres. Of these, 71,000 were in the province of Ulster, not very far from one-half of the entire.

But there are four counties in Ireland which, perhaps, any one would select as displaying the largest amount of prosperity and comfort in the general class of the occupiers of the soil. I exclude Derry, because the ownership 'of a great portion of it, by the London Companies, introduces distinct elements of calculation; the other four counties are unquestionably Antrim, Down, Tyrone, and Armagh. In these four counties there are nearly one-fourth as many holdings, between five and fifteen acres, as in all the rest of Ireland put together. Of a total, in round numbers, of 150,000— there are in the county Down 10,700, in Antrim 6,000, in Armagh 9,400, in Tyrone 9,000. Mr. Donnelly's returns enable us to fix the proportion which the emigration from these counties bore to all that from Ireland in the last fifteen years; it is as follows:—

Antrim,	-	-	6·19
Armagh,	-	-	2·33
Down,	-	-	3·64
Tyrone,	-	-	3·20

15·36

statistics, page lxvii., will prove. Leinster, area 4,876,211 acres, number of holdings in 1864, 104,438; Munster, area 6,096,990 acres, number of holdings 114,921; Ulster, area 5,478,867 acres, number of holdings 203,066; Connaught, area 432,043 acres, holdings 120,698.

"Thus, according to Lord Dufferin's argument, the emigration of farmers ought to have been, from Ulster, at least two to one as compared with Munster, whereas the proportions are reversed. Has tenant-right nothing to do with this?

"Again, Lord Dufferin states that the emigration from Ulster is as 23 to 27 as compared with the other provinces, and therefore he argues, tenant-right has nothing to do with it; but as he mixes here the emigration of the labourers with that of the farmers, he does not state the case quite fairly. I will however take it in this way (though it has only an indirect bearing on the argument), and what is the truth. The decennial census of 1861 (the last) tells us that the population of Ulster in that year was 1,914,255, exceeding that of Leinster by 456,843, of Munster by 400,697, and of Connaught by 1,001,247; and yet with this enormous excess of population in Ulster, the proportion of its emigrants to the total population is less than the average from the other three provinces.

"'Parliament,' exclaims Lord Dufferin, 'parliament and unjust landlords, we are told, are depopulating the south; what occult agencies are depopulating the north!'

"I think I may now answer this question in the orthodox Irish fashion:—'What occult agency checks its depopulation.'"—Irish Peers on Irish Peasants, by Gustavus Tuite Dalton.

It is not possible to glance at these figures without being struck by the disproportion between Antrim, and the other three counties. Antrim included almost the entire of the manufacturing population of Belfast.

In the above figures I have taken only the farms above five acres. The result will be equally striking if we extend it to all above one acre. To include holdings below one acre is only to mislead, as such holdings include, of course, tenements in towns and villages—houses, and not lands. I may observe that the four counties I have chosen are not the best for my argument, but they are the fairest test of Ulster.

We may expect, I think, emigration to be from any district— first, absolutely in proportion to its population; next, in proportion to the number of small holdings to be found in it; next, in proportion to " the disturbance of the equilibrium between land and the population dependent upon land"—in other words, we would expect emigration from agricultural districts to be greatest where there were most people on each acre of arable ground; and lastly, we may fairly expect emigration to be swelled by the migratory and unsettled habits of a manufacturing population.

Let us apply these tests to Ulster emigration, and so far from coming up to its share of Irish emigration, it is plain that it is not one-third of that which our experience of the rest of Ireland would lead us to expect from districts peopled and occupied as those of Ulster are.

The best and shortest way of dealing with this is to extract from Mr. Thom's valuable statistics a tabular statement of the quantity of arable land in each of these four counties—its population, the number of small holdings, and the number of emigrants, and leave it to every one to work out the problem for themselves :—

	Acres of arable land	Population 1861	Holdings between 1 and 15 acres, 1864	Emigrants, 1851 to 1864
Antrim,	500,000	378,000	8,000	95,000
Armagh,	265,000	190,000	14,000	36,000
Down,	514,000	300,000	15,000	56,000
Tyrone,	450,000	238,000	12,000	49,000

I will add to these figures the statement that of the population of the County Antrim, more than 100,000 are in the town of Belfast, and that the total emigration from Ireland from 1851 to 1864, was 1,546,000. I believe any one studying these figures must come to the conclusion that as compared with the rest of Ireland there has been some powerful influence checking in Ulster the tendencies which in the other portions of the country led to a large emigration. Between 1851 and 1861 the population of all Ireland diminished 11½ per cent., that of Ulster but 4. The character of the emigration from

I

Ulster is indicated by the fact that "*the decrease in the number of families has been least in that province, where it amounts only to* 3,686, *or* 0·97 *per cent.*" * We cannot have a better test of the character of emigration than is afforded by the inquiry whether it is the departure of families or of individuals. That of individuals may be it often is a healthy and natural emigration. When that of families is general it is the departure of a people from their homes.

Mr. Dalton has well pointed out that we have no means of distinguishing between the emigration of the labouring classes and the tenant farmers. We have, however, valuable, although imperfect, information from these statistics of Ulster emigration. In the first place we have the emigration from Ulster in proportion to its population, just one-half of what it is from Munster. Taking the rural counties of Tyrone and Armagh, we find them to contain a proportion of farms, between five and fifteen acres, nearly an eighth of all such holdings in Ireland, while they supply to the emigrants of Ireland a little more than five per cent. We have not the statistics which would enable us to carry our deduction beyond these general results. These general results establish by figures, which, no more minute investigation could alter, that the emigration from Ulster, tried by any test that could possibly be suggested, falls far short of that from the rest of Ireland. To gain all the instruction we could from these statistics, we should have them illustrated by living evidence. In the case of the southern emigration we have this. The testimony of the Roman Catholic Bishop of Cloyne has told us, from actual inquiry, the elements of which emigration from the port of Queenstown is composed. He has emphatically told us that in no instance has he been able to trace a single instance of an emigrant who held a lease. Similar information might have been given to us as to the northern emigration. It might have been told us by witnesses acquainted with that which is actually going on, how many of the Ulster emigrants are from that manufacturing population, which must, in every country, supply a large addition to those who are leaving the country. We might have been told whether, in fact, emigration goes on from estates on which the custom of tenant right is still religiously observed. We might have learned how many of the emigrants have been crushed from their farms by the growing consciousness that the Ulster tenant right no longer supplies a security against eviction. All these things were within the enquiries of the Committee of 1864. The landlord interest had its able and intelligent advocates on that committee. Lord Dufferin himself was examined as a witness in defence of his order; from beginning to end of that evidence we have nothing to establish that Ulster farmers are emigrating where Ulster tenant right is established and is observed.

---

* "Statistics of Ireland." *Thom's Almanac*, 1865.

I have scarcely a doubt upon my mind that if the question were thus examined it would be found that even the small proportion of Irish emigrants which come from Ulster, compared with its population, is supplied almost entirely from its great manufacturing districts, from the parts of it in which tenant right is not acknowledged, or proceeds in the tenant-right districts from that landlord tampering with tenant right of which Lord Dufferin is the ingenious and able, although I cannot say the successful, advocate. We have no official means of ascertaining the relative proportions of Protestants and Roman Catholics among the emigrants from Ulster. There is no doubt whatever that by far the greater number are Roman Catholics. I am not about to advert to any of the questions connected with the general position of the Roman Catholic people of Ulster. They are every day made to feel in many of the old modes the oppression of the ascendancy which still insults and crushes them down. This is a subject beyond the limits of this letter, and I cannot enter on its discussion. I confine myself entirely to their position in relation to the custom of tenant right. Taking the whole Roman Catholic population scattered through the nine counties of the province, they have not the benefit of that custom at all to the same extent as the Protestants. Upon estates like those of Lord Abercorn, upon which tenant right is respected in all its integrity, the Roman Catholic tenant enjoys it equally with the Protestant. I hope there are not many properties—there are some—upon which indirect attempts are made to get rid gradually of a Roman Catholic tenantry. There are many upon which Protestants are more favoured. But I am now comparing the professors of the two religions over the entire surface of the province, both in the districts in which tenant right is fully or partially recognized, and those in which it is not—in the mountain districts, to which a large and poor population, in many instances exclusively Roman Catholic, have been driven—as well as in the well-cultivated hills of Down, or the rich corn lands which lie round the banks of the Foyle.

Looking at the whole province in this way, and including all the people that dwell from Farney to Fairhead and between Strangford Lough and the point where the western cliffs of Donegal meet the billows of the Atlantic—of the persons who within these nine counties really enjoy the security of tenure which is conferred by the custom of tenant right—the immense majority are Protestants. If this be so, and if, on the other hand, the vast majority of the emigrants be Roman Catholics, it leads inevitably to the conclusion that emigration is not supplied from the class that are protected by tenant right. Bishop Keane has told the Committee of 1864 that by personal inquiries he was able to say that he had never known a southern emigrant who had held by lease.

If a Protestant Bishop had been examined, equally well acquainted by personal observation with the circumstances of the poorer portion of his flock, he would have told the Committee that the emigration of a family from an estate where tenant right is observed is very rare. And yet we must remember that when a tenant gives up, or even is evicted from his farm in such a district, he has generally the means of emigrating—he derives them from the proceeds of the sale of his tenant right. The evicted Munster tenant scarcely ever has.

I have used the expression "emigration of a family," because this is the emigration which really shows that the people are flying from their country. Younger sons and younger daughters have at all times gone, even from well-to-do households, to better their fortunes in other countries. When a whole family leave their native land we may well suppose that it is some pressure drives them away. Between the years 1851 and 1861, Ireland lost 76,000 families. Of these, but 3,600 had gone from Ulster,* although a third of the entire population are within the limits of that province.

The change in the character of Ulster, indeed of Irish, emigration has been very remarkable, in respect to the religion of the emigrants. Not very many years ago it was believed to be draining Ireland of its Protestant population. About the year 1830, the emigrants were very generally Protestants. They are now almost exclusively Roman Catholics. In connexion with this subject, it ought not to be forgotten that emigration from Ireland began with the Protestant people. Primate Boulter's letters complain of a passion having seized on the Protestants more than 150 years ago. The denial of security of tenure was then the cause of that emigration. There were Protestant emigrants who were driven, by the State trials of 1773, to swell the ranks of American revolt. Thirty years ago Protestant emigration was the great grievance constantly put forward by Protestant partizans. The explanation is to me obvious. It is notorious that Protestants, up to a very recent period, held a higher position among the peasantry than Roman Catholics. They were, therefore, the first to feel the growing pressure of landlord domination, the downward tendency of the country, and accordingly they left it.†

---

* "Statistics of Ireland." *Thom's Almanac*, 1864, p. 774.

† In a previous note I have adverted to the Protestant emigration of the last century. About the period of Catholic Emancipation a rage for emigration seemed to have seized on the Protestant people. They went in such numbers as, among Protestant politicians, to give rise to serious alarm. The emigration from Ireland was almost then exclusively Protestant. The cry was raised that the Protestants were driven out of Ireland. Very influential persons started a scheme of "Protestant colonization;" large sums were subscribed, and a few "Protestant colonists" were actually settled upon wild waste lands in the county of Donegal, the estate of the late Sir Edmond Hayes.

I believe that in the text I have assigned the main reason for this strange passion for emigration seizing on a whole class; but other causes, no doubt, contributed to it at the time.

Political questions exercise, a very great, and, to superficial observers, an unaccountable, influence over the movements of both of the great religious divisions of the Irish people. Each party believe, their personal welfare, if not their personal safety, to be

Lord Dufferin then adverts to the fact, that since 1841 the number of holdings in Ireland between 15 and 30 acres has increased   Lord Dufferin thus states the proposition :—

" But it so happens that the total number of holdings in Ireland containing 15 acres and upwards has increased enormously since 1841. In fact, there are now nearly twice as many small farmers—using the term even in its most modest acceptation—as there were before the famine. This, will, undoubtedly, be considered an extraordinary statement, but it is nevertheless, the fact, that holdings between 15 and 30 acres have increased by 61,000, or 75 per cent., within the last 20 years; and holdings above 30 acres by 109,000, or 107 per cent., during the same period ; the emigration, so far as it has affected the occupying class at all, having been almost entirely confined to the poor people who attempted to get a living out of bits of land ranging in size from half-an-acre to five or six acres."

As to the increase in the number of the larger holdings we need no statistics to tell us this. As farms were consolidated and the occupiers of small farms exterminated, the numbers of large holdings must increase. There is no mystery in these statistics; I take the numbers from Mr. Donnelly's statistics for the year 1864. In that volume we will find the increase or decrease of each class of holdings between 1841 and 1864. The figures differ slightly from those of Lord Dufferin, probably because those I quote are brought down to a later period.

Between 1841 and 1864 the holdings in Ireland, between one and fifteen acres, diminished in number 315,000, the diminution of those under five acres being 222,000. Between fifteen and thirty acres they increased by 57,000, over thirty acres by 109,000. On the entire number of holdings over an acre the diminution amounted to 138,000.

Many very amazing things have occurred in the progress of these discussions, but none more amazing than this—that Lord Dufferin, or any one else, should have imagined he had made any discovery in these figures, or that they tell us anything which can exercise the slightest influence upon the question at issue.

bound up in the triumph of their cause. The victory achieved by the Roman Catholics in carrying Emancipation, and the depression of what was called the Protestant interest, had its effect in making many Protestants emigrate to Canada.

But there was also another cause. The old system had been, on the whole, to show favour to Protestants in the occupation of land. They held, to use the expression of Arthur Young, " at favoured rents." In many cases they were placed above their Roman Catholic neighbours. As liberal opinions prevailed, this preference gave way; and many of the landlords displayed their liberality by no longer allowing the Protestant any favour in his rent ; they were depressed to the common level of the Irish peasants, and they went away.

After all, the first Protestant emigration from Ireland is that recorded by Nicholas Pynnar, in his *Survey:*—

" The tenants have no leases ; they said they never could get anything but promises, and therefore, for the most part, they are leaving the land."

Three hundred and fifteen thousand holdings, under fifteen acres, have unquestionably disappeared. Of course the number of holdings over fifteen acres has been increased. Two millions of acres,* which we may assume to have been included in the extinct holdings, have not been suffered to lie waste; neither have they been all consolidated into gigantic farms like those described by Arthur Young. What has happened is exactly that which Lord Rosse describes in his pamphlet, but which everybody knew. The holding of the going away tenant is added to that of his next neighbour. It so happens that in the returns we have of the sizes of farms, there is a division made at thirty acres. We have three classes distinguished: a class of farms below fifteen acres, a class of farms between fifteen and thirty acres, and a class above thirty. When a man of ten or twelve acres is driven out, his farm is annexed to the adjoining one. It may happen to raise that farm from the second class to the third, by swelling its size above thirty;† it may raise it from the first to the second, by bringing it above fifteen acres. In point of fact, by far the greater portion of the two millions of acres have been annexed to the larger farmers. The third class of farms, those over thirty acres, have been increased by 109,000, the second class, that between fifteen and thirty, by only 57,000.

Lord Dufferin may indeed fairly say that he has proved that these small holdings have not as yet been consolidated into farms of very overgrown dimensions. But as no one ever said or ever imagined that they had, the discovery, is not one of very vital importance. The reference to these statistics exactly leaves the

* I assume with Lord Dufferin the small holdings average six acres.

† Mr. Dalton has, with his usual clearness, pointed out the real effect of Lord Dufferin's statistics :—

" 1st. An emigration of over two millions of souls from a purely agricultural country has had the effect, according to Lord Dufferin, of increasing the number of small farmers. This, unless there has been a simultaneous immigration of the same class (which is not the case) is either, unless subtraction be equivalent to multiplication, pure nonsense or a miracle. To prove his position, however, Lord Dufferin points to the fact that the *holdings* between fifteen and thirty acres have increased by 61,000, or 75 per cent. It is simply the necessary consequence of so large an emigration from a country of such small holdings.

"In one sense, indeed, it does by a sort of fantastic arithmetic, increase their number. It has turned many a large farmer, as we understand the term in Ireland, into a small one, by adding to the size of his farm, thereby increasing his expenses and diminishing his capital. We have more small farmers in the true sense of the word—that is, farmers with small capital—than we had before the famine.

" The increase in the number of holdings over fifteen acres has been effected in the worst possible way. A ten-acre farmer has been converted into one of twenty acres by the Procrustean device of stretching him. With his limited capital, in many cases diminished by the purchase of the good-will of the outgoing tenant, he is called upon to do twice as much as he had to do before, and he can not do it. Nor is he the only loser by the transaction. As the emigration goes on the Government statistics, on which both Lord Dufferin and I rely, prove that the yield per statute acre of every crop, both green and cereal, is gradually decreasing. The decrease from 1847 to 1865 inclusive is considerable. Comparing 1847 with 1865, the exact decrease in the principal crops is per cent.—oats, 16·3 ; flax, 47·9 ; turnips, 36·1 ; potatoes, 50·. Some years would show a greater decrease, but on the whole it has been gradual since 1849.

matter what it was. Where three holdings of eight acres have been destroyed, they have been in many instances consolidated in one of twenty-four.

Lord Dufferin may, of course, say that it is better for the country that there should be one holding or farm of twenty-four acres on land which before there were three of eight acres. But it does not throw much light upon this question to cite elaborate statistics to prove the marvellous discovery that the result actually is—that there is one more farm of the extent of twenty-four acres than there was in the island before. As for the statement that "there are now twice as many small farmers" (meaning holders of farms between fifteen and thirty acres) "as there were before the famine," it must be remembered that even where a holding is unaltered in its dimensions it does not at all follow that a farmer has not been driven out. Lord Dufferin himself tells us that in many cases cottiers or labourers have been promoted to be farmers. The farmer who has 'still something to lose throws up his farm. He is replaced in that very farm by a man of an inferior class. The result is that diminution in the agricultural produce of the country which Mr. Dalton has pointed out.*

In the beginning of the process of consolidation we must, of course, expect that the farms of the more moderate size will increase in number. The great majority of the holdings are small, and two farms of ten acres can only make one of twenty. As the process advances, the consolidation will be with still larger farms. When the man who has got the two united farms of ten acres each leaves the country his going will add twenty acres, not ten, to the holding of his neighbour, and accordingly we find the process has reached this stage. In 1864, 3,777 holdings between five and fifteen acres were given up. But these, instead of being attached to farms under thirty acres, were all merged in farms of larger size. Even Lord Dufferin's small farms, those between fifteen and thirty acres, diminished in that year in number by 1,962, and this diminution has been steadily taking place every year since 1861. In the year 1864 all holdings over five acres diminished by 5,842.

It is well to understand these things. It is worth while even to see clearly what Lord Dufferin means. His assertion means this— the consolidation at present tells more largely on small farms. As the process advances we must expect it to be a little slower. The landlord is not himself prepared to meet the expense requisite to fit up a large farm, and he cannot always meet a tenant qualified to undertake one. When farms of thirty acres or upwards are thrown up

---

* I do not desire to involve myself in any disputed statistics, but I believe I may say that, after a sifting and full discussion, a statement made by Mr. Heron at the Statistical Society, and by Mr. Fisher at the Royal Dublin Society, may be considered as established :—

In 1847 the crops of Ireland were worth fifty-two millions, in 1861 they were worth thirty-four millions.

it will therefore frequently be relet to a new tenant, instead of being thrown into the adjoining farm. Yet in the year 1864 2,000 farms of this class have disappeared.

Lord Dufferin's real argument, put into a strange statistical form, is this:—Emigration has as yet done no harm, for it has only lessened the farms below fifteen acres. Judge Longfield has given his opinion that this is the smallest farm upon which a farmer can live comfortably, and therefore it is not desirable that any such should exist. This may or may not be so. I only repeat that Lord Dufferin's statistics leave the question exactly where it was before.

These statistics do not affect in the slightest degree the arguments that have been used. It is impossible to deny that the Irish people are leaving their native land. Of what avail is it to tell us that there are more large farms now than there were in 1841? That the small holdings of which the occupiers have been banished have been consolidated into larger ones, I readily admit, and this is all that Lord Dufferin's statistics prove.

Does Lord Dufferin mean to tell us that every holder of a farm between 15 and 30 acres is now secure in his position, that the process of consolidation and extermination will have reached its terminus when it has swept away all the holders of farms under 15 acres. If he does not mean this, his statistics are only calculated to mislead.

I have already said that emigration has actually mitigated the evils resulting from the present system of land tenure. It was far better for an evicted tenant to go away than to remain at home to be a burden on the poor rates. It was better for the agricultural labourer to earn a sufficient livelihood in America than to waste away a miserable life in Ireland upon a pittance that barely kept body and soul together. Nobody in his senses ever denied this. But what many men in their senses did say and think was, that the necessity for his going arose, to use the language of Lord Dufferin, from some malignant " human agency," that blasted and blighted with " perennial desolation " the rich resources of his native land.

But there is now, beyond all question, an emigration of a different class going on, an emigration which is no relief to the misery of the country, but an aggravation of it. Men are going away who have means, and industry, and strength, and who, if permitted to remain in their native land would, even under existing circumstances, add something to our stock. It is said, and it is proved,* that men like these are leaving Ireland because the insecurity of tenure which is now the necessary condition of an Irish farmer's life, deprives them of all opportunity of bettering their condition at home.

The whole argument founded on emigration is this:—The people are leaving the country, because a vicious system of land tenure

* *Ante,* the evidence of Bishop Keane.

has depressed the whole industry, lowered the whole character, and condemned to barrenness the whole resources of the country. Does it matter, in the slightest degree, to this argument, to show that as small holdings diminish larger ones increase—more of small holdings than of any other class must disappear because small holdings are the most numerous class. What avail the manipulations of letting which have substituted one set of miserable, because dependent, set of occupiers for another? What use to establish, which is not established, that the tillers of small farms have been the first to go? I am sure that many of those who have left the country have occupied farms far above the size of Lord Dufferin's magic " fifteen acres." Any one acquainted with arithmetical calculations will see that *if the farms actually " consolidated" in each class has been exactly proportionate to the number of the class, the result would be exactly the same as that deduced from the tables upon which Lord Dufferin relies.*

I have used the expression, " the first to go." Lord Dufferin, and Lord Rosse, and all those who coincide in their views, contemplate a still larger emigration of the people. If this be so, of what use is it to tell us the number of the farmers holding farms under 30 acres who are waiting their turn to be driven out.

I bring no charge of inhumanity against such men as Lord Dufferin and Lord Rosse because they so contemplate a large emigration of the population that still remains. We are dealing with questions of fact, and not of sentiment. The question is, can we devise means of supporting the people at home. If not we ought not to keep them. I will even go farther, and say that if our present system of land tenure is to continue, the only chance of seeing rich and prosperous farming in Ireland is the extermination of the people. If we could only quietly get rid of its present inhabitants we might divide Ireland into vast tillage, or better still, pasture farms, for which, probably, English or Scotch, or even some Irish undertakers might be found. I really believe that this is the inevitable result of the reasonings of those who defend our present system of land tenure. It is not necessary to say that their reasonings are fallacious. Their defect is that they overlook the trifling difficulty in the way, that of shipping off the people. While the people remain our present system of land tenure must keep that people miserable and poor.

Lord Dufferin is unquestionably justified in saying that, twenty years ago, and long before, many men of strong national feeling— the ardent and sincere advocates of popular right—regarded emigration not as a means of remedying the evils of Ireland, but as a palliative of the miseries of the people. Even then there were those who regarded these opinions as wrong, and who thought that if human law did not mar the bounty of Providence there was abundance to sustain them in their own land. But twenty years ago the great preponderance of educated opinion was with those who desired to see emigration encouraged and even aided by the State.

This supplies no authority whatever for the views of those who now look forward to a more extended emigration as an indispensable condition to their plans of Irish prosperity. The emigration that is now going on is of a character wholly different from any that was then thought of. The population, in the first place, has fallen from more than eight millions to less than six. It is a totally different thing to desire emigration in the one case and in the other. Those who thought the country might well spare some from a population approaching nine millions, might yet be startled at hearing that it is necessary to reduce it below five.

Besides, it is a total confusion of the subject to confound the emigration which was then recommended with that which is now going on. They have no resemblance except in name. " Voluntary emigration," wrote Sir Robert Kane in his work on *The Industrial Resources of Ireland*, contrasting " voluntary" with aided emigration, " carries off just the class of persons whom it is most important to keep at home—persons of both foresight and enterprise, and possessed of some small capital." This is exactly what is now going on. The men who are going are those who, in the language of Lord Rosse, put together something before they go. The emigration which it was proposed thirty years ago to aid would have been the emigration of the indigent— of those who had neither means nor employment. The voluntary emigration of an entire class can only result from something that makes that whole class miserable at home. The persons who go under such conditions are not emigrants but refugees.

There is, indeed, a voluntary emigration which no one in his senses would deprecate; if we mean by emigration that movement which carries off bold and adventurous or even restless spirits from the old abodes of civilized man to carry intelligence and civilization to the remote and unpeopled regions of the globe. This is indeed, the fulfilment of the Divine precept, which, when it commanded men to increase and multiply, bade them also to go forth and replenish the earth. This was the emigration which, in the palmiest days of Greece and Rome, bore their hardy sons to found colonies in distant lands. It is that by which England has settled a new Anglo-Saxon race beyond the western ocean. It is that by which the vast centre of Europe sends every year thousands and tens of thousands to swell on the western prairies the still advancing European population, who have made the great American people.

Is this the emigration that is now drawing away the life-blood of the Irish nation? The Irish is not an emigration from the people but of the people. It is not the bold, the adventurous, or the indigent who are going. The emigrants are not confined to the young and the enterprising. Whole families are leaving their native land. Old men take their departure. Men of staid and sober habits—the fathers of the village—desert the home of their manhood—men whose emigration would in any settled state of society, be heard of with amazement, and whose leaving is, in any state, a portent and an omen of ill. This emigration is one that tells of the upheaving of its inhabitants from the land. It is vain to speak of this as the ordinary movement which at all times stirs some of a population to wander from their home. If all the landlords of Ireland were suddenly to sell their estates, to abandon their ancestral homes, and leave Ireland for ever, would this be accounted for by telling us that in every state of society, even the most prosperous—adventurous spirits have been found among landowners, who have parted with their home possessions, and sought the perilous and daring prospects which open to the imagination of the adventurous, in climes that are attractive because they are distant and unknown? Can we account for an equally strange and equally signal departure of other classes of the people by the remembrance that at all times many of those classes have sought a new fortune in a new land?

Common sense tells us the wide difference between one class of emigration and the other. It is trifling with a solemn subject; it is almost jesting with the agonies of the Irish nation to pretend not to know to which class the emigration that is now going on is to be referred.

But more than this. Passionate appeals were made to the Government during the famine years to provide means of enabling the people to emigrate, and these appeals were unheeded. With corn and cattle going literally to waste in other countries, our rulers were implored, if they would not bring food to the people, to carry the people to the food. It was a time when the saving of human life was the first grand consideration. The people were starving at home. There seemed no choice between this and their going to other lands.

Who would hesitate in the choice? Who would hesitate now between emigration for the Irish people and their continuance at home in their present misery and serfdom? Let us not mistake the issue. The complaint is not that emigration is preferred either by the people or any one for them. The complaint is that such a choice is the only one offered to them—that home is made by human law a place unfit for them to live.

I agree with Lord Dufferin in this. If our present "desolation" is to be "perennial," emigration is a boon to every Irish peasant whom it carries from Ireland to any other region upon earth. If our present condition cannot be remedied except by parting with our people—then, for their own sake, for the sake of humanity, let the people go. But it is because it can be remedied by other means that we protest against a contented acquiescence in their flight.

The choice is not between emigration and keeping the people in misery at home; it is between driving them, "sorrowing and reluctant exiles," from their native land and giving them that security of tenure which would make them the happy and industrious occupants of the Irish soil. And even now, if our present state must be perpetuated by a refusal to give security of tenure to the tenant; if serfdom is to be the perpetual doom of those who remain at home; if, in a word, we are to despair of any improvement in the land laws—to give up all hope of any legislative protection for the occupiers of the soil—surely he would be the best friend of the Celtic race who would advise the old people, with one consent, to go—and leave their curse and their country to the malignant " human agency" which drives them from their fathers' homes.

Fortunately we have indications that all, even of Irish landowners, do not take the same dismal view of our position as that which is taken by Lord Dufferin and Lord Rosse.* There are those who recognize a duty to the Irish people distinct from that of driving them from their native land, and who admit that before we fling them away like " weeds," some effort ought be made to provide for them at home. The Marquis of Abercorn, himself an

---

* I should be very sorry to do Lord Dufferin any possible injustice; and it is right to say that, in a letter to the *Daily News*, of which I will have a few words to say presently, he has very indignantly disclaimed that which he considers an imputation, that " he is anxious to see the population permanently reduced."

"To any one who cares to study my opinions with candour it will be apparent, not that I do not regard emigration as *per se* a great calamity, but that I consider as long as people find themselves in straitened circumstances at home it is folly to expect them to stay there; that an endeavour by artificial means to tether down to the soil more persons than can be maintined in comfort by its cultivation is likely to prove abortive ; that the true remedy for emigration is the development of the country's industrial resources ; and that in the meantime, the opening presented by America to those who can find no opportunity at home for the remunerative employment of their energies is an unspeakable blessing."—*Letter to the Daily News*, January 24th, 1867.

I perfectly agree with Lord Dufferin, that "the true remedy for emigration is the development of the country's industrial resources ; " although he will pardon me for saying the phrase " development of Ireland's resources" has long since degenerated into a cant. The only way I know of to "develope" our two great "industrial resources," land and labour, is to give to every occupier an interest in improving by his industry the land.

I presume that Lord Dufferin, among other right-minded men, would, as an abstract question, much prefer that our population should remain in comfort at home, just as he would wish, as an abstract question, that every man could dine every day upon roast beef. I think I see the means by which they can live in comfort at home. I presume Lord Dufferin does not, or he would not have concluded his first letter to the *Times* with the sentence :—" For these reasons I believe that emigration has been, and will continue to be a blessing to Ireland ; and I disagree with those persons who consider that the Almighty pronounced a curse, and not a blessing upon his children when he told them to go forth and multiply, and replenish the earth."

This bears out the only assertion I have made on the subject—the prospects of Ireland, which Lord Dufferin and those who think with him set before us, involve a further expatriation of our people.

It does not affect the question in the least that Lord Dufferin contemplates this feature in his prospect with regret.

Irish peer and an Irish landowner, thus spoke, a short time ago, at the inaugural banquet of the Lord Mayor:—

"Closely connected," said the Lord Lieutenant, "with the happiness and the well-being of the people is the subject which of late has been prominently before the public, and has been ventilated by many writers of great ability—I mean that of emigration. I will venture in reply to say a few words upon it; and in what I say, I wish to speak, not with reference to the past, but solely as to the present and the future. I am aware that according to strict economic principles, the population of Ireland is somewhat in excess. I admit that if you were to make a new Ireland you would arrange to have a somewhat smaller population. But this is not the question. YOU MUST TAKE IRELAND AS IT IS. YOU MUST TAKE THE POPULATION AS YOU FIND IT. MEN AND WOMEN ARE NOT CATTLE OR MACHINES, TO BE PLACED 'OR DISPLACED AS THE EXIGENCIES OR THE WHIM OF THE MOMENT MAY SUGGEST. YOU MUST TAKE THE POPULATION AS IT IS, AND DO THE BEST YOU CAN FOR IT. You must find the means of livelihood—you must find employment, and you must advance their social and moral well-being. This is the problem which those who have the interests of Ireland at heart should study—not relying upon the deportation of a population which, after all, is but little in excess of what the rules of economic principles allow. Let me not be supposed to deprecate a wholesome emigration, such as that which flows from the superabundant population of the sister isle. An emigration of that nature is a proof, not of weakness, but of strength. It is the superabundance of vigour and enterprise as well as of numbers. But when emigration reaches excess it becomes the hemorrhage which drains the life-blood, while it evidences the disease which lurks beneath."

I will not stop to cavil at the unsound political economy which teaches his Excellency that the population of Ireland is even "a little" in excess. I do not think that if his Excellency were to make a new Ireland he would need to "arrange to have a somewhat smaller population;" he would not do so if all the occupiers were treated as they are treated on his own estates. That which concerns the Irish people is this—the representative of their Sovereign has told them that:—"Her Government must take Ireland as it is. Must take the population as they find them." That "men and women are not cattle or machines, *to be displaced as the exigencies or the whim of the moment may suggest.*"

We must form plans of improvement "NOT RELYING ON THE DEPORTATION OF THE POPULATION." These are noble words.

I am no partizan of Lord Abercorn's administration. But it is impossible to withhold from language like this, spoken with the authority of a Viceroy, the tribute of admiration and respect.[*]

---

[*] It is an act of simple justice to Lord Abercorn to say that his acts as a landlord are, if report speaks truly, in perfect accordance with the sentiments he thus expressed.

It is strange to observe that in Pynnar's Survey, the lands of "the Earl of Abercorn" were among the few upon which he found an "estated tenantry" placed.

It would throw some light upon Lord Dufferin's statistics if his Excellency would inform us how many families have emigrated from the Abercorn estates.

By a singular coincidence the chief magistrate, who was his entertainer, had but a short time before expressed very similar sentiments, both on his own behalf and on that of an Irish nobleman like Lord Abercorn, the owner of great possessions in our land. In replying to a deputation of tenantry who presented him with a well-deserved testimonial of their regard, the Lord Mayor had used this memorable language, worthy of one chosen, solely by the force of his ability and his character to fill the first civic chair of our country:—

"Emigration is the hemorrhage which drains the life-blood of Ireland away; and I deeply regret that a noble lord, of hereditary talents, of great parts and accomplishments, should have reanimated the Sangrado prescription of more blood-letting and hot water. Ireland has too much of that already. I fear to face the future, when one and a-half million of our population is to be reduced. I fear to face the deep and untold misery to thousands—the quenched fires, the household gods scattered, the trading classes in the towns still further reduced and ruined, and the professional and middle classes feeling the want of that life-blood which it is the duty of true statesmen to keep in the body politic, and, above all, arrest its continual flow."*

But while I cheerfully pay my tribute of respect to language such as this, whether spoken by a Viceroy or a Lord Mayor, let me say also that when spoken by a ruler imposes a deep responsibility upon him who uses it. It conveys an invitation to the Irish people to remain at home. They will be justly regarded as cruelly deceiving them, who, from the place of authority, so invite them, unless they use their utmost efforts to make their native country one in which the people can live. That can only be done by making it a country in which they can expend their industry on its fields with a certainty that the fruits of their industry will be their own.

An inspired apostle has warned us of the hollowness of the charity which contents itself with words:—

"If a brother or sister be naked and destitute of daily food, and one of you say unto them, Depart in peace, be ye warmed and filled ; but, notwithstanding, ye give them not those things which are needful to the body—what doth it profit?"—(*St. James*, ii. 16).

* Mr. Wm. Lane Joynt, the present Lord Mayor of Dublin, is the manager of Lord Annaly's estates in the county of Clare.

It was in reply to a deputation from the tenantry of that estate that he used the language I have quoted above.

He was able to tell that deputation that on a large property only three tenants had been evicted in the course of ten years.

On that estate a custom of permitting an outgoing tenant to sell his interest has been introduced. I have been assured that from the whole of that estate not a single family has been contributed to swell the emigration.

It is by examining individual instances of this nature that we can really learn the causes that are driving the Irish people from their homes. If I found whole families flying from the estates of Lord Abercorn in the north, and Lord Annaly in the south, I would begin to distrust my own opinions as to the connexion between emigration and the want of tenant right.

The charity would be worse than hollow; it would be a cruel deception which, when " the brother or sister naked and destitute of daily food," were about "to depart in peace," would say to them, " Remain at home and be ye warmed and filled," if, notwithstanding, ye give them not those things "which are needful for the body."

The first is the charity of those who adopt the views of Lord Dufferin and tell the Irish people to go to—America, and there be "warmed and filled." The second would be the worse charity of those who use words like those of Lord Abercorn, unless when they tell them to remain in Ireland, they really intend to secure them the means of living in their native land.

Sentences like those, spoken by Lord Abercorn, will be treasured up in the hearts of the people to add to the bitterness of disappointment if the hopes they create, are once more dashed in cruel mockery to the ground.

In passing, let me say that I cannot admit that which Lord Dufferin assumes, that it has been an advantage to the country to turn out every man who held a farm under "fifteen acres." I could almost fancy Lord Dufferin had been led astray by some confused memory of the traditions of our early years when he invites us to a controversy on these everlasting " fifteen acres." Except in these recollections there is no magic in the phrase. These small holdings existed principally in Ulster, and above all counties in Ireland in Down and Armagh. You could almost measure the prosperity and the comfort of the population by the multiplication of these holdings. In an excellent tract, to which, I regret to say, I can only refer from memory, the late Mr. Sharman Crawford bore conclusive testimony upon this point to the condition of the county Down. Mr. Blacker, whose name will long be remembered in connexion with the improvement of Irish agriculture, bore similar testimony as to the county of Armagh. Sir Robert Kane,* in his work on the industrial resources of Ireland, quotes, with approval,

* From a very admirable essay in the *Industrial Resources of Ireland*, I extract a few passages, the statistical facts of which are sufficient, at all events, to show that we must not take it as an established principle in Irish social science, that the existence of farms under 15 acres is destructive to the prosperity of the country, or inconsistent with the comfort and independence of the occupiers of the soil.

" By the returns of the census of 1841, the number of farms in Ireland, and their magnitude, was

Provinces.	Farms from 1 to 3 acres.	Farms from 5 to 15 acres.	Farms from 15 to 30 acres.	Above 30 acres.	Total.
Leinster,	- 49,152	45,595	20,584	17,889	133,220
Munster,	- 57,028	61,320	27,481	16,557	162,386
Ulster, -	- 100,817	98,992	25,099	9,591	234,499
Connaught,	- 99,918	45,221	5,790	4,275	155,204
Total,	- 306,915	251,127	78,954	48,312	685,309

" The following table exhibits the number and the average size of farms, compared with the total area and area of arable land of each province :—

a calculation of that gentleman, that if all Ireland had been tilled and occupied like Armagh, Ireland could have supported in comfort more than double her then population.

Armagh supports, for each square mile of its arable ground, by far the largest population of all the Irish counties. Down comes next in the number of its population compared with its cultivated soil. In Down, the population on each square mile of arable ground is 317; in Armagh, 387; in Tipperary, 146; and in Cork, 148.*

Yet between 1851 and 1861, as I have already pointed out, the whole province of Ulster lost but 3,886 families, a decrease of not quite one per cent.† A large share of one year's proportion was supplied by the evictions of Glenveagh.

It does not at all follow that the labourer who held a few acres of land, or even a smaller portion, was therefore entirely dependent on it for support. In many instances, especially in the north of Ireland, the system assumed a form very nearly equivalent to that allotment system which persons have taken so much pains to introduce into many parts of England. The man who worked as a day

Province.	Number of Farms.	Total area in acres.	Area of arable land.	Average size of farms.
Leinster, - -	133,220	4,860,642	3,961,188	29·7 acres.
Munster, - -	162,386	6,049,886	3,874,613	23·8 „
Ulster, - -	234,499	5,466,648	3,407,539	14·5 „
Connaught, - -	155,204	4,388,166	2,220,960	14·3 „

"It is thus seen that in every province the great majority of the farms are under fifteen acres, and the average magnitude of the farms in the north and west, appears to be but one-half that of the southern and eastern provinces. The geographical association is very much at variance with other social circumstances, and it will form just now an interesting object of inquiry."   .   .   .   .

"That the greater or less magnitude of farms is not in any way necessarily connected with the condition of agriculture, or with any other elements of social comfort of the population, becomes fully evident on reference to the table of the sizes of farms given in page 305. It is there seen that in Connaught the average size of farms is almost exactly the same as in Ulster, and yet these two provinces are the extremes of ignorance and of intelligence, of activity and of industrial indolence, which this island presents. The difference has certainly nothing to do with the smallness of the farms."

The following is the extract from Mr. Blacker's work entitled *Ireland as it Was, Is, and Ought to Be:*—

"The county of Armagh contains 212,755 acres, and a population of 220,653 souls, and that the entire kingdom contains 17,190,726 acres, and 7,839,469 souls ; now, in the county of Armagh, by a recent survey, more than one-seventh of the surface is taken up by lakes and unprofitable land, and the remainder is, for the greater part, but indifferently cultivated, and yet the peasantry are better clothed, lodged, and fed, than they are in most other counties in Ireland. I cannot, therefore, be accused of taking away from the comforts of the rest of the kingdom, by taking the county of Armagh as a standard, and its proportion of unprofitable surface is not very remote, I believe, from the average of the others; if, then, 212,755, the number of acres in Armagh, give a population of 220,653 souls, 17,190,726 acres, the entire contents of the kingdom, ought to give a population of 17,828,888, in place of 7,839,469, the population at present. It, therefore, appears, that supposing the other parts of Ireland to be as well cultivated as Armagh, it would support about two and a half times the number of its present inhabitants, and be able to export provisions largely besides ; for Armagh, notwithstanding its population, exports pork, butter, and grain, in great quantities."

* "Statistics of Ireland." *Thom's Almanac,* 1865.   † Ibid.

labourer held with his cabin a small patch of ground, upon which he worked at extra hours, and which enabled him to supply the deficiencies of his wages. Various forms of domestic, or even outdoor employment, gave opportunity to members of his family to assist in obtaining the humble livelihood of his little household. In such a life as this many an Irish family has lived happy and contented with their lot.

But, surely, in Ireland it is not open to us to choose between the one system and the other. We have a population living upon small farms. We have them so after all the pitiless exterminations of the last thirty years. It is impossible to discuss the question without taking the existence and, as I think, the interest, of these people into account. All government ought to be carried on for the benefit of the Irish people—that is, for the good of the men, women, and children now living on the Irish soil. What are we to think of reasonings which begin by asking us to exclude a large number of these men, women, and children from all our calculations. But the condition of these very people is a far greater subject, in any rational estimate of the duties of Government, than the condition of all the landlords in Ireland put together. I say with Lord Abercorn, " we must take Ireland as we find it," we must deal with " the population as they are." We have to deal with human beings " our own flesh and blood," and " not with cattle or machines." I ask, what is to become of the two millions of Irish men, women and children who now depend for their existence upon small farms. Are we to " displace them as the exigencies or the whims of the moment may require?" Are we to have no " fear to face the deep and untold misery of thousands, the quenched fires, the household gods scattered." In the name of the God of mercy, has there not been in Ireland enough of this for one country and for one age? Yet surely I may say, that all those who use the reasonings I am combating content themselves by quietly assuming that the country would get on better if they were out of the way. I deny that any question which affects the homes—the daily bread, the very existence of a large number of our people, is to be determined by considerations of what can be most profitably done for the landowners with our fields.

This question really lies at the root of all our discussion. Whose interests are we to consider in legislation as to land? The social compact is not one between the owners of property binding them to maintain its rights against those who have none. It is a compact between all the people who are living in the land—and every man whom you bind by virtue of that supposed compact to obedience to your laws, is entitled, by the reciprocal obligation of obedience and protection, to have his interests considered in any deliberation on any question affecting our social state.

No statesman and no Legislature has a right to adopt a scheme

K

for the improvement or the settlement of Ireland in which no provision is made for the great mass of the people. The social system fails in its first and most sacred obligation, under which any man, without any fault of his own, is excluded from the means of living in his native land. If we must resort to the first principles of human nature—to what would the first law of our nature, that of self-preservation, lead those whom you thus deliberately exclude from the great partnership of society?

It is not my fault if we must revert to propositions like these. Those who propose to carry out the improvement of Ireland after the departure of the Irish people compel us to recur to the first principles of government and of society. They are the revolutionists who, by proposing to rest national prosperity on the expatriation of the people, subvert all the principles upon which the fabric of society is based.

There may be revolutionary theories which subvert the sacred rights of the people as well as those which subvert the less sacred rights of property. When either are propounded it is the duty of those who hold by the principles upon which the authority of all government, and the foundations of all society are based, to restate these principles, and call on all lovers of social order to uphold them. I brand as "revolutionary" every theory of national improvement in which the well-being of the great mass of the Irish people has no place—and in this I mean by the Irish people the human beings who are now living and moving on this Irish soil.

In this view of our condition and our duties it is a delusion to discuss upon the abstract grounds, upon which the question has been discussed, the relative merit of large or small farms. The true question is, by which system can provision be best made out of the resources of Ireland for the people that rightly or wrongly, fortunately or unfortunately, are located upon our land.

Before I pass from these earlier letters of Lord Dufferin I am bound to notice a statement quoted by your Lordship—that to which you refer when you say:—

"Next as to the prices of labour, we are told by Lord Dufferin that 'in the west of Ireland some fifteen years ago the rate of agricultural wages varied from 2s. 6d. to 5s. a-week. Ever since it has gradually advanced, ranging in the south and west of Ireland from 10s. 0d. to 12s. 0d.' In this neighbourhood, the rate of wages has risen from 2s. 6d. and 5s. a-week to 6s. 0d. and 9s. 0d."*

Your Lordship has not done altogether justice to the statement of Lord Dufferin. He describes agricultural wages in the south and west as "ranging from ten to twelve, *or even fourteen shillings* a-week," *and rising even higher in Ulster.* When your Lordship speaks

* Lord Lifford's letter to Mr. Butt—page 11.

of wages as having risen in your neighbourhood to six or nine
shillings a-week, I believe I may understand you as meaning not
that any labourer can get regular and constant employment at any
thing like nine shillings a week; but that the remuneration of
labour under ordinary circumstances is but six shillings a-week,
rising in exceptional cases, or at seasons of unusual demand to a rate
as high as nine.

With regard to the rate of wages paid in former years, there is some
difficulty in fixing it. The very expression "2s. 6d. and 5s." shows the
uncertainty of the statement. The table prepared by the Commissioners of Poor Enquiry, in 1836, exhibits a remarkable variety in
the wages in different districts of Ireland.* But they were not
uniform even in the same locality. In the district to which your
Lordship refers, I know that cottiers living on the glebe land nearest
to your Lordship, a great many years ago, received rather regular
employment—not from farmers of the very highest class—at the
rate of tenpence and one meal a day. At the same period I have
not the least doubt that, within a very short distance, there were
men often working at a lower rate.

There can, however, be no doubt that before the famine, agricultural labour could in many districts of Ireland be obtained at a rate
of wages miserably low. It is equally certain that over the whole
surface of Ireland a very great improvement has taken place, but I
think I may say it is equally certain that the passage which you

* This table, referring to the year 1835, states the average rate of wages in Donegal
to be a shilling a day. In Antrim and Derry, in Armagh and Down it was tenpence
in Winter and a shilling in Summer. Generally throughout Ulster it varied from tenpence to a shilling. It was only in a few districts that even in winter it fell so low as
eight pence.

A rate so low as sixpence a day appeared to be unknown, except in Connaught and
some of the wildest districts of Clare, Kerry, and Cork.

In Connaught it was in few places above eight pence; in the barony of Mohill, in
the county in which the town of Boyle is situated, in summer it ranged between eightpence and tenpence.

In Leinster it generally rose to tenpence, and this was the lowest in the Summer
months.

In Munster it ranged from eightpence to tenpence, the lower rate more generally
prevailing.

This table supplies us with an approximate estimate of that, which at first sight,
appears a still more important element in the labourer's condition—the constancy of
his work. In this respect the variation is very great. In Ulster, generally, the
labourers were supposed to find employment at the wages specified for about half
the days in the year. In parts of Mayo they could find employment at sixpence for
only thirty days in the entire year.

But even this latter element is far from an unerring test of the labourers condition.
Most of these labourers, especially in the West, had their small plots of ground on
which they worked themselves, the rents of which they paid by working for their
landlord. I can perfctly recollect many years ago, when I did take an interest in the
condition of a few cottiers in Lord Lifford's district, some of them refused to bind
themselves to work for the farmers for more than three days in the week, even
when guaranteed tenpence a day and their breakfast.

There are many, very many, elements to be considered before we can form a perfectly just estimate of the relative condition of the Irish labourer at any two given
times.

have quoted from Lord Dufferin is a wild and monstrous exaggeration of that improvement.   When even your Lordship's knowledge of rural affairs, with the power of testing it derived from your own experience in a district at least as prosperous as most of these in Connaught, has been led astray by that statement, we must not wonder if it has received implicit credence from those who had less opportunity of being informed.   I am quite sure that in all investigations connected with the land question the condition of the mere agricultural labourer has an importance which has not been sufficiently regarded.   But I advert to this singular statement of Lord Dufferin's not only on account of the intrinsic importance of the subject to which it relates, but also because it appears to me to supply a very striking illustration of that strange facility of rushing to conclusions without any examination of the steps by which they are reached by which Lord Dufferin has been able to invest even his statistical deductions with all the wildness, and, I admit, with much of the interest.which belong to the fictions of a romance. Laputa or Utopia does not differ more from any existing country than—in respect to the labourer's condition—the Ireland which Lord Dufferin describes does from the Ireland of real life.   If there were any subject upon which we might presume it impossible for Lord Dufferin to fall into error, it would be on the subject of agricultural wages, especially in Ulster, and considering the weight and importance which have been attached to the statements of Lord Dufferin, it may not be without its use to try by this very simple test his claim to be the infallible instructor of the English nation upon Irish affairs.

Those who believe that emigration has proved a blessing to the Irish people, at least to that portion of them who have remained at home, must of necessity contend that the outgoing of the labouring population has bettered the condition of the labourer who remains. Lord Dufferin, in support of his argument, describes in very strong terms the improvement.   He actually goes the length of stating that

"THE IRISH LABOURER HAS ALREADY RISEN FROM A SERF TO BE HIS EMPLOYER'S EQUAL!"

Again, he asserts that the evicted tenant has been converted from a struggling farmer into "a well-paid labourer."

Again, " the wages of labour have doubled within the last fifteen years."

And, finally, he clearly and unequivocally asserts that throughout the South the wages of agricultural labourers "RANGE FROM TEN SHILLINGS TO TWELVE SHILLINGS, OR EVEN FOURTEEN SHILLINGS, A WEEK."

These are clear and distinct statements of very great importance if they be accurate, but statements by the accuracy of which we may fairly try the right of the noble lord to be considered an unimpeachable authority upon Irish affairs.

It is quite true that emigration has already caused farm labour to become scarce—that is, there are not quite so many idle hands as formerly always at the disposal of the person who may desire at any time to employ extra labourers. But I am very much afraid it would be inaccurate to say that wages have risen at all in proportion to the diminution in the number of labourers.

The strangest feature of our present condition is, that while our labouring population is so much diminished by emigration, the wages of those who remain have not increased at all in proportion to the diminished supply—apparently a proof that the demand for labour must be lessening. The wages of agricultural labour have unquestionably increased; I am not sure that they have increased in a ratio much greater than is measured by a corresponding rise in the price of all the necessaries of life, especially if we take into account, as we must do, the difference of the diet to which the failure of the potato has compelled the labourer to have recourse. I am quite sure that they have not at all increased as much as we might have expected from the reduction in the number of those seeking for employment.* We must not be led astray by the accounts which are occasionally published on this subject— accounts in which exceptional rates of wages, under the pressure of some unusual demand, are confounded with the ordinary payments. In this way, I confess, I was disposed to account for the strange passage which your Lordship has partially quoted from one of Lord Dufferin's letters to *The Times*—letters intended to inform the English people, upon the authority of a resident proprietor, of the actually existing condition of Irish rural affairs.

That whole statement is this:—

" When I was in the west of Ireland, some fifteen years ago, the rate of agricultural wages varied from half-a-crown to five shillings a week. Ever since it has gradually advanced, ranging in the south and west of Ireland from ten shillings to twelve shillings, or even fourteen shillings a

---

* In some parts of the country, and at some times of the year, labour is unquestionably deficient, and I have heard apprehensions expressed that if emigration continued there would be a difficulty in obtaining a supply sufficient for the proper cultivation of the soil.

These complaints come, it must be remembered, from persons who have all their lives been accustomed to a state of things in which there was no difficulty in obtaining any amount of extra labour—in which Irish labourers went over to England to supply that very extra labour at the time of harvest.

There is not employment in Ireland for all those who are seeking for it.

Bishop Keane says, in his evidence in 1864 :— " I can state, of my own knowledge, that I am not acquainted with a single town in the diocese of Cloyne, or of Ross— with which I was formerly connected—where almost every day throughout the year, except during three weeks of harvest, and occasionally for a short period during the spring or seeding time, men having families will be looking for an occasional day's work and cannot find it."—*Evidence of Bishop Keane.* Question 3,341.

week; while in the north the labourer is almost absolutely master of the market, and can dictate what terms he pleases."

There could be no mistake as to the meaning of this sentence in the mind of any one who read it. It was introduced to support the argument that emigration was really bettering the condition of the labouring classes, both of those who went and those who remained. It refers distinctly to "agricultural wages," to the wages of labourers who, to Lord Dufferin's own knowledge, fifteen years ago, were paid wages so low as five shillings and half-a-crown a week. And the statement made is that the rate of these identical wages has ever since gradually increased, and that the same labourers who were thus paid, fifteen years ago, five shillings, and sometimes half-a-crown a week, are now, owing to the effects of emigration paid at the rate of ten, twelve, or even fourteen shillings a week.

But this is not all. The northern labourer is still better off. His condition is contrasted with even that of the Connaught labourer, receiving fourteen shillings a week. " In the north the labourer is almost absolutely master of the market, and can dictate whatever terms he pleases."

If there be meaning in words it means that the labourers in the north can dictate terms exceeding fourteen shillings a week, and that the wages mentioned are not an exceptional rate, but the ordinary wages of ordinary agricultural labourers.

I am the very last person in the world who would wish to take advantage of the unguarded expression of an opponent. I know by experience how very easy it is for a quick and impetuous reasoner to fall into error in writing upon such subjects. But with all this I must say that if any confusion of thought or hastiness in writing has led Lord Dufferin into an erroneous statement in the passage I have quoted, it is impossible to regard his Lordship as a safe guide to follow, even as a witness, in the tangled complication of Irish affairs.

Let any Englishman who is, or has been, disposed to accept Lord Dufferin's representations of Irish affairs—let him read over and over again the sentences I have quoted. Let him rejoice, as I am sure every true Englishman would rejoice, in the prosperity of Ireland which enables us to pay our agricultural labourers ten, twelve, or even fourteen shillings a week, and when he has pondered a while upon this happy state of things, let him hear what, unhappily, is the truth—

The average rate of agricultural wages throughout Ireland does not exceed seven shillings a week.

And in that highly favoured North, in which the labourer "can dictate what terms he pleases," Lord Dufferin's own labourers, when he wrote these sentences, were paid eight shillings a week.

Upon the very day on which I read your Lordship's letter referring me to Lord Dufferin's statement, it so happened that I was engaged as " a Nisi Prius Advocate" in a trial in which it became necessary for a very respectable farmer, residing in the County Leitrim, to produce the account books of his farm for the harvest months of the year 1865. I saw with surprise that he was paying his labourers tenpence a day, with an additional allowance of twopence for their night's lodging, when they were required to work at a distance of nearly six miles from home. There seemed to be no difficulty in getting extra labourers at the same rate. This was incidentally proved in a court of justice, of course without the slightest reference to any inquiry into the general rate of wages. These labourers were working close to the town of Boyle.*

I need not say it is not easy for a private individual, unacquainted practically with rural affairs, to ascertain the average rate of wages throughout Ireland. Still I made such effort as was in my power. From every part of Ireland I received assurances that a rate of wages such as that mentioned by Lord Dufferin was unknown. Mr. M'Carthy Downing writes to me that throughout the whole southern and western districts of Cork, the average rate of wages does not exceed seven shillings a week. Your Lordship publicly tells us, with Lord Dufferin's statement before you, that in your neighbourhood, one in the far North, they range between six shillings and nine. In Donegal, a gentleman residing in the same neighbourhood as your Lordship informs me that he gives his farm labourers six shillings a week, with a house and a potato garden. Throughout Connaught I am told a shilling a day is considered high wages. In Down and Antrim I was assured that, except in the immediate vicinity of Belfast, the general rate of wages does not, on the average, exceed eight shillings. Of course all doubts were set at rest when I soon afterwards read Lord Dufferin's own statement that, in the best part of the County Down, his own labourers were receiving eight shillings a week—"from 1s. 4d. to 1s. 6d. a day." All information points to one result, and I fear I am exaggerating, not diminishing the rate, when I say that, excluding the vicinities of large towns, the ordinary wages of labourers throughout Ireland do not average more than seven shillings a week. Labourers cannot get constant employment even at that rate.

I need scarcely say that this state of facts is entirely irreconcilable with the plain and literal meaning of the passage I have quoted from Lord Dufferin's letter in *The Times*. His statements having been challenged by Mr. Dalton, in a letter to *The Daily News*, Lord Dufferin, in a letter to that journal, of the 24th of January, thus explained, or qualified, or retracted them :—

" With regard to his criticisms on my estimate of the present rate of wages in the South and West your correspondent has greater justification.

* See table of wages referred to in note to page 147.

But though my words quite bear the interpretation he has put upon them—what I alluded to when I named ten or twelve shillings a week was, not the wages of the ordinary farm servant—though I admit I have inadvertently used the term agricultural in the previous sentence—but of the best description of unskilled manual labour. I merely repeated, in fact, a statement made in the speech already quoted, which referred to such labour as that which is employed on railways, and by contractors. The point is of no importance to my argument; for if agricultural wages are still so low it only proves that, at all events till now, the emigration of the labourer has not been excessive. But in justification of my general statement as to the rise of wages, I may mention—in his evidence before Mr. Maguire's Committee—that Judge Longfield estimated the increase between 1844 and 1860, at from 25 to 80 per cent. I myself have been paying from 1s. 4d. to 1s. 6d. a day; in the County Down, during harvest, a labourer cannot be had under 2s., or 1s. 6d., with his food supplied."   .

I hope I will not be accused of " ruthlessly gibbetting" any land-lord, past, present, or to come, if I place in parallel columns that which Lord Dufferin wrote, and that which we now know he meant :—

" When I was in the West of Ire-land, fifteen years ago, the rate of agricultural wages varied from half-a-crown to five shillings a week. Ever since it has gradually advanced, rang-ing, in the South and West, from ten shillings to twelve shillings, or even fourteen shillings a week; while in the North THE LABOURER is almost abso-lutely master of the market, and can dictate what terms he pleases."—Lord Dufferin's first letter.

" What I alluded to when I named ten or twelve shillings a week was, not the wages of the ordinary farm servant—though I admit I had inad-vertently used the word agricultural in the previous sentence—but of the best description of unskilled manual labour. . . . . . I myself have been paying from 1s. 4d. to 1s. 6d. a day."—Lord Dufferin's second letter.

Whatever Lord Dufferin thought or meant it is as clear as words can make it that the sentence in his first letter contained a precise and circumstantial statement of the rate of agricultural wages in the South and West of Ireland, and in the North; representing them in the first as "ranging from ten to twelve or even fourteen shillings a week," and as rising still higher in the North.

The explanation certainly invites criticism. I have too often admired, on other subjects, the happy elegance of Lord Dufferin's light and graceful style not to feel an interest in the comparison between these two sentences. We now know that the mistake proceeded from the "inadvertent" use of the word "agricultural" "in the previous sentence." The "previous" sentence is, "When I was in the West of Ireland, fifteen years ago, the rate of agricultural wages varied from .half-a-crown to five shillings a week." The next sentence—"It gradually rose until." As a full stop intervenes, its intervention is perhaps to be considered, in courtesy to the monarch of punctuation, to constitute two sentences; but a full stop never yet divided words which looked more like a continuation of one. " Fifteen years ago the rate of agricultural wages varied from two-and-sixpence to five shillings a week. It rose." What varied, and what rose? " It" seems very like a mere repetition of " the rate of agricultural wages." This unfortunate "it" is the point of the whole confusion—a huge mistake has hid itself in that little word. " It" plainly means " agricultural wages," but " it" does not mean "it;" but when "it" is mentioned "it" means the wages of the best " unskilled manual labour," whatever " it" may be.

I confess I cannot see why in the explanation the farm "servant" is introduced. He is not exactly the personage whom we had known in the previous statement as the agricultural " labourer." Neither his position or his wages are the same. But images elude our closest observation as they glide into each other in the marvellous disappearances of that dissolving view in which all that Lord Dufferin said so exquisitely vanishes into something that he meant.

But not satisfied with leaving us even in this perplexity, Lord Dufferin entangles us in still more hopeless bewilderment when he tells us that the mistake arose, not in the " it," but in the " inadvertent use of the word 'agricultural' in the previous sentence," or, as I should say, part of the sentence. It was "inadvertent," and, therefore, erroneous, to describe the wages which fifteen years ago varied from half-a-crown to five shillings a week, as " agricultural" wages. In the name of common sense what wages were they then? No flattery can possibly congratulate Lord Dufferin on the clearness and felicity of his explanation. There is, however, one consolation. Lord Dufferin is very angry with Mr. Dalton for having described him as advocating emigration when he said that " emigration was, and would continue to be, a blessing to Ireland;" but he graciously admits that for the second mistake there is " more" excuse. When Lord Dufferin wrote the sentence—" fifteen years ago the rate of agricultural wages varied from half-a-crown to five shillings a week. IT has ever since gradually advanced, ranging now, in the South and West of Ireland, from ten shillings to twelve shillings, or even fourteen shillings a week"—he admits that his words " BEAR THE INTERPRETATION" (! !) that agricultural wages have risen to ten, twelve, or fourteen shillings a week. Giving Lord Dufferin every credit for the candour of this admission, it would have been very desirable if he had " condescended"— if I may use a phrase of his own—to suggest any other conceivable interpretation which the most strained or the most perverted ingenuity could put upon them.

Were I disposed to pursue this criticism I might remind Lord Dufferin that his first statement can scarcely be called an " estimate," it was an assertion of a matter of fact. I might even ask him what wages he intended to " estimate " when he spoke of

the half-crown wages of fifteen years ago and the fourteen shillings
of the present day. I might even inquire who is "the labourer,"
emphatically "THE" labourer, whom he describes as "dictating his
own terms" in the North. Perhaps I might even suggest that it
is a strange thing for a resident country gentleman to support any
statement he makes on the subject of agricultural wages by the
authority of Judge Longfield. Judge Longfield has, perhaps,
rather less opportunities of learning them than I have myself. I
would have thought that if either Judge Longfield or I had
wanted information on such a subject we would have been only too
happy to receive it from Lord Dufferin. I confess I would be
scarcely satisfied with Judge Longfield's information if he left me
to make out the truth between the rather vague and indefinite limits
that range "from 25 to 80 per cent."* Lord Dufferin might also be
reminded that in letters professing to deal with the great improvement in the condition of the agricultural labourer this is the
only passage in which he makes any estimate of his wages. There
were repeated statements of a general rise of wages of agricultural
labour—that they were doubled—that the evicted tenant had
been elevated from a struggling farmer to a well-paid labourer—
that the labourer, "the agricultural labourer," is become the
master of his employer. The only particular statement of the rate
of wages—upon the very subject upon which, of all others we
would look to Lord Dufferin for information, is that statement
upon which I have been commenting.

If Lord Dufferin is to be judged, as every public writer, no matter
what may be his rank or his ability, must be judged by that which
he has published and deliberately given to the world; it is difficult
to suggest an excuse for the carelessness of this statement. The real
wages are little more than one-half of that which Lord Dufferin assured
the English people Irish labourers were receiving. The statement

---

* Lord Dufferin says, "In justification of my general statement as to the rise of
wages, I may mention that in his evidence before Mr. Maguire's Committee, Judge
Longfield estimated the increase between 1844 and 1860 at *from 25 to 80 per cent.*"
I confess I do not know the meaning of a rise from 25 to 80 per cent. Neither
advance would bear out Lord Dufferin's statement that "the wages of labour (I
presume Lord Dufferin here means agricultural labour) have doubled within the last
fifteen years."

I am disposed to think that in quoting this, as Mr. Longfield's evidence, Lord
Dufferin has fallen into some mistake.

I have searched in vain through his printed evidence for such a statement.
"From 25 to 80 per cent." is very unlike the accuracy of that distinguished
gentleman.

I have, however, found in the evidence of Mr. M'Carthy Downing an important
statement that in his opinion the Irish labouring class were not in a better condition
in 1864 than they were in 1846.

He made to this statement the remarkable and important addition that the late Mr.
Senior, whose position unquestionably gave him better means of judging than any man
in Ireland, had very strongly the same opinion.

It is quite plain that this is a subject deserving of much more investigation than it
has yet received.

was made with all the circumstantiality of time and place. " Fifteen years ago, when I was in the West." It pledged Lord Dufferin's personal knowledge to a part of the statement, it appeared to pledge it to the whole. And this was done in a controversy in which Lord Dufferin had volunteered to come forward as the impugner of the accuracy of others—to convict Mr. Maguire and Mr. Bright of having inaccurately represented to the people of England the condition of Ireland. For a misrepresentation so wonderfully incorrect in its general statement—so marvellously, I might almost say miraculously, put together, as to convey a wrong impression in every detail of the combination of its words—nothing in Lord Dufferin's explanation furnishes anything like a sufficient excuse.

No one will suppose that in his original statement, precise and circumstantial as it was, Lord Dufferin had any intention of deceiving the English people, whom he undertook to inform. Apart from higher reasons, the very nature of the subject forbids even the suspicion. It was a public matter upon which no one could expect a misstatement to pass uncorrected. Nevertheless, the statement was—as I have said, a positive, precise, and most circumstantial testimony as to a state of things alleged to exist in Ireland—in its plain and literal meaning, entirely contrary to the fact. Lord Dufferin fell, no doubt, into some strange confusion between some exceptional high wages of which he had heard, and which were running in his memory, and the ordinary rate of agricultural wages of which he was writing. But, unfortunately, those who read letters in the newspapers know only what is written or printed, and have no means of even guessing at the confusion in the writer's mind which makes him say one thing when he means another. Indeed, in the case of Lord Dufferin, the suspicion of such a confusion is the very last thing that would enter into his reader's mind. The more clear and lucid the style the less could he imagine it. The mischief is as great as if the misleading had been intentional. Lord Dufferin's original statement was given to the public with all the weight and authority of Lord Dufferin's high character and name. It was so given in the most influential organ of opinion and information in the world. It was even believed by thousands and tens of thousands of Englishmen who are desirous of obtaining accurate information on the state of Ireland, and who, not unnaturally, received with implicit credence any statement made by Lord Dufferin in a letter to *The Times*. It is still believed by many of them—for the retractation has not been as full, as distinct, or as widely circulated as it ought to have been. Lord Dufferin has never written to the journal in which his statement was published to confess his mistake. No statement could be more calculated to injure the cause of Ireland. What sympathy could any Englishman have with those who complain of Irish misery while we are rich enough to pay our agricultural labourers a higher rate than

Englishmen receive? It brands as deceivers those who have said that want of employment is driving the Irish people from their homes. And this statement, thus wholly misrepresenting our condition, has been circulated throughout England on Lord Dufferin's authority, and as a fact within his knowledge, and except in the meagre and bewildering explanation I have quoted, no retractation of it has ever yet appeared. Lord Dufferin has published none in the great journal in which he gave the statement to the English nation.

But Lord Dufferin's explanation, or rather his original statement as amended by that explanation, is open to a graver, or at least more important criticism—the criticism which denies, or at least questions, the existence of any remuneration for " unskilled manual labour in Ireland" to which the description of Lord Dufferin can possibly apply. Lord Dufferin gives us no more accurate account of the occupation he means than by calling it " the best description of unskilled manual labour," and in another passage " such labour as is employed on railways and by contractors." If by the labour employed by railways, he means the men employed as porters, and in other inferior capacities, I believe he has exaggerated their wages ; but whether or not, such wages are fixed by railway companies to give their servants good places, and supply no test whatever of the general condition of the country. It would be a perfect absurdity to say that the wages of such persons have been doubled within the last fifteen years. If they have been raised at all they have been raised merely to meet an increase in the price of the necessaries of life. As to the labour employed generally through the south and west of Ireland by contractors I am utterly at a loss to know what it is. I cannot reason upon an unknown quantity. If Lord Dufferin speaks of the workmen known as " navvies," the whole assertion, as applied to them, is unspeakably absurd. Their labour is certainly not generally classed with " the best unskilled manual labour."

Even in the difficulty of dealing with an unknown quantity, and groping and guessing at the meaning of these hieroglyphical expressions, I think I may venture with confidence to say that there does not exist in Ireland " any unskilled manual labour," of any class or kind, to which the expression could be applied, I will, not say with accuracy, but without palpable absurdity, that within the last fifteen years " their rate of wages gradually advanced, in the south and west, from half-a-crown and five shillings to a rate ranging from ten shillings to twelve shillings and even fourteen shillings a week, while in the North the labourer is almost absolutely the master of the market, and can dictate whatever terms he pleases."

At all events, so far as relates to the wages of agricultural labourers, into whose condition alone we are enquiring, in connexion with the land question, Lord Dufferin's dream of wages ranging from ten to twelve or fourteen shillings a week in the South and West of Ireland, and the labourer dictating his own terms in the

North, must be classed with the unrealized visions of Irish prosperity, which are so often and so cruelly mocking our hopes.

Lord Dufferin's letters have never been published in a collected form. Such a publication has been expected, if not promised. If ever the expectation or the promise be realized, I venture to predict that the publication will be accompanied by a retractation, or a modification for all purposes of argument equivalent to a retractation, of many of the most striking statements they contain.

I hope I will be forgiven by Lord Dufferin if I say that it is not only in his historical statements, and in his estimate of the present amount of wages, that we can detect the traces of a similar inaccuracy of thought. Could there be a greater instance of it than that which occurs in the following passage in his second letter :—

"But it is well known that vast numbers of the cottier tenantry, instead of emigrating, were converted into labourers, and either found employment in the neighbourhood of their own place, or removed into the adjoining town, or came over to England, while hundreds of others were provided for by being placed in possession of some of the 160,000 farms which, as I have already stated, have been created since the famine year."

ONE HUNDRED AND SIXTY THOUSAND FARMS CREATED SINCE THE FAMINE YEAR; and these farms have provided for the evicted tenants ! The landlords have turned their tenants out of one farm to place them upon another ! !

" The cottier tenantry removed into the adjoining towns ! ! ! "

I must quote, in contrast with this passage, the description given of this very removal of these cottiers, by Mr. James O'Connell, in a speech I have already quoted, at a meeting in Tralee :—   .

"They were hunted like wild beasts. . . . I say with as much solemnity as if I were giving testimony in a court of justice, that it would be impossible for me to describe the odious acts of oppression that were then perpetrated. . . . The poor were driven into the town, estates were cleared, and notices to quit were served. If that did not answer, the houses were levelled. Perhaps fifty families were cleared for every three or four kept. The only refuge of those poor creatures then was to go into the town. The young and healthy, and those who could afford it, left the country for England or Scotland ; for emigration to America was not as easy then as it is now. The old, the indigent, and infirm, came into the towns, went into those dens that Mr. Downing described, and dragged out a miserable existence, at most for a few years, and then become chargeable on the town electoral division." *

This is the process which Lord Dufferin describes by the euphemism, the evicted " cottier tenantry removed into the towns." And it is by a reference to this process he discreetly vindicates the

* Speech of Mr. James O'Connell, *ante*—Note to page 123.

Irish landlords against the charge of having caused emigration by their evictions!

Those who were evicted did not emigrate—they went into the towns. It is quite true, my Lord—Lord Dufferin forces me say it—THEY DID NOT EMIGRATE, they had not the means—and they were not given them—they went into the towns to meet the fate which Mr. O'Connell describes, or—I say it with shrinking—they crawled to the poorhouse, or they perished—many of them did so—by the way side or in the fields.

But as to the creation of 160,000 farms—how is this proved? The proof is that holdings over fifteen acres have been increased by the very simple process of the consolidation of farms. Lord Rosse, as we shall presently see, correctly describes that process as frequently consisting of the addition of the holding of an evicted tenant to the farm of his next neighbour. Of course there is one farm of twenty acres where before there were two of ten. This process cannot go on without multiplying the number of the larger farms, and this Lord Dufferin treats, in reasoning, as the creation of 160,000 farms, affording a place for the very tenants whose eviction caused the consolidation. In truth, throughout every one of Lord Dufferin's letters it is taken for granted that the effect of all the evictions has been to increase the number of farms. His syllogism is this:—A farm of fifteen acres is the smallest farm which a tenant ought to hold. The evictions have increased the number of farms over fifteen acres—therefore, they have increased the number of farms. In subsequent reasoning this proposition is used as if it were established that there has been a numerical increase in the actual farms. It is obviously a very different thing to say that farms have increased in number, if we mean agricultural holdings above fifteen acres in extent, or to use the very same set of words with the meaning that the number of all actual agricultural holdings has increased. Lord Dufferin begins by proving the first proposition—he uses it afterwards as if he had established the second. And yet even Lord Lifford regards this reasoning as unanswerable! and the most intelligent of English journalists adopt the formula, when quoting Lord Dufferin's assertion, " Lord Dufferin has proved!!"

I may refer to the same class of statements the guarded and softened language in which Lord Dufferin speaks of the evictions of former years. In his very first letter, while Lord Dufferin gives the hesitating admission—

"That many acts of harshness and cruelty have been perpetrated in Ireland, more particularly during the time of the famine, I have no doubt."

He qualifies it by the addition—

"In all countries there have been unrelenting creditors who have insisted on their pound of flesh; but would it not be unreasonable on that account to stigmatize the recovery of debt as injustice?"

Any language which implies that the clearances which were made some years ago on Irish estates were the mere isolated instances of harsh enforcement of legal rights which occur in every state of society, does not accurately describe the events that did occur. To say that the acts then perpetrated were not acts of injustice because law was on the side of the perpetrator, is to confound all the distinctions of right and wrong. Lord Dufferin "has no doubt" that many acts of cruelty "were committed," just as "in all countries there have been unrelenting creditors who have insisted on their pound of flesh." There is not a man in Ireland who has a doubt, that, even before the introduction of poor laws, still more at the time of the famine, a system of general eviction was adopted upon a large number of estates, a number large enough to prevent us from treating them as altogether "exceptional" cases. The phrase which designated such a process as "a clearance" became a household and familiar word in Ireland. There were many counties in Ireland in which popular indignation fastened the odious epithet of the "crowbar brigade" upon those who levelled the habitations of the poor. The extermination that was thus carried out did not consist of mere isolated acts.

There are many districts in Ireland, which bear to this day the traces of that relentless havoc. I know nothing more intensely painful in a travel through Ireland, than to cast one's eyes over rich and verdant fields, and see everywhere the roofless walls of dwellings that had once been human homes—to perceive the traces of the "leveller" upon the half-tumbled gables of the peasants' habitations—and to be told, when you enquire, that these are the marks of the desolating "clearance." Let us argue this question fairly on its true grounds; we do not so argue it when we start with palliative descriptions of that mighty extermination. It was no casual exercise of individual hardheartedness—it was no isolated oppression by a creditor here and there enforcing his pound of flesh. It was too often wide enough and general enough to be regarded as the movement of a class. It would be hard, it would be unjust, even under the indiscreet provocation of the palliatives of their advocate, to speak thus of a whole class. There were landlords, ay, many landlords in Ireland, who nobly struggled to aid and support their tenantry in the sore visitation with which it pleased God to visit the land. But it is vain to deny it, there were whole districts of Ireland where extermination was the rule. I have no wish to bring back these things to mind. But the question between the landowners and the Irish people cannot and must not be argued upon the supposition that acts of oppression and cruelty have been "few and far between." With just as much truth might we say that the visits of the leveller "were like angel's visits." These acts of cruelty and oppression would be most unjustly imputed to all, or even the majority of Irish land-owners; but they were quite numerous enough to entitle us, for the purpose of practical legislation, to regard them as the acts of a class. There is but one way in which landlords, as a class, can escape the odium of these acts, and that is by consenting to lay down the power which enables them to be committed.

I reserve to a future page some observations which I propose to offer on a letter from Lord Dufferin which has appeared in *The Times* of the 1st of February, in which he distinctly criticises the plan I have prepared; and I proceed, in the first instance, to make some comments on a publication which seems to me to be one of the most instructive that has ever appeared upon the subject of tenant right, although I am not sure that the instruction I gather from it is that which its noble author intended it should convey. It comes, however, from a nobleman eminently entitled, by his scientific attainments, his ability, and his character, to command for everything that falls from his pen the respect of his countrymen. I refer, I need scarcely say, to the pamphlet of Lord Rosse.* Of the fifty-three pages which that pamphlet contains, twenty-three are devoted to an examination of the arguments of Mr. Mill, drawn from the science of political economy, in favour of the system of peasant proprietors. In any observations I may make upon his pamphlet, I will confine myself to the first thirty pages, in which his Lordship professes to deal practically with the land question, and with the suggestions made in relation to it; among others, with the possibility of passing a measure, the description of which I believe I may fairly regard as intended for the "Act of Parliament" which I have myself pro-posed:—

"*A cunningly devised Act of Parliament which would break through the contract, and give the tenants, without purchase, some of the privileges of owners.*"

It is impossible for any one carefully to read these thirty pages without seeing that Lord Rosse admits the whole case, which incon-testably establishes the necessity of legislative interference. He admits, and he justifies, the refusal of leases, not on any grounds connected with property, but on political considerations. "There

---

* *A Few Words on the Relation of Landlord and Tenant in Ireland and in other parts of the United Kingdom. By the Earl of Rosse.*

is no doubt," says Lord Rosse, " a strong objection to make leases."
There are apprehensions entertained in which Lord Rosse does
not share—that Parliament may be induced to pass some measure
of tenant right:—

" So long as these apprehensions exist many will be reluctant to make
leases. *They think if they have to contend for their rights they had better do
so with their hands untied.*"

And more than this—I pray the attention of every reader to
what follows. They are the words of Lord Rosse:—

" The apprehension with some goes even further, extending not merely
to the leasing BUT TO THE LETTING OF LAND. Some people ask the question—is it not safer to farm the land ourselves? And, in point of fact,
a great many small proprietors, just as in England, have long farmed
their own estates, and with, I understand, a favourable pecuniary result."

What is the obvious meaning of these sentences? Plainly this—
that the owners of the soil in Ireland have such a distrust of the
occupiers that they will not trust them with leases, but insist on
keeping them as tenants at will.

With what object? " That if they have to contend for their
rights THEY MAY FIGHT THE BATTLE WITH THEIR HANDS
UNTIED."

Their hands untied by leases. In other words, their distrust of
the occupiers is such that the landlords think it necessary to retain
in their hands the power of driving the people from the soil whenever such a measure will aid them in fighting the battle for that
which they please to consider their right.

But Lord Rosse's description of the state of feeling on the part
of the landlords to the tenantry does not end even here. " The
apprehension extends not merely to the leasing BUT EVEN TO THE
LETTING OF THE LAND." That is, there are landlords who distrust the people so much that they will not even trust them with a
tenancy from year to year, but to avert the creation of such a
tenancy cultivate their own estates. What is this but the extermination of the people? The cultivation of his own estate is
adopted by the landlord not because he believes it the best for his
interest, but because he has " apprehensions" which cause him to
refuse to permit tenants to exist on that estate. Is not this to say—
and say in the strongest words—that the relations of the owners
and occupiers are not regulated by any economic laws, but by the
rankling and deep-rooted hostility between classes, which disturbs
the natural operation of all these laws. The comparatively few
persons who possess the land in Ireland find it necessary, for the
defence of their rights, that they should either at once drive the
people from the soil, or retain the power of doing so, in order that

L

when the proper time comes "they may be able to fight the battle with their hands untied."

In the *Plea for the Celtic Race* I ventured to make, in milder terms, this very statement of the feelings and motives which I believed to be most unhappily influencing the landlord classes in Ireland. I endeavoured to point out that the distrust—to use no stronger phrase—which exists between the owners and occupiers of the soil had led latterly to a systematic refusal on the part of landlords to grant leases; and to all the consequent evils of insecurity of tenure and resulting serfdom on the part of the tenant. All these assertions are now more than confirmed by the distinguished authority of Lord Rosse, with this significant addition, he tells us, that this distrust has led landlords, in some instances, not only to refuse any security to the occupier, but absolutely to deny him a place in which to live upon his native soil.

This testimony, borne by such a person as Lord Rosse, is surely calculated to excite grave and melancholy reflections in the mind of any man who will weigh and consider all that it implies. What peace or prosperity can there be in a country in which such principles guide the actions of the landlords? What man with any spirit or independence will remain in a country in which he can only obtain a place to live, upon terms which leave his landlord's hands "untied" to strike the fatal blow that is to ruin him, whenever the caprice or the passions of that landlord will tell him that the blow is necessary in the contest for his rights? What tenant will improve his lands on such a tenure? In the absence of a lease, Lord Rosse tells us, "the landlord's honour is the tenant's security for fair dealing." The honour of a landlord who tells him fairly that he refuses him the lease that he may keep his hands untied in the battle which he anticipates!

To me the most melancholy feature of this dismal picture is the fact that Lord Rosse gives to such a landlord policy more than the implied sanction of his character and name. When Lord Rosse, speaking for the landowners, says that, looking to a battle for their rights, they think it better "to keep their hands untied," it surely is not too much to describe the present relation of landlord and tenant as one of "suppressed civil war."

With such an avowal on the part of Lord Rosse, extending even to the statement that the owners of land are "asking the question IS IT NOT SAFER TO TILL THE LAND OURSELVES;" of what use are all Lord Dufferin's statistics to prove that emigration is not caused by the landlords. When landlords ask "of themselves such questions must not tenants ask of themselves" another—whether it be not safer for them at once to fly from their native land? Where landlords act upon the principles of Lord Rosse emigration is the only safety for the tenant.

The statement is so important, as throwing the clearest light on what is passing in the minds of landowners, that I must quote it at length:—

"Many are dissatisfied that leases are not freely given by Irish landlords. In the absence of a lease, the landlord's honour is the tenant's security for fair dealing ; and, throughout the greater part of the province of Ulster, where the tenant by old customs dating many generations ago enjoy certain privileges, that security has been found sufficient. An attempt was made in 1852, upon imperfect information, to improve that security ; but it was soon found that the opposite effect would be produced, and it fell to the ground.

"There is no doubt a strong objection to make leases; every one well recollects the ruin brought upon estates by the subdivision of land, which took place under them. There is, perhaps, no one thing which injured the agricultural districts so much as such leases : the estate of Lord Palmerston, already referred to, is a sample. In 1828 an Act was passed to prevent subdivisions : in 1832 that Act was virtually repealed, it was said, under pressure from Mr. O'Connell—that was the year of the Reform. Another Act was passed in 1860, containing a clause against subdivision ; there is still a strong feeling of doubt as to whether that would be effectual. There is also another objection. In the counties there is an occupation-franchise ; in many the occupiers have swamped the owners, and members have been returned to Parliament unconnected by property with the county. As they have no standing in the county they must rest their claims upon the promise of political services, and could they but persuade the occupiers that the land having been once let to them, it would be possible to procure a cunningly-devised Act which would break through the contract, and give them without purchase some of the privileges of owner, the prospect would be very tempting, and a better election-cry there could not be. Some, no doubt, rather scrupulous, would say that the proceeding would not be honest ; it would at once occur to them that it was like the case of the man who had lent his horse to his friend to ride, and the friend having cut off the mane and tail, brought in a large bill for improvements, and upon the strength of it demanded joint ownership. However, such scruples are often easily reasoned away, when clever men undertake the task. The members thus returned for the counties would find many powerful auxiliaries in the boroughs; to this body of some thirty or forty members would be added such men as have expressed strong opinions adverse to the rights of the landed proprietor, whether English or Irish. They fear lest this powerful body, watching their opportunity, taking advantage of the exigencies of party, might succeed in inflicting upon them some grievous wrong. I have no such fear. Parliament would never pass such a measure : it would affect English property almost as soon as Irish. No special pleading would succeed in devising an excuse for treating property as one thing in Ireland, and another thing in England, Wales, and Scotland.

"It cannot, however, be said that such apprehensions are unreasonable; and so long as they exist, many will be reluctant to make leases. They think if they have to contend for their rights, it will be better to do so with their hands untied. This apprehension with some goes even further, extending not merely to the leasing, but even to the letting of land. Some people ask the question, is it not much safer to farm the land ourselves? And, in point of fact, a great many small proprietors, just as in England, have long farmed their own estates and with, I understand, a favourable pecuniary result. It is very desirable that the farmers should calmly consider all this, and ask themselves whether it is just to blame the landed proprietors, who, under these circumstances, hesitate to let on lease; and whether, if they were in their place, they would not perhaps do the same."

Let us examine this statement with the attention which it deserves as an authoritative exposition (at least an exposition upon the highest authority attainable in such a case) of the feelings and motives which influence the landowners in refusing leases to their tenantry—and so keeping them without any security of tenure. This is exactly the information which is required for the adoption of satisfactory legislation on the Irish land question.

The first object of the landlords in refusing leases is a social or economic one; there is the danger, that once the landlord's hands were tied, the tenant might permit an increase of population upon his farm. Lord Rosse, it will be remembered, is here not speaking for himself, but giving us an account of the feelings and motives which influence the landlord class, especially in the refusal of leases. One of the reasons of that refusal is the fear that granting leases may lead to an over-population of the country.

It is not easy to deal with this part of the question, and yet this very declaration opens up to us one of its most important portions.

So far as the granting of a lease may tend to promote an excess of population by the subdivision of farms, Lord Rosse appears to think that there are decisions of the Irish Courts of Justice which interfere with the enforcement of clauses in leases, prohibiting sub-divisions. I do not know of any such. I am quite sure that it is not only possible, but easy, to draw covenants in a lease which would give to the landlord the most effectual power of prohibiting a subdivision. If I may venture to refer to my own "cunningly devised Act of Parliament," which gives the tenant a 63 years lease, it gives it to him with restrictions against subdivision, which the shortest and simplest appeal to a legal tribunal could most certainly enforce. It is one of the few subjects connected with this question upon which I may assume to know more than Lord Rosse; and, I think I may venture to assure him that he may grant leases to his tenants, and insert in them covenants against subletting which no court of justice, not even an Irish one, can possibly refuse to enforce.*

---

* Lord Rosse in his pamphlet mentions two cases—one his own, the other Lord Derby's, in which it was found impossible to enforce covenants against subletting :—
"There was a lease apparently drawn with great care to prevent subdivision, ending with a sweeping covenant against alienation. The tenants were still in the act of

But there is, unfortunately, more—much more—in the statement than this. The dread of an excessive population has become an active and moving principle with most Irish landowners. I will not now stop to inquire whether this fear of the presence of human beings be not in itself the deepest proof of the wretchedness of our country. It is enough for us to know that events have happened which have burned and branded this fear of over-peopling deep upon the hearts of the proprietary class. We did not need even the testimony of Lord Rosse to assure us that the protection which the landlord seeks is one against the multiplication of people on his estate. This, as I have already pointed out, is the inevitable effect of the poor law, enacted without a law of settlement. So long as there was no obligation on property to provide for poverty, many of the landowners never troubled themselves about the subdivision of farms; they let cottiers multiply, because cottiers swelled their rents. When there was a prospect of a poor law some of the most prudent, or the most hard-hearted, began to clear their estates. When the law actually passed, numbers of others followed their example.* To this hour one of the actuating motives with the proprietary class in refusing leases is to keep the occupiers so entirely under their control that they may prevent the settling on the land of a single human being who may afterwards, by possibility, come upon the rates. Hence it is that with every Irish landlord the most popular remedy for every evil of the country is emigration. Hence it is that no man, not even Mr. Mill, knows even the elements of political economy unless he adopts, as an axiom, the theory that Ireland is over-peopled. Hence, too, many of the restrictions, which it seems at first sight a mere capricious tyranny to impose upon Irish tenants at will.

When we read of a widow lady being evicted because she brought a widowed daughter to reside in her house—of "rules of the estate" which punish with eviction any tenant who marries, or permits any of his family to marry, without a written license from the agent—of injunctions enforced by the penalties of eviction that

subdividing the land, and the farm besides had been alienated. This appeared to me to be an extreme case, and the best counsel's opinion was taken; but the opinion was decisive that nothing could be done. Lord Derby produced a similar lease in the House of Lords, upon which he had taken counsel's opinion, and with the same result; so that it was quite clear that the courts had been so hampered by previous decisions that they could do nothing."

Either the covenant must have been very ill drawn or some act of the landlord himself must have waived the forfeiture which the violation of the covenant created.

English not *Irish* decisions have long since determined that if such a covenant have been once waived by the landlord, it is altogether gone. This was probably the difficulty in the cases to which Lord Rosse refers. The Irish Judges are not answerable for it. It is as old as the days of Lord Coke.

* "Nearly two-thirds of the whole of the lands of Ireland have fallen out of lease, and are now held by occupiers at will. The landlords are rapidly clearing their estates in apprehension of the effects of the poor law."—*Sir Matthew Barrington's Letter to Sir Robert Peel,* 1844—*Land Tenure in Ireland,* p. 44.

two families should never live under the same roof—of rules made peremptory on all tenants that they should not harbour a visitor or a lodger—of stern decrees which prohibit them from giving a night's shelter to a homeless wanderer, we, at first, regard these things as the mere caprices of a wanton and objectless tyranny.*

* Very few persons are aware of the extent to which restrictions of this nature are enforced upon Irish estates.
I brought forward in the *Plea for the Celtic Race* some instances of this nature which have fallen under my own knowledge (Third Edition, pp. 36, 37). I invite the special attention of the reader to the testimony of Mr. Molloy, which I there cited—a testimony amply confirmed by all the information which I have since received from many independent quarters.
These restrictions are as old as the institution of the Poor Law. Perhaps the most remarkable instances of their cruel operation is to be found in an occurrence which, as long back as the year 1851, was brought before the readers of *The Times* by that excellent and truly philanthropic writer who has made the initials "S. G. O." familiar to all those who love justice.
On the estate of the Marquis of Lansdowne, in Kerry, an order of this nature had been issued. I will not attempt to weaken the effect of the narrative of "S. G. O." by any paraphrase:—
"On the estate of the Marquis of Lansdowne there lived, a few months ago, a man and his wife, Michael and Judith Donoghue; they lived in the house of one Casey. An order has gone forth on the estate (a common order in Ireland) that no tenant is to admit any lodger into his house. This was a general order. It appears, however, that sometimes special orders are given, having regard to particular individuals. The Donoghues had a nephew, one Denis Shea. This boy had no father living. He had lived with a grandmother who had been turned out of her holding for harbouring him. Denis Shea was twelve years old—a child of decidedly dishonest habits. Orders were given by the driver of this estate that this child should not be harboured upon it. This young Cain, thus branded and prosecuted, being a thief—he had stolen a shilling, a hen, and done many other such crimes as a neglected twelve-year-old famishing child will do—wandered about. One night he came to his aunt Donoghue, who lodged with Casey. He had the hen with him.
"Casey told his lodgers not to 'allow him in the house,' as the agent's drivers had given orders about it. The woman, the child's aunt, took up a pike, or pitchfork, and struck him down with it ; the child was crying at the time. The man Donoghue, his uncle, with a cord tied the child's hands behind his back. The poor child after a while crawls or staggers to the door of one Sullivan, and tried to get in there. The maid of Sullivan called to Donoghue to take him away. This he did; but he after-wards returned with his hands still tied behind his back. Donoghue had already beaten him severely. The child seeks refuge in other cabins, but is pursued by his character—he was so bad a boy, the fear of the agent and the driver—all were forbidden to shelter him. He is brought back by some neighbours, in the night, to Casey's, where his uncle and aunt lived. The said neighbours tried to force the sinking child in upon his relations. There is a struggle at the door. The child was heard asking some one to put him upright. In the morning there is blood upon the threshold. The child is stiff dead—a corpse, with its arms tied ; around it every mark of a last fearful struggle for shelter—food—the common rights of humanity.
"The Donoghues were tried at the late Kerry assizes. It was, morally, a clear case of murder ; but it was said, or believed, that these Donoghues acted not in malice to the child, but under a sort of sense of self-preservation ; that they felt to admit him was to become wanderers themselves. They were indicted for man-slaughter, and found guilty."
Those who know the superstitious charity with which the Irish people entertain strangers, the warm and tender affection with which they cherish the feelings of kindred, will understand the terrible coercion under which this poor boy was driven from the doors.
Yet the estates of the Marquis of Lansdowne are considered among the best managed in Ireland. It suggests very strange reflections to observe that several times during the examination of witnesses before the committee of 1864, those who cross-

They are not so. They are the result of a determination, at all hazards and by any means, to keep down the poor rate. To prevent the possibility of the people multiplying, the occupiers must be kept in a state of serfdom.

Statements of this nature suggest the reflection that in this, perhaps, short-sighted view of their position, the Irish landlords are interested in diminishing and getting rid of the population, as well as in preventing its increase. But if the owners of the soil are taught to believe that the country is over-peopled, and if they think it their direct interest to prevent or diminish the presence of an excessive population which one day or other may be a burden to themselves, can we wonder that some how or other the people are driven out?

The second objection is a political one :—

"There is also another objection. In the counties there is an occupation franchise. In many the occupiers have swamped the owners, and Members have been returned to Parliament unconnected by property with the county."

This is the second objection to the granting of leases. Lord Rosse appears to consider the right of choosing representatives to be vested not in the occupiers but in the owners, and he regards persons connected by property with the county as having an exclusive right to its representation. This may be the theory of the British constitution or it may not, but when it is assigned as an objection to granting leases that the occupiers have presumed to "swamp the owners" by choosing the persons whom they thought best fitted to represent them, the meaning is, that the tenants must be kept in a state of practical servitude lest they may exercise independently their political rights? The landlord's "hands must be untied," in order that if they vote against his wishes he may be able to turn them out.

The third objection is one compounded of the other two— Irish landlords hesitate to give leases or even to create a tenantry on their estates because they apprehend that legislation might possibly be adopted which would confer some rights upon any person who should be a tenant at the time of its adoption, and therefore, in the emphatic words of Lord Rosse, "Some people ask themselves the question is it not much safer to farm the lands ourselves?"

examined the "tenant right" witnesses repeatedly put questions as to this very estate, as if it were one with regard to which no one would dare to suggest the necessity of legislative interference.

I believe that if the whole truth were known the "best managed" properties are often those upon which the serfdom of the tenant is the most abject and complete.

Similar edicts are at this moment enforced upon hundreds of Irish estates.

This is exactly what was said last year when the late Government proposed their measure of tenant compensation—Ministers and Parliament were distinctly warned that if such a measure were likely to pass, it would be a signal throughout Ireland for one universal notice to quit.

Except for that which I regard as a calamity—the implied approval which Lord Rosse expresses of the feelings and policy of his class, I cannot find one word to object to in his statement. That statement, unhappily, contains all the elements upon which I relied on as making out the argument for legislative interference. The Irish landowners are keeping the occupiers under their absolute dominion. And this I traced to the operation of the poor law—to the granting of the elective franchise to the occupier—to the political antagonism which exists between landlord and tenant—and to all the causes which have resulted in relations of hostility and distrust.

But again I said that this state of things was of recent origin—that in old times leases were granted. I quote again the testimony of Lord Rosse, omitting the intervening sentences in which he refers to the evil of the increase of population. That is a matter of opinion. Here is his testimony as to facts:—

" I well recollect the glowing terms in which several old people in our neighbourhood were wont to speak of the plenty in their younger days—bread, meat, and the best ale being the ordinary peasant's fare."

" It was the practice then to do that which is now so much recommended—to make long leases."

Lord Rosse is of opinion that these long leases enabled the tenant to subdivide his holding, and that this has been the origin of our evils. Even if this were true the natural inference would seem to be this:—We should return to the system of long leases, which produced the comfort, and prohibit the subdivision which destroyed it. I have already offered some observations on this subject of "middlemen" and subdivision. Lord Rosse's testimony confirms what I have said; but I am now only anxious to direct attention to the remarkable testimony contained in this passage. There was a time when, in Ireland, bread, meat, and the best ale were the ordinary peasant's fare. We are distant only by two links of tradition from that time.* This tradition of prosperity

* I may observe to Lord Dufferin that this must have been *after* all restrictions on the woollen manufacture had been removed, and *after* all the mischief created by the restrictions had been done. Lord Rosse is, most probably, preserving the traditions of the period just before the Union, when Ireland had improved in commerce, in agriculture, and in manufactures, faster than any nation upon earth.

There are strange traditions of the abundance experienced by some classes even in olden times. Living was not dear in Kerry when salmon was bought for a penny a pound, lobsters for one penny, rising to two-pence each, fat turkeys for nine-pence each, is not inconsistent with the stories of wretchedness which written accounts have shown.   There was a class of that people whom that prosperity did not reach.   The " ordinary peasants," described by Lord Rosse, were the higher class of tenants who lived in the farm houses of the farms now occupied by the serfs.

Let me call attention to another passage in Lord Rosse's tract. This is his prospect for the future :—

" The value of land, no doubt, will rise.   It is not in the nature of things that so great a disparity in this respect between England and Ireland will long continue.   As land becomes more valuable farm buildings will be provided everywhere.   No farm unprovided with proper buildings will then command a tenant, and there will be no want of capital for the purpose, *as is evident from the purchases in the Landed Estates Court*, and the large deposits in the banks (£17,000,000).   The tenant will say to the landlord, if you do not provide farm buildings as good as the English tenant has I will not take the farm.   I am willing to pay a fair rent, and I am entitled to suitable buildings."

And Lord Rosse adds—

" I believe that time will soon come, unless progress be retarded by injudicious legislation."

I earnestly wish that Lord Rosse had pointed out the process by which such a state of things can be brought about in Ireland, that land will be let in the same manner as in England, or in which the landlord's farms will remain unlet unless he is prepared to make the outlay required to put them into the same state as that in which an English farm is let.   I am unable to see how the £17,000,000 deposited by the tenant farmers in the banks will be available for such a purpose.   That sum will only be expended when you give the tenant security for his tenure.   Lord Rosse contemplates an expenditure by the landlords amounting to very many millions on their estates.   The only hint he gives us of

and mutton for two-pence a pound.   Yet Arthur Young gives us this enumeration of the prices of his day, and tells us that in Limerick he knew a gentleman "keeping a carriage, four horses, three men, three maids, a wife, three children, and a nurse, all for £500 a year."—Vol. ii., p. 7.

Yet it was in Kerry—but a few years afterwards—that the misery of the labouring classes provoked the first revolt of the Right Boys, and on an estate near that very city of Limerick, were gathering and clustering on the richest soil in Europe the most miserable population of cottiers upon earth.

Well might Bishop Berkely ask, some years before :—

" Whether we are not in fact the only people who may be said to starve in the midst of plenty ? "

It is strange how throughout all the eventful history of Ireland we find this admixture of plenty and starvation, of happiness and misery, in the lot of a people dwelling on the same soil, as if they had been so left side by side, the one to prove how God and nature blessed the country, the other to show how it had been cursed by man.

the source from which this expenditure is to be supplied is the reference to the £25,000,000 expended in purchases in the Landed Estates Court. Does this imply that landlords unable to make the expenditure are to be sold out? The reasoning of Lord Rosse is that such a state of things will arise from a vastly increased emigration. I describe this by saying that I am sure it never could occur until the greater proportion of our people are exterminated. I believe that it would be also indispensable to the process that a large number of the landed proprietors should be sold out. In other words, Irish prosperity is to commence when we have got rid of the largest proportion of the Irish nation. The project is not new. Sir W. Petty once proposed to carry over the Irish people bodily to England, and turn the whole island into a dairy farm, to be managed by 200,000 dairy maids and herds.

Lord Rosse's hope for Ireland is in the advent of a state of things in which tenants would be so independent as to reject a farm unless it is let to them with all farm buildings and in perfect working order, and in which Irish landlords will be so full of money as at once to meet the requisition. I wish that some person of judgment and experience would now form an estimate of the sum which would be required to put all the land of Ireland into the same condition as English farms. It was one of the very first considerations which suggested itself to the acute and business-like mind of Arthur Young when he contrasted the English and the Irish mode of letting. He estimated an expenditure of eighty-eight millions as the very lowest sum which would fit Irish farms for English farmers. He did not forget that when the farms were improved, the farmer must have a capital of his own in addition to that expended by the landlord—this he calculated at twenty millions more.[*] In 1810, Mr. Wakefield, after carefully examining the subject, and with Arthur Young's estimate before him, calculated the sum requisite to put Irish farms into the same letting order as the English, at one hundred and twenty millions. Mr. Fisher, in one of his instructive publications, tells us that in a recent parliamentary debate the sum requisite was calculated at one hundred

---

[*] "I have reason to believe that five pounds sterling per English acre, expended over all Ireland, which amounts to £88,341,136, would not more than build, fence, plant, drain, and improve that country to be upon a par in those respects with England. And farther, that if those 88 millions were so expended, it would take much above 20 millions more (or above 20s. an acre) in the hands of the farmers in stock of husbandry, to put them on an equal footing with those of her sister kingdom ; nor is this calculation so vague as it might at first sight appear, since the expences of improvements and stock are very easily estimated in both countries. This is the resolution of that surprising inferiority in the rent of Ireland : the English farmer pays a rent for his land in the state he finds it, which includes, not only the natural fertility of the soil, but the immense expenditure which national wealth has in the progress of time poured into it ; but the Irishman finds nothing he can afford to pay rent for, but what the bounty of God has given, unaided by either wealth or industry."— *Arthur Young's Tour in Ireland,* Vol. ii., part ii., p. 12.

and fifty millions, or ten pounds for each acre of cultivated land.* A very moderate estimate suggests that taking one farm with another, and supposing all Ireland at the disposal of some layer-out of farms, no "contract company" could have a profit who would undertake to level all the ditches, make new and proper fences, lay down farm roads, thorough drain the soil, build suitable farm houses and offices—in a word, divide all Ireland into large and well-appointed English farms at a contract price of five pounds for every acre of the cultivated land. If the landlords found the seventy or eighty millions, the seventeen millions of tenants' money in the savings' banks would scarcely supply them with the additional capital necessary for the cultivation of such farms.

I cannot help thinking that I answered, by anticipation, the argument which is founded on the assumption that there is the slightest rational prospect of such a result arising from the present state of things.

"I know that there are persons who will say, 'We do not wish to continue the existing state of things; but that state of things is exactly breaking up in the very emigration to which you point. The process is going on by which Ireland will gradually become assimilated to the agricultural districts of England and Scotland, and large farms and capitalist farmers raise off the soil the largest amount of produce for the sustenance of man.'

"The first answer to this is, that it involves the extermination of the people. But we must think, apart from all other considerations, of the long delays, the difficulties, and the dangers of the process.

"If, however, there be any one who thinks that Ireland would be a happier and a richer country if we were to assimilate it to England in its great agricultural forms—I ask him, first: whence is to come the expenditure that is to fit the land for such a state of things? Are Irish landlords prepared at once to incur the expenditure which, in England, has been the slow and gradual accumulation of a long series of years? But I ask him next: is he prepared for the process by which it must be accomplished—the extermination of the people? In England the

---

* " A large outlay is necessary to increase the productiveness of the soil, and expand the wealth of the people. As that outlay will not be made by the landlords, we must consider upon what terms it should be done by the tenants, and whether the equivalent of a lease for thirty-one years is a sufficient compensation.

"Under a lease the tenant contracts to maintain the improvements he may make, and to give them up to the landlord at the expiration of the term—the landlord becomes heir to the tenant's outlay.

" *Will leases for thirty-one years induce the tenants to make the outlay which Ireland requires?*

" One of the advocates of the Bill before Parliament estimated the necessary outlay at *one hundred and fifty millions sterling ;* this is about *ten pounds per acre* on the arable land of Ireland."—*The Land Question,* by Joseph Fisher. Dublin : M'Glashan and Gill.

Mr. Fisher himself estimates, but apparently upon indefinite ground, that it is absolutely necessary to spend fifteen millions upon improving Irish farms ; but this, it is to be observed, is not a calculation of what would be required to bring them *to the English state.*

consolidation of farms has also been slow and gradual. There has been no violent dispossession of occupants : it has been the almost unnoticed result of the operation of causes which caused no rude disturbance—of the growth of manufactures—of the opening up of modes of employment and enterprise, which gradually withdrew the people from the soil. The process in Ireland would be one by which a whole population would at once be driven from their land, their country, and their home. There is a great difference between the adoption of a system by the growth of circumstances and time, and the forcing of that system upon a country in a manner which makes it a revolution. Whether such a change would be desirable or not, it is one that involves the extermination of the greater proportion of the present inhabitants."*

" Unwise, indeed, would be the policy of any British statesman who would secretly acquiesce in the expatriation of that people, in the belief that large farms and English and Scotch farmers might well replace the small farms and Irish cottier tenants that are gradually swept away. Still more desperate would such a policy be on the part of the Irish gentry. The process is one which no interest in Ireland could survive. By the time the land would be cleared of her people all classes would be destroyed, and English proprietors as well as English tenants would be called on to take the place of the present proprietors of the soil."†

Surely in contemplating the state of things described in the passage I have quoted from his pamphlet, Lord Rosse never permitted his mind to dwell upon the intermediate steps that must be gone through before the country could arrive at it. Between us and that state of things a great gulph is fixed—a gulph in which a large proportion of our people, and many, very many, of our landowners must be swallowed up.

I will venture to quote from this remarkable pamphlet one or two passages entirely confirmatory of some other views I have expressed—

" A great change has taken place in Ireland, Now when a farmer is beginning to fail he puts together what he can, and emigrates. The landlord, perhaps, loses two years' rent or more, *but he is compensated in the comfort and happiness resulting to all parties.* The farm is annexed to that of the adjoining tenant."

Is not this just the process which I described as " RAPIDLY COMPLETING THE EXTERMINATION OF THE OLD CELTIC RACE."

Lord Rosse confirms my opinion that the emigration of late years has assumed a new character. The farmer who now throws up his farm is one that can " put together" something wherewith to go. It is not the evicted tenant who now swells the tide of emigration, but the farmer who has still something to take with

---

* *Land Tenure in Ireland,* p. 65.
† *Land Tenure in Ireland,* p. 92.

him, one who—as Lord Rosse describes it—feels himself beginning to fail; as the Bishop of Cloyne tells us—who feels himself unable to bear up against the fatal effects of insecurity of tenure which leaves him no place for his industry.

If this be the character of the recent emigration, of what avail are Lord Dufferin's statistics, cited for the purpose of proving that emigrants consist generally of other persons than evicted tenants?

But has the landlord nothing to do even with emigration like this? With what feelings does the landlord regard the removal of that tenant? He looks upon him as an incumbrance of which he is delighted to be rid. Away with him from his native land! He is not fit to live upon the soil. Even for the loss of two years' rent the landlord is amply compensated in seeing one more of his natural enemies go. Is it likely that a landlord actuated by such feelings will do anything to make that tenant stay? As surely as such feelings influence the landowner so surely will they work the tenant out. Lord Rosse too truly describes the feelings with which the occupier is regarded by his lord.

" The farm is annexed to that of the adjoining tenant." In the face of testimony like this, of what avail are land statistics which show that in this exterminating process farms over fifteen, still more those over thirty acres, are multiplied in number. Of course they are so—because two or three smaller ones are " consolidated" into one.

I say that this farmer fails, and emigrates, exactly because under our present system of land tenure he has no fair play at home, and no confidence that he will have any. Is it possible for him to have it in a country in which it is avowed on the part of the landlords that they will not give him any security of tenure; because, in the battle for their rights they must have their hands untied. Nay, he is further told that the opinion is gaining ground that it is not quite safe to let him occupy even as a tenant at will, and that landlords are asking themselves the question, whether it would not be safer for them to cultivate the lands themselves.

To many of the Irish peasantry these words will have a deep significance. They are no idle threat. There are districts in Ireland in which landlords have cultivated their estates themselves, in which thousands of acres have been cleared of the old people. The owner for a time, has farmed for himself, and after a few years the land has been set in large farms, frequently to English or Scotch tenants.

I admit that the present laws of property would permit of the carrying out of this threat. It would be in the legal power of the Irish landlords to turn off their tenantry and cultivate their estates themselves. When the simultaneous extermination of a whole people is spoken of—as a matter of serious contemplation—it is

high time for legislation to interfere and protect the right of the
people to live upon their native soil.

A threat like this may help us to judge of the claims of proprietary right put forward on behalf of the Irish landlords. It may help
us also to judge of the right of the Legislature to interfere. Suppose
an attempt were made to realize that threat; suppose, upon a given
day, notices to quit were served upon every tenant in Ireland, and
that, with one consent, all Irish landlords were to set about
clearing their estates and cultivating the land themselves. Will it
be said that the Legislature ought to suffer this to be carried out?
Ought the Irish people submit to it if the Legislature did so suffer
it? Is there, after all, such a very great difference if the very same
thing be done piecemeal which if attempted by one fell swoop would
demand legislative interference, and in its absence justify national
resistance? Caligula wished all the Roman people had but one
neck; but it would have made very little difference to the Roman
people if, even with a multitude of necks to deal with, he had
succeeded in chopping off all their heads in detail.

And in a state of society in which the feeling between landowners
and occupiers is such that the landlord will not trust his tenant
with the ownership of the land for the shortest lease and under the
most stringent covenants—in which he must regard that tenant as a
robber in dealing with whom "he must keep his hands untied;" the
occupier is expected to be contented and happy in trusting to the
honour and the mercy of that landlord for the very means of existing in his native land, and for the enjoyment of the fruits of his
industry and toil!

In my view of the land question Lord Rosse's pamphlet is a
most valuable contribution to the cause which is known as that
of " tenant right." It was impossible for Lord Rosse to write on
any subject except truthfully and with knowledge. Because he
has done both he has borne testimony to a state of things
which makes it impossible for Parliament any longer to leave the
relations between landlord and tenant to the uncontrolled operation not of economic laws, but of the evil passions which distract
and divide the proprietary and occupying classes in this country.
The real value and the real importance of the pamphlet consists
in this: we have a clear and frank, although most temperate,
account of the opinions and feelings which influence those who are
now absolute masters of the Irish soil. Do these opinions and
feelings qualify them to exercise absolute dominion over the Irish
people? It is no common or ordinary right of proprietorship
which the Irish landlords have assumed. They have departed
from the old established usages of the country, and insist that " their
hands shall be untied," to deal at any moment with the occupiers as
in their discretion they think fit. They claim to be "the managers"
of their own estates, to have everything controlled by their direction,

and subject to their rule. They take the place—not of proprietors receiving their rents, and, so long as covenants are observed, leaving their tenants to themselves—but of proprietors governing by their authority every movement upon their estate; and in order that they may so govern they are keeping the Irish natives as their tenants at will. The Irish people are to be in a state of pupilage under the mastership of the proprietors.

But among these proprietors we know and are assured that there exists a very strong objection to the over-peopling of the country—that there is a dread of the increase of human beings, and that most of them believe, honestly and fairly believe, that to promote the well-being of the country a large number, even of the existing inhabitants, ought to go away. Is it difficult to see to what the combination of such opinions and such powers must necessarily lead? In the case of landlords thus circumstanced these convictions cannot remain as mere abstract opinions. Unconsciously it may be to themselves, they must influence their conduct.

I have already instanced three most remarkable cases of rules adopted upon estates, by which every tenant is prohibited from receiving even a relative as an inmate on his estate. I believe that we have a very imperfect idea of the extent to which such estate legislation is in force. The " rules of estates" constitute local codes of law, which regulate many acts of the tenant's life. There is certainly one estate—there are, I believe, very many more—upon which the rule is in force to which I have already adverted, the rule which prohibits any marriage taking place among the tenantry without the license of the agent. We have seen that upon another estate a Roman Catholic dignitary was evicted from his farm because he did not dismiss his curate who had made a speech improperly ridiculing the proprietor in the excitement of an election. There is, as in greater jurisprudence, the unwritten as well as the written law; the latter too often resides in the breast of the agent, or even the inferior minister of the estate. This is not the tyranny of middlemen, or of landowners of lower rank. " The rules of the estate " are often the most arbitrary and the most sternly enforced upon great estates, the property of men of the highest station, upon which rents are moderate, and no harshness practised to the tenantry who implicitly submit. Such rules are tyranny and feudalism the moment they go beyond the mere conduct of the tenant in that relation, and attempt to regulate his domestic relations and his home. Every day these rules are extending further and further in that regulation. What shall we say of that rule which is, perhaps, the most general, that which forbids the harbouring of any except the tenant's immediate family in his home.

Rules like these, I repeat, are not confined to tyrannical or bad landlords; they are as general as the dread of over-peopling the land. Is the tenant who is bound to observe such a rule, who fears to violate it even at the bidding of humanity, in a condition as high as that of a serf? What romance that borrowed its " sensational " descriptions from the grim tales of feudal tyranny has ever drawn a darker picture than that of a peasant shutting his door against the benighted traveller because the lord of the neighbouring castle had forbidden strangers to be entertained? If English travellers brought home such tales from Styria or the Tyrol, or even that wilder region,

> " Where the rude Carinthian boor
> Against the houseless stranger shuts the door ;"

how would they speak of feudal serfdom as existing in the Austrian dominions !

I have already adverted in a note to a portion of the statement made by " S. G. O." of one striking instance of this nature. Let me earnestly implore the attention of every right-minded man to the words of the judge who passed sentence on the peasants who, in the execution of one of these inhuman orders, had been accessary to the death of the poor helpless victim of the barbarous policy of a " well managed" estate. The Chief Baron, in passing that sentence, thus addressed these miserable serfs :—

"The poor boy whose death you caused was between twelve and thirteen years of age. His mother at one time held a little dwelling from which she was expelled. His father was dead. His mother had left him, and he was alone and unprotected. He found refuge with his grandmother, who held a farm, from which she was removed in consequence of her harbouring this poor boy, as the agent on the property had given public notice to the tenantry that expulsion from their farms would be the penalty inflicted on them if they harboured any persons having no residence on the estate. This poor boy was then left without a house to shelter him or a friend to assist him. He was an unhappy outcast. . . . He went to the house of a man named Coffey, whose wife humanely gave him a little food, but she was afraid to shelter him in her house, as the agent had given orders that distress for twelve months' rent would be made on any tenant who should harbour persons not resident on the estate, and that they would also be expelled from their farms. He is turned adrift to the world, friendless and unprotected. He came to Casey's house, where you, his uncle and aunt, resided. He applied for relief, as he was in a state of destitution. Casey, with whom you lodged, desired you to turn him from the house, as he was afraid the orders of the agent would be enforced against him. . . . You committed the offence, not with a desire to inflict death, but influenced by fear that Casey would be expelled from his holding. The poor child is turned out of doors; and the next proof was, that you, Judith, took a pike-handle and beat him violently with it while lying on the ground. . . . He implored of you to spare him, and he promised to leave the place. He raised himself from the ground, and bound, as he was, went tottering along from house to house, but there was no refuge for the wretched outcast. As a last resource he turned his steps to Coffey's house, but some of the neighbours threatened to tell the agent if Coffey harboured him. Coffey had, however, the humanity to take him to Casey's house, where you resided. He fell twice from weakness and the result of the injuries you inflicted on him. He is supported to the house, and a scene ensued which I find difficult to describe. The door was opened by you, Judith, and a struggle ensues. Coffey and another man endeavoured to force the boy in—you keeping him out. He bleeds profusely. The threshold is smeared with blood. You succeed in keeping him out; and he, unable to walk, rolls himself along the ground, till he gets to the wall, where he remains. Night passes over him, and on the following morning he is found by the neighbours, cold, stiff, and dead. . . . I do not think, however, that you inflicted the injuries with an intention to cause death, it was through fear that the threat would be carried out against Casey. Casey acted under the influence of the threats of those in authority, but such is no justification for the offence. It forms no defence, that such an order was given as that which appeared in evidence on the trial. For an order from the execution of which death ensues is not only not sanctioned by law, but is directly at variance with it."

This is one of the revelations of the actual life of the people which are sometimes made in courts of justice. These tenants resided on an estate, the landlord of which was held up as the very model of a kind, a just, and a liberal landlord. Could any description of human serfdom exceed the picture of abject terror in which these tenants lived? We must argue from individual instances, for it is only by individual instances we can form our judgment. The words I have quoted are the staid and sober words of judicial calmness. Let us see what was proved at this trial.

It was proved that on this estate an order was issued against harbouring in a house any person not a resident upon it.

It was proved that this order was enforced by the sanction of the dreaded penalty of eviction. The Chief Baron's words were:—

" The agent of the property had given public notice to the tenantry that expulsion from their farms would be the penalty inflicted on them if they harboured any one not resident on the estate."

That penalty was actually enforced against a widow for giving food and shelter to a destitute grandson of twelve years' old:—

" The poor boy was between twelve or thirteen years of age. His mother at one time held a little dwelling, from which she was expelled; his father was dead. He found a refuge with his grandmother, WHO HELD A FARM, FROM WHICH SHE WAS REMOVED FOR HARBOURING THE POOR BOY."

The peasant to whose door he comes implores of an inmate of

his house "to turn him away, lest the penalty should be enforced against him."

These miserable serfs, even under the shadow of darkness, feared to do the stealthy charity of giving to the outcast child the shelter of a roof   When one more bold or more tender-hearted than the others offered to receive him—the neighbours rose in terror, and threatened to give information of the broken rule. The terrorism of landlord dominion was complete; and driven from every house, torn by violence from the sacred threshold to which his despairing struggles clung, the miserable child lay down to die, and morning dawned upon his cold and stiffened corpse. This is no fiction. Could, I ask again, any picture of abject—miserable—serfdom be more complete? In what land of slavery, in what clime of eastern oppression, do human beings crouch down in abject terror, from the very instincts of their nature, as these miserable Irish men and women cowered down that night? Is it right or fitting that man should hold over his fellow the terrible dominion to which these poor miserable people sacrificed that wretched child?

The accident of death resulting in this instance caused the revelation of the rule, the penalty, and the terror. But for this accident the deep and wretched slavery of these peasants would have been unknown. How many Irish peasants are crouching and cowering in secret under tyranny like this? Upon how many Irish estates is the order at this moment enforced which forbids a night's lodging to a houseless wanderer, under that terrible penalty, the dread of which froze up every warm gush of charity in the hearts of these Irish and Christian men and women?

Let those who blame me for calling the condition of the Irish tenant serfdom realize if they can the scene of that poor child's death. The terror which the bare thought of sheltering him caused—the crowding of the terrified cottiers to prevent an act that might end in their extermination—the fact, the miserable, the damning fact, that there was not one who dared to violate the edict to save a homeless child from perishing—and let them tell me by what milder terms can such a state of abject submission be called.

Nothing is more vain and unprofitable than a controversy about names. In this instance we see despotic dominion binding men's souls and consciences by a law as absolute and exacting as that by which the slave driver can bind his slave. I care not whether it be called the tyranny of law, or the sacred right of property, or feudal oppression. It is the condition in which Irish people are living under English law. That condition is enforced by that law. If any one of those cottiers had harboured the outcast on that evening, the tribunals of justice would have awarded—if necessary all the power of the executive would have enforced—the penalty of eviction, which would have been inflicted as the punishment of his crime. Had they given way to the instincts of humanity the very same judge who pronounced the just sentence which punished their obedience to an inhuman edict, might, in that very same court-house, have been compelled to award the sentence of eviction, which, disguised under the assertion of a civil right, would really have been the adjudication of the landlord's sentence of punishment for disobedience to his law.

It is impossible for law to be, either in the sight of God or man, altogether irresponsible for the wrong and the tyranny to which it is every day giving effect.

I ought not, perhaps, to pass from Lord Rosse's pamphlet without noticing an objection which he makes to any measure which involves what he regards as " exceptional legislation." I understand by this any legislation which will deal with the relations of landlord and tenant in Ireland—differently from the laws which governs them in England. The assumption that this is a decisive objection to any proposal runs through his entire pamphlet. After stating the rather questionable propositions that the interest of the tenant is to have new purchases made of Irish property, which would give him " a wealthy proprietary, able and anxious to assist him in getting forward," he adds, " the slightest approach to *exceptional* legislation would be a warning to the capitalist to keep off."* " It only remains," he says in another place, "to inquire whether the relations of landlord and tenant could be improved by any measure not open to the very grave objection of being *exceptional*."† Proposing to extend the Montgomery Act to Ireland, he observes in the same page:—" As that Act is still law in Scotland extending it to Ireland would not be *exceptional* legis-lation."‡ Again, in another place, " no special pleading would succeed in devising an excuse for treating property as one thing in Ireland and another thing in England, Wales, and Scotland."§

With reference to the argument which tells the Irish tenant that his true interest is to invite wealthy proprietors to invest capital in land—it plainly points out to the " selling out " of a large number of the present landowners. I am not sure that the experience of many Irish tenants will confirm the assertion that they have found themselves better off under " wealthy proprietors," who have been invited "to invest capital in Irish land," than they were under the old and "insolvent" proprietors. ‖ The question is one involving too many considerations to be incidentally discussed.

* Lord Rosse, page 24.   † Lord Rosse, page 26.
‡ Lord Rosse, page 26.   § Lord Rosse, page 23.
‖ Upon this point the evidence given before Mr. Maguire's Committee, especially the evidence of Judge Longfield, gave us most valuable information. The purchases under the Encumbered Estates Commission have been among the many concurring causes which have been driving the Irish people from their homes. No illustration of this can be stronger than the evidence to which I have already adverted—evidence in which he tells us that he has been compelled to sell estates upon which the custom of tenant right prevailed to a purchaser who bought them with the intention of robbing

I may, however, observe, that in reading arguments of this
nature by which those who use them believe that they show conclusively that it would be greatly for the interest of Ireland to replace by others all the existing class of proprietors and occupiers; it has sometimes occurred to me to ask myself, what is
the meaning of such a proposition. I have been accustomed to
understand by Ireland, not merely a country possessing certain
geographical features, but a country inhabited by a certain people
whom I know; I care nothing for the abstract prosperity of
mountains, and villages, and plains—I care a good deal for the
comfort and happiness of the people whom God has now placed
on them. I understand, in a word, by Ireland, the Irish people;
and when any man proposes to me a plan to create prosperity
in Ireland by substituting a new class of proprietors and
occupiers for the present, I am very much disposed to ask him
whether the present occupiers and proprietors do not in reality
constitute the Irish nation—whether any plan to benefit the
Irish nation must not be a plan to benefit them; and whether
a proposal which gravely proposes to create Irish prosperity by
putting capitalist landlords and capitalist tenant farmers in
place of our present ones be not a proposal to make Ireland a
great country by destroying the Irish nation, I am not capable
of understanding this singular survivorship, and I believe, with
Lord Abercorn, the true question for every statesman is to consider how to make prosperous and happy those who, whether as
occupiers or as owners, are now living upon the Irish soil.

Passing from this, however, let me ask whether there be really
this conclusive objection to "exceptional legislation." I believe
that all legislation must be adapted to the circumstances with
which it deals, and more than this, to the feelings and wants of
the people whom it is to govern. If the circumstances of landed
property in England and Ireland be the same, if the feelings of the
English people and Irish people in respect to it be the same, then,
indeed, it follows that the same legislation on this subject is
applicable to both countries. If the circumstances be wholly
different, if the feelings be wholly dissimilar, no words can
express the folly as well as the wickedness of insisting on the same
legislation for both. The bed of Procrustes fails in supplying
us with an adequate illustration. The very same laws which
in one state of things are beneficent and wise, in another state of
things are inhuman and cruel. The accident of being incorporated
in the same empire does not necessarily alter or assimilate the
conditions of things. When sumptuary laws were in force I can

the tenants of that right, and just because they did so intend were enabled to outbid
competitors who would have respected it.
     Could there be a stronger proof of the necessity and the justice of a measure which
would protect by law the Ulster custom of tenant right.

conceive a law regulating dress very proper in Ireland, which in Canada would have comdemned people to be frozen to death. If any man had insisted in those days against exceptional legislation either for Canada or Ireland, supposing both to have been subject to the dominion of the British Parliament, I do not believe the absurdity would have been as great as that of insisting on treating in the same way the relations of the capitalist farmer to the capitalist landlord of England—and the relations of the Irish tenant farmer, who has not the most remote conception of what capital practically means, to a landlord who would denounce you as a revolutionist, or, if possible, something worse, if you told him that he was bound to let his farms with all proper farm buildings and all proper appliances of cultivation.

When I read some of the proposals that have been made, it seems to me that the great principle is forgotten that no legislation is wise which is not so framed as to be adapted to the wants and the habits of the people. You cannot apply to a country of small holdings and poor tenants the principle which you borrow from a country of great farms and capitalist farmers. Ireland is a country of small holdings, with a great agricultural population settled on the land. We must adapt all our legislation to this state of things. If you tell me that all the condition of our social system must be changed, that all our small farms are to be consolidated into great ones, our poor tenants driven away and capitalist cultivators put in their place, I answer that this is the project of a social revolution—a revolution as great and, at least, as cruel as that which would be accomplished by driving out all the landlords and dividing the estates among a large number of peasant proprietors.

Even this does not express all or nearly all that can be urged in reply to such an argument. If England had been at the time of the Revolution subjected to a confiscation which vested all the property of the country in alien proprietors—if the memories of that confiscation were still branded deep in the hearts of the English people—if a Roman Catholic minority had seized on all the land, all the political power, all the Church revenues, all the social position of the English nation—if English proprietory rights were enforced solely by foreign bayonets—then Irish landlords might say that no rule should be applied to them which was not applied to English property in land.

And if, more than this, it could be shown that every English proprietor held his land upon conditions which bound him not to create a state of things which had now arisen—if it could be established that his very title deeds involved a trust which had never been fulfilled, and imposed conditions which up to this hour were broken—if the result had been in England agrarian crime and national beggary—if the whole English people were flying from

their native land to escape the pressure of English landlordism—
then, and then only, might Irish landlords object to exceptional
legislation.

The advocates of Irish tenant right are those who might justly
denounce exceptional legislation. There is exceptional legislation
for Ireland, because there is legislation which induces an exceptional
state of things. This is the only true test. Give us, on this land
question, equality of legislation. I do not mean in saying so to
refer to the differences between English and Irish law—all of
which, and they are many, are, as we shall see, against the Irish
tenant. Give us equality of law, tested, as law only can be tested,
by its practical result. The tenant in England practically enjoys
independence and security of tenure. Frame your law so as to
give to the Irish tenant the same. The identity of law, even if
it existed, which would not do this, would be only a mockery and
a cheat. The late Sir Robert Peel truly expressed this when, in
promising identity of law between Ireland and England, he reminded the House of Commons it must be an identity not in
letter, but in spirit. " It is true," he said, " of political as of
higher things, the letter killeth, but the spirit giveth life."

It has been true that in the application of the English land law
to Ireland, " the letter has killed"—killed! literally killed! con-
signed to death multitudes of the Irish people. The spirit of
English law even yet applied to our land question might give life
to the dying energies of the Irish nation.

The true test, if we really wish to establish identity of law
between Ireland and England, is to apply to any condition of
things existing in this country exactly the same legislation which
would be adopted if the same condition of things existed in England. Would, I ask, the condition of serfdom which is now the lot
of the Irish tenant farmer, be tolerated in England for one year?
Would the English tenant endure to be served with annual notices
to quit? would he endure notices served by " a driver " that he
must not dare to give a relative a night's lodging, or marry a
son or a daughter without a license from the officer of the estate?
If a wholesale eviction like that of Glenveagh had occurred in one
of the central counties of England, does any man who knows the
English House of Commons, or the spirit of the English people,
believe that such an eviction would ever have taken place in
England again? The laws which, in the circumstances of England, leave the tenants freemen, in the circumstances of Ireland,
make them slaves; and therefore, upon the very principle of giving
Ireland English freedom, in Ireland they must be changed.

But am I to be seriously told that Irish landlords object to exceptional legislation for Ireland? Since the Battle of the Boyne there has
been nothing but exceptional legislation for Ireland. The Irish landlords have maintained their power by legislation not merely excep-

tional, but directly opposed to the letter of the statutes declaring the British Constitution, and wholly abhorrent to the spirit of British law. Let us take the history of Irish legislation since the Union; what is it but a miserable series of exceptional legislation, of legislation specially applied to the coercion of Ireland; of arms acts, of insurrection acts, of all the devices and contrivances by which English ministers and Parliaments have annulled or suspended the British Constitution in this country. Every man in England is at this moment entitled to bear arms. No man in Ireland can possess a pistol except with the permission of the police. One of the very first measures for which Lord Rosse was called on to vote when Parliament assembled, was an act suspending the operations of the *Habeas Corpus* Act in some of its most essential provisions. Was he prepared to vote against such a proposal on the ground that it was " exceptional legislation ?"

The whole government of Ireland, from the Battle of the Boyne to the present day, is one long-continued exception of Ireland, not only from British law, but from the British Constitution. I speak not of particular acts; I speak of the whole purport and polity of our laws and our administration. All the statutes which secured English liberty at the period of the revolution of 1688, were framed with the avowed object, and for the express purpose of making it impossible to govern England except with the assent of the English people. There has not been a statute passed for Ireland which has not been subordinate to the one great object of enabling Irish government to be carried in defiance of the wishes of the Irish people.

Is it only in matters of temporary—or at least, nominally temporary—enactment that " exceptional legislation" has been applied to Ireland? Are our corporation laws the same? Every insignificant town in England has its mayor and its corporation. In all Ireland eleven municipal bodies represent the most ancient element of the British Constitution. Do even these eleven enjoy the privileges of English corporations? Is Lord Rosse prepared to vote for a measure which will place the election of sheriffs in the hands of the corporations of Cork and Limerick, and Dublin and Waterford? It is " exceptional legislation" that vests it in the Crown? Is he prepared to abolish that " exceptional legislation" which entrusts, in Ireland, the whole county taxation to twenty-three gentlemen selected by the sheriff, an officer appointed by the Crown? In every department of our affairs " exceptional legislation" meets us. Uniformity of law or of administration is never thought of when the object is, by exceptional legislation, to trample down and to crush the Irish people. The cry for it is only heard when some measure of justice—redressing some exceptional wrong—to the oppressed and down-trodden Irish people is proposed.

Whenever, in relation to any subject, the circumstances existing

in Ireland and England are the same, then I believe the same legislation should be applied. Upon any subject in relation to which
the circumstances of the two countries differ, the very principle
of equality of laws compels us to vary our legislation with the
varying circumstances to which it is applied.

Lord Rosse, I perceive, includes Scotland in his area of uniform
legislation. Is he prepared to apply to Ireland the principle which
has been established in Scotland in relation to the most important of
all matters—that of the national religion. The example of Scotland prohibits him from saying that the Church of England is the
established Church of the United Kingdom. In England the
State establishes the Church of the majority of the people; in
Scotland the law establishes the Church of the majority of the
people. In Ireland—is Lord Rosse prepared to put an end to
exceptional legislation?

Are the rights of personal liberty less sacred than of landed property? Is Lord Rosse quite sure that when the suspension of the
Habeas Corpus Act is next proposed, " special pleading will not
succeed in devising an excuse for treating" the right to personal
liberty " as one thing in Ireland and another thing in England,
Wales, and Scotland?"

A vote for that measure is justified by saying that the persons
entitled to personal liberty in Ireland use it in a different
manner from that in which it is used by the persons entitled to it in
England, Scotland, and Wales—and therefore the public safety
demands and justifies restrictions which are not needed in England,
Scotland, and Wales. Be it so. I say that the landowner in Ireland uses his right in a manner different from that in which it is
used by the persons entitled to it in England, Scotland, and
Wales, and therefore the public safety demands and justifies restrictions which are not needed in England, Scotland, and Wales.

But if we wanted an illustration of the absurdity to which such an
argument leads has not Lord Rosse himself supplied the most striking
one? He advocates the extension of " the Montgomery Act" to
Ireland, on the ground that it would have " the advantage of not
being exceptional legislation." The Montgomery Act was an Act
passed some years ago for Scotland, founded on some peculiar
circumstances connected with the Scotch law of entail. This law is
not in force either in England or Ireland, and is, therefore, clearly
" open to the grave objection of being exceptional legislation." We
have never heard of any Scotchman objecting to legislation adapted
to the peculiar circumstances of his country upon such grounds. I
rather think Scotchmen have always insisted on " exceptional"
legislation—that is, in other words, legislation adapted to the
peculiar circumstances, the peculiar wants, and the peculiar wishes
of the country. But Lord Rosse, who objects to all exceptional
legislation, proposes to extend to Ireland this statute so excep-

tionally passed for Scotland. He will not have an act specially framed to meet our own case. His objection is removed if it was specially framed to meet the circumstances of a country wholly different from Ireland.

The argument as to "exceptional legislation" is, in truth, a delusion. The whole question resolves itself into this:—Are the circumstances of Ireland and England in relation to landed property so identical that whatever law works well in one country must necessarily work well in the other.

I do not believe, when the question is stated in this broad and plain way, there is any man in his sober senses who will say that they are.

That to which Ireland is really entitled, in comparison with England, is to have laws which will practically secure the same result which English law secures to England, and emphatically to the same rights and privileges for the Irish people which the English people enjoy. Any other "uniformity of legislation" is a mockery and a cheat.

But let us see if there has not been, if there is not now, an exceptional state of law in Ireland upon questions directly relating to property in land.

From the close of the 16th century, there has been a poor law in force in England. In Ireland, up to the year 1839, there was none. We must allow our minds to dwell upon this statement before we can realize all that it conveys. In England, when the confiscation of the church and monastic property deprived the poor of the provision which had been made for them by the piety of olden times, a law was enacted which gave to the labouring peasant in each parish a first charge on all the property in that parish for an amount of wages sufficient to support himself and his family in at least a moderate degree of comfort. English labourers were actually receiving this out of a rate levied on all property during that dismal period in which we have been tracing the condition of the Irish labourer, compelled to work as a bondsman for a pittance barely sufficient to sustain life. To the people living as labourers on the soil it is impossible to conceive a wider or more complete variation between the laws and institutions of the two countries. The Irish and the English labourers were living under systems of government as different as those of England and Russia. No illustration, no language, can convey an adequate idea of the difference between the position of an English labourer, entitled to demand from the guardians as many loaves of good wheaten bread as he and his children, however numerous, could eat—and that of the miserable Kerry cottier described by Lord Clare.

In the position of the landowner—in his relations and his obligations to the people around him, the difference was nearly as great. It is plain that if the poor law of Queen Elizabeth had been extended to

Ireland, the state of things which we have been describing never could have existed. If it had been introduced even at a much later period, the clearances of estates and the extermination of the people never would and never could have occurred. The English landlord was bound to support every man born on his estate. It is to this very difference between the law of England and Ireland, maintained throughout a period of 250 years, that we may trace many of the difficulties which now surround the question of land tenure in this country. But that difference was the necessary result of the policy of conquest—it was an indispensable condition of carrying it out. It would have been inconsistent with that whole policy to tax the conqueror for the benefit of the conquered race.

Exceptional legislation for Ireland began with the reign of Henry VIII. Up to that period it had been the invariable practice of the parliament of the pale periodically to revise the statute roll of the English legislature, and extend to Ireland "all good and wholesome statutes lately made in the realm of England concerning the common weal." * It was thus that all the earlier statutes which secured the liberty of Englishmen were incorporated in Irish laws. The last of these revisions was effected in a memorable parliament, convened at Drogheda by Sir Thomas Poyning, the deputy of Henry VII.

From that day to the present no similar extension of good and wholesome English statutes to Ireland has ever been enacted. Unhappily the great charter of the English labouring man was adopted after the last of these assimilations.

For 250 years Irish property in land was exempt from an obligation which constituted a heavy burden upon all English estates. It might almost be said that the exemption bequeathed to the modern owners of the estates the accumulated obligation with the gathering pauperism of these 250 years. In the meantime the hard toil of the Irish peasant was making rich the land, from which law gave him no right to support. If pauperism was gathering and obligations accumulating, so was capital in the improvements of the soil—and rents were swelled by the unrequited labour of the serf. The rental of Ireland represents to a large extent the result, not of capital expended, as Lord Dufferin supposes, by any present owner or by any one whom his ownership represents, but of toil and labour vested in the lands by the occupying serfs and cottiers— by the industry of bondsmen for whom their masters never incurred the English obligation of supporting them.

---

* It is a common mistake to suppose that this was done once for all by the act passed in the parliament of Poyning. This was only the last of a series of acts passed at intervals for the same purpose. A similar statute had been passed not thirty years before, in the reign of Edward IV. The real Poyning's law was the law enacted at the same time, which prevented the Irish Parliament from originating any bill of which the heads had not been sanctioned by the Irish Privy Council, and declared that no acts should be valid until the Royal assent was given *under the great seal of England*. The latter provision continued law until the Union.

When at last the voice of indignant humanity compelled the establishment of a legal provision for the poor, the English precedent was not followed. The Irish poor law lacked the great principles of that precedent. It contained no law of settlement, and it gave no right of relief. This may have been right, or it may have been wrong; but it was highly exceptional legislation. It was exceptional legislation which enabled the Irish landowners to evade the burden of the poor law. Every Irish landlord who has cleared his estate has done so with impunity, by virtue of exceptional legislation. If that exceptional legislation were repealed to-morrow—if the property from which starving tenants have been "cleared" or "weeded," were now placed under the English law, and made liable for the support of those that were driven out, there are prosperous estates of which the whole rental would not pay the poor rate. There are landowners in Ireland, the most ready to insist on English proprietary rights, and join Lord Rosse in protesting against "exceptional legislation," who could scarcely retain an acre of their estates if they were not protected by "exceptional legislation" from the obligation to which every English owner of property is subject.

But let us throw over the law of settlement, and let me ask— Is Lord Rosse ready in all other respects, to apply the English poor law to Ireland? Is he willing to consent to an equally liberal administration of out-door relief? If upon this all-important, this vital question, which regulates the relation between landed property and the people, men will not, even now, adopt the English system—it is vain to tell us that any "special pleading" is requisite to show that landed property is, and has been, "one thing in Ireland and quite another thing in England and Wales."

But to come still more strictly to the very subject with which we are concerned, I ask is Lord Rosse prepared to give up the benefit of the Irish statutes which give to the Irish landlord facilities for ejectment utterly unknown to the English law? *facilities but for which the wholesale evictions of the last twenty years would never have been carried into effect?*

This is a part of the subject which has not received all the attention it deserves. The Irish landlord has by the law of Ireland facilities for crushing a defaulting tenant which are unknown in England. I will endeavour in a few words to explain this even to those unacquainted with the forms of legal procedure.

There is no abstract principle of law which entitles a landlord to recover possession of his land as soon as his tenant fails in the obligation to pay his rent. The rent is a debt for which the landlord has the same remedies as any other creditor has against the goods and person of his debtor. He has, furthermore, the extraordinary remedy of distress which gives him an advantage over other creditors of his tenant. But the common law does not regard a default in paying rent as creating any forfeiture of the interest which a tenant may have in his land.

The right to recover possession in such a case rested, and still rests, in England, upon provisions in the lease or instrument creating the tenant's estate, provisions reserving to the lessor a right to resume possession if certain prescribed covenants are not observed. The principle applies to other covenants beside that of payment of the rent. The ejectment for nonpayment of rent is simply that which is called in law "an entry for condition broken." It rests entirely on the contract embodied in the original grant. In the generality of leases there was retained the right to recover the land on breach of the covenant to pay rent as reserved—either absolutely or in the event of no distress being found upon the land. But in any lease in which this provision was omitted the landlord, while of course he had his remedies for recovery of the rent, had no power to treat the tenant as forfeiting the estate. Even in cases in which the provision was made it not unfrequently happened that in the devolution of the title to estates the person receiving the rent had not the power of enforcing the forfeiture.

And lastly the enforcement of the right of forfeiture could only be resorted to after the fulfilment of preliminary ceremonials which at all events interposed some difficulties in the landlord's way. The common law of England, and the tribunals which administered it, discouraged the forfeitures of tenants interests, and when a landlord came to enforce one he was held strictly to every requisite of the law. Forfeitures were odious in all English courts.

Irish legislation has exactly reversed these principles. Commencing in the reign of Queen Anne contemporaneously with the Popery laws, a number of acts of Parliament have been passed constituting what is known in Irish jurisprudence as "the ejectment code," a code to which Chief-Justice Pennefather applied the memorable declaration that it was a code of law made solely for the benefit of the landlord and against the interest of the tenant, and that it was upon this principle that judges must administer and interpret it. The whole object of that code was to expedite and facilitate the eviction of the tenant—to get rid of every formality and difficulty by which the good old wisdom of the common law obstructed the forfeiture of a tenant's estate, and lastly to extend that forfeiture to cases in which, according to the common law, it did not exist. Statute after statute was passed for those purposes. If defects were discovered in the old penal law they were met by a new one. As some latent principle of the common law protection was discovered undestroyed, a new and more stringent enactment mowed it down—until, as I said, the whole principle of the common law was reversed, and to make forfeiture easy has been judicially declared to be the duty of judges in administering this code.

And all this while the English landlord has been left to his common law remedies. Of all these voluminous ejectment statutes just one, and that an unused one, has found its way into English legislation. So little influence has this act upon the proceeding that it is actually not noticed in some of the best commentaries on the English laws of landlord and tenant. In our Irish commentaries, of all subjects connected with that law, the ejectment statutes have occupied the largest space and the most prominent position.

The result of the law in the two countries is this:—In England the landlord who resorts to the process of ejecting a tenant who has not paid his rent can only do it according to the forms and the principles of the common law.

In Ireland, by statutes passed for the special benefit of landlords, every difficulty which the requisitions of that common law interposed in the way of such an ejectment is swept away. In England it is the duty of Judges to administer the law so as in every doubtful case to protect the tenant. In Ireland it has been judicially declared to be their duty in every doubtful case to facilitate his eviction.

But this is not all. The landlord seeking to evict a tenant was formerly obliged to proceed in one of the superior courts of law. This proceeding is attended with expense and with delay. In Ireland immediately after the peace, and just at the time when I have pointed out* that the cessation of war prices made it difficult for landlords to enforce the exorbitant rents at which land had been previously let, a statute was passed† enabling the landlord to evict for non-payment of rent in the civil bill or county courts. This power was extended to every case in which rent was due upon a lease, whether the landlord had a right by law to recover possession or not. By the combined operations of the ejectment statutes and the cheap tribunal—the landlord was saved all difficulty, all expense, and all delay. The process of eviction was reduced to the very minimum of time, of trouble, and of cost.

From 1816 to the present day the Irish landlords possessed these extraordinary facilities for evicting tenants for non-payment of rent. Whether these facilities be right or wrong they were, and are, peculiar to Ireland. In 1856 a jurisdiction in such cases was conferred on the county courts in England,‡ but a jurisdiction very different from that which has for fifty years been exercised by the Irish local tribunals. All this was not enough. Even under the Irish "ejectment code," the eviction for non-payment of rent did not extend to tenancies not created by writing. It did not include the general class of yearly tenants in Ireland. The tenant who held from year to year was in a position in which he might at any time be dispossessed by a notice to quit, but that notice must expire with the termination of the year

* *Ante* page 90.　　　　　　† 56th George III., c. 88.
‡ 19th and 20th Victoria, c. 108, section 52. Any one reading this section will see how totally different it is from the similar enactments in Ireland.

of his tenancy, and be given six months before. If a tenant held his farm from November to November, after the landlord let the first of May pass in any year, he had no power of recovering possession of the farm for 18 months, even though in the interim the tenant fell into arrears of his rent.

Here was a new difficulty. The highly penal ejectment code had been framed for a tenantry holding under leases. The landowners had ceased to give leases. They had preferred to have a dependent tenantry holding as yearly tenants. It had been forgotten that in creating such a tenantry they had exempted them from all that carefully drawn machinery of Irish statute law which enabled the landlord to pounce upon the tenant the moment he fell into default. As usual the difficulty was met by a new penal legislation. A few lines—indeed a few words, dexterously inserted in a statute for regulating the civil bill courts extended the ejectment for nonpayment of rent to tenancies from year to year.

So that in Ireland tenants holding from year to year, constituting now the immense majority of Irish tenants, are subject to ejectment for non-payment of rent—a process which in England cannot be used against such tenants. That process is enforced under a penal code against the tenantry, which is unknown in English law, and it is enforced in a local tribunal and in a summary and expeditious manner, while in England, the landlord seeking to get rid of such a tenant, must first serve him with notice to quit, and then proceed to evict him by the costly and dilatory process of an action in the superior courts.

The result is that in England a recourse to ejectment is a rare and exceptional resort. In Ireland it is an ordinary occurrence—actually a part of the routine management of some estates—employed upon others, as Lord Dufferin tells us, as a pressing mode of demanding the rent.

With all these advantages specially created for him by Irish legislation—with principles, tribunals, and procedure—all newly invented for the very purpose of enabling him at once to crush out his defaulting tenant—an Irish landlord can hardly be heard objecting to "exceptional" legislation.

It is scarcely necessary to say how unwise and mischievous was this policy of speedy enforcement of landlord rights. As O'Connell long since pointed out it destroyed the value of character to the tenant. The more summary the remedy of the landlord the less the necessity for care in the selection of his tenant—the greater the temptation to hazard the acceptance of an offer of high rent from a tenant whom the landowner had completely in his power. It was not possible to conceive a code of law more calculated to destroy all true relation of trust between landlord and tenant. It treated the tenant as a knave, and this was to adopt a very effective means of making him one. The law that made ejectment easy invited the landlord to be a tyrant and the tenant to be a cheat. The ejectment statutes were the penal code which oppressed the peasant in his land tenure—they had their origin with the penal laws which oppressed him in his religion. They almost kept pace with them in absurdity and mischief.

If the subject were less solemn, it would be inexpressibly ludicrous, to hear those who have in their favour an ejectment code like this, a code based upon the supposition that the tenant is not to be trusted even for one year—gravely tell us that everything is to be settled between landlord and tenant by mutual confidence and good will.

I trust, my Lord, you will forgive me for using the opportunity which your Lordship's letter afforded me, not only to reply to your own objections, but also to notice the publications of Lord Dufferin and Lord Rosse. I have not professed to give a formal and full reply to all that has been written by either of these noblemen; still less to have met in these pages all the objections that have been urged by others against the proposal I have made.

In one respect I have perhaps gained the object which I proposed to myself in the publication of that proposal. Discussion has been at least excited upon its nature, and I may even hope that in that discussion some persons have been led to regard the question of Irish land tenure in a point of view in which it had not been presented to them before. Subjects have certainly been considered in public journals and writings in connexion with the Irish land question, which, when I published the *Plea for the Celtic Race*, I felt had been entirely lost sight of.

It may perhaps be my obstinacy or my presumption, but after weighing as best I can all the objections that have been made, I adhere with unabated confidence to the opinion I expressed, that it is vain to expect a settlement of that question except by a measure which will give to the occupier of the soil a tenure for a certain period, without any power in the proprietor to interfere with or prevent it. Nay, I feel satisfied that whatever attempts may be made to settle that question by measures short of this will prove failures, either in their proposal or in their execution, and that in the end the very necessities and nature of the subject will compel men either to abandon the effort or to adopt the principle for which I have contended.

It would indeed be presumption to say that I have devised the best mode of carrying that principle into effect. The provisions I sketched were intended mainly as suggestions to be moulded and re-formed by the judgment and experience of others. The details of any measure prepared entirely by one mind must of necessity be imperfect.

Many of the objections which have been made against that measure have been founded on a misunderstanding of its nature. It
has been urged that it would revive the mischiefs which are stated
to have existed in the case of the long leases of former days,
and pictures have been drawn of lands held under such tenures,
at low rents, yet covered with pauper tenants, with a wretched
people and an ill-cultivated soil. Such an argument could not for a
moment impose upon any man who had given attention to the
proposal I have made.

The tenures I propose do not bear the remotest analogy to those
leases. The leases I suggest would be given to the occupier, and
the occupier alone. The leases to the middleman did nothing for the
occupying tenant, who was still subject to the exactions or the caprice
of the middleman, the only landlord he knew. Security of tenure
to the middleman was far from being security to the tiller of the soil.
I propose that every tiller of the soil should have a secure tenure.
Under these old leases the occupiers paid exorbitant rents. I propose to secure to every occupier that he shall only pay a moderate
one. Lastly, those who say that I would overrun the country with
the small tenements of former days, have overlooked the fact that
*I make subdivision impossible except with the landlord's consent.**

* While Irishmen ought to acknowledge the fairness and candour which have generally of late marked the discussions of the Irish land question in the English press, it
is impossible to observe without surprise the ignorance of Irish subjects which sometimes marks the mode in which they are treated even in the best of the English
journals. Of course the dogmatism and confidence of assertion are exactly proportioned to the ignorance displayed.

To take a very humble illustration—humble at least in respect of one of the parties.
A writer in the *Saturday Review* thus conclusively disposes of the proposal to give a
sixty years' lease to the occupiers :—

"At present, the peasant has no means of vindicating his title, except by an armed
insurrection; and of this there is no immediate prospect. But if he could only get the
stand-point of a sixty years' lease, made obligatory by act of Parliament, he would trust
his sons' wits and the wits of his grandsons to keep the landlord out of possession till
the longest day that time should see. People in England, when they hear of a sixty
years' lease, feed their innocent minds on the green pastures of improved cultivation
which the term suggests. The Irish agitator, when he makes a sixty years leasehold
tenure his platform cry, and defies the Government to reject his appeal, knows as well
as his shouting followers that it means a possession which, once obtained, the Irish
peasant and his children would clutch as an indefeasible inheritance, and only part with
at the cost of life. We know too—for the report of the Devon Commission was not
written in vain—what a state of things leases for lives once brought about, and how far
they contributed to the grim terrors of the great famine."

I have pointed out the error involved in supposing that any proposal has
been made to give a sixty years' lease to the occupier, which could possibly revive the
evils of the middleman's lease. I pass by the somewhat singular argument that the
Irish tenant ought not to get such a lease, because at the end of that term his grandson
may possibly endeavour to find means of denying possession to the landlord of
that day—an argument, I admit, about as wise as most of the ravings of the calum-
niators of the Irish people. I very respectfully take exception to the description of
"the Irish agitator," "making a sixty years' lease his platform cry—defying the
Government to reject his appeal," and "all the while surrounded "by shouting
followers," who know as well as himself how the grandson of the Irish tenant will
behave at the end of sixty years.

It so happens that no person but myself has ever made the proposal of a compulsory

I am not expressing an opinion one way or another upon the expediency of preventing the subdivision of farms. I have already shown that in past times it has been in Ulster, not inconsistent with prosperity—in Munster it has been rather the result than the cause of the wretchedness of the occupiers. But I am pointing out that the proposal I have made does not give, or tend to give, the slightest facility for such subdivision. On the contrary it prohibits it, because it makes the covenant against it a universal one, and it gives to the landlord increased facility for enforcing it.

Were my proposal adopted it would not even prevent the consolidation of farms, if it be true that this consolidation is the necessary result of the laws which regulate our present progress; or if the creation of manufacturing industry made it more profitable for a tenant to devote himself to the pursuits of that industry than to cultivate a small farm. Whenever, from any cause, it became advantageous for an occupier to part with his holding, he would sell it with his lease of 63 years, exactly as the Ulster tenant now sells his tenant right. If the tendency of progress leads to large farms, that holding would be purchased up by his neighbour, who would add it to his own. Economic laws would still have full and perfect play. Mens interest or necessities would lead or force them to conform to these laws. The only difference would be that these laws would exercise their proper and natural influence uninterrupted by a vicious and unnatural state of things. If an occupier abandoned his farm it would be because he found he could do better than devote himself to its cultivation; not as it is now, because our system of land tenure prevents him from cultivating it at all. Under that system economic laws are marred and disturbed in their operation. The "malignant human agency" is interposed by a land law which declares that the tenant shall not have freedom in the cultivation of his lands.

Neither would my proposal prohibit, or even interfere with, emigration, if emigration is, from circumstances, the best thing for the Irish people. It would only give each tenant the free choice between cultivating his farm at home and seeking his fortune in another land.

I only ask that before the Irish race are driven from Ireland they should be given the opportunity of making the most of the

lease for sixty years. The only suggestion at all resembling it was one thrown out before the House of Commons Committee in the evidence of the Roman Catholic Bishop of Cloyne, and he did not propose to make it compulsory. I have never in my life attended a tenant-right meeting—I have never made a speech on the subject of tenant-right from a platform or anywhere except in the House of Commons. The proposal of a sixty years' lease has never been even adverted to by any one in any platform speech.

The "Irish agitator," the "platform cry," and "the shouting followers," are all pure and not very lively fiction, without even the smallest foundation in fact.

This is not the spirit in which Irish questions ought to be discussed, especially in journals to which Irishmen naturally look for better things.

Irish soil; of trying whether the industry of Irishmen cannot raise from it enough to support us all in comfort.

If it be true, as Lord Dufferin states in one of his letters, that the circumstances of modern farming have brought about "a desire on the part of the owner and occupier to increase the size of existing holdings," I quite agree with him that "when such a feeling exists in the minds of the parties chiefly interested, the tendency will not be averted by legislation"—*assuming always that the tendency is really the result of the laws of human progress, which legislation is powerless to control.* If the tendency is created by some human influence, then legislation may remove that influence, and leave the laws of progress to their unimpeded action. In Ireland, I repeat, the laws which enable landlords to prohibit the industry of the tenants prevent the free operation of these laws. I surely propose nothing that is even an attempt to control that operation. If Lord Dufferin be right, although every tenant in Ireland held by a lease for 60 years, the peaceful operation of economic laws would infallibly bring about the consolidation of farms. At present that consolidation is to be traced, not to these laws of progress, but to the vicious system which refuses to every tenant farmer the opportunity of being industrious.

I have already quoted some passages from the evidence of Bishop Keane to show how this want of security for improvements is driving the people out of the country, and so directly forcing the consolidation of farms. Let me quote one more to prove how it operates in preventing improvements on the part of those who remain:—

"I will mention," he said, "another case—that of a parishioner of my own. He had a farm of about 120 acres, 90 acres of which were under cultivation, and producing fair crops, considering the state of the country. He had about 30 acres of cut out bog; that is, waste. I said to him— 'Why do you not endeavour to improve your farm? You could make it valuable for yourself and your family.' . . . His answer was—'If I were sure that I could calculate on the fruits of my own industry I would set about it at once; but being uncertain whether I may not be holding out an invitation to the landlord to turn me out, not only of that portion of the farm, but also of the other portion, I will leave the farm as it is.'" *

"The second case is the case of a man who took a farm of land on condition of improving it. The landlord said—'I will give you that side of the hill on the condition that you improve it.' I pass by that place four or six times every year regularly, and I see there crops where formerly there was nothing but barrenness. *The man got the farm on condition of improving it. He was a poor man, with no capital except his strong*

* Bishop Keane. Question 3,353.

*arms, stout heart, and willing mind ; and the result is that he has beautiful crops now where there was nothing but barrenness and sterility before."**

Again he illustrates the question by an instance of four tenants, who were able to obtain a lease from one of the abused middlemen who held himself by a long tenure. These leases were taken in the year 1837—they were of land " on the skirt of the brown, barren mountain, growing nothing but heath and coarse grass." Of one of these tenants he tells us—

" The first two years you may suppose how valueless the land was, when I tell you that for that period he was to pay no rent at all. There was not a road within a mile of the place. He took lime by the high road 10, 12, or 14 miles—*he was obliged to take it then on his back, and on the backs of his children for the remainder of the distance.* On the slope of 20 acres there was neither house, nor fence, nor green field . . in the course of 26 years that man, to my certain knowledge, was able to rear his family in comfort. He was able to convert that very slope of 20 acres into the state in which it now is, producing green crops, corn crops, and anything he likes to put into the ground. He has fenced it, he has built a house upon it ; he has gone to incredible labour in taking out stones that were in his way ; and the result is, that it is now quite a pleasure to look at his farm."†

I cannot quote such evidence as this without remembering that there is a strange sameness in the story of the hardworking industry of the Irish peasant as there is in that of the discouragement and oppression which has kept him down. Exactly one hundred years have passed since an instance almost exactly similar came under the notice of Arthur Young. Sir William Osborne was then the owner of a property in Tipperary, residing within two or three miles of Clonmel. At the time when the Levellers or White Boys were rife, Sir William " met with a manly-looking fellow of forty, followed by a wife and six children, who begged." In reply to remonstrances upon the scandal of begging, he said he could get no work. " Follow me," said the baronet, " and I will give you some." " He gave him five acres of a heathy mountain, built him a cabin, and lent him £4 to stock his ground." " The fellow flourished, he went on gradually, repaid the £4, and presently became a happy little cottar." Twelve years afterwards, when Young wrote, he was able to say—" He has now twelve acres under cultivation, and a stock in trade worth at least £80."

Twenty other persons made similar applications, and were settled in the same way. " THEIR INDUSTRY," writes this English traveller, " HAS NO BOUNDS, NOR IS THE DAY LONG ENOUGH FOR THE REVOLUTION OF THEIR INCESSANT LABOUR."

* Bishop Keane. Question 3,366.
† Bishop Keane. Question 3,354.

Yet these are the people of whom Lord Dufferin tell us that if we give them leases for a long tenure and at a moderate rent, they will not be able to hold them, if we only add the un-Irish conditions, which would oblige them to pay their rents, and be industrious upon their farms.

Sir William Osborne's tenants had been actually engaged in the insurrectionary movements of that day.

Arthur Young continues:—

"It shows that the villainy of the greatest miscreants is all situation and circumstance: EMPLOY, DON'T HANG THEM. Let it not be in the slavery of the cottar system, in which industry never meets its reward; but BY GIVING PROPERTY TEACH THE VALUE OF IT; BY GIVING THEM THE FRUIT OF THEIR LABOUR TEACH THEM TO BE LABORIOUS. All this Sir William Osborne has done, and done it with effect, and there probably is not an honester set of families in the county than those which he has formed from the refuse of the White Boys."[*]

This industry was not exceptional. Wherever Young found the Irish peasant encouraged, there he found him toiling in an industry which, he admits, accomplished results which no Englishman could have produced.

"In the mountainous districts I saw instances of greater industry than in any other parts of Ireland. Little occupiers *who can get leases of a mountain-side*, make exertions in improvements which, though far enough from being complete or accurate, yet prove clearly what effects encouragement would have upon them."

It is not surprising that he should say of this class of Irish tenants:—

"It is, from the whole of the evidence, plain that they are, in no common degree, masters of the art of overcoming difficulties by patience and contrivance. . . . Give the farmer of twenty acres in England no more capital than his brother in Ireland, and I will venture to say he will be much poorer, for he will be utterly unable to go on at all."

I return to the proofs of the same spirit of enterprise, and the same industry existing in the peasants of our own day supplied to us in the evidence of Dr. Keane.

The value of evidence like this is, as I have before observed, that it does not consist of opinion or speculation, it is testimony as to matter of fact. .These instances, striking as they are, are but samples and illustrations of the general conditions of Irish life. I will ask of any one to read over carefully these three brief narratives of actual fact, and then ask himself the question—does our present system of land tenure discourage and prevent improvements which under a system that gave security would certainly be made?

---

* *Arthur Young's Tour*, Vol. ii., p. 173.

Many and many a man, with the "capital of a willing mind, a strong arm, and a stout heart," is pining hopelessly in the workhouse, or wandering a reluctant exile from his home. There is many a man who, rather than leave the old country, would carry the lime upon his back up the weary hill-side to build himself and his children a home—many a one who would gladly toil in cheerful industry upon "the skirt of the brown and barren mountain," and whose toil would cover the wild upland with luxurious crops.

There is the land lying waste—there is the labourer, THE REAL CAPITALIST, driven from his country, or perishing in the pauper's home. Cannot we see where is the malignant "human agency" which blights our noble country with "perennial desolation."

But I use this evidence for one purpose, and for one only. Is there a man in the enjoyment of his natural senses that can doubt the fact, that insecurity of tenure prevents improvement on the soil?

Of what is that insecurity of tenure the result? Of no natural law of human progress, but of the fact that territorial arrangements, the effect of the confiscations of conquest, have vested in a small number of proprietors the dominion over the Irish soil, and that this dominion is so exercised—by a combination among these proprietors, arising from the social and political antagonism of classes, and creeds, and races—so as to deny to the occupier the security which is the only condition on which he can improve.

Then, if the industry of the tenant be not free—if human agency drives him from the waste he would reclaim, and human authority tells him that on his own farm it is "irregular" to improve, it is vain and trifling, it is "darkening counsel by words without knowledge" to talk of economic laws as applicable to a state of things in which the freedom of human industry, which is the essential element of these laws, is wanting.

Let no one call this "declamation." It is strict and stern reasoning. We have but one fact upon which we must make up our mind. Does the present system of land tenure prevent the occupier from expending his industry on the soil? All that we know of human nature tells us that it must. All the principles of economic science—principles that are nothing more than formularies, generalizing the inferences to be drawn from the motives of industrial and commercial action—teach us that it must. Evidence, clear, conclusive, and overwhelming, establishes that it has done, that at this hour it is doing, so. All rude and untutored common sense—all the educated common sense, which men call science—all the teachings of books, all the lessons of the past, all observation of the present, coucur in the testimony—that by maintaining precariousness of tenure we are putting a check upon industry, and preventing the occupiers from making improvements which, had they security for their holdings, they would effect upon the soil.

If this cardinal fact in all reasoning on the Irish land question be established, it meets us in all the varying circumstances under which that question can be presented to our mind.

I have shown how it meets us in the attempt to attribute to the natural laws of human progress those strange phenomena of our social state which perplex every one who attempts to solve the problem of that state by any application of these laws.

Are we to be told that Ireland is over peopled while we deliberately maintain and enforce a system which prohibits the population from raising all they can from the resources which a merciful Creator has given us in the soil?

Can we listen to any argument which tells us that our poverty is the inevitable result of our want of manufacturing industry while we permit a vicious system of land tenure to deprive our people of the opportunity of employing their industry upon their own land?

Are we to turn in senseless resentment to rend England for having put down our woollen manufacture a century ago, while before our own eyes and in our own day—the great manufacturing industry of the country—the industry that creates produce from the soil, the industry that tills the ground, is blighted and blasted by unwise and pernicious land laws; and while those who ought to live by that industry are brought to beggary and ruin? There is no magic in words. Never did the suppression of the woollen trade more directly throw out of employment the combers and weavers of wool, than does the system of land tenure which prohibits agricultural industry throw out of employment the farmer and the agricultural labourer who depend upon that industry for their support.

And lastly, this fact meets us in the great and vital question—Is it just to drive away the Irish—to drive them away without giving them a chance of making all they can on their own land? Is it just or right to drive away such men as the narratives of Bishop Keane describe? to deny to them the privilege of toiling on the barren mountain side, in order that proprietors may retain their influence or dominion, and that the lands of Ireland may be preserved for the holders of great consolidated farms, who are in "the good time coming"—the millenial blessedness of landlords—to occupy the places of the humble and industrious tenants that are remorselessly to be swept away.

Anxious as I am to meet every fair objection to the proposal I have made, no time at my command would enable me to reply to all the criticisms I have received. There are some on which I would wish to offer a few words of comment.

It has been said, and truly, that my proposal will not restore the tenants who have been cruelly evicted within the last twenty years, and that therefore I am inflicting a penalty upon the landlords who have exercised their rights in a humane and forbearing spirit, while

I would leave those who have acted harshly to enjoy a kind of premium in the comparative freedom which they would have in the
management of their estates.* No human legislation, it is true, can
undo the cruelty and the injustice which have been inflicted upon
the Irish people. But this surely forms no valid reason why we
are not to prevent them in future. Such an argument is a bar
against all improvement. The instances are rare in which we can
remedy the wrongs of the past. It is not always possible to deprive the perpetrators of the wrongs of the advantages they have
gained. But legislation must look only to the future. And after
all, if we be compelled to leave undisturbed the fruits of past,
while we prevent the possibility of future injustice, I am not sure
that we can very deeply sympathise with the complaint of the man
whose grievance is that he did not rob in time.

I am, however, far from admitting that such a measure as I suggest is a penalty upon any landlord. I believe that were it passed
there is not a landlord in the country who in four years would not
be far better off than he is now. We must not be deterred from
this measure of good to all by the argument that the men who have
acted worst will profit most. That argument is not true. The man
who has evicted his tenants unless in the rare instances in which he
has kept his land unlet, would be subject to the law I propose
equally with the man who has permitted his tenants to remain
upon his estate. Even when he had his estate in his own hands he
would be bound not to let his land except upon the terms of the
new law.

A more specious objection, urged by the same authority, is that
I would deprive proprietors " of the first great right of an owner—
that of tilling his own land himself."

It is important in matters of this kind that we should be accurate
even in words. I do not propose to deprive any proprietor of " the
right of tilling his own land himself." That of which I do deprive
him is the right of arbitrarily evicting the present occupier for the
purpose of tilling the land himself. As to the latter right there are
cases in which it would be impossible to deny the power and even the
duty of interference. Suppose a combination of all the proprietors
to lay down their lands in grass and drive out the whole people—
no one, I apprehend, will say that against such a project of extermination Government ought not to interfere; or if Government
failed, that the people should not protect themselves. For such an
extermination the plea would in vain be urged that the landowner
were only exercising the first great right of an owner, that of
" farming his land himself."

In the criticism on which I am commenting even its able and
candid author falls into a fallacy which pervades almost all the

reasoning of those who oppose legislation on the Irish land question.
He does not sufficiently attend to the distinction between acts which
are the isolated doings of individuals and acts which are the
habitual and general practises of large classes of men.   The latter
may frequently be the proper subject of legislative interference
where the former would not.   The distinction is that which pervades all jurisprudence, even that of our criminal law   Acts which
are regarded as innocent, or at least not the object of punishment
when done by an individual acting singly, are high misdemeanours
when done in combination with others.   Combination is power.
The combination of many individuals is, in effect, the enacting of a
law.   And when a large class all pursue the same conduct because
they are guided by the same interest and the same passions, they are
acting in combination.   Indeed, the refusal of each landowner to grant
leases can scarcely, in any instance, be said to be his own solitary
act.   He often pursues that course in deference to the opinions and
prejudices of his order.   In every instance he is supported by them.
Legislation, as well as jurisprudence must recognize the distinction.
Evil things that are only the isolated offences of individuals must
often be left to the correction of general opinion and individual
conscience.   But when these evil things become the habits of whole
classes they are public mischiefs, and the legislative power must
interfere to put them down.   These are principles of common application, and they are the principles upon which legislation upon the
Irish land question must rest.   One landowner might not be prevented from turning his estate into a desert—all the landowners in
the country could not be indulged in a similar caprice.   One landowner may refuse leases without justifying an Act of Parliament—
when all combine to refuse them the Legislature must interpose.

But can it really be said even of an owner of a district—of an estate,
suppose of 20,000 acres, in a thickly populated country—that he has
a right to pull down villages, to level all human habitations, and to
till or pasture that 20,000 acres himself ?   Has anything like this
ever been done in England since the clearance of Hampshire for
the New Forest?   On a smaller scale it has been attempted, and it
has been punished.   But the very assertion of such a right drives
us back to the origin of property in land.   Fortunately, in Ireland,
that origin is not lost in the obscurity of remote and unknown days.
All proprietary right in Ireland can be traced to the time when
" waste and unreformed countries" became vested in the English
Crown.   No Irish proprietor ever obtained from that Crown a right
to till the land himself.   Such a right was distinctly and positively
withheld from him—as to all but a specified portion of his grant.
For the rest his only right was to receive rent from " estated"
tenants whom he was bound to place upon the land.

So far from admitting this to be "the first great right of an
owner," I would say that in the case of the monopoly of great

tracts of country by one proprietor, he has not and he never had such a right. In Ireland the very terms of every grant exclude it. Even in England the condition of all grants was to have men ready for the service of the lord when required. In no country in Europe has the land been given to a few with a right to exclude the people. And plausible, nay even true as this statement of an owner's rights may be in individual cases, it is not true when it is applied to the great mass of property throughout the kingdom. The owners of land as a class have not the right to till their own land and sweep from its surface the people. The question is entirely one of degree— where interference with such privileges should commence? I answer as before, whenever the claims of the owners to till their own lands amounts to a public mischief and a public wrong.

I may observe, in passing, that the measure I have suggested was framed with the most scrupulous care to preserve to the personal occupation of the landlord every portion of his estate which had been usually tilled by the owners of that estate. It is exactly in conformity with the policy of James I. and Sir John Davies, to which I have already referred. It leaves in his own hands all that he has ever held as demesne land, and it confirms the tenants in the possession of the rest. It takes away from him the power of turning out people for the purpose of extending his demesne—of "adding field to field" until for the peasantry "there should be no place." This, so far from being an ancient right of property, is made a crime by many old statutes. Acts against depopulation were passed by the Parliaments of the Plantagenets and the Tudors; very "strong" ones are to be found on the statute book of Henry VIII.

I cannot forbear from quoting from the works of Sir Thomas More, a description of "a clearance," which would almost impress us with the belief that he had an Irish eviction present, in prophecy, to his mind—

"Therefore it is that one covetous and insatiable cormorant and very plague of his native country, may compass about and enclose many thousand acres within one pale or hedge—the husbandmen he thrust out of their own; or else either by covin or fraud, or violent oppressions, they be put beside it, or by wrongs and injuries they be compelled to sell all. By one means, therefore, or other, either by hook or by crook, they must needs depart away—poor, silly, wretched souls—men, women, husbands, wives, fatherless children, widows, woeful mothers with their young babes, and the whole household—small in substance but rich in numbers—as husbandry requires many hands. Away they trudge out of their known and accustomed homes, finding no place to rest in. All the household stuff, which is very little, worth nothing, it might well abide the sale. Yet, being suddenly thrust out, they be constrained to sell it as a thing of nought. And when they have wandered abroad, and that be spent, what can they do but go steal, and then justly perdue, be hanged; or else go about a-begging, and then also be cast into prison as vagabonds, because they go about and work not, whom no man will set to work, though they never so willingly proffer themselves thereto."

It was probably under the influence of such feelings that the Chancellor of Henry VIII. drew up some of the statutes on the subject of depopulation which were passed in the reign of that King.

I have frequently thought it strange how readily the advocates of the oppressions of power refer to the old principles of the law and the constitution, never remembering how they protected and vindicated popular right. No one who has read the statutes against "depopulators" can doubt that if, under the Plantagenets the English landowners had ventured on a third of the extermination of which Irish landlords in our time have been guilty, the Parliament of that day would not have scrupled much about such rights of property as are now claimed, or hesitated to discover rather violent means of reminding the "depopulators" of their duty to their country and their king. The remedy of some of the earlier statutes was a very simple one. The landowners who had cleared their estates and pulled down villages were compelled, by a very summary process, to rebuild the villages and replace in them the people they had turned out.

With the enactment of the poor law of Queen Elizabeth the English clearances came to an end. Singular is the fatality which seems to attend all legislation for this country. In England the institution of a legal provision for the poor was the most effectual means of stopping extermination. In Ireland it led to the driving of thousands and tens of thousands from their homes.

The same high authority upon which I have been commenting, suggests another objection. Speaking of the evictions, the writer in the last number of the *Edinburgh Review*, asks:—

"Is it equally certain that any alteration of the land laws, even one giving fixity of tenure at a reserved rent, would have kept all these people at home? The returns of evictions lately moved for by the Earl of Belmore, show, that in the last six years, there have been in all Ireland, 37,164 ejectments. Of these two-thirds were for non-payment of rent. Now, as payment of rent is included amongst the obligations to which, under Mr. Butt's scheme, a tenant would be subjected, it is not clear that fixity of tenure on those terms would have saved those 25,000 poor ruined people from eviction."

Even to raise the question, we ought to know how many of these evictions were for exorbitant rents.

But I must observe, in the first place, that by far the greater number of these ejectments were brought against yearly tenants. Nearly all the ejectments for non-payment of rent are so. I have already pointed out that such an ejectment is wholly unknown in England, and is a novelty even in Irish law.* An ejectment for non-payment of rent is adopted as the quickest mode of getting rid of a yearly tenant instead of waiting for the slow process of notice to quit. Every tenant who is thus evicted must, it is true, owe a year's rent; but it does not at all follow that he might not find means of paying the rent, and so stopping the ejectment, if he had any interest which it was worth his while to retain. Once his landlord had determined to get rid of him, paying up his rent would only put off the evil day. Any inferences drawn from ejectments for non-payment of rent against yearly tenants are liable to many elements of uncertainty. So far as they rest on any analogy with English ejectments, they are only calculated to mislead. It does not at all follow in case of any one of these evicted tenants that he was not in a position to protect his interest by paying up his rent, if he had any interest to protect.

But apart from this, and even if we could suppose that these ejectments represent the evictions of tenants who were hopeless defaulters, this passage involves, I must say, the very same fallacy into which Lord Dufferin has fallen. It assumes that those who have been unable to pay their rent under the present system would be equally unable to pay it under a system which, by conferring on them fixity of tenure would give them security for the application of their industry to their farms. But if the argument for fixity of tenure be worth anything, it is this—that it would encourage and stimulate the industry of the tenant—that he would, under its encouragement create, by improvements, a property in his farm. It is impossible to argue from the default of the miserable serf, who has no field for his industry, that the same default would occur when you had elevated him to the condition of an independent and therefore industrious tenant. Punctuality in his rent would become his habit when you had given him a property which that punctuality would preserve. Every perch of ground he reclaimed would be an additional security for the regular payment of his rent. To assert that evictions for non-payment of rent would be as frequent with fixity of tenure as they are now is only to say, in other words, that fixity of tenure would have no effect in improving the condition, elevating the habits, or stimulating the industry of the occupier of the soil.

This brings me at once to Lord Dufferin's letter in *The Times* of the 1st of February—a letter in which he distinctly criticises the plan

* *Ante* page 189.

I have proposed. Before I saw this letter the greater portion of these pages were actually in print.

Lord Dufferin classes that plan among proposals which "involve the transfer of a large amount of proprietary rights from the landlord to the tenant."

"I do not deny," he says, "the right of the State to deal in a very peremptory manner with private property of all kinds, and especially with landed property ; but, in assuming this right, it must be made clear that its exercise will be of indisputable benefit to the community at large, and the individual to whose prejudice it is enforced must be compensated at the public expense to the full amount of the injury he sustains. The safety of a nation may depend upon the security of an arsenal, and that of the arsenal on the conversion of a hovel into a redoubt ; yet the engineer in command dare no more remove a brick from the obnoxious premises without the sanction of an Act of Parliament, and an elaborate valuation, than he dare blow up St. Paul's. But considerations such as these the authors of the various schemes 'for dealing vigorously with the Irish landlords' deem beneath their notice. The most notable plan is one lately promulgated by Mr. Butt."

I certainly have not deemed considerations like these beneath my notice. I venture to say that any one who has read the tract on Land Tenure will find them very fully discussed. I can only say, that whether successfully or not, I at least elaborately attempted to show that all established principles of jurisprudence justified the interference I proposed. The arguments by which I attempted to prove this may be weak or they may be foolish, but I scarcely think they are answered by an assertion that I deemed the considerations arising out of the rights of property beneath my notice.

The argument of Lord Dufferin—if it be intended as one—has the disadvantage of leaving us in doubt as to which of two grounds it takes. It may mean that the passing of such a measure as I propose would entitle the landlord to receive compensation for the depreciated value of his estate; or it may mean that the same principles of respect for private right which in other cases compel us to give compensation when we take away property, ought in this instance to prevent us interfering at all.

In either view I do not admit the argument to be well founded. I have already stated that if proprietary rights in Ireland really interposed any obstacle to giving fixity of tenure, the cheapest expenditure of money which England ever made would be that which would purchase them all up.* But let us just suppose a landlord making a claim for compensation because he had been compelled by law to give his tenants leases at the fair letting value of their farms. Of what pecuniary benefit is he deprived ? What injury inflicted on him are a jury to estimate ? What right is

* *Land Tenure*, pp. 75, 76.

taken away from him, the value of which they are to ap-
praise? In what honest way can any landowner make money of
the dependence and the serfdom of his tenants? Is he to claim
compensation for the loss of the power of appropriating the fruits of
their industry?—of exacting extortionate rents?—of driving out his
tenants while they are punctual and industrious? Could a jury be
empannelled in any county in Ireland which would award to any
landlord one shilling compensation for the loss of these rights?

The admitted right of the public is to take away or injure any
man's property when public good demands, paying him such compensation or purchase as the verdict of a jury would award.

If Lord Dufferin's property were taken for a railway to-morrow
what compensation is he entitled to receive? Exactly the selling
value of his land. If it had been taken for public purposes, under
any of these acts which at various times authorized the taking of
property for a term of years at a fixed rent, what would he receive?—
a rent fixed by the letting value of the land at the time that it was
taken. If public purposes require it the State has a right to take
his property, paying his present selling value. If public interests
demand it, the State has a right to take his property on a lease for
a term of years, fixing the rent at that which any one would now
contract to pay in such a lease. Does not a compulsory sale at
the present price of the property deprive the landlord of any advantage to be derived from the future contingent increase in the
value or the prices of the soil? Is a compulsory lease at a given
rent a greater interference with the rights of property than a compulsory sale at a given price?

It is, of course, another and a different question, whether this
principle can be fairly applicable to a measure such as I propose.
I admit at once that it is one thing to force a lease for a barrack or
a gaol and another thing to force a lease for an occupying tenant.
But Lord Dufferin it is who points out the analogy. If the principle
be an accurate one, I do all that ever the Legislature feels itself
bound to do in such cases.

I might therefore content myself with denying that any compensation is required for the Irish landlord. But the measure which I
propose so far from injuring would benefit him. Were such an
act to pass there is not a proprietor in Ireland whose estate would
not be increased in value.

I might ask if any one has ever yet heard of compensation being
given to men for a legislation which prohibited men using their
property in such a manner as to work public mischief and wrong.
In such cases the question is not one of taking property; it
is one of regulating its use. The principles which govern compensation have no relation to the subject. The fallacy lies in
supposing that when you control the exercise of proprietary
rights in land you more or less take the land from its owner.

Such a fallacy never could exist for a moment undetected if it were not that real property is something tangible and immovable. But you no more take away land from the landlord when you prohibit him letting it at extortionate rents or on precarious tenures, than the usury laws took away the money of the banker when they restricted him in the terms of his loan. It is needless to refer to the numerous instances of regulation in which property embarked in various pursuits—in factories, in passenger ships, in furnaces, in many other employments—has been subjected to laws imposing conditions, sometimes very onerous ones, upon its use. To cases like these the principles which regulate compensation have no application.

And once more I ask are we to overlook the fact that Irish estates were granted subject to the express condition of placing on them "estated tenants?"—that every precarious tenure that exists on an Irish, at all events on an Ulster estate is a violation of the compact still subsisting, by which the owner of that estate is bound to the nation and the Crown?

I content myself by repeating, that as a question of political jurisprudence, no clearer case was ever made out than that which justifies, by all the principles of the social compact, the regulation of Irish property which I suggest.

The next objection made by Lord Dufferin is founded on a state of things actually existing on his own estate.

He instances a case in which he is the owner of a strip of land adjoining Belfast Lough—a strip suitable for villas, " which may eventually become a favourite resort of the inhabitants of Belfast." It is now in the hands of tenants holding by beneficial leases, but about soon to expire:—

" We will suppose that Mr. Butt's Bill passes; the accidental occupants of this property become tenants for an additional term of 63 years; I am unexpectedly precluded from adding some thousands to my rent-roll, and a project which would have diffused the wealth of a rich community over a large agricultural area is indefinitely postponed—unless, indeed, I choose to buy back my own property, at a price, probably, not much lower than the original value of the fee simple, from tenants who have neither legal nor equitable claims against me."

It appears to me that precisely the same curtailment of the landlord's right exists wherever the Ulster custom of tenant right is recognized.

I do not admit that the adoption of my measure would preclude Lord Dufferin from adding to his rental. He appears to assume that the new rent to be paid would be the same as the old. In fixing the rent to be paid for the term of 63 years, the letting value to be reserved on such a lease must obviously include the advantages of site and position which would raise the letting price in the market. If they are such as would not do this they are mere speculative advantages, incapable of appreciation.

What would become of them if the very same property were taken for a railway, in which an arbitrator would be sworn to give the proprietor the fair selling value of the land, and no more?

In a lease to be granted under the measure I propose, I actually reserved to the landlord the benefit of a rise in the value of the land at a future time from such incidental and extrinsic causes. I have admitted that the details I suggest may be imperfect, and even faulty. I meant to secure this—that when his land was demised for 63 years, there should be reserved to the landlord the fair rent which ought to be paid for the land on such a lease, taking into account all its advantages, whether of fertility or situation; and I meant further, if unforeseen circumstances made that situation a more valuable one, to secure to the landlord, as far as it could be possibly accomplished, a proportionally increased rent.

If the land were to be subdivided in building plots, I left to the landlord the full power of insisting on a share in the increased value. I proposed to prohibit subdivision without his consent.

But supposing even that, in instances like this—some scheme of improvement of an enterprising landlord might be impeded—the question is whether we are to leave in the hands of the landlords an arbitrary power of eviction, in a thousand instances working injustice and wrong, for the sake of one case in which it may facilitate improvements? Are we to keep the whole population serfs, and encounter all the terrible evils of that serfdom, for the sake of Lord Dufferin's projected villas on the shores of the Belfast Lough?

There is in the paragraph I have quoted a strange fallacy, tacitly assumed, which runs through all the reasonings, both of Lord Dufferin and all the advocates of the extreme views of proprietary rights—the assumption that all improvements must be effected by the landlords, or at least under landlord supervision and control. The project which would diffuse the wealth of a rich community over a large agricultural area is indefinitely postponed, if tenants acquire any permanent interest in the land. I believe that if the site be the best adapted for villas, and villas are wanted by the rich community of Belfast, villas would be built there, even though there be tenants on it holding by leases for 60 years. Such leases, indeed, are not usually considered a hindrance to building speculations. On the contrary, wherever there is property entailed by marriage settlement, containing land suited for building purposes, a power is, in all well-drawn settlements, reserved as to that portion of the estate, of granting leases for a still longer period than 60 years.

Lord Dufferin asks why I have chosen the exact number of 63 years. I answer, because it was necessary to choose some exact

number—because 63 is a multiple of 21, and because I came
to the conclusion that a lease of a duration of somewhat about
that term is the very shortest which would offer, in the circumstances of Ireland, sufficient inducement to the people to remain
in the country, and to improve.   I freely admit there is no magic
in the precise number of 63.   I would myself very much prefer 99.

When Lord Dufferin apprehends that leases for 63 years will doom
land suited for building purposes to continue unimproved, I may remind him that, in the opinion of many of the persons best qualified
to judge, Belfast owes no little of its rapid increase to the very fact
that many years ago long leases, and, in many instances, perpe-
tuities were granted at low rents upon the vast Chichester estate.
It is no disparagement to the present representatives of a great
family to say that there would not be so many villas around Belfast
if there had been no leases for 60 years, and if all building improvements had been left to the enterprise of the successive owners of
the Donegal estates.

Lord Dufferin assumes, in his own instance, that all improvements of this nature can only be effected by himself.   To give
long leases to the tenants is indefinitely to postpone them.   It is
very curious how this supposition, never plainly stated but always
tacitly assumed, runs through all arguments like his.   In another
passage of this letter Lord Dufferin says:—

"Mr. Butt, like the malevolent fairy in the tale of *The Sleeping
Beauty*, would curse us with the doom of rigid immobility for the greater
portion of a century, without the prospect of that magic 'after-glow' of
renewed life and vigour which completes the story."

In this passage, brief as it is, there are condensed the elements of a
great question, the principles of two rival systems.   All of us desire
to see Ireland rise from her present low condition.   No man could
describe our country as Lord Dufferin has done who did not feel his
heart stirred by the hopes for her that have so often been the dream
of the patriot.   There are those who believe that if ever the country
is to rise from her misery it will be by the emancipated energies of
her people.   There are those who think that it is only in her upper
classes that the elements of her regeneration are to be found.

And, accordingly, when I propose to elevate into independent
leaseholders 500,000 tenant farmers who are now but tenants at the
will of the landlord—to give to each and every one of them the
opportunity of improving his fields and creating a property for himself—to call out whatever energy he may possess, and bring into
action whatever motive for industry may lurk within his breast—
Lord Dufferin tells me that I would curse the country with the
doom of a rigid immobility for the better part of a century!   All
progress and improvement would be stayed during all the period
in which the Irish peasant could hold any property in the soil!

National progress depends upon leaving to the landowner free and uncontrolled dominion over the land and its occupiers. According to this policy we will better promote national industry and improvement by making 10,000 landlords absolute than by making 500,000 occupiers independent. According to this policy the more we destroy all freedom in the occupier, the more industrious he will be.

The statement as to "immobility" rests solely on the assumption that the tenantry will not improve. There is frequently a difficulty in answering a writer like Lord Dufferin who constantly exhibits a marvellous facility of unconsciously condensing into one compendious error a contradiction of the whole history and the whole experience of the nation.* I had thought it one of the admitted facts of our social history that such improvements as have been made either in or upon the soil of Ireland have been generally made by the occupiers of the soil. Are we to go back upon the proof—to collect together all the testimonies from all the books that ever have been published—from all the speeches that ever have been made—from all the evidence that has ever been given on the subject of the occupation of Irish land—to establish this universally conceded fact, that while in England and Scotland there has been a large outlay on the part of proprietors in bringing the soil of the country to its present state—in Ireland almost all that expenditure has been made by the occupiers of our soil.

It is easy to show that of late years there has been much more activity and improvement among the landowners. There has been a stimulated energy from the circumstances in which the country is placed. Men who purchased under the Incumbered Estates' Commission have expended money in improving their purchases. Landowners have been driven in many instances by the necessities of their position to devote themselves to making the most of their lands. Large works of drainage have been executed by money borrowed by the landowners. All this nobody denies; but all this has no appreciable effect upon the general result of the character of Irish progress. That progress has, on the whole, been effected at the cost and by the labour of the tenants.

It is not meant by assertions of this nature that there were no improving landlords in old times. I believe there were more then than are now. The improvements effected by Chief Baron Foster at Cullen, so graphically described by Arthur Young, were greater than those of which any landlord of our own day can boast, at all events they were calculated to benefit a larger number of people. At that period there were many, very many, landlords in Ireland who deserved equal praise. I am disposed to think that improving

---

* Truth is to be sought only by slow and painful process. Error is in its nature flippant and compendious ; it hops with airy and fastidious levity over proofs and arguments, and perches upon assertions which it calls conclusions."—*Curran.*

landlords ceased very much at the Union, and that in the early years of this century the tenants were the only improvers. But be this as it may, when we assert that all improvements in Ireland have been effected by the occupiers what we mean is this. The Irish soil has been cultivated, improved, and raised in value by the industry of man. Fences have been made, houses have been built, stones have been removed, rushes dug out, water drained off, and waste and barren land brought under the dominion of the plough or the spade. Since the beginning of the last century the value of the agricultural holdings of Ireland has increased by many millions. This increased value represents many millions worth of labour expended in or on the soil. By far the greater portion of this expenditure has been made by the occupiers. From the days of the "settlement" to the present day the custom of the country has been that the owner in letting his land made no expenditure in putting it into order. He demised nothing to the tenant but the bare power of the soil with whatever improvements previous occupiers had made. Tenants so long as they had any security of tenure improved their farms. Landlords improved their demesnes. The improvement on the demesne was on a large scale—it was striking, and it was well executed. The improvemnts on the farm were small, unnoticed, and most probably ill-done. Yet the sum of many small things far exceeds the amount of a few great, and the aggregate of the occupiers' expenditure represents a proportion, so great as to be almost the entire, of the value added by human industry to the Irish soil.

Let us reflect for a moment upon what has been done by the despised and condemned Irish occupiers before we acquiesce in the conclusion that to entrust them with an interest in the soil is to curse us during the period of that interest with "immobility." I presume I am correct in supposing that this means a condition stationary in respect of improvement. Let us see what they have done. Let us remember the rents they have paid—that they have tilled our soil under every circumstance of difficulty. Without capital and

* I have not thought it necessary to enter on any estimate or calculation of the value thus added by the labour or capital of the occupiers to the Irish land. I am quite safe in saying it must be very many millions. Arthur Young calculates the rental of Ireland at five millions ; the Poor Law Valuation amounts to twelve millions.

Bishop Keane, on data that appear correct, has estimated that between the date of Young's work and 1840, the improvements on the Irish soil equalled in value upon each acre those made in England in the same time.—*Evidence*, 1864.

All such estimates must be but remote approximations to the truth. There is nothing more difficult than to arrive at any tests by which we can accurately compare the condition of a country at one time with its condition at another. It may be assumed as certain, that since the Revolution there has been an immense expenditure, which has permanently added to the value of the land. If some miracle could throw the land of Ireland into the state in which it was the day of the Battle of the Boyne, an expenditure of very many millions would not be sufficient to place it in the state in which it is now. Is it an over estimate to say that the expenditure of one hundred millions would not suffice ?

without encouragement—reclaiming their twenty acres of wild mountain where an English traveller tells us Englishmen would have starved—all the while oppressed by cruel laws—treated with contumely and insult—without any of the outward incentives which stimulate selfishness to industry, and cheered in their toil only by those domestic affections which have been to the Irish people the redeeming spirit that has gone with them through the furnace. Take as an example the poor cottiers of Sir Wm. Osborne or the reclaimers of the mountain heather described by Bishop Keane. It is unjust to compare what the Irish occupiers have done for Ireland's improvement with the progress of any country in which liberty has been known, and in which industry has had its reward. The proper comparison would be with some of the eastern territories in which oppression has laid waste the energies of the people. But let them be compared with any country we will—let us make allowance for all the difficulties of their position, and measure their industry by the improvements actually made upon the Irish land, and I venture to say the history of mankind supplies no such instance of patient, enduring and ill requited labour as that which during that period is furnished by the maligned and persecuted Irish race.

Why are we to contradict all our history—and disregard all experience by assuming that if we give such people an interest in our soil all improvement is to stop? For two centuries the "immobility" has been on the side of the landlords who left it to this very people to effect all that has been effected to break in upon the desolation of our uncultivated resources. All that has been placed upon the soil by the industry of that people the landowners now claim as their own, and tell us that property in land represents the accumulated capital of many generations which they or their predecessors have expended on that land. To this an enemy might reply, that this is to rest the moral as well as legal right of Irish property upon confiscation. It is a legalized wrong which has vested in the landowners all the improvements which the toils of many generations of occupiers have effected. But while landowners are actually enjoying the benefit and the ownership of millions of property invested by the people in the soil—millions to which they themselves have added little or nothing—it is too much now to tell that people they cannot remain upon the land because their doing so is to condemn the country to the curse of immobility.

Of course it is possible that the existence of a lease may stand in the way of some supposed or some real improvement. I have not a doubt that Naboth's vineyard was a real obstacle in the way of a real improvement. But a tenant's lease is not the only ownership that may be such an obstacle. The life estate of many an owner stands at this moment between sites very suitable for building and the erection of the buildings. The ownership in fee of many a great proprietor's estate in England and Ireland is the positive

obstruction to many projects that would diffuse wealth and employment through an entire district. How many railways have been
sent far from a town by an extorted reverence for the sacred
precincts of the great man's demesne? How many places suited
to be great seats of trade and commerce are kept back by the
whims or the caprice of the territorial lord? It is the influence of
great estates that really curses whole districts with "immobility."
If the argument of "immobility" is to have weight, it is a strong
one for breaking up large properties. Lord Mansfield, I think it
was, who said "the strong bent of the Saxon mind has ever been
that land should be free." It was this strong bent that employed
in courts of law judicial fictions to defeat the statutes by which
feudalism endeavoured to prevent the free transfer of estates. It
is not by long leases of small portions of land to tenants, but by
the accumulation of great properties in individual hands that immobility is inflicted upon nations. But these are matters which we
need not discuss. The real question is by what means are we most
likely to get the whole soil of the country improved. All experience
tells us that which common sense points out—give to the Irish
people an interest in it, and over the whole extent of Ireland improved cultivation and gladdened industry will work, in one twelve
months, throughout all the cornfields and meadow lands of Ireland,
improvements compared with the value of which all the villa
residences which all the landlords of Ireland could build in twenty
years would sink into insignificance and contempt.

I believe that it is from the 500,000 occupiers, and not from the
10,000 landowners, that the national improvement must spring.
That while the latter are kept in serfdom, and deprived of the
rewards, and therefore destitute of the incentives of industry, it is
vain to expect true national improvement from any amount of
energy and exertion of the former. Unless indeed we mean the
improvement which consists in driving the people out. There is
one "immobility" with which I would wish to see us "cursed," and
that would be—if I may use the expression—the "immobility" of
the people from their native land. There is one progress I could
wish to stay, and that is the progress of the emigration that is
draining away our strength.

Of all real improvement of Ireland we must lay the foundation
by elevating the character and condition of the people. This we
never can do while we keep them serfs—while they are so, we will
indeed be cursed by the "immobility" of which we have had the
experience long enough—the "perennial desolation" which has
never yet known a change.

I have observed that this assumption runs through all the arguments made for the continuance of the absolute dominion of the landlord—the assumption that no improvement can be effected except
by the immediate agency of the landlord, or under his superin-

tendence, or control—that we are to trust nothing to the energy or the enterprise of the tenant—and that it is impossible for any but the landlords in Ireland to be the real improvers of the soil. It might shake our faith in the soundness of such an opinion to reflect that it is contradicted by all experience—that the only improvements that ever have been effected have been so where the occupier has been protected either by a lease or by the custom of tenant right. Experience only confirms that which we might infer beforehand from the circumstances of the country. The occupiers hold the keys of the improvement of the soil.

Lord Dufferin is constantly arguing on this assumption—that none but landlords can improve.

In another letter he actually claims for the landlord the right of turning off his tenants exactly as he would his farm servants whenever he chooses to consider them deficient in energy or skill:—

"It is a mistake to imagine that non-payment of rent is the only circumstance which can justify evictions. Any one acquainted with the management of land is aware that an unskilful farmer, even though he pay his rent, may do his landlord's property more harm than an industrious tenant who is occasionally in arrear. Few things are more liable to deterioration than land, and the value of a field may be as completely annihilated for a certain number of years as that of a house off which you have taken the roof. Now, one of the landlord's most important duties is that of insuring the consummate cultivation of his estate, and to hold him up to obloquy because he makes a point of *weeding his property of men whose want of energy, or skill, or capital* renders them incapable of doing their duty by their farms, and replacing them by more suitable tenants, is hardly reasonable."

According to this theory, the tenant is, in fact, to be a species of bailiff or deputy of the landlord; the landlord's chief duty being not to benefit his tenants, but to ensure "the consummate cultivation of his farm," and for this purpose to "WEED OUT" the tenants when they fail in the energy, the skill, or the capital that is necessary for that purpose. If this be not an approach to the "metayer" system it certainly makes the landlord the superintendent of the cultivation. But I protest I think this is very like an open avowal of a policy of extermination; it is so if extermination be necessary for the discharge of the chief duty of the landlord, the ensuring of "the consummate cultivation of his farm."

Surely, if Lord Dufferin intended to point out the odious nature of the power which he claims, he could not have devised a phrase better calculated to accomplish it than this very one of "weeding." One of the most important duties of a landlord is to cast out his tenants whom he may think deficient in energy, or skill, or capital; to pluck them up like noxious "weeds," and fling them over the bounds of the estate to wither and to die. And this, be it observed,

in the case of tenants who pay their rent. The whole of this
singular but deeply instructive passage is an expansion of the
statement with which it commences that "it is a mistake to suppose
that it is only non-payment of rent that can justify ejectment." If
anything were wanting to justify "strong and vigorous dealing"
with the Irish land question, it will be found in such candid
avowals of what is passing in the minds of the proprietary class.

I pray the earnest attention of every reader to the real character
and extent of this process of " weeding."

Lord Dufferin leaves us in no doubt upon these points. I put
two sentences of his letter together, and I prove to demonstration
that whether he means it or not, his theories of landlord right
and duty involve the extermination of the greater proportion of the
present occupiers of the soil. In one passage, he writes:—

" Bad husbandry and non-payment of rent constitute, even according
to Mr. Butt, just occasions of eviction. By the inflexible application of
these principles there is no property in Ireland which would not be
cleared of a large proportion of its occupants in ten years, and the immediate effect of his beneficent efforts would be universal discontent and
an enormous stimulus to emigration, counterbalanced perhaps by a rapid
improvement in cultivation, and a brevet promotion for some hundreds
of thousands of agricultural labourers at the expense of a corresponding
number of tenant farmers."

That is, if even in leases for 63 years, at a moderate rent,
conditions be inserted that tenants must pay their rents and properly cultivate their farms, with all the stimulus which leases at fair
rents would give to industry and improvement—these conditions
in ten years would drive the greater proportion of the occupants
from their farms.

Why? There can be but one reason—because the great majority
of the occupants, even were they granted a fair lease, would not pay
their rent, and would not properly cultivate their farms. Here, then,
is a clear, distinct, and most positive statement of the character of
the present occupants of the farms. They cannot hold their farms
if landlords insist on the conditions of payment of rent and proper
cultivation of their farms.

But how are landlords to deal with these very same tenants,
holding within the next ten years as tenants from year to year—
tenants, be it remembered, incapable of holding on the condition
of payment of rent and proper cultivation? I quote Lord Dufferin
again:—

"Non-payment of rent is not the only thing which can justify ejectment. . . . One of the most important duties is that of insuring the
consummate cultivation of the farm; to hold him to public obloquy
because he MAKES A POINT of weeding his property of men whose want
of energy, or skill, or capital, makes them incapable of doing their duty
by their farms."

I ask of any rational man to read these sentences—dismal and unhappy sentences—and say if they do not mean?

The present occupants cannot hold their lands if payment of rent and proper cultivation be insisted on.

No landlord will let a tenant remain who will not pay his rent.

It is the actual duty of a landlord to weed out those who cannot or will not do their duty to their farms by " consummate cultivation." Is not the inference inevitable?

Therefore, the present occupants must be driven away, or to use that which, I suppose, is the proper, or at least the newest phrase, " weeded out." It is a happy variation of the old term of " clearance." Estates were " cleared " of Irishmen as Indian plains are cleared of jungle and wild beasts. Lord Dufferin, more delicately, " weeds" out the occupiers as men weed out the hemlock and the thistle from their fields.

It is impossible for Lord Dufferin to write half a dozen sentences without impressing on them the leading idea that has unhappily taken possession of his mind.

" One of the greatest benefits to Ireland has resulted from the legal machinery invented to transfer the estates of incumbered proprietors to the hands of persons with sufficient capital to improve them. Surely the same policy ought to be pursued in facilitating *the transference of farms from the impoverished agriculturist to the man of energy and capital.*"

That is—exactly as the Incumbered Estates Commission sold out the old proprietors, a process of " weeding " must be applied to get rid of the present occupiers of the soil.

I do earnestly pray the attention of every reader to this clear and distinct declaration. The true policy for Ireland is :—

" To FACILITATE THE TRANSFERENCE OF FARMS FROM THE IMPOVERISHED AGRICULTURIST TO THE MAN OF ENERGY AND CAPITAL."

Not, be it observed, to help the impoverished agriculturist—not to seek out and, if possible, to remove the causes of his distress—but to transfer his farm to the man of energy and capital. Surely this describes a policy of getting rid of the present occupiers of the soil, in order to replace them by " MEN OF CAPITAL."

Whenever the County of Down is " weeded" of all occupiers holding less than fifteen acres, and when all who hold over fifteen acres, but have not energy and capital, are replaced by men who have, I venture to believe that it will not be the happy and prosperous county that it is now.

I must add that if we wanted proof of the state of thraldom in which the occupiers are kept by insecurity of tenure—nothing could be more suggestive of it than Lord Dufferin's statement, that even on an estate, which we must presume to be well and liberally managed, an ejectment is served as an ordinary mode of quickening the tenant in the payment of his rent.

"To serve an ejectment is frequently the only way of inducing a dilatory tenant to pay up an arrear of rent, in which case it bears the same relation to an eviction as a lawyer's letter does to an action at law. On my own estates, dozens of ejectments have been served for one eviction that has taken place, and the more indulgent the landlord, the more disposed will some of his tenants be to wait for this proof of his patience being exhausted."

The service of an ejectment, even in the inferior court, is rather an expensive attorney's letter. But is it possible for tenants living under such a system to be really independent? Will they ever be secure in their tenure, or can they have any assurance that the ejectment may not turn out a reality? Between landlord and tenant ejectments are dangerous playthings. Could such a thing occur upon any English estate? Or can there be confidence between a landlord and his tenants in a state of society in which the proprietor finds, or thinks it necessary to adopt such a mode of stirring up a lagging tenant to pay his rent?

I do not stop to point out many inconsistencies which present themselves in this commentary of Lord Dufferin. The Act for the sale of incumbered estates contained provisions annulling contracts, and interfered with rights of property far more violently than any regulation I propose as to tenants leases. It ruined many a proprietor and many a creditor who, if the sale of estates had been left to the operation of old laws, might and would have preserved their properties. Its advocates justified it because it was necessary for public purposes to obtain a solvent proprietary. Its operations were carried out in disregard of the ruin and misery which, in individual cases, it entailed. Lord Dufferin praises that Act, but he will not tolerate a measure which would give a solvent and contented tenantry to Ireland, because it might interfere with contingent rights of property in projected villas near Belfast Lough.

In one sentence I am told that I am condemning Ireland to "immobility" for 60 years; in the next, that my plan would lead to a sweeping revolution in the occupation of Irish farms, to a great improvement in agriculture, and to a "brevet promotion" of agricultural labourers to be tenant farmers.

And this very process, which is made an objection to my bill, is the very process to which Lord Dufferin points as the only one that is to remedy the present state of things.

Let me deal at once with this most singular objection, that I still leave the tenant open to eviction, because I insist as the condition of his holding upon the payment of a moderate rent and on the proper cultivation of his farm. I have taken especial care to frame the latter condition so as to prevent it ever being used as an instrument of oppression. It can only apply to cases in which the tenant is really destroying the property in the farm. But I deny that if they were granted leases of long tenure and at fair rents, the Irish occupiers would not observe these conditions. To assert the contrary is to adopt that system of depreciation, not to say slander, of the Irish people which has been too often the resource of those who have desired to deprive them of their political and social rights. Why should we assume that if an Irishman is given a farm at a fair rent and with a reasonably framed covenant against waste by improper cultivation, he will not be able to retain it. What is there in the character or history of our people which justifies this? Is it proved by the industry, the energy, and the enterprise they exhibit in every country except their own? Is it proved by what they have done, in spite of every discouragement, in their own? Is it consistent with the eulogium—Lord Dufferin's own eulogium—on that people? Will any man believe it who reads the instances I have selected from those proved before the Parliamentary Committee of 1864? No one can have read Lord Dufferin's letters without seeing that he is constantly assuming propositions, from which, when they are plainly put to him, he shrinks. Never was there a writer who so successfully used the sophisms of the Enthymeme to impose upon himself. The suppressed proposition of his syllogism upon this point is, that an Irish occupier is incapable of being a punctual and improving tenant. I have traced that proposition to its inevitable conclusions, according to his own words. I am quite sure he will not abide by it when it is removed from the haze of his own imaginative logic, and plainly put before him, with all its necessary consequences, in print.

If the Irish peasant is capable of being a punctual and improving tenant, surely he will be able to retain the interest conferred on him by the measure I propose. That measure, at all events, offers him all the inducements possible to habits of punctuality and improvement. If he be capable of acquiring these habits, and if we place him in the position in which he has the strongest motives to adopt them—if experience can tell us anything of human nature, he will be very likely to be both punctual and improving.

If it were really true that it is not possible, under any modification of our present system of land tenure, for the Irish people to keep their ground in their native country, then the reflection would suggest itself that this system must be wholly unsuited to the country, and that it must be altogether changed.

I do not need to resort to this argument. Lord Dufferin tells me that even if the people obtained the leases I ask for them they still must go. I only say, let us try to give them at least the last chance of living in their own land, and before we drive them to exile let us offer them the opportunity of making out life at home by securing them a tenure of their holding such as will give them the opportunity of being industrious if they will.

Is this too much to ask for the old people of any land?   Is it too much to ask for a people such as Lord Dufferin describes?

Are we, my Lord, without an effort to help them, to let that people go?

Will any man living deliberately tell me that we discharge our obligations to the millions of human beings now located on this Irish soil when we say to them—go to another land—without caring for their condition—without troubling ourselves to inquire what becomes of them when they do go—without even providing them with the means of going?

Has anything like this ever been done by any civilized or uncivilized government upon earth?

I have really thought it very strange that, in all the writings I have read upon this subject, no one appeared to think that the people now living in Ireland have any claim of any kind either upon the Government which claims their allegiance or the country in which they have been born.   I have already pointed out that if an Irish evicted tenant emigrates to America he cannot, by that act, escape the duties of his allegiance to the Queen.   At home he has no means of living.   The troops of his Sovereign have been employed in guarding the servants of the landlord who have pulled down his house.   He has been turned adrift upon the road, it may be from fields that his own hard toil, or the hard roil of his father, has made fruitful.   He emigrates.   By the valley of the Mississippi or the Ohio he finds, under American law, the opportunity of industry which is denied him at home.   Prosperity, and even affluence, reward his industry in his new abode   A war breaks out between the country that has thrust him out and the country that has given him protection.   If British troops invaded the country of his adoption—I ought to say the country to which British law has flung him—and if he took up arms in defence of his home, British law would inflict on him the penalties of treason, and were he seized in arms, like Wolfe Tone, that law would visit him with a traitor's doom.

If allegiance and protection be reciprocal it is impossible to say that we have nothing to do with the two or three millions of our people who are doomed to emigration but to thrust them out, with hot haste, as quickly as we can, that when they are gone the estates of the landlords may become more productive of fat cattle and of rent.   I say, on the contrary, that all the conditions of the social compact, all the principles of civilized and Christian jurisprudence, oblige the statesman who deals with Ireland's social condition to think of these two millions of Irishmen and to provide for them a place and a livelihood at home.

" Every man," says Edmund Burke, " has a right to all that society, with all its combinations of skill and capital, can do in his favour."   It was by maxims like these that this greatest of political philosophers stayed the spread in England of the principles of revolutionary France. What answer could we give to the Irish emigrant who, sorrowful and reluctant, embarks at Queenstown to leave for ever his native land because his landlord denies him the tenure which would enable him to exercise his industry at home—what answer, I say, could we give him if he were to ask us:—" Is this all that British society, with all his combination of skill and capital, can do in my favour?"

Emigrate! emigrate! emigrate! Is America to take the place of Connaught in the ribald cry of a new war of extermination against the Irish race. Many parallels have been drawn between the servitude of the Irish and that of the Israelites in Egypt. Is the resemblance to be complete, even in the last scene? After centuries of oppression of the Irish race do their oppressors " hasten" at last " to thrust them out ?"*

I have adverted at, perhaps, unreasonable length to the statements which have been given to the public by your Lordship, Lord Dufferin, and Lord Rosse. Upon this question these writings are not merely arguments, they are facts. They are revelations of what is passing in the minds of Irish proprietors. I am not about to cavil at words, or rest an argument on isolated phrases. But no man can attentively read the publications of Lord Dufferin and Lord Rosse, or even your Lordship's own letter to me, without feeling that in their general purport they express, on the part of the proprietors, a distrust of the occupiers, which makes them determined not to give those occupiers an interest in the soil. This is the leading idea, if I may use the expression, which pervades and guides all the reasoning of these publications. It finds its expression in Lord Rosse's avowal that the landowners are resolved to fight the battle with their hands untied; in Lord Dufferin's argument, that it is the duty of the landlord to weed his estate of tenants who have not the skill or the capacity to do their duty in consummate cultivation of their farms; and in your own denunciation of my proposal of compulsory leases as one calculated to deprive the Protestant proprietors of all influence with the people and of all control in the management of their estates.

The result of all is that Irish proprietors generally think it expedient to keep the tenants entirely under their control, and this feeling is influenced, to some extent, by religious—to some

* "The Egyptians were urgent with the people that they might send them out of the land in haste."—*Exodus*, xii. 33.

extent by political, motives, and also by the belief that, to ensure
a proper cultivation of the farms, it is necessary that the tenant
should be under the supervision and direction of the owner of the
estate.   I am not now discussing the reasonableness or unreasonable-
ness of these feelings.   I only state, as a matter of fact, that these
feelings are entertained.   The view taken of the position of Ireland
by those who represent the opinions of the proprietors is that, from
one cause or other, it is necessary to have a dependent tenantry,
acting under the control and subject to the power of the proprietors
of the soil.

It is of the utmost importance that we should bear these things
in mind when we come to consider the measures of practical legislation which have been proposed.   There are now two proposals of
this kind before Parliament and the country—one the proposal of
the late Ministry, embodied in the bill brought in by Mr. Fortescue;
the other that of the present Ministers, contained in the measure
offered to us by Lord Naas.

In all that I have written on this subject I have endeavoured to
avoid canvassing the merits or demerits of any proposal that has
been made.   I have contented myself with stating my own views
of the indispensable requisites of any measure that will really relieve
Ireland of the disgrace and misery of our present system of land
tenure.   But strongly as I hold these views, I am far from wishing
to discourage any effort which is made by any person in office or out
of office to settle the land question of Ireland, even upon conditions
which I believe to be inadequate to attain that result.   It is scarcely
possible to legislate upon the subject without recognizing some of
the principles upon which true legislation must be based.   There
is something gained when we induce the British Parliament "to
touch, even with the tip of their finger," the heavy burden that
English rule has laid upon the Irish nation in the system of land
tenure which it maintains.

I regard either the measure of Mr. Fortescue or that of Lord
Naas as a last attempt to remedy the most flagrant evils of the
insecurity of tenure without interfering with the landlord's absolute
dominion.   In the state of feeling which exists between classes in
this country, I believe the problem to be an impossible one.   It may
be well, however, that the experiment should be tried.   Is it possible
so to legislate as generally to encourage improvements and give the
tenant security for his industry while you leave to the landlord the
power of arbitrary eviction, and the uncontrolled right to do what
he will with his own?   These were really the conditions of the
problem which both Lord Naas and Mr. Fortescue had to solve.

Accepting these conditions, the bill of Mr. Fortescue was framed
with great care and with great liberality.   It was drawn with the
most scrupulous care to avoid the slightest interference with what
are termed the rights of property.   It left every existing contract

perfectly untouched.   It permitted every landlord in future to let his land upon whatever terms and on whatever terms he pleased. But it did all which could be done by any legislation, restricted within such principles, to enable the tenant to acquire by his improvements a property in his farm.

This will be apparent to any one carefully examining its provisions—they are, indeed, few, and easily understood.   It permitted the tenant to make certain specified improvements* on his farm with or without his landlord's consent. Upon the termination of his interest he was to be paid a sum equivalent to the value of the increase which these improvements caused in the letting value of the farm.   A possession of 41 years was to be considered as a sufficient compensation for the improvements; and if the landlord chose to grant or offer a lease for 31 years at the old rent no further claim could be made against him.

Then followed a clause absolutely necessary on the principles upon which the bill was framed. *Tenants were prevented from obtaining any compensation for improvements which any written agreement prohibited them from making.*

And finally, a still more important limitation—*exempted from the*

* In all the observations I make upon either of these measures I do not mean to express an approval of the restrictions they both contain as to the classes of improvements for which compensation is to be made. I am sure that it would be possible for an occupier very greatly to enrich his farm, while his improvements could not be specifically brought under any of the descriptions given in either bill. Fully to apply the principle of compensation it would be necessary to adopt the rule of saying that if the tenant gave up his holding in such an improved condition that it would let for a higher rent than it would bring in the condition in which he got it, the value he had so created should belong to himself. Of course there would be great difficulty in applying such a rule, it might be, after an interval of years—the very difficulty which Lord Dufferin points out in the working of Mr. Fortescue's bill. These difficulties are not insuperable—and the rule is the only way in which the principle of compensation can be fully carried out.

In Mr. Fortescue's bill the improvements for which a tenant can claim compensation are—
1. The thorough drainage or main drainage of land.
2. Reclaiming of land from tidal or other waters.
3. Protection of land by embankment from tidal or other waters.
4. Reclaiming bog land, or reclaiming or enclosing waste land:
5. Making roads or fences.
6. Erection of farm buildings, houses for stewards, labourers, or other persons employed in superintending the cultivation of, or in cultivating, land, and of other buildings for farm purposes.

Under the bill of Lord Naas it is proposed to compensate the tenants for improvements of any of the following classes—
1. The thorough drainage or main drainage of land.
2. The reclaiming of bog land, or reclaiming or inclosing of waste land, or clearing land of rocks or stones.
3. The removal of useless fences.
4. The making of fences.
5. The making of farm roads.
6. The erecting of a farmhouse or other buildings solely for agricultural purposes suitable to the holding, or the rebuilding or enlarging the same.

The three first may be made and charged for ever against the will of the landlord. The three last require his assent.

operation of the Act all tenants holding under leases made before its passing.

This Act, therefore, dealt only with tenants holding as tenants from year to year to year and with tenancies to be created by future leases.

I pass by altogether the provisions intended for the ascertainment of the compensation payable. These are matters of detail which do not affect in the least the principle of the measure. The proposal may be open to the criticism of Lord Dufferin, that it might be very difficult to ascertain exactly the value added to the farm by the improvements after the lapse of an interval of some years. There would, however, be far greater difficulty and inconvenience in enforcing any provision which would require the tenant to value and register his improvements at the time when they are made. Apart from every other objection, it would be at once inviting, with his landlord, an occasion of quarrel and dispute. Such a provision would destroy even the slender chance that there is of the measure in any case being of use.

What Mr. Fortescue's measure really effected is this:—It incorporated with all future lettings of land a contract that the tenant shall be at liberty to make improvements, and be paid for them in all cases in which the agreement for letting is silent on the subject. But by permitting the landlord to make his own terms it still left all contracts perfectly free. The landlord still could do what he liked with his own. The bill simply proposed to apply to contracts of tenancy a principle much more rational than that which now regulates them. In the absence of any express contract every such tenancy would in future imply an agreement that the tenant, when giving up his holding should be paid for any addition he may have made by his industry or his expenditure to the value of the land.

I am far, very far from undervaluing the establishment of such wise and rational principles. It would be an immense improvement in our jurisprudence. Even in a country like Ireland it would, probably, in the course of years, effect an alteration in the habits and customs connected with the letting of land. It is very difficult to see upon what rational grounds such a measure was resisted. It would have left every landlord in Ireland with just the same power and the same privileges as he has now.

The bill introduced by Lord Naas deals somewhat differently with the question. He also proposes to permit a certain class of improvements to be made with or without the landlord's assent. But he requires notice to be given to the landlord, and plans to be submitted to an officer of the Board of Works; if approved of by him the improvements may be carried on in defiance of the landlord's dissent. And this measure holds out to the tenant a further inducement to improve, by offering him a loan from Government to be a charge upon the farm, both in his own hands and in that of the landlord after the reversion of the tenant's interest has fallen into his hands.   Unlike the bill of Mr. Fortescue, that of Lord Naas does apply to existing leases, and it enables the tenants who hold under such leases to make improvements and acquire a right to compensation even against the dissent of their landlords.

Whatever opinion may be formed of the value of either of these measures, it is of vital importance that their actual operation should be understood—that no false hopes should be excited—and that the Irish people should not suppose that they accomplish purposes which neither of them profess even to touch.

In the first place, both of them deal only with a limited class of improvements.   Lord Naas's bill still further limits them by making it necessary to submit them beforehand to an officer of the Board of Works; this would, in truth, be prohibitory of the small improvements which Ireland most needs.   Mr. Fortescue's encumbers the right of the tenant to make improvements with no vexatious restrictions; it harasses him with no preliminary impediments or conditions; it leaves him perfectly free to improve, so long as his landlord does not interpose to take that liberty away.   On the other hand, it leaves it perfectly optional with the landlord whether the measure shall have application to a single tenant on his estate.   Lord Naas's has just the same effect as to all the yearly tenants on the estate. Its provisions apply to every tenant holding by lease in spite of the landlord's dissent or even his strenuous opposition.

In considering measures of this nature we must always remember that we have to estimate its effect upon two different classes of tenants—upon those holding by lease and those who are tenants from year to year, or, in other words, virtually tenants at will.   The latter class include the vast majority of the Irish tenantry.

As to tenants holding under existing leases, Mr. Fortescue's Bill would have no effect whatever.   They are expressly excluded from its operation.

As to future leases, no one can doubt that every such lease in the rare instances in which it will be granted would contain a special agreement superseding the provisions of the Act.   It is quite vain to say that this would be discreditable to the landlord— that it would be an evasion of an Act of Parliament.   It would be neither one or the other.   If Parliament means to take away the discretion of the landlord, nothing is easier than for Parliament to say it.   If the discretion is left to him it is plainly intended he should exercise it.   It is only where the lease is silent that the statute steps in.   The effect might possibly be to encourage arrangements in future leases upon the subject.   But the landlord who really believes it essential for him to retain the management of his property in his own hands will always in granting new leases make stipulations which will leave the question of improvements entirely under his own control.

But let us see how either measure—that of Lord Naas or of Mr. Fortescue—will practically act in the case of the great mass of the Irish tenantry, those holding from year to year. Under Mr. Fortescue's Bill the very humblest tenant may make improvements himself, and, *if his landlord does not interfere,* he will, no doubt, acquire a property in his land. Under Lord Naas's Bill the small farmer will never be in a position to take the preliminary step—as to him the Bill will be completely a dead letter. The yearly tenant who is rich enough, and contemplates improvements considerable enough, to bear the expense of an application to the Board of Works, can acquire a property, or subject his farm to a Government loan, but upon the very same condition that his landlord does not interfere. In every case of a tenant from year to year, the landowner holds the power in his own hands. The notice to quit puts an end to the arrangement. The landlord must be an acquiescing party to the improvements, whether they are made by the industry of the tenant or carried into effect by the cumbrous and costly process of a Government loan from the Board of Works.

I admit at once that under Mr. Fortescue's Bill the occupier of a small farm might possibly, in some instances, succeed in effecting improvements without provoking the interference of an indolent or careless proprietor. At all events, this Bill would accomplish that in which Lord Naas's entirely fails—it would make it impossible that acts of robbery should be committed as to future improvements. If a landlord, whether from carelessness or design, permitted his tenant hereafter to expend his industry upon improvements, he never could seize on the fruits of that industry for himself. He must interfere to warn the tenant, or he must leave him the value of the improvements he makes.

I believe, however, the instances would be rare in which the industry of the tenant would thus steal a march on the dominion of the landlord. It never would happen on estates that are called well managed, one of those estates on which notices to quit are a part of its ordinary management, or on which scenes like those which were described in the trial for murder at the Kerry assizes, could occur.

On the other hand, Lord Naas's Bill would apply to a case which Mr. Fortescue left wholly untouched, and it is the only instance in which either measure would be really effective. A tenant holding by lease a farm of considerable value may desire to make large improvements upon that farm. It may be worth his while to incur the expense and trouble of an application to the Board of Works, and the improvements may be of such a character that this machinery may be applicable. In this instance Lord Naas's measure enables such a tenant to effect them, even in defiance of his landlord's dissent, if the public officer determines that the improvements are such as ought to be made.

I do not undervalue such a provision, especially in the principles it establishes. But it is one that will affect very few. It will do nothing for the great mass of the Irish tenantry, who do not hold by lease, and who, if they did hold by lease, have not the means of defraying the cost of an inquiry by a public officer, and cannot effect improvements upon the scale which alone could justify such an inquiry.

I am not incorrect in saying that the practical effect of either Bill would be this. Lord Naas's Bill would enable the substantial farmer, who holds under a lease, to make improvements on his farm, even against his landlord's will, provided he obtained the sanction of the Board of Works. Under Mr. Fortescue's Bill the poor but industrious farmer might acquire, from a careless or inattentive owner, some little property by the expenditure of his industry on his farm. In every other instance, under either Bill, the permission of improvements would be just as it is now, a matter in which the tenant is dependent solely on the good will and pleasure of his lord.

Mr. Fortescue's measure would be an admirable one if all the lands in Ireland were held from year to year, and all landlords were willing that their tenants should acquire a property by improvements in their farms. Lord Naas's would be still more useful if all tenants held by lease, and were rich enough to make improvements which would bear the expense of a survey by the Board of Works. Unhappily the circumstances of Ireland are not exactly those for which the provisions of either bill would appear to be framed.

But let us see how far either Bill may go in recognizing principles which lay down useful guides in legislation on this subject.

Mr. Fortescue's Bill generally recognizes the principle that in future when land is once entrusted to a tenant's care the landlord who does not interfere to prevent him from making improvements shall never be permitted to seize on these improvements. Is it going much further to carry back that very same principle to the past—to adopt the "retrospective clause of Lord Derby's Bill of 1852," and to give some real protection to the occupiers of the Irish soil? This would be accomplished by carrying the very clause which was framed by Lord Naas, approved of by the Conservative Cabinet of that day—adopted by the Cabinets both of Lord Aberdeen and Lord Palmerston—sanctioned by statesmen of all parties, and carried by decisive majorities through the House of Commons.

But in the very case in which the measure of Lord Naas will be effective is there not a complete recognition of the principles for which I contend? In the case of a tenant holding under a lease it permits him to effect improvements against his landlord's will. It

P

allows him to charge these improvements upon the land—I care
not whether by a direct charge in his own favour or by the
machinery of a loan from the Board of Works.   What then
becomes of the inviolability of contracts?

"It is not so written in the bond."

The provisions of the lease are distinctly set aside.   Its covenants
bind the tenant to surrender the land to the landlord at the expiration of the term, free of all charge, and " with all improvements
made thereon."   You make these covenants absolutely waste paper.
You hinder the landlord who has parted with his property on the
very faith of these covenants from enforcing them, and you enable
the tenant, who got possession of the property by entering into a
solemn contract to observe the covenants—to charge permanently
the land which was so entrusted to his care.

Is there anything in what I propose more subversive of property?
more inconsistent with that which is called proprietary right?

If all tenants held under leases, and had farms large enough to
bear the expense of the inquiry this very clause would accomplish
almost all that is needed.   If once you permit the tenant, against
the will of his landlord, to acquire an interest beyond the letter
of his bargain, no reason can be assigned why your legislation
should not be so framed as to extend that privilege to those
who hold from year to year.   If you are prepared to interfere
with the contracts and the rights of property—that is, if you
prevent the landlord from exacting his "pound of flesh," why
is this to be done only for the rich and prosperous tenant, whilst
you do nothing for the poor and the humble man—the man
who most needs your protection?   In Lord Naas's Bill, it is
literally the old story, one law for the rich tenant and another
for the poor.   Nay, more, there is one law for the good landlord
and another for the bad.   The only landlord whom it coerces
is the man who has given leases on his estate.   As to the landlord who has kept his tenants in his power it leaves him " with
his hands untied."

But I do earnestly pray the attention to this of all persons really
anxious to solve the difficulties of the Irish land question.   Here
we have two measures—each prepared by an Irish gentleman of
practical acquaintance with the subject with which he deals—both
of them prepared with very great skill; one of them with great and
even generous liberality.   Both these measures are designed and
framed for the very purpose of securing to the tenant compensation
for the *bona fide* improvements he may effect—of giving him, in
fact, the long coveted opportunity of expending his industry upon
his farm.   Up to a certain point the arrangements of both seem
excellent, if not quite perfect.   At that point each of them breaks
down.   It is just the point where the notice to quit intervenes.

Both measures fail in the objects at which they aim. They fail, not for want of skill or of inclination on the part of their framers, but because they were dealing with occupiers who are completely under the dominion of their landlords, and upon whom, so long as you leave them so, you can confer no rights. It is vain to attempt to attach the privilege of improvement to a tenure that perishes in the very creation of the privilege. No human legislation can enable a tenant to improve his farm without his landlord's consent while he is left in a position in which he ceases to be tenant at the pleasure of that lord.

Does this legislation really amount to more than this?—Every tenant in Ireland may improve, and be paid for his improvements, provided always that his landlord does not exercise his power of declaring that he shall not be so ?

Of what avail is this to meet the state of serfdom and subjection in which the occupiers of the soil are held? You ask the Irish land-lords to make their tenants independent by permitting them to acquire a property in their farms. Surely, if the Irish landowners desire so to make their tenants independent, they may do so now. Are we to forget the systematic refusal of leases for the express purpose of keeping the tenants under their dominion, or the management of their estates in their own hands? The whole tendency of the management of landed property has been every day more and more to reduce the tenant to the condition of a servant of his lord, to impose upon him restrictions more and more coercive and vexatious. The great principle of Irish landlords, of late years, is that "the land-lords hands must be untied,"—that the improvement of the country depends upon the landlord having the management of his property— that the political and social elevation of Ireland can only be effected by means of their mastery over the people. Is all this to be changed by the magic of a few lines? Are all these cherished principles of action at once to be abandoned? Can we expect the very men, who now refuse to give their tenants the shortest lease, to be found cheerfully to assent to their acquiring something like a permanent interest by the improvement of their farms?

Are the Irish serfs to be emancipated by the declaration that they are to be independent of their landlord's will whenever it is the will of their landlord that they shall be so independent?

Nothing can be further from my thought than to discourage the efforts which any person may think it right to make in support of the measure of Mr. Fortescue, or to blame those who expect good to follow from that of Lord Naas. No one will more sin-cerely rejoice than myself if in either shape the experiment shall succeed, if it be found that either of these measures place on Irish estates an independent tenantry acquiring a property for themselves, and enriching the country by the application of their industry to the soil. If the experiment fails its failure may prepare men's minds for bolder and more effectual legislation. Another " conspicuous failure" may perhaps convince all men that no skill, and no industry can unravel the intricate involvement in which two centuries of mismanagement have tangled the relations of our land tenure. The Gordian knot must for ever remain knotted or it must be cut. But surely I am justified in saying that even since last year the question is changed by the revelations of the feelings of the landowners which have been elicited in the course of this discussion. Whatever hopes may have been entertained last year that the landowners of Ireland would not interpose their veto against the application to their estates of a measure like that proposed by Mr. Fortescue, he will be very sanguine who will read over Lord Rosse's most instructive pamphlet and really entertain that expectation now.

The effect of every legislative measure must be calculated by the prejudices, and even the passions of those by whom it must be carried into effect. This legislation is to act on a state of things in which the tenantry have no greater tenure than that of a yearly tenancy, and in many instances not even so great, in which leases are almost unknown, and in which the greater number of landlords regard it as their interest, or their duty, or it may be as both their interest and duty to keep their tenantry in a state of subjection to themselves. Applied to this state of things the measure, either of Lord Naas or Mr. Fortescue may in some few and exceptional instances be the means of accomplishing good. In the generality of Irish estates the landlords will exercise the power which in either bill is left them of preventing its operation. They can do so by the very simple process of intimating through the bailiff their desire that no tenant shall make the improvements which Lord Rosse calls irregular without some special sanction and agreement. In the case of properties on which the system of government is not so perfect in its arrangements it will be done by the more clumsy process of tendering new agreements which every tenant must sign under the penalty of the notice to quit. The landlord will retain the very same power which he now has of prohibiting or assenting to improvements at his own absolute discretion, and when he does assent to them of dictating whatever terms he thinks fit.

The extent to which the system of coercive agreements is already resorted to is much greater than is generally supposed. I have already mentioned an instance in which notices to quit were served on the whole tenantry of an estate, and in which they were left the option of remaining only on the condition of signing agreements which bound them to consult the agent of the property in the minutest points of the cultivation of their farms, and in which I was compelled to advise them that they had no choice but to submit. I have been assured by respectable authority that agreements of this nature are not uncommon. There are written agreements upon

Irish estates which bind the tenant not to give more than one night's lodging to any one not a resident on the estate, and not to permit any of his family to marry without the agent's consent.

Among the petitions presented to the House of Commons in the Session of 1866 was one from some tenants on an Irish estate. In the printed copy of the petition published by the House of Commons the name of both the estate and the landlord were suppressed. But the facts stated are that a number of tenants who had long been in possession of their farms, who had expended money upon them, were served with notice to quit, and as the condition of its abandonment were asked to sign a new agreement which bound them to give up possession if demanded on the 7th of November in each year. If they held over after this demand, or violated any of the rules laid down in the agreement, *they bound themselves for each month they did so to pay a ruinous penal rent.* No one can say that this agreement was not binding in law.

Conditions of this nature are not uncommon in Irish tenures, even those supposed to be leasehold. I have heard of an estate on which most of the tenants hold leases for lives, but *every one of the leases contains a covenant that it is to be surrendered on demand, and that it is to be void if the surrender be not made.*

Both the measures on which I am commenting are open to the observation that they fall far short of doing to the tenant the justice which was effected by the provisions of the measure introduced by Lord Naas himself in 1852. In the tract on land tenure I have already pointed out all that is involved in the Cabinet and Parliamentary sanction which was so solemnly given to the " retrospective clause" which that measure contained.* It is sufficient to say now that neither of the measures at present offered to Parliament contain it.

Both of them, again, are open to the observations which I have made, as to all measures intended to deal with the Irish land question.† Neither of them places the occupiers of the rest of Ireland in as good a position as the Ulster tenant is placed by the custom of tenant right. " It fails, therefore, in one of the essential objects of doing equal justice to all; and more than this, it incurs a danger surely not to be despised—that of supplying a plausible pretext for reducing the Ulster custom to the privileges conferred by the Act."†

When Lord Dufferin proposes to engraft on Mr. Fortescue's measure a loan from the Government to enable landlords to buy up the improvements of their tenants, it is plain that in Ulster such a loan would be sought, and sought for the purpose of buying

---

* *Land Tenure in Ireland,* page 78 to 89. I know of nothing more instructive in connexion with the land question than a study of the Parliamentary history of that celebrated " retrospective clause." It is sketched in the pages to which I refer.

† *Ante,* page 18.

out tenant right.   This would, of course, be the extinction of the
custom.   No landlord who had once bought up the tenant right
of a farm would ever on that farm permit the custom to be renewed.

I have, in a former page, quoted Lord Dufferin's inadequate, and
worse than inadequate, definition of the Ulster custom.*   Tenant
right, is something very different from a custom "that the landlord will allow the outgoing tenant such a sum as will remunerate
him for improvements upon the soil."   It has been rightly pointed
out, that to identify the tenant right of Ulster with the claim to
compensation for improvements, is to confound two wholly different
things.†   The tenant right does not depend upon the fact of
improvements having been made.   It is not measured by the value
of those improvements.   The purchase of the tenant right of an
outgoing tenant is the purchase of a right of occupancy in a farm,
and that right of occupancy is treated as a property, although it
is invested with no legal protection, and rests wholly on a provincial
or local custom, enforced by sanctions very different from those of
law.‡

This property, though clothed with no legal form, has been the
subject of repeated transmissions by purchase and by descent.   It
has been left by will, and been regarded as the provision for families.
In some instances it has been the subject of marriage settlements;
in instances innumerable marriages have been contracted on the
faith of its possession.   There is not an estate on which it prevails,
on which it has not been repeatedly recognized by the owner.
Scarcely one in which he has not pocketed the arrears of a defaulting
tenant out of the purchase money of the incoming one—none in
which he has not been frequently called on to approve of and accept
the purchaser as the new tenant of the farm.

This right of property, whatever be its origin, is something
wholly distinct from the claims of a tenant to be compensated for
improvements effected on his farm.   When this property began to
be made the subject of inquiry, it was natural that its holders should
be anxious to invest it with the moral sanction of the argument that
it is now in reality the value of the accumulated result of the capital
and labour of successive occupiers, whom the present owners represent.§   But just in the same way the owners in fee endeavour to

---

* *Ante*, page 108.
† Q. " You are aware that the sums paid for tenant right represents a sum paid for
occupancy and not a sum paid for compensation ?
A. " Yes ; certainly so.
Q. " Whenever you introduce the custom of Ulster tenant right, and bring it into
the consideration of questions of compensation you are mixing totally different things ?
A. " They are totally different things."—(Evidence of Judge Longfield, Land
Tenure Committee, Questions 325–326).
‡ See evidence collected, *ante*, pp. 78–79.
§ Lord Dufferin's evidence before Land Tenure Committee, question 966.

surround their rights with the very same sanction, by the statement that all property in land is really now the result of expenditure by past generations; but in neither instance is this the foundation of the right. The property exists wholly independent of this expenditure. That expenditure constitutes a very strong reason, in justice and in good conscience, why the property should never be disturbed.

Neither is it correct to define tenant right as a custom under which an outgoing tenant is permitted to obtain a sum of money from the succeeding tenant for giving up to him possession of the farm. This definition is deficient in not recognizing any interest in the seller, and *not describing what that interest is.* It is the right to hold at the old accustomed rent, with the understanding that this rent will only be varied when circumstances exist which entitle the landlord to increase it without disturbance of the property really represented by the tenant right. In the admirable report of Mr. O'Connell to the Repeal Association, to which I have already referred,* this element, perfectly essential to any definition of the true custom, is very well expressed. The custom is thus stated :—

" According to the practice of this right no person can get into occupation of a farm without paying the previous occupier the price of his occupation or good will, whether the land be held by lease or by will."

It is quite obvious that such a custom would mean nothing if the price of the good will were not calculated on the rent which the out-going tenant is paying. The landlord is, therefore, made a party to the purchase by the new tenant of a good will which is estimated at the old rent. Equity precludes him from ever after insisting on its arbitrary variation. The custom, in the language of the Report, precludes the landlord of a farm

" FROM SETTING IT AT SUCH AN INCREASE OF RENT AS TO DISPLACE TENANT RIGHT."

This is really the essential part of the custom, and it is upon the observance of this that the twenty-four millions of property,† which is the value of the Ulster tenant's property in their farms, depends. The Ulster custom of tenant right is one that entitles every tenant to fixity of tenure at his accustomed rent, except some circumstances entitle the landlord to increase that rent without taking into account the improvements the tenant may have effected on his farm. There is, of course, a sense in which " compensation for improvements " forms a part of the price of all interests in land. Every purchaser of that interest, whether it be the fee-simple or the leasehold, will give more for the land when it is improved, and in the increased price every seller receives compensation for his

* Report of Parliamentary Committee of Repeal Association. Vol. ii., p. 289, *ante,* page 107.
† Mr. Heron calculates that property as worth twenty-four millions. *Ante,* page 79.

expenditure in the improvement of the soil. In this sense, and in this sense only, does " compensation for improvements" enter as an element into the sale of the outgoing occupier's tenant right.

When pressed before the Land Tenure Committee, Lord Dufferin virtually admitted this :—

"Then if I understand you aright, the tenant right of the North is a kind of user or custom that has sprung up, and is allowed by the landlords, that a dealing shall take place for the goodwill of a farm, and a sum be paid for it by an incoming to an outgoing tenant, that sum consisting in part occasionally of compensation for any improvements that may be upon the farm, and in part for the privilege of coming into the enjoyment of the land?—Yes; I think that is so.

"I PRESUME THAT THE SAME RENT IS PAID, AS FAR AS THE LAND IS CONCERNED, AS THE OLD TENANT PAID?—YES.

"Is it not the fact that although that sum paid for tenant right is occasionally compounded of those two sums for the compensation for improvements, and for the value, if it can be called so, of the outgoing tenant's interest in the farm, it is very frequently paid for the latter of those two things alone?—Certainly.

"Entirely irrespective of any compensation for improvements on the farm?—Yes.

"Which may or may not exist, or have been made by the outgoing tenant?—Certainly." *

I believe it is not possible for any one to read over the extracts I have made from *Pynnar's Survey* † to entertain a doubt that this right of occupancy in the tenant originated in the evasion by the grantees of Ulster property of the conditions imposed upon them to place an estated tenantry upon their lands. But whatever be its origin the custom has now existed for a period which in fact, if not in law, is " time immemorial;" for time " whereof the memory of man runneth not to the contrary." I have already pointed out that in England copyhold tenures in reality originated in a similar custom. ‡ All considerations of justice and equity make it imperative that if necessary this immemorial custom should be declared to be the law. Precedent is not wanting in the statute by which Irish landowners in the Irish Parliament, protected their estates, which they held by " a custom of the country unrecognized by law." § In spite of all the objections that are made to the custom, the prosperity of Ulster is the decisive proof of its value. Wisdom as well as justice tells us that it should be maintained. And I earnestly hope, as I confidently believe that the day will never come when the British Parliament will lend money from the Imperial Treasury to Ulster landlords to enable them, under the guise of paying their tenants for improvements, in reality to buy out the Ulster custom of tenant right.

* Lord Dufferin's evidence before Land Tenure Committee, Questions 1126–1130.
† *Ante*, note to page 37.
‡ *Plea for the Celtic Race*, p. 49.
§ *Post*, page 281.

I have been able to do little more than glance at this portion of the subject—I mean the present position of the Ulster custom of tenant right. Is the continuance of that custom secure? I have adverted to some of the warnings which indicate its extinction at no distant day, unless legislative protection be given to the tenure of all the occupiers of the Irish soil. It is not possible too often to refer to the evidence given by Judge Longfield, that land jobbers in the Landed Estates Court were every day purchasing up Ulster properties with the very intention of making money by confiscating the property which the custom secured to the tenant in his farm.* He earnestly pressed upon Parliament the absolute necessity of protecting the interest of the tenant holding under such a custom in cases of sales in the Landed Estates Court. His proposal was, in all such cases, to enable the court to give the tenant a lease in order to protect the tenant in an interest which " had been recognized from time immemorial;" an interest which no good landlord would disturb, but by disturbing which an unscrupulous man received a bonus on his purchase. "Land jobbers," he told the committee, "were buying those estates with the intention of squeezing the tenants out of the estate." This is the testimony of the judicial personage who actually is obliged by law to sign the conveyance, which is the authority to the purchaser to commit this great robbery and wrong.

It is plain that any principle which would justify the compelling of a lease in the case of a sale under the Landed Estates Court would justify it in any case in which the custom of tenant right exists, and in which it is likely to be disturbed. " The custom of the country " is, in many instances, law. It ought always to be so. I shall presently show that when the interests of the gentry were concerned the landowners of Ireland made no scruple of violating the legal rights of property by doing substantial justice in making the custom of the country law.† But I now refer to this evidence for the purpose of showing that the property of the Ulster tenants now vested in tenant right requires the protection of law.

This is a matter of no light moment. It is of the gravest moment to every one who appreciates the value for Ireland of that strange and wayward, but, after all, that noble race who constitute the Protestant population of Ulster. They have their faults, their great faults of ancestral intolerance; but with that intolerance they have inherited from their covenanting or Puritan ancestors, from whom many of them are descended, some of the stern, but still sterling, qualities which make a people great. What lover of Ireland would wish our country to lose that bold and manly freedom, that proud, albeit it may be, that harsh spirit of independence—

* Evidence Land Tenure Committee, Questions 135, 136, 620, 638, 652, 697.
† *Post* page 241.

that prudent, even it be sometimes cold and ungainly, thrift—that
patient yet unconquerable energy, which are the qualities that in
their combination have made Ulster what it is? Take tenant right
away, and the Protestant people of Ulster—as we know and pride
ourselves on that people—will not long survive its loss. Unless
fixity of tenure be secured by law the Ulster custom of tenant
right is doomed.*

But upon the general question let me say, once for all, without meaning to undervalue the vast importance of a measure
which would secure to the tenant the right to make improvements
and be paid for them—even such a measure would never compensate for the absence of some security for tenure. Men are
influenced in expending industry upon their farms, not by
the hope of being paid for it, but by the hope of enjoying its
fruits. The incentive to this industry is weakened, if it be not
gone, when you tell the tenant he may be turned out to-morrow;
but if he is that his landlord must pay him for what he is doing.
In many cases the payment might, in very many it would, fall
far short of the worth of labour that is expended. Men give
their labour and their strength to ornament and improve that
which is their own. They expend industry upon neatness,
upon appearance, in the pride of ownership. This pride it is
that cherishes the very feelings and habits in which our people
are deficient. Slovenliness and want of order will be the charac-
teristics of the man who improves under the liability of eviction:
even though you tell him he will be paid. On our Irish
farms and farmhouses the industry which it is most desirable to
encourage is exactly that which will not bear to be reduced to
measure and rule. When men plant trees the thought that
rises to their minds is that they and their children will walk under
their shade If the cottier spends his leisure hours in adorning
his home, or in adding to it another room, the motive present to
his mind is that of living on in the place which he is making
neat or convenient If, year after year, he carries earth to enrich
the still ungrateful soil, he is cheered in his labour by the belief
that, a year or two more, and he will reap the crop of corn
from that field. You will never get from human occupiers all the
energy of improvement of which they are capable unless you give
them a tenure long enough to enable them to feel that their improvements are their own.

And this is just the industry and the improvement which Ireland
wants. In the county in Ireland in which, I still think, above all
others, the land, in proportion to its natural resources, is made the
most of, you will not see, as a rule, great improvements carried on
under the superintendence of the Board of Works. What you

* See this question discussed more fully in the tract on Land Tenure, pages 45-52.

will see is a number of small holdings, upon each of which great and constant industry has made small improvements—upon which cultivation has been gradually carried to the hill top, and by the patient care of many a year the cut out bog has been trained to grow waving corn or luxuriant grass—holdings in the midst of which the whitewashed cottage, with its neatly trimmed thatch, is ornamented with its little garden of flowers and fruit trees before its door. These are improvements and this is industry incapable of being submitted to the approval of a landlord. They cannot be mapped and measured by any officer of the Board of Works. You can only attain them when you give security of tenure to the occupier of the soil.

It is, perhaps, necessary my Lord, that before I proceed to offer a few closing observations on the general effect of all that I have written, I should advert in a very few words to some other topics to which your Lordship has referred. It is due to your Lordship that I should do so, especially to the views you express on the subject of the Church Establishment. I need scarcely say that in attaching the importance which I have done to this subject of our land tenure, I have never meant to say that there are not other questions which are of great moment to the Irish nation. But I believe that the land question is above and before them all, exactly as the life of a nation or an individual is before and above any question relating to the condition of that life. The policy of conquest pervades our whole system; but it rests, as its basis, on the serfdom of the occupiers of the soil. It is there—in our system of land tenure—that it presses on the nation's life. I might almost say that we must elevate the great mass of our countrymen to the rank of freemen before we can determine upon any subject under what laws it is fit for freemen to live.

Upon the question of our ecclesiastical establishment your proposal is that a portion of the revenues now belonging to the Established Church should be applied to the purposes of general education, and that in lieu of the charge from which the Exchequer would thus be free, the nation should provide for each Roman Catholic priest in Ireland an estate—it is scarcely right to call it a glebe—of the average value of £200 a-year.

May I ask your attention to the fact, that of all the writers in the Conservative Press who have heaped their praises upon your Lordship for your resistance to fixity of tenure, there is not one who has even mentioned your proposal in relation to the Church. You thus state the plan by which you propose to remedy the grievance involved in the appropriation to the Church of a small minority of the revenues devoted and intended for providing religious ordinances for the people at large:—

"I conceive, then, that a large portion of the revenues of the Established Church might be legitimately applied to national education. This would save to the State a considerable sum, now applied to education, and the State could, therefore, better afford to use a large sum for a purpose, which would go far to remove the stigma of an anomaly from the Reformed Church, would be a great pecuniary boon to the poorest class, and would do much to secure, to the side of order, the most politically powerful class of men in Ireland—I mean the providing glebes for the Roman Catholic clergy, subject to a payment to their bishops. Justice is seldom done to the Roman Catholic clergy by those opposed to them. They are judged of in England by a few noisy members of their body, who make themselves conspicuous in elections; but little is known about the great body of the Irish priests—their genial kindness, and their influence over their flocks for good. When I recollect that they are sprung from the people; that in their earliest years they imbibed the thoughts and opinions of the people—dangerous, and grounded on false notions of history, and of their rights, as I have stated those opinions to be; that they associate invariably with the people, and, though often men of refinement of mind, induced by a superior education, seldom with the higher classes, my wonder is, not that they are sometimes coarse and unscrupulous agitators, but that they are so generally charitable and self-denying parish priests, the strenuous advocates and enforcers of morality, order, and submission to the law. Be that as it may, in every case of attempted or contemplated rebellion against the Queen's Government for the last half century, the Roman Catholic clergy, in conformity with the laws of their Church, and from their knowledge of what is the best interest of their flocks, have used their powerful influence on the side of loyalty.

"Now, is it just, is it politic, to leave these men under no reciprocal obligations to the State? They are educated men, and are aware of what goes on abroad, and they know the folly of the political fancies of a most impulsive and deluded people. Is it wise to leave them dependent for their support on the poorest and most ignorant class, even though there is no danger of that support failing? It is not a question of religion. Religion never was promoted by endowments, nor checked by persecution. It is a pure question of justice and of wise policy, except so far as it greatly affects the power of defending the Established Church, by making its position less anomalous.

"There are about 1,050 parish priests in Ireland. Supposing a power were given by Parliament to purchase a glebe for each, of the average value, some more some less, of £200 a-year, this, at 4½ per cent., would take a sum of about five millions; a sum about the cost of the new drains in London, the annual interest being about the price of one iron-clad. Of the £200 a-year coming to each parish priest, £30 a-year would be made payable to his bishop, which would give to each Roman Catholic bishop, after expenses were paid, an average income of about £1,000 a-year. Religious equality and its consequence (spoliation apart), the payment by the State of the Roman Catholic clergy, were part of the old and far-sighted policy of Mr. Pitt. So was Reform of Parliament. So was Free Trade. The temporary repudiation of two of these great principles of their greatest leader has, with short exceptions, deprived the Tory Party of office for more than thirty years. These principles might have been a tower of strength to the Tory Party; the two last have proved tremendous weapons against it. In the present loosening of party ties, it remains to be seen who will take up the first in its integrity, not for mere party purposes, but in the spirit and power of Pitt; and thus preserving the property of the Established Church to its original uses, remove the last trace of religious ascendancy, and give a boon to the Irish people patent in every parish in Ireland."*

I will not be drawn, even by these passages, into a discussion of the question to which they refer—a question, beside, although not altogether foreign to, the subject which I have undertaken to discuss. I will only say that I am sure that, to give permanent or real contentment to Ireland, we must abandon the policy of conquest upon all questions of religion, as well as on those relating to the tenure of land; we must banish from every part of our legislation, from every nook and corner of our administrative system, every vestige of the policy which would treat the religion of the vast majority of Irishmen as a proscribed or inferior faith. We must banish it from all our arrangements of national education, whether for the higher, the lower, or the middle class. We must banish it from all our laws which dispose of the property which the piety of past generations has consecrated to the service of religion. In each and every of these questions—in every department of Irish government—we must, once and for all, and with an honest and unfaltering purpose, dismiss and destroy for ever any lurking notion that we can subject the religion of the immense majority of Irishmen—that which is the faith of the old nation—to any brand of degradation or inferiority on the Irish soil.

I am bound to state these convictions lest I might seem to dissent from the opinion which your Lordship so clearly expresses as to the absolute necessity of establishing " religious equality " in Ireland. I express no opinion upon the particular measure which your Lordship recommends. It is only justice to say that it is very different from a proposal to make the Catholic clergy stipendiaries of the State—a proposal to which they have told us they will never give their assent. I forbear further to pursue a subject which, as I have said, is beside the question on which I write.

* Lord Lifford's Letter to Mr. Butt, pp. 17, 18, 19.

But, my Lord, it is not beside that to point out that the hope is
vain that any endowment, or any establishment, even of the fullest
religious equality, will detach the Roman Catholic clergy from the
cause of the people. You can win over the priesthood of Ireland
by doing justice to the people. I am not sure that I would say
with you that the influence of the Catholic priesthood has been
used on the side of "loyalty," if you mean by loyalty that
attachment to existing institutions which can only result from
contentment under them ; but with some little knowledge of the
two attempts that have been made in our generation to excite
insurrection in Ireland, I can and must say that I believe the
influence of the priesthood—an influence quietly and unostentatiously exerted, which sought no favour from Government, and
made no parade of loyalty before England—has been in both instances
used to dissuade the people from joining in the projected revolt.

But it is another and a very different thing to expect that the
Catholic priesthood will inculcate on their flocks contentment with
the system of land tenure which is keeping their people in misery
and serfdom. I do not believe all the gold in the British Treasury
could buy them to this; and if it could they would fail. If you
could ally the Catholic clergy with "landlordism," you would only
destroy their influence with the people; and in severing the peasant
from his pastor you would snap the last link that binds him to
order and to patient endurance of his wrongs.

But I cannot refrain from reminding you that there is a subject
upon which the Roman Catholic clergy have made a request—a
plain and a simple one—and it has not been complied with. They
have not asked for the glebes which you offer them. They have
asked that in the administration of the funds which the nation
votes for Irish education—the teaching of those who adhere to the
faith, which is the faith of the Irish people—should be free. They
ask that in the national schools of Ireland the Irish Catholic priest
and the Irish Catholic bishop should have the same liberty of
teaching which in the English national schools is allowed, not only
to the Catholic priest, but to the Jewish rabbi. The answer to
that request by our rulers is the maintenance of a system of Irish
national education opposed to the whole wishes and feelings of the
Irish nation—a system which would not be freely adopted by a
vote of any parish in Ireland, and which I do not believe would be
forced upon this island if we were a distinct and independent
colony, without the advantage or disadvantage of having one single
representation in the Imperial Parliament

Again:—That clergy have asked for a Royal sanction to a
University founded on principles in accordance with those of the
Church to which the great majority of the Irish people belong,
and—would it be possible in any other country upon earth?—that
sanction is refused.

There are other matters as well as the land question upon which the spirit that enacted the penal laws is not extinct.

And surely I may venture to say that even in the views you have expressed upon the Church question, there is a proof that there is no prejudice so strong that in honest and upright minds it will not yield to the " irresistible logic of events " to the force of reason and truth. Am I wrong in saying that there was a time when you yourself would have regarded as revolutionary a proposal to appropriate the Church revenues in the manner you now suggest? I am sure that it will be read with approval, or at least acquiescence, by many who would a short time ago have so denounced it. I think I can see in that very proposal the struggle between honest and high-minded prejudices and the conviction forcing itself, in spite of them, that an unjust ecclesiastical ascendancy, cannot and ought not to be maintained. Even on the land question I do not despair of seeing similar prejudices give way.

There is but one secret in governing Ireland as there is in governing any country. Let it be governed for the good of the whole people. Let us abandon the policy of maintaining any English interest, or any Protestant interest, or any class interest, or any interest but that of the Irish people. When every measure of government and every institution of the country are moulded and adapted to meet the wants, the wishes, and the capabilities of that people—when, in a word, Irish legislation is influenced as exclusively by reference to the wants and wishes of Ireland as English legislation is by a reference to those of England, then, and then only, will Ireland be governed as a free country.

Let me turn again to the great question with which I have been attempting to deal. It is more than time that this letter should draw to a close.

" Immensum spatiis confecimus æquor."

Before I make an effort, at its conclusion, to condense into a brief space some few of the conclusions which seem to follow from all that we have reviewed, I must ask your Lordship's forgiveness for having permitted myself to be led on far, far, beyond the limits of a reply to the letter which you did me the honour to address to me. I feel, my Lord, how many apologies I owe to you for having introduced into this letter the discussion of many topics connected with this question with which I had, perhaps, no right to associate your Lordship's name. When I began to write I had no intention of doing so. Nearly four months have passed since I commenced this letter. When I commenced it I intended to write a short tract—I have been insensibly led on to write a large book. Each day brought me some new statement to be answered, or opened up some new view to be discussed, and the result is that there are many things in these pages which do not properly belong to a mere reply to your Lordship's letter. But I confess I was not sorry in a discussion in which I must of necessity say hard things, or those which may seem to be hard things, of a class—to feel myself constantly under the restraint of addressing a member of that class. Nothing could more forcibly remind me of the distinction which every just man must draw between individuals and a system ; or more effectually prevent me from forgetting that against the opinions I am expressing a great deal of worth and of virtue may be arrayed. Combating opinions entertained by your Lordship, I never could forget that no matter how wrong or mistaken, or even mischievous, I might regard them, individuals hold them who are entitled to all respect. Neither did I regret throughout this letter to feel myself in the position of reasoning not against but with an Irish landowner, one whose mind can I know do full justice to my argument, and one of whom I believe that, if I did convince his judgment, neither class interest nor class prejudice or any view of private interest would prevent his acting on the dictates of his reason and his conscience.

In this spirit, my Lord, at the close of this long letter, with all the light that discussion has thrown upon this question, I appeal to you to reconsider your judgment upon my proposal—to say whether it is really communistic and revolutionary—or whether it be not in truth an assertion of just claims that have been too long neglected—an eminently conservative adjustment of differences, the very existence of which is a state of chronic revolution—and the staying of the progress of a violent social change which is now driving the Irish people from their homes.

The principle of that which I propose is this. The occupier of the soil ought to be secured in its possession by a lease. We ought not to base our land system on short and uncertain tenures.

Is this proposal a new one? Have I not shown it to be incorporated in the very foundation of all Irish proprietary right—interwoven, if I may so speak, with the very texture of the title deeds of every Irish estate. Up to our own day it was recognized by a custom stronger than law I am only asking of Irish proprietors to return to a custom which our grandfathers and great grandfathers followed. This may be unwise or impolitic ; but surely it is scarcely revolutionary even to enforce the old custom of the country by law.

In fact, my Lord, it is by virtue of an enactment not dissimilar in principle that a very large portion of the property in Ireland is now enjoyed by its present owners. Your Lordship's ancestor presided in the Irish Court of Chancery, and over the Irish Peers, when the English House of Lords, the supreme tribunal of appeal, pronounced a decision which actually vested in the chief lords the greater portion of the interests which were held under "leases for lives renewable for ever." That decision declared the law—the law common both to England and Ireland— How did the Irish Parliament of landowners deal with it ? They passed a statute, recognizing what was rightly termed the old custom and the old equity of the country, and by that statute they vested in one set of proprietors a large amount of property which was actually ascertained to be the legal property of another. That precedent, my Lord, would exactly and precisely justify legislators in giving legal protection to the Ulster custom of tenant right. There was not an argument advanced in favour of the "Tenantry Act" of 1779, which would not justify such a measure. That Act was passed to protect property which legally belonged to one person, but which "the old custom" and "the old equity" of the country had always considered as morally and equitably vested in another. When the harsh application of legal principles attempted to confiscate that property, the Irish Parliament interposed, by legislation, to do justice, even at the expense of legal rights; and under an Act so passed, a very considerable portion of Irish property is now enjoyed by its present owners. "The old custom" and the old equity of the country might be pleaded with even more truth and justice on behalf of the property acquired and enjoyed under the Ulster custom of tenant right.

Writing to your Lordship I could scarcely omit this illustration, but I do not need it.

It may be said that I go further than compelling the landlord to give a lease—I compel him to give it at a fixed rent. I do so, because without this it is utterly impossible to carry out the first object. A law which would compel a landlord to give a lease, but permit him to insert in it any reservation of rent he pleased, would be in the circumstances of Ireland so nugatory as to be absurd. If it be necessary to enforce by law a return to the once universal custom of leases, the second proposition is involved in this—not that we should fix the rent, but that we should fix its maximum, and fix that maximum at the highest amount which any tenant can reasonably pay. Considering the hopeless state of dependence in which the great majority of Irish tenants are placed, the prohibition of a bargain for an extortionate rent is, in itself,

Q

nothing more than an application to the case of landlord and tenant of some of the most established principles of jurisprudence.

I admit also that I compel the landlord to give that which I may call the right of preemption to the tenant occupying the farm. This is also but a necessary conseqence of the enforcement of a lease. The proposal could not be carried out in any other way without exposing all existing tenants to eviction. Unless we are to permit the landlord to defeat the whole measure, by taking the land into his own hands, somebody must get the preference. The occupying tenant is the person entitled to it. He is there by the landlord's act and choice. I give to the landlord the power of getting rid of him unless he proves himself a good tenant—good both in payment of rent and in the proper cultivation of his farm. Ought any landlord object to keep a tenant who is both punctual in his payments and careful in his cultivation of the land? I remind you again that even in so forbidding the landlord to take into his own hands lands usually let, I am following out old precedent and adhering to the spirit and even to the letter of the conditions upon which the greater portion of Irish property was vested in its present class of owners.*

If any one is prepared to concede the principle that landowners ought to be compelled to observe the ancient custom of letting land. I do not believe it possible to carry out that principle by any measure which will interfere with their dominion less than does the measure I propose.

If there be difficulty or inconvenience in making this the subject of legislation it is caused by the landowners who have in truth created a social revolution by adopting the determination of insisting on the totally new principle of universal tenancies-at-will.

This is a matter of recent origin. Let me earnestly implore the attention of those who may be disposed to condemn novel proposals, to this fact, that THE STATE OF THINGS WITH WHICH WE ARE DEAL-ING IS ONE ABSOLUTELY AND ENTIRELY NEW. The general in-security of tenure which arises from a general and combined refusal of the landowners to grant leases is entirely the creation of the last few years. For the first time in the history of Ireland the people occupy their native country at the mercy and by the sufferance of the comparatively few persons who have acquired the ownership or lordship of the soil.

Is not this in itself an answer to a great deal that has been said against measures such as I propose? It is quite true that tenant right and fixity of tenure are but recently pressed as popular demands. The necessity for them has only recently arisen. O'Connell, to-wards the close of his life, perceived the growing evil, and did con-template fixity of tenure. But it may be that this question of land tenure was even in old days of more importance than was supposed.

---

* Sir John Davies, *ante* page 44.

It may be that a law against extortionate rents would, at any time, have been a wise measure for Ireland. I am far from saying that it would or it would not; but this is not the question now. That of fixity of tenure is forced on us by a state of things such as never existed in the country before. It requires a mental effort to realize all that is involved in the condition of land tenure in which the landowners of a great country generally insist on holding all its cultivators as tenants-at-will. It requires a greater effort still to accustom our mind to think of the measures by which an evil so novel and so gigantic must be met.

This great change in our customs was not that which grew up in the gradual moulding of habits to the altered circumstances of time. It is a sudden and violent revolution brought about by the strife of classes—the determination on the part of the landowners to use their dominion over the soil to keep the people in their power. This is not matter of conjecture. It is explicitly avowed. Leases are refused because the landowners think it necessary to retain a dominion which is really that of vassalage over those on whom they confer the privilege of being tillers of the soil. It is useless to inquire to whose fault we are to trace this state of things. I know all the answers that would be given to that question by bigotry, by passion, or by prejudice, on one side and the other. It is enough to know that the claim is asserted, and most effectually enforced, and that in our generation there is not the slightest prospect of the passing away of the circumstances or the motives which have caused it. We must work a moral miracle, and wholly change the nature and the feelings, possibly even the religion, either of the Irish landowners or the Irish peasantry before those circumstances or those motives pass away.

The people refuse to remain as tenants-at-will to the landowners, and they are going away.

Surely I am justified in saying that this is a national condition altogether different from the ordinary social difficulties which, in civilized countries, statesmen are called upon to solve. And surely the statesmen who are not prepared boldly and effectually to deal with it, are really letting Ireland drift either to ruin or to revolution, or to both. I say boldly—for never was there a subject which more required and justified bold and decisive expedients—it is not one that is to be dealt with by palliatives that bring, in the end, no alleviation, or mild remedies that effect really no redress. Never was there a question of which it might more truthfully be said—

> "The foolish cant—'He went too far'—despise,
> And know that to be brave is to be wise."

Unless we go far enough to meet the mischief, we will act at least as wisely by not interfering at all. The real evil is the universal insecurity of tenure preserved by the general determination

of landowners to let no one occupy the soil of Ireland except
as a tenant-at-will. This is a claim on their part, founded, I admit,
on the legal exercise of proprietary rights, to keep the people in
their power. The real question is, shall the nation acquiesce in
that claim. It is impossible long to evade the decision of that
question; and all legislation that postpones it is only tampering
with a subject upon which every statesman who deals with Ireland, unless he is wholly unfit for his position, must very soon, one
way or other, make up his mind. If the resolution be come to to
acquiesce in that claim, nothing remains but to uphold extreme
proprietary rights, and warn the people that they have nothing
to expect; and the more clearly and distinctly this is done the
better will we discharge the only obligation to that people, and to
humanity, which it will remain for us to fulfil. If we are not to
acquiesce in that claim, let us devise the measure which, with the
least disturbance of the present condition of property, may yet
adequately meet the evils of this novel and unheard of state of things.

I say "novel and unheard of!" Could there, I ask, be a greater
social revolution than that which, in a country like Ireland, voluntarily altered the whole tenures of the country from leases to
tenancies-at-will? Compare one of these estates like that which
Arthur Young describes, on which every Protestant tenant held by
a lease for three lives, every Roman Catholic tenant by a lease for 31
years, with the same estate as it is in the present, with no tenure
on it beyond a tenancy from year to year—very likely reduced to
an actual tenancy-at-will, by the contrivance of an annual notice to
quit, or by an agreement binding the tenant under a heavy penalty
to give up possession whenever he is asked. The change is not
a mere formal one as it might be in England. The lease is
refused for the express purpose of enabling the landlord to evict
the tenant whenever he pleases. Let us dwell on all the effects
of such a change in the case of one tenant—then in the case of
an entire estate. Let us enlarge our view to all the estates in the
island—suppose the same change upon each of them, and then we
may fairly estimate the extent of the social revolution through
which Ireland is past. The edicts of Stein and Hardenberg scarcely
effected a greater practical change in the land system of Prussia
than that which has been effected in Ireland by the edict of the
landowners, which has degraded the tenantry from freeholders into
"villeins"—an edict by which the lords of the soil are to be the lords
of the people, not by any penal enactment—not by any law of feudal
privilege—but by a combined exercise of proprietary rights.

But not only is it new in Ireland. It is new in history. I remember no instance in history in which such a combination has
taken place. In what country supposed to possess free institutions
and a free government has such an attempt ever been made? The
landowners of the country with one consent agree that no one shall

cultivate the Irish soil unless he places himself in a state of vassalage, and they leave to the people the alternative of submitting or going away. No passage in history supplies us with any guide—no lesson of political philosophy ever contemplated such a social condition. There is but one country on earth in which it could happen. Such a state of things could only exist in that unhappy land in which alien proprietors have held its soil for two centuries without either subduing or conciliating its people—in which the sins of the fathers are literally visited on the children, not unto three, but unto seven generations—in which even as the seventh generation is passing to its grave, the descendants of the conquerors and the conquered still stand aloof from each other in angry distrust, and in which, under the semblance and forms of civil society, the relations of owner and occupier are still guided by the maxims and agitated by the passions of civil war. Time that heals the wounds of other dissensions, but rips open the scars of ours, and makes them bleed afresh. The evil deeds of former days still follow us remorselessly with their curse, as though some old guilt unexpiated and unpardoned still rested on our soil, as evil spirits are said to haunt the places where great crimes have been committed, and the stains of human blood remain indelible upon the stones into which they have once eaten, reappearing after a lapse of years, during which it might have been thought that the rains and winds had long since washed and worn them away.

Was there ever a chain of evidence more complete than that by which, even in the imperfect tracing of those pages, our present insecurity of tenure is connected in "unbroken links of causation" with the policy and the passions of our confiscations? Up to the time of the Union we find an English colony settled in an enemy's country which had been "reduced by the sword to a sullen and refractory allegiance"—proprietors whose "common title was confiscation—hemmed in on every side by the old inhabitants of the island brooding over their discontents in sullen indignation." "The people of the country divided into two distinct and separate castes, one possessed of the whole property and power of the country, the other expelled from both."* We find penal laws enacted to crush down the conquered enemies, statutes to prevent them acquiring long interests in the land—every relaxation of these laws opposed upon the ground that it might weaken the titles acquired by confiscation—even the acts of mercy by which British sovereigns proposed to remove unjust attainders defeated upon the same ground.† We

* Lord Clare.
† " Among the few occurrences which disturbed the Duke of Devonshire's long administration, which passed with unusual tranquillity, was the alarm given to the possessors of confiscated estates, by an application of the Earl of Clancarty to the king for the restitution of his estates, which had been forfeited in the Rebellion (!!) of 1688 ; and were supposed to be worth £60,000 annually at the time when he applied. The Earl had obtained the consent of the British Cabinet that a Bill should be brought

have proprietors to this day "persuaded that every change of policy
or isolated disturbance threatens" their titles—"a gentry who think
they only garrison their estates, and look upon the native occupants
as persons merely to eject them on a favourable opportunity;"* and
we have that gentry now refusing to give any security to these
occupants with the very object that the occupants may have no
hold whatever on the soil, and that when the landlords " fight the
battle for their rights, they may do so with their hands untied." †
    I have endeavoured, as nearly as possible, to condense this
evidence in the words of others. Was I wrong in saying that
while the arbitrary power of eviction lasts, the sword of Oliver
Cromwell is suspended over every peasant's door?   Until you give
that peasant security of tenure, so far as he is concerned the penal
laws are unrepealed.
    In old times a penal law prohibited the " Papists" from acquiring
a freehold interest in land, or even a long or beneficial term of
years.   This law and the corresponding law denying them the franchise,‡ were justified upon precisely the same grounds upon which
Lord Rosse rests the present refusal of the landowners to give leases.
It was said that if these concessions were made to them, farms would
become divided into a number of small holdings—that the " Popish"
tenantry would return men unconnected with the county by property, and that measures would be passed in Parliament dangerous
to the influence, the rights, and even the title of the landowners.
All the reasons which, we are assured, influence now the landlords to refuse leases, influenced their ancestors to pass the penal
laws.   It was even said that those who cried " down with landlordism, also cried down with the British Crown."   Over and over
again it was pointed out that the title of the House of Hanover to
the throne, and the title of the Irish landowners to their estates,
both rested on the exclusion of the old possessors—and loyalty
and self-interest, and the rights of property, were all alike invoked
as a justification of the policy which deprived the Irish people of all
freedom or independence upon the soil of their native land.
    To protect the titles, the influence, and the position of the landed
proprietors, was the policy and the object of the penal laws.   The

into the Irish Parliament *for the reversal of his attainder*; but the measure was re-
linquished, in consequence of the vigorous resolutions of the Irish Commons, who had
addressed his majesty for that purpose in 1728 and 1735 ; and again, in the session of
1739, voted, that any attempt to disturb the Protestant purchasers of estates forfeited
by rebellion, would be of dangerous consequence to his majesty's person and government."—*Gordon's History of Ireland*, Vol. ii., page 217.
    * Mr. Otway's Report, *ante* page 67.
    † Lord Rosse, *ante* page 165.
    ‡ It was said in the Irish Parliament, by the advocates of the Catholics, that up to
the first year of the reign of George the Second there was no legal exclusion of Roman
Catholics as such from the elective franchise.   It was insisted by their opponents that
they had been excluded at a period much nearer the Revolution.   The point was not
of much importance then.   It is of none now.

same policy prompted the worse administrative oppressions by which the people were crushed down. The excuse was then as it is now, that it would be unsafe for the landowners to trust the people with the privileges of freemen and freeholders on their estates. To keep them down from that position was the object of the penal code. The same distrust prevails now. The laws proscribing religion have been repealed. Civil and religious disabilities have been removed. The right of the elective franchise, and that of holding long leases have been conferred. But the very policy of the penal code is carried out by a mode more suited to that which we are pleased to call the liberality of this generation, at all events more adapted to the prejudices of the commercial spirit of the age. Driven from penal laws and legal disabilities the policy of conquest has resorted to a far more coercive power, that resulting from the legal ownership of the soil. The landowners have discovered the force of the tremendous weapon which, in that ownership, the law has placed in their hands. In old times they chained the arm of the occupier; they have now found out that it is enough if in the use of that terrible weapon, their own hands are left untied. But all this is but the continuation under novel forms of the one undying conflict. The refusal of leases is only a new strategy of the old civil war.

And now the Irish peasant is plainly told that he is perfectly free— that he enjoys the protection of the best laws and the privileges of the freest Constitution in the world, but that as he is a dangerous person to his landlord's rights, if he remains in his country, he must do so as a tenant-at-will—that is, in a state of servitude in which he has not one hour's security, and in which he cannot call his industry, or even his home his own. He must submit to be his landlord's bailiff in all that concerns the cultivation of his farm*— a mere farm servant retained only until it may suit his landlord's convenience that he should go†—his landlord's serf even in the domestic arrangements of his home‡—his landlord's vassal in the exercise of the franchise which the law has nominally given to himself§—a bondsman in all respects but one. His master retains the power of turning him adrift upon the world when he will.

The Irish peasant knows law, not by what is written in the statute book, but by that which comes home to his roof-tree and his fireside. Can any man say that as to him the practical operation of the old penal laws is gone?

Must not every right-minded man ask himself whether the position of a tenant at will upon an Irish estate is one in which any man ought to be contented to remain? In any case he must be content to banish all real sense of independence from his heart. Every man must do so who agrees to live dependent upon the will

---

* Lord Dufferin, *ante*, page 213.   † Lord Rosse, *ante*, page 170.
‡ *Ante*, page 178.   § Lord Rosse, *ante*, page 172.

of another for his very means of life. He must submit to whatever "rules of the estate," the folly, the caprice, or the tyranny of his master may enact; he must be ready at the bidding of 'the driver' to turn away his nearest relative from his door. Even if he is an educated clergyman, a dignitary of the church of the people, he must see that all his curates measure their language or he will not be suffered to live upon the estate. No matter how vexatious may be the petty persecutions of the rules, he must submit—and all the while he is shut out from the real exercise of the only industry he can employ. Round the humble home of the peasant lie stony fields and thorny brakes, and banks of heather upon which he would be glad to labour until "the live long day would prove too short for his untiring toil."* But if he toils he has no assurance that ever the fruits of his industry will be his own. He looks out from his door in listless but angry inaction, and broods over a sullen but surely not unnatural discontent. Even of the continuance of such a life he has no security. Very probably the annual notice to quit reminds him that he is only "a pilgrim and a stranger" in his native country, and that he knows not the hour when some "improvement" may require him to leave his home and give up his bit of ground.

You ask me, my Lord—"How would an Irishman like to be obliged to obtain leave from the police to marry, and to be refused leave if the police officer thought he did not possess a sufficiently large farm?"†

There are many "well managed estates" in Ireland on which he must obtain the same leave from an "agency" between which and him their exists far less sympathy than there is between the Bavarian peasant and the police. There is, at all events, this difference—the refusal of the Irish agent is one against which he has no appeal.

Let us try and realize to ourselves, if we can, the daily life of a man who passes it in such a position as this—a man, it may be, with feelings as proud and as sensitive as our own—a man with the consciousness that his Creator has implanted in his bosom thoughts and faculties that were not given him to fret and pine away in an existence like this. While men are kept in this position have we any right to be surprised at Irish discontent? In the estrangement of classes, those of the higher order know but little of the thoughts and feelings that control the people's inner life. Occasionally some glimpse reveals them. We know, from evidence taken before a Parliamantary Committee, that in Ireland that unerring sign of an oppressed people, the actual hiding and hoarding of money, still prevails—guineas are still hid in the thatch, concealed in the old

---

* Arthur Young.
† Lord Lifford's Letter, p. 12.

stocking, or buried in the earth. A dread of their landlord pervades many of the peasantry, as unreasoning it may be as the fear with which "the rising" of the people is regarded in that landlord's home. There are districts of Ireland in which actually the tenants fear to show any sign of comfort, or to permit the females of their families to go well dressed to Mass. Some undefined sense of insecurity pursues them in all they do; a vague sense of some coming mischief, if not from the landlord from some one who has access to his ear. Timorous apprehensions of a rent to be raised, of fields to be taken from him—of the great man displeased—disquiet with forebodings of ill the life of many an Irish occupier of the soil. On many an evening the shadow of "the malignant human agency" darkens his hearth.

Is not this, the old serfdom, continued to this day? Where, or when, has it been changed since the day when confiscation placed alien proprietors over the old people? I have endeavoured, in a laborious, and, I fear, too minute and tedious enquiry, to trace back the stream of oppression to that source. Let us carry back our views over the oppressions of two centuries, and rest upon the point where they commence—the day upon which the soldier of fortune, the follower of Ireton, of Cromwell, or of William, was placed in possession of his Irish land. Upon that land had dwelt a number of the people from the conquest of whom his title was derived. He came with all the haughty passions, all the cruel fears, of the conqueror in his breast. He did not come, as is often the case of a seizure by conquest, to take the place of the former owner in the arrangements of the country and of the estate, a seizure in which—except in the presence of a new proprietor—all things go on as they did before. The old people were driven out as well as the old lord. The new owner was sent—not to conciliate that people—but to crush them. He would have been false to his principles, and false to his comrades, if he had permitted them to occupy on his estate any position but that of slaves. They were tolerated, but not pardoned rebels—men whose enmity was to be kept down, and every privilege conceded to them was a danger to the dominion of their lords.

Before time could soften these relations—law embodied, in penal enactments, the angry passions and the jealous fears that might have been forgiven in the first heat of conquest. The religion of the old people was proscribed by persecuting laws. The physical resistance of that people was rendered powerless by enactments depriving them of arms. Their political influence was destroyed by the law that excluded them from the franchise and from juries. Their moral and social importance was put an end to by the laws which prohibited education and excluded them from the learned professions and all corporate privileges—while precaution was taken against the chance liberality of any of the conquerors, by the enactment which prevented the granting to any of them of a lease beneficial either in interest or in tenure.

Can we wonder, in such a state of things, that upon each of the estates I have described, successive generations of owners and occupiers passed away without any change in the first relations of passion, and resentment, and distrust? The law had written its commandments of hatred and disunion in tables as enduring as those of stone. The representatives of the new proprietor and of the old occupiers lived nominally, as landlord and tenant under the same law. Nevertheless, they belonged to two separate nations. They could scarcely be said to belong to the same country. In the Ireland of the old people the master of the estate was an intruder and a stranger—and that master knew and felt it. Their people were not his people, their religion was not his religion, and their country was not his. Generation after generation we can trace the unchanged position of both—in the testimony of Arthur Young in 1777, of Sir Laurence Parsons in 1793, of Lord Clare in 1800, of Edward Wakefield in 1810, of Lord Rosse in 1867. At the end of two centuries the occupier and the owner are as estranged as were their ancestors on the day when the new proprietor came to his estate. We are still in the presence of the passions, we are face to face with the difficulties, of that day. The representative of the crushed and conquered occupier has never yet been raised to the dignity of a free and independent tenant. It is not thought safe by the landowners that he should be so. He is an enemy with whom, at any time, his landlord may be called on " to do battle for his rights."

This history of the country has been represented on a small scale upon many an Irish estate.

But even this sketch would be incomplete if we did not remember that a dominion originating in conquest has been ever since maintained by that which for this purpose we must call foreign military force. If English arms created, English arms maintained the proprietary right. We must cast our eye back over the history of those agrarian crimes in which individual cases of oppression were too often avenged—the roll of those organized conspiracies and insurrectionary movements which Mr. Grant so vividly described in the speech which I have quoted.* We must remember and weigh the fact which in that speech is so forcibly pointed out, that all these insurrections had been put down by the overwhelming strength of English military force while not a single attempt had been made to redress, or scarcely any to discover, the grievances which caused them.†

* *Ante*, page 81.

† At the period at which Mr. Grant spoke, the *Edinburgh Review* thus described the military occupation of Ireland.

"They," the Irish people, "hate the English Government from historical recollection, actual suffering, and disappointed hope ; *and, till they are better treated, they will continue to hate it.* At this moment, *in a period of the most profound peace, there are*

From the accession of George the IV. to the present day, frequent disturbances have been in the same way put down by force. How often have we known the Irish executive, congratulated on its vigour and its success when an insurrection act has crushed down the violence of crime in a district? or a special commission by its fearful, although necessary examples of retributive justice has terrified agrarian turbulence into temporary quiet? Congratulations of this nature have been actually spoken from the throne as if Irish government—no one dreams of Irish statesmanship—could set before it no other object or contemplate no higher duty than that of trampling down all resistance. This has been our whole policy— to bring the great power of England to put down every Irish effort at revolt—and the only foresight in which that policy ever made provision for the future, was to make such a display of power as to convince the people of the hopelessness of every attempt to resist.

Let any one seriously reflect upon all that is involved in this state of things. The result is that all the force of the English Government is exerted to maintain the extreme proprietary rights of landowners, no matter with what cruelty they are exercised—and to crush the resistance of the peasantry, no matter by what oppression it is provoked. Can any system of government be more fatal to national improvement, more destructive of every hope of that adjustment of differences by mutual forbearance and concession which in all other nations has reconciled the angry war of classes? I know of no greater curse to a country than to have its local oppressions maintained by the force of another nation. If real grievances be at the bottom of all these agrarian disturbances, every time that English power tramples down an insurrectionary movement, it is only widening the breach between classes—it is adding to the haughtiness of the oppressor—it is deepening the hatred that rankles in the bosom of the oppressed. This is the system of government which has identified "landlordism" and the authority of the British Crown.* On all orders of men, from the highest to the lowest, its evil influence has been felt. It has lowered

twenty-five thousand of the best disciplined and best appointed troops in the world in Ireland, with bayonets fixed, presented arms, and in the attitude of present war: *nor is there a man too much*—nor would Ireland be tenable without them." "When it was necessary last year (or thought necessary) to put down the demand for Reform, we were forced to make a levy of fresh troops in this country—not a man could be spared from Ireland."

At this moment, including 11,000 constabulary who are in truth a trained, a disciplined, and efficient military force—a standing army without the annual consent of Parliament—Ireland is at this moment (April, 1867), held by thirty thousand armed men.

"Ireland" continued the writer in the *Edinburgh Review*, "*till her wrongs are redressed*, and a more liberal policy is adopted towards her, will always be a cause of anxiety and suspicion to this country ; AND IN SOME MOMENT OF OUR WEAKNESS AND DEPRESSION, WILL FORCIBLY EXTORT WHAT SHE WOULD NOW RECEIVE WITH GRATITUDE AND EXULTATION."

* Lord Lifford's Letter.

our gentry as much as it crushed the people. It has inflamed the oppression of agrarian tyrants—it has degraded even that oppression by giving it a demoralizing and cowardly confidence in external support. It has armed the resistance of the oppressed with the energy and fierceness of desperation, while it has imparted to agrarian crime all the guilt, and something of the dignity of national revolt. It has arrayed against proprietary rights those instincts of nationality which are strong in the Irish heart, while it has set against the authority of government the angry feelings which individual oppression kindles in each breast. Converting British authority in Ireland into military rule, it has too often debased Irish loyalty into a selfish and a cruel passion. No part of our social system has escaped the mischief. In the eyes of the Irish people and of Europe it has brought the authority and even the name of the British Sovereign into unmerited odium and disgrace.

After all this miserable experience, may we not ask—Is there a prospect of this wretched and humiliating condition ever terminating unless by the extermination of the old inhabitants, or by some great and wise measure of conciliation which will destroy the policy as well as the letter of the penal laws, and place THE IRISH PEOPLE as freemen on THE IRISH LAND?

If these things be so, I ask of your Lordship—I ask of every calm thinking and intelligent Irish landowner—can these things last? Can they be tolerated in the boasted enlightenment and freedom of this nineteenth century? Is the spirit of feudal oppression driven from every other country in Europe to find a refuge and to inflict its last wrong and mischief upon mankind here? *

* In the above rapid sketch I have not stopped to notice a peculiarity connected with Irish property—a peculiarity often remarked, and which I am persuaded has had no little influence in creating the present mischievous relations of the owner and occupier of the soil.

It has been often said—perhaps it cannot be too often repeated—that in the letting of Irish land the landlord never makes, and never has made, the expenditure which both parties to an English letting would consider it indispensable the owner should make. "The English farmer pays a rent for his land in the state he finds it, which includes, not only the natural fertility of the soil, but the immense expenditure which national wealth has in the progress of time poured into it ; but the Irishman finds nothing he can afford to pay rent for, but what the bounty of God has given, unaided by either wealth or industry."—*Arthur Young.*

It is not altogether easy satisfactorily to account for this great difference in the arrangements of the rural economy of the two countries.

In lands let to the occupants who constituted the class whom I designate as serfs, it is very easily understood that setting the farm into tenantable order was a process wholly inapplicable to such lettings.

But all the lettings of land were not of this character. There were many, very many, farms in Ireland let to tenants just as independent and as substantial as any English farmer.

It would be very well worth inquiring how lands were formerly let in the old and long settled districts of Leinster—those, for instance, included in the old English Pale districts, which, just because they were long settled, differ in many very material respects from the rest of Ireland.

Something, of course, must be attributed to the character of the persons who generally received the grants of confiscation. They were not those in whom we would

Shall I be forgiven if I address a few words of respectful but earnest remonstrance to a numerous class of critics—may I venture to place your Lordship among them?—those who admit the evils which I point out—admit that they ought to be remedied by legislative enactment, but still object to the measure I propose? In this class I certainly may reckon a gentleman who has written upon this question with great ability and great knowledge, and who is pleased to say, "that, though Mr. Butt's remedy for Ireland is visionary in the extreme, and would cause more ills than it would cure, yet few have equalled him in the diagnosis of the disease;" and adds that my " scheme is never likely to become law, or even to gain a serious hearing in the House of Commons, *at least in our day.*"*

To a gentleman so well informed and liberal-minded as the writer whose criticism I quote, I need not suggest that there are many schemes "visionary in the extreme" when propounded, which yet have become law even in the day of those who proposed them. Every man is a visionary who is a little, even a very little, in advance of the prejudices which surround him. Every man is more or less a visionary who foresees that the power of truth and the irresistible march of events must yet break down the prejudices of class. But let me earnestly—and I will say it, solemnly—ask of all that thus criticise me, can they suggest any measure falling short of the principles of mine which will really remedy the evils that exist?

> " Si quid novisti rectius istis.
> Candidus imperti, SI NON HIS UTERE MECUM."

I will only ask them to remember the evil with which we have to deal. It is one that affects the very life of a nation, the right of the Celtic race to live in their own land—it is one that approaches the very foundation of society and proprietary rights. Let us not disguise from ourselves its importance—it is one that touches the deepest susceptibilities of a noble but passionate people—it is one

---

expect either the means or the inclination to put their estates into perfect order by the expenditure of large sums of money.

More, perhaps, is due to the unsettled state of the country. There were periods at which no one seemed to regard himself as having any permanent interest in Irish property. The business of every one appeared to be to make what he could of it for the time. When a change took place in this respect the custom of letting it the other way had become inveterate, and custom has, upon matters of this nature, an influence that is all-powerful.

The general rule in Ireland has certainly been, as stated by Arthur Young, that the landlord lets his farms without making any expenditure upon them, and this fact has exercised upon the whole system of Irish land tenure an influence far greater than we might at first suppose. Contrasted with English landlords the Irish landowners who gave the tenant nothing but the bare produce of the soil were not lettors of "farms" but exactors of rents. "The farm" which the English landlord let was a thing wholly different from anything for which an Irish tenant paid rent.

This subject, in all its bearings, is well worth a more extended and minute investigation than I can bestow upon it.

* *Irish Peers on Irish Peasants.* By G. T. Dalton, Esq.

with which we must not and we dare not trifle. If we propose any remedy at all, it must be one of which we can honestly say, before God and our country, that it will give redress.

If we are to approach the question in this spirit—the only spirit in which Irishmen ought to approach it—then, I ask, if I have correctly described the evil, can the wit or ingenuity of man devise any remedy for it that must not involve, of necessity, the very principle I suggest?

I know but of one safe mode of legislation. Nations drift to ruin by the statesmanship which has no higher wisdom than the cunning which suggests that "something must be done." No wise or great measure ever yet originated in the mere desire to produce something that will meet a demand for the manufacture of laws. We must first clearly and distinctly ascertain the evil that requires a remedy, and then, according to our resources, endeavour to apply it. If I am to adopt the medical metaphor of my critic, we must act upon " the diagnosis." " ' Occidit qui non servat' was the tremendous sentence passed by the great physician of the Augustan age upon negligence or incompetency in his own profession."* The surgeon would justly subject himself to this condemnation who gave cough mixtures, or even contented himself with putting on a straight waist-coat, when a fatal tumour requiring amputation was swelling on some limb. In politics, as in medicine, the first step is to see clearly the mischief, the next is to see the remedy by which it is to be removed. " Occidit qui non servavit " is the sentence which history will pro-nounce upon the statesman who looks on with folded arms while an evil system of land law is hurrying on the extinction in Ireland of the Irish race. With a more certain and a deeper condemnation will it be pronounced on those who attempt to deal with the evil that is crushing them out by palliatives, that cannot arrest the mischief that is destroying a nation's life. We must remember, in every question relating to Irish land tenure, that we have to deal with a class of proprietors among whom the impression is prevalent that either their religious, or their political, or their pecuniary interests are involved in keeping their tenantry in a state of dependence. In many, perhaps in most, instances the im-pression has reference to these three interests combined. All this may be—it is, perhaps, the natural and necessary result of the circumstances in which Irish proprietors are placed. It may be even produced by acts on the part of the tenantry themselves. But no matter how it may be accounted for or explained, or justified, the fact remains a real actual fact in Ireland's social state.

What then is the evil in our present condition of Ireland? It is the general insecurity of tenure, produced by a general determination of the landowners to refuse leases. Turn the question as we will

---

* Sir Philip Crampton.

devise expedients as we may, wrap it up in all the disguises that we can—the point comes simply in the end to this. We have but one remedy to meet that refusal, and that is to compel them.* It is a simple but it is an efficacious one. It is just as simple and just as

* There cannot, to my mind, be a more instructive proof of the rabid obstinacy with which some landowners—I hope they are not many—cling to the obsolete traditions of proprietary right than is to be found in the denunciations which have been uttered against the very innocuous measure proposed by Sir Colman O'Loghlen and Mr. Gregory. That measure proposed *that in all future lettings, if no term is mentioned,* the letting should be assumed to be for 21 years.

This measure, exactly like Mr. Fortescue's, did nothing more than alter, in the case of future lettings, the implication which the law now draws from the silence of contracting parties upon certain points. Where parties let and take land without saying anything of the terms, the law supposes them to mean that they contract for a tenancy to be determined by a six months notice to quit, and to continue for ever, unless either party give that notice. It also supposes that as to improvements, they mean that they shall belong to the landlord.

These implied contracts are solely and entirely the creation of law. They arise only in the absence of express provisions. If parties choose to let, the law make their contract for them, they do so with their eyes open. A measure altering the implication in no way interferes with the freedom of contracts. It leaves the landlord perfectly free to let his land upon whatever terms he pleases, and for whatever period he thinks fit. It only tells him that if he chooses to do certain things the law will put upon his act a certain meaning. Mr. Fortescue's bill told the landlord, " If you do not mean your tenant to have the benefit of improvements, say so—or you will be supposed to mean that he shall have it.

Sir Colman O'Loghlen's bill tells him—if, when you let your land, you do not say that your tenant shall not have a tenure of 21 years, the law will suppose that you intend he should have it. A pamphlet, written under the name of an "Irish Peer," describes this measure as "useful as showing the utter disregard of right and reason shown by some of the party," as only second, and scarcely second, in enormity to the measure proposed by myself, and excuses Mr. Gregory's support of it on the ground that he knew it could not pass—just as the "Irish Peer" goes on to say that "no man can better than myself appreciate the ludicrous and preposterous inequality, in operation as well as in justice, of such a bill" as that which I have proposed.

I would scarcely think it necessary to advert to such a matter if it were not that I am anxious to call attention to a very remarkable passage in the letter, in which Mr. Gregory thought it necessary to vindicate himself against the imputation conveyed in the excuse made for him:—

"The origin of the bill is this:—Sir Colman O'Loghlen and myself, and many men of experience and large property in Ireland, some of them members of your house, have long felt that the real cause of discontent among the Irish peasantry has arisen, not from occasional cases of hardship proceeding from the tenant being deprived of the value conferred on land by his improvements, BUT BY REASON OF THE UNCERTAIN TENURE WHICH PREVAILS IN IRELAND. WE CANNOT FIND SUCH A TENURE TO BE THE RULE IN ANY CIVILIZED COUNTRY IN THE WORLD. We have endeavoured by this bill to arrest that evil."

Thus clearly and distinctly stating the mischief, the insecurity of tenure which prevails in Ireland, but is unknown in any other civilized country ; can the framers of this bill upon reading such a letter as Lord Rosse's expect upon full reflection that such a measure will "arrest the evil?" Can this great mischief be arrested by a measure which only enacts that in future every tenant must sign a paper saying he is tenant from year to year—or if not that he will be a tenant for 21 years.

The effect would, of course, be that whenever the landlord did not intend him to hold for 21 years he would be asked to sign such a paper. The result most likely would follow, that the paper would contain stringent conditions of which, but for the necessity of having a written paper, the landlord would not have thought.

I have already pointed out in, commenting on Mr. Fortescue's bill, that the result of enactments altering the nature of the implications arising from silence in future contracts will simply be, in some instances, to surprise careless or inattentive landlords

effectual as the masterly manœuvre by which the evil spirit of "landlordism" has defeated all the long course of legislation by which an attempt has been made to elevate the Irish peasant to the rank of a free man. It is not matter of inference or of speculation, it is demonstration, that influenced by the passions and the fears of the old feud, landowners can use, and have used, and are using, nay more, that they intend, and will continue to use the proprietary rights which the law attaches to the ownership of the soil, so as to give to the occupier the choice of leaving Ireland or remaining in it as a serf. There is one way, and but one, of meeting this. We must submit, or we must pass a law enacting that proprietary rights shall not be so used. To this plain and simple issue the question must at last be brought.

I ask those of them who are not willing to submit, but who object to my proposal, to tell me by what other conceivable means, except a measure based on the principles of that proposal, is an absolute and unconditional submission to be avoided. To my mind no mathematical demonstration was ever plainer than the reasoning which asserts that if it be necessary to "arrest" in Ireland "the evil of insecurity of tenure," this can only be done by a measure which will compel the landlord to give security of tenure. The evil proceeds, and proceeds solely, from the determination of the landlords that the occupiers shall not have any fixed or secure interest in the soil. In the name of common sense how are we to overcome this by any measure which professes to give security to the tenant, but still leaves it to the landowners to determine whether the occupiers shall have that security or not?

I have already pointed out the great difficulty that meets us in every measure intended to secure compensation for future improvements, and so permit the industrious tenant to acquire a property in his farm. We have to deal with occupiers who are tenants at will, and owners who have avowed their determination that they never shall be more. While we leave the occupier in that position, the working of the most skilful, even the most liberally-framed measure of compensation must really be dependent upon the landlord's will.

A measure securing compensation for past improvements would, of course, give a certain fixity of tenure to every tenant who has improved. Such a measure was more than "entertained" by Parliament, it was sanctioned by three successive Cabinets. It passed the House of Commons by majorities great in number, but greater

into concessions to their tenants which they did not intend. They cannot, within the range of human possibility, have the slightest influence upon those landlords who in dealing with their tenants are determined to keep their hands untied.

Let us endeavour to evade it as we will, no human intellect or human ingenuity can escape the "mathematical demonstration" mentioned in the text.

Nothing can be more full than Mr. Gregory's admission of the evil, and of the necessity of "arresting" it.

in the character and influence of those who composed them.* If it had not been for a change of ministry it would probably have become law.

Fourteen years ago the "retrospective clause" was carried through the House of Commons. The intervening period has, no doubt, far diminished its value. Much of the property it would have protected has been seized. Defective as that clause may have been, if it had become law as it passed the Commons, it would have saved us many an eviction since; and at the cost of creating much and perhaps angry dispute and litigation between landlord and tenant, it would in many instances have left the tenant in peaceable possession of his farm—in all it would have embarrassed and impeded the proceeding of the landlord to turn him out.

The more we reflect upon the subject, the greater will appear the difficulty of dealing with that which is the real question—are we to submit to the claims made, openly made, upon the part of the landowners, such as I have described? I think I have proposed a measure by which we can escape that submission without in the slightest degree countenancing any interference with the true rights of property. In the fearful timidity which always attends the possessors of Irish property they talk of such proposals as sanctioning the doctrines of men who say the tenantry should hold the lands without paying rent. It is not too much to say that if such measures are entertained the measure I propose if adopted would for ever crush them. It would make punctuality in payment of rent the condition of holding the farm ; but it would tell the occupier that so long as he paid a fair and moderate rent he might defy the landlord, the bailiff, and the notice to quit. Who that knows the real feelings of the Irish tenantry does not know what would be the effect of such a legislative declaration? The more he dreaded and disliked his landlord the more earnest would be his efforts to be ready with his rent. The very feelings which now make him lawless and violent would prompt him to industry and thrift. He would defy eviction, not by the threatening notice of the ribbonman, but by the labour, of which he would know the fruits would be his own. Were such a measure accepted by the tenant farmers of Ireland, as a final settlement of the question, it would give, in the minds of the people, a new and a national title to proprietary rights ; were it offered by the landowners it would conciliate to those rights the good will and the conscience of a people who now regard them with dislike.

I do not believe that the Irish tenant farmer is influenced by the desire imputed to him, of holding his land without paying rent. He is influenced by the strongest, the most passionate wish to have secure possession of the land he cultivates, and of the home in which he

* *Land Tenure in Ireland*, 3rd edition, p. 85.

R

dwells. Give him this on fair terms and he will be content. Designs, no doubt, have been entertained against all rights of landed property; and the people sympathise with, even when they have not taken part in, such designs. But both the designs and the sympathy originate in the conviction that proprietary rights are used so as to be inconsistent with the right of the people to live and prosper in their own land. It is not the rent but the insecurity and the serfdom which the Irish occupier hates. Give him security and freedom, and I do not believe you will find a people on earth more ready, loyally, and in good faith, to recognize all the existing arrangements of ownership, or more ready to toil honestly and laboriously to fulfil all the obligations which that ownership has a right to exact.

But it has been actually said that such a measure tends to disturb the title to Irish estates! that my arguments if they were valid ought to be followed out by a proposal for the repeal of the Act of Settlement and the restoration of the forfeited estates!!!*

---

* I have, I confess, seen with some surprise an objection of this nature even suggested (although perhaps only in a passing jest) in a very well written, and in many respects very sensible, tract, entitled, *A Demurrer to Mr. Butt's Plea*, by an Irish Land Agent.

This tract has reached me just as I have been closing this letter, or I would gladly have noticed some of the passages contained in it. I have not the remotest idea who the writer may be, but his tract bears internal evidence both of knowledge and truth-, fulness. This makes me the more regret that I cannot now notice some statements which are, I am sure, worthy of great consideration, but from which I draw inferences very different from his. Many, indeed, of the facts included in his statements I have already commented on in my observations on the publications of Lord Dufferin and Lord Rosse.

I was, of course, prepared for the usual statement that no one has any right to give an opinion upon such subjects except a landlord or a land agent, or, mayhap, in some rare cases, a tenant farmer. But I scarcely expected, within a few pages of this claim for exclusive knowledge on the part of "practical men," to find the following passage :—
"No doubt," he says, "they "—that is, the occupiers—"are all in favour of owning their farms, or of long leases and low rents, but it does not follow that a man is always the best judge of what is good for himself, and an Irish tenant's opinion on many points is not exactly infallible."

Is it treason to ask whether an Irish landlord's, or even an Irish agent's, is! Practical men, we have seen, sometimes fall into strange mistakes, even on a matter so simple as the rate of wages.

The Irish Land Agent has, however, completely answered his own statement—that "the complaints of the present system of land tenure do not come from the sufferers."

I might also suggest to him that if he correctly describes the feelings of the occupiers in the passage I have quoted, he scarcely offers an adequate explanation of the fact he mentions—that he has not found them very anxious to accept the leases which he has known them offered.

Considering the class of men who are aggrieved by the present system of land tenure, there is something very comical—I can use no other word—in this demand of landlords and land agents that the discussion of this question should be left to the parties themselves. It would certainly be a most admirable arrangement if it could only be contrived that the only person entitled to reply to Lord Dufferin would be a landlord or one of the evicted tenants.

I remember an instance of a very similar demand. I have read in some memoirs of Wilberforce, of a West India planter convulsing the House of Commons by saying that no complaints of the cruelties of the slave trade had come from any of the kidnapped negroes, and adding, in phrases more vehement than polished, that in the absence of

We might have expected this miserable cry by this time to have died away. It has been the excuse or the pretence for all the oppression and misgovernment of Ireland. It was the origin of the penal laws. It was used to resist the granting of electoral privileges to Roman Catholics. It constituted no small part of the arguments against emancipation. It was employed to terrify the landlords into supporting the tithe system. To attack tithes was to assail rents. It has been used to frighten them against yielding to any concession on the subject of the Church—" Think you no spark will fall upon your evil deeds when the muniments of the Church are blazing," has been the language in which they have been addressed in many a powerful and eloquent appeal. Surely it is time that the right to landed property may rest in Ireland, as it does in all other countries—upon its own strength. Surely Irish landowners are wise enough to see that to use such language is to imply a weakness in their title in which nobody except themselves believes. The territorial rights that can only be guarded by out-works of oppression are far from being secure.

The measure I propose would put an end for ever to these miserable fears. It would take from proprietary rights in Ireland everything that still identifies them with confiscation and conquest. It would repair the fatal error—it matters not whether in the design or the execution—of that which was called the settlement of Ireland—that of trusting to the jealousies and the passions of the new proprietors, the condition of the old Irish people on their native soil. Were such a measure passed, in ten years after its becoming law, no cause of anxiety would exist in the relations of landlord and tenant in Ireland. Both the owners and the occupiers would feel themselves at home in their native land.

And may it not, my Lord, even on lower grounds that considerations of national peace and prosperity, may it not be the interest of Irish landowners that such a settlement should take place? I need not remind your Lordship that measures absolutely scouted as " revolutionary " and "impracticable" have yet passed—and passed in the end without the safeguards and restrictions by which an early concession would have been accompanied.

I ask, once more, is it possible for our present condition of land tenure to last? Is it possible for a few landed proprietors, like

such complaints "it was great presumption in honourable gentlemen, who knew nothing of West Indian property, to interfere between him and his slaves."
Is it not something of the same feeling which resents any discussion on the Irish land question by any one outside the privileged circle, even by the press? All others must be " persons seeking political, capital, profit, or notoriety; or to a certain class of newspapers, who find an increase to their circulation by the introduction of high-seasoned articles."
Is there in Ireland a landlord or land agent who can believe that his cause can be served by nonsense like this. Far better to blurt it out with the honest blunt-ness of the old West Indian slave driver—" It is great presumption in them ——— fellows to interfere between me and my slaves."

those of Ireland, really to maintain their claim to hold the Irish
people as serfs? Is it possible for them really to enforce a decree
of expatriation against the Irish race? We read history in vain
if we are not able to discern the great lessons which teach us the
vanity of such a thought. I do not believe it possible for a people
like the Irish thus to be driven from their native land. I believe
implicitly in the emancipation of that people from serfdom, because I
have implicit faith in the power of principles which must control in
the end the destiny of nations.

> " There is a Providence doth shape our ends,
> Rough hew them as we will."

Have you marked,* my Lord, that the whole intelligence of
Europe is against you? No traveller from any continental country
has ever written his impressions of his visit to Ireland without
pointing to "landlordism" as the cruel origin of Ireland's misery
and discontent. In what French or German publication are Irish
affairs ever discussed without a condemnation of our system of land
tenure, far more sweeping and severe than any I have ventured to
pronounce? The voice of Christendom is raised against you. Do
not believe that there is no power in that voice.
Can you say that you have the intellect of England, or even the
active and thoughtful intelligence of your own country, on your
side? Where do you take up any intelligent treatise on Irish
affairs, written by an impartial person, without a discussion more
or less favourable to a system of peasant proprietors?* How many
reflecting men have urged this? Where will you find a man who

---

* I need scarcely say that the creation of peasant proprietors, as far as it goes, is
a displacement of the landed gentry.
I would see with great satisfaction a return to a state of things which formerly
prevailed to a large extent in England, and to some, although not to so great an
extent, in Ireland—that of an independent yeomanry, cultivating their own fee
simple estates The tendency in both countries has been to absorb such properties
into those of the great landowners. I have been told that this has occurred even
in that peculiar district of Wexford known as the barony of Forth, a district still
peopled by the descendants of a colony from Pembroke, who landed with Strong-
bow. I believe that before the Union there were in this district many small farmers
who were owners of their farms. I am afraid that many, if not all, of them have sold
their fee simple, and pay a rent for what was once their own estate.
I speak naturally with some distrust of my own opinion, but I must say that I
do not believe there is generally the slightest ambition on the part of the Irish
farmer to become an owner in fee. There is an intense desire for fixity of tenure,
but this desire is perfectly satisfied by a secure tenure, under a good landlord, at a
moderate rent. I believe that the majority of tenants so circumstanced have not
the slightest desire to be possessors of the fee, and that most of them would decline
to purchase it if it was offered at a fair price. This peculiarity in their character
may be accounted for by the old traditions of the country, possibly by traditions
descending through the character of the people from the old Irish tenures. Very
probably they are not yet trained to those feelings of independence which would
enable them to appreciate an ownership in fee.
It has been said that "every man in Ireland desires to be a landlord." There is

is not a landlord to say that he is satisfied with the present condition of the occupiers of the soil?

Let me ask your attention to the language in which Irish proprietary rights are spoken of both in England and Ireland. I am not about to weary, perhaps offend, your Lordship, by extracts from the writings of men who exercise no small influence upon the educated opinion of the nation. In every place, even in the English Universities, wherever in speech or in writing Ireland is made the subject of intellectual discussion, there Irish landlordism is arraigned, and tried, and condemned. I will not even quote the language of Mr. Bright, which Lord Dufferin places at the head of his letters; yet, my Lord, you must not forget that upon this, as upon other subjects, Mr. Bright represents the feelings and sentiments of great masses of his countrymen. I will ask your attention to the language of one distinguished among our own countrymen— of one who has vindicated the promise held out even in the high honours and distinctions of his University career. I quote from a paper read at a meeting of the Irish Statistical Society, in May, 1864, by Mr. Heron :—

"Under the present laws no Irish peasant able to read and write ought to remain in Ireland. If Ireland were an independent country, in the present state of things there would be a bloody insurrection in every county, and the peasantry would ultimately obtain the property in land as they have obtained it in Switzerland and in France."

This is not the language of a revolutionist or a communist, it was written by a man subject to the responsibilities which I admit belong to the position of "one of Her Majesty's Council learned in the law." He had filled the office of professor in one of the Queen's Colleges. He is a distinguished writer upon jurisprudence. In little more than twelve months after he had written and publicly read this passage his professional character and position forced him into the service of the Government. These words were not spoken at any excited popular meeting, carrying away the speaker

a sense and an extent in which and to which this is, unhappily, too true. But it means a *landlord having a tenant under him*, not an owner in fee cultivating his own little bit of ground.

I am bound to say that, so far as my opportunities of judging of the feelings of the peasantry extend, while they have an actual passion for fixity of tenure, I do not think it has taken the form of a desire to be absolute owners of the land they till.

If we grant them fixity of tenure we give to the industrious and improving tenant an opportunity of acquiring an interest which would make him a part proprietor, and carry with it perhaps most of the advantages of an entire ownership. Upon this point I am quite willing to accept Lord Rosse's description of "the cunningly devised act," it would "give the tenant, without purchase, some of the privileges of ownership," it would do so without taking anything from the landlord. It would vest in the tenant the ownership of a new property which his industry would create. It would probably give him the desire to acquire that ownership, and would fit him for doing os whenever the opportunity arose.

by the passions of a crowd. They were read at a meeting of a scientific body, a body presided over by grave and eminent personages, enrolling in its list of members many who rank among our foremost men, and in the transactions of that society they first were submitted to the light of publication.*

As to Irish opinions, I content myself with this one quotation. I could have cited many others from men in somewhat similar, although less distinguished positions, to show you how far the educated opinion of your own country is arrayed against you.

Let us turn to the evidence of English opinion. I do not speak of popular opinion, nor even of the high class of that which is generally termed so. Of this it were easy to collect evidence. I might even recall the memory of the fierce and scornful invectives with which but a few years ago Irish proprietors were visited in the columns of that great journal, which upon this, as upon many other subjects, too faithfully represents the passions and the prejudices of England. I am speaking of a different and more formidable condemnation, the condemnation of our Irish system of land tenure, which has been pronounced in the calm and tranquil judgment of those who are, after all, the guides and the instructors of rational thought. Let us see how Mr John Stuart Mill speaks of that system, not in any political discussion, but in a treatise from which many educated Englishmen will learn the principles of social Science—" The land" of " Ireland," says this great thinker:—

" The land of Ireland, the land of every country, belongs to the people of that country. The individuals called landowners have no right, in morality or justice, to anything but the rent or compensation for its saleable value. . . . When the inhabitants of a country quit the country en *masse* because its government will not make it a place fit for them to

---

* Since writing the above I have seen a suggestion from Bishop Keane, in a letter to the National Association, that a measure securing future compensation should be accompanied by a clause providing that *the power of arbitrary eviction should be suspended until the tenant should have time to improve*:—

" In order that improvement may be sure and quick, that, unless in the case of non-payment of rent, no tenant be liable to eviction for such a number of years as good landlords and intelligent farmers, thoroughly acquainted with the present state of things, may think necessary, that the tenant may have time to make improvements."

Without some provision of this nature it would be plainly impossible that any measure securing compensation for future improvements would be effectual.

I have often thought of suggesting, as I propose in a future page, that, with a view of keeping the people at home, a short measure should be passed, suspending the power of eviction for two years, and empowering, in the mean time, a Royal Commission to collect evidence, so as to ascertain the real condition of the Irish occupiers, and after ascertaining the views both of landlords and tenants, recommend some measure which might adjust the relations of landlord and tenant in such a way as to secure the landlord his rights, and yet give to the occupier the power of applying his industry on the soil.

Had such a measure been announced in the Royal Speech it would, indeed, have been a message of peace to Ireland. It would have stayed insurrection more effectually than all the flying columns that traverse the country, and all the iron clads and gun boats that blockade our coasts.

live in, the government is judged and condemned. It is the duty of Parliament to reform the landed tenure of Ireland."

And again :—

"Nothing can be done for Ireland without transforming the cottier tenantry into something else. But into what? Those who know neither Ireland nor any foreign country propose the transformation into hired labourers; I contend that the object should be their transformation, as far as circumstances permit, into landed proprietors." *

And even among British statesmen, by cold, cautious, and reserved British statesmanship, in the high places of British council, what language has been held?

How has " the Irish question" been described in the House of Commons by a statesman who surely could have no motive for using this language except a deep conviction of its truth? When on a former occasion ministers appealed to Parliament to suspend the protection which the Constitution gives for personal liberty, Mr Disraeli said :—

" He wished to see a public man come forward and say what the Irish question was. Let them consider Ireland as they would any other country similarly circumstanced. They had a starving population, an absentee aristocracy, an alien church, and in addition, the weakest Executive in the world. This was the Irish question. What would gentlemen say on reading of a country in such a position? They would say at once in such case, the remedy is Revolution—not the suspension of the Habeas Corpus Act. But the connexion with England prevented it—therefore England was logically in the active position of being the cause of all the misery of Ireland. What then was the duty of an English minister? To effect by his policy all the changes which a Revolution would do by force." †

It is impossible not to feel that these are the words of deep thought as well as deep conviction. They are the words of the statesman to whose guidance the Conservative party are now trusting in the unprecedented perils and difficulties which surround them.

And yet men tell me it is vain to hope that ever English statesmen will yield the just demands of the Irish people—and Irish landlords tell us they may safely defy the opinions and the resentments of their own countrymen, because they are sure of the perpetual support of England's overwhelming power.

Has no warning voice been heard in the chamber where your Lordship sits, in the assembly where the rights of property are supposed to be held peculiarly sacred? The warning came from no ordinary source. It came from a nobleman who had but a short

* John Stuart Mill.
† Mr. Disraeli—*Parliamentary Debates.* 1848.

time ceased to represent his Sovereign in this country—and who must have spoken under the sense of the deep responsibility which that position imposed upon him. These were the words of Lord Kimberley, spoken in the House of Lords:—

"It was impossible for England to perform its duties to Ireland so long as no attempt was made to deal with the important question of the tenure of land. He implored the Irish landed proprietors not to pass it by. The landed proprietors were supported by the force of the United Kingdom in maintaining themselves in a position which, he was convinced, if Ireland stood alone, they could not possibly maintain, and this country was strictly responsible for seeing that its military force was not applied in perpetuity to save the landowners from measures which they have neglected to provide, and which might otherwise be forced on them."*

Surely, my Lord, for those who can read it, "the handwriting is on the wall." It needs no Daniel to interpret a portion. The "landlordism" which after two centuries of mastery can do nothing better for the Irish people than drive them from their native land is a system that cannot be maintained Of a system proved and condemned as this has been we may truly say, "it has been weighed in the balance and found wanting." Let us remember that the dominion of which such words as I have quoted have been spoken and written, is one that could not last a year if English troops did not garrison our island to support it. Let us weigh these words of British statesmen, let us estimate the weight of opinion by which our land tenure is condemned. When all these things are put together—and when we add to them all the deep and burning hatred of the Irish people to the system, the voice of condemnation that has been uttered from all Europe, the indignant murmur of the exiled Irish that comes over the ocean from the other side of the Atlantic—the weary and the shame to England of Ireland's perennial desolation and perpetual discontent, it needs no deep political sagacity to see that the system which has all these elements of power arrayed against it cannot last.

* Lord Kimberley's Speech, August, 1864.
I have been accused of being a Revolutionist for giving expression to the very same sentiments.
"I have already ventured to advert to one feature connected with Irish land tenure. It is upheld against the will of the people by the power of England. If Ireland were an independent kingdom in the middle of the Atlantic, the present arrangements of landed property would not continue unmodified for one year. If British power forces the present system upon Ireland, it is not only the right, but the duty, of that power to examine and control the exercise of the rights which it enforces. Irish proprietary right depends upon the support of England, then English statesmen and the English nation are bound to see that their power is not exerted to perpetuate grievances which in any ordinary measure of national movements would long since have been redressed. The nation that is called on to uphold proprietary rights for one class in another country is certainly justified in looking narrowly to the mode in which these rights are exercised."—*Land Tenure in Ireland*, pages 72, 73.

And yet Irish landowners dream of maintaining their high and arbitrary views of proprietary right—they tell us of the necessity of "keeping their hands untied"—of the power and duty of "weeding" unsatisfactory tenants from their estates. Those who do so refuse "to discern the signs of the times." The Irish people are flying from the Irish soil. It is impossible for British statesmen much longer to look on as mere spectators of that flight. It is trifling with a great question to shut our eyes to the fact that it is the old, the never decided struggle, between the Irish landowners and the Irish people. The Irish difficulty is now to reconcile proprietary rights with the continued dwelling of that people in their own land. Can we really suppose that this question must not be adjusted, that England will not call on the landowners whose power her military force maintains " to set their house in order," so that they and the Irish nation may live in one house. It will not do to answer that appeal by saying " we have got the land, we are satisfied, and if the people do not like our arrangements they may go." The part of the porcupine in the fable may not always be successful, and every year that a final and complete adjustment of the land question is postponed the less favourable will the final adjustment be to proprietary rights.

Let no man misunderstand, or pretend to misunderstand me, when I speak of the conflict between proprietary rights, and the dwelling of the Irish people in their own land. I mean this—I believe that no one can patiently and carefully give his attention to all the evidence that throws light upon the emigration of the people without coming to the conclusion that it is impossible to keep the people at home unless we can give them security or fixity of tenure, I care not by what name you call it—and that there is not the slightest prospect of their obtaining this, while we leave our land tenure to be regulated by the uncontrolled exercise of proprietary rights.

The statesmen and legislators are fortunate who have only to deal with a state of society like that of England—a state in which no man can say there is any conflict between the right of every proprietor to do what he likes with his own and the right of every Englishman to live in his native land. Unhappily—most unhappily—every man who approaches an Irish social question meets this conflict encountering him at the very threshold of his enquiries. If that conflict existed in England, no one doubts for a moment how it would be solved. The conditions of property would be moulded to the wants and necessities of the people. If Ireland were an independent country no one can doubt that the solution of the problem would be exactly the same. If such a measure as I propose be necessary to protect the right of the Irish people to live upon the Irish soil, it ought to be passed just as surely as any measure would be passed which were necessary to ensure the right of the English people to live upon the English soil.

If, in any other country in Europe, a state of things existed, such as now exists in Ireland, would there be an hour's hesitation on the part of its government in adopting a remedy far more peremptory and decisive than that which I have proposed. I care not what may be the form of that government, from the absolute despotism of the Czar to the free democracy of the Cantons of the Alps, there is not a government in Europe that would not interfere in such a case between the landowners and the people, and protect the people in the occupation of the soil. The English Government is the only civilized government on earth that would look on and see a whole people driven from their homes.

And surely if this state of things were to come at once upon the English Government and people—if it had not grown up, as it were, day by day before their eyes—it would not by either of them be tolerated for an hour. If we could suppose that at the time of the Union all communication from Ireland to England had been shut out—that while England still sent her troops to keep Ireland in subjection, no accounts had ever reached her of what was going on— and that now, at the end of sixty-seven years, a commissioner was sent over to examine, for the first time, into what had been doing for those sixty-seven years—and that commissioner reported what is going on around us, that the whole nation was flying away because landowners refused the security of tenure to the occupiers of the soil—that the result was national misery and universal discontent— will any man believe that one year would pass over before fixity of tenure would be throughout Ireland established as the law?

Let us suppose that the question related, not to Ireland, but to some remote dependence of the British empire, to some conquered province of India, or even one of the " Crown colonies" in some West Indian island. The statement laid before an English minister is this :—There is a country subject to the British Crown, and under the control of the British Legislature, in which the cultivators of the soil are subject to the dominion of a few persons claiming proprietary rights ; these men—it matters not whether they call themselves zemindars, or slave-owners, or chiefs, or feudal nobles, claim the right of enforcing from the peasant an arbitrary tribute—of imposing on him any rules and conditions they think fit—of seizing on any little property he may have created by industry in improving his small plot of ground, and of turning him out of his home and his farm whenever they think proper. These powers are sometimes exercised with cruelty and under circumstances of great hardship— they everywhere create in the minds of the occupier's dissatisfaction and discontent.

Is there a man who reads this who doubts what the remedy would be. The British minister who had to deal with such a case would say at once :—Commute the arbitrary exaction into a fixed rent proportioned to the real value of the holding—settle the conditions upon which he is to hold, and give him such a tenure as will protect him against arbitrary eviction by the zemindar, the slave-owner, or the feudal noble.

Is not this exactly the state of things which exists in Ireland ? and is not this precisely the remedy I propose ?

Let us suppose, in addition to this, that this occurred in a country in which the property had been taken away from the native proprietors and conferred upon English settlers, placed in it for the express purpose of conciliating the people to English rule, and most strictly enjoined to forbear uncertain exactions and precarious tenures. Let it be a conquered province of India. Complaints come home that these proprietors have recently changed all the customary lettings of the country, that the ryots—we must not call them tenants—dissatisfied with the condition to which they are reduced, are committing frequent outrages—that they are flying from the country in immense numbers, while those who remain are engaging in plans of revolt. Let me suppose your Lordship were sent as a Commissioner by your Sovereign with plenary powers to settle the differences that distracted such a province. On calling all classes together you find that the poor " ryots " would be peaceable and contented if you assured them of their holdings at a moderate rent, and on a tenure of 60 years. I believe, my Lord, that after settling such a measure you would return with pride to your Sovereign, and tell her that you had executed her commission with an ease and a satisfaction which surprised you.

And if to such a moderate request the English zemindars—I must not call them landlords—refused their assent ; if you had the power you would give the people what they asked in spite of the zemindars. If you had not that power you would, I think, tell the " zemindars " that they would dissent at their peril, and that if they refused to settle their difference with the " ryots " upon such moderate and equitable terms, they must not expect that the troops of the British Sovereign would any longer support them in enforcing rights which were really oppression and wrong.*

---

* This very question of the right of a landlord to the protection and for the aid of the executive in committing acts which endanger the peace of the whole country, gave rise to rather a curious correspondence with the Government of Lord Carlisle, when the Sheriff of Donegal sent a requisition for a military force to accompany him in carrying out the evictions at Glenveagh. The entire of the correspondence which ensued between all parties was published in a parliamentry paper, and may be read a with great advantage by those who desire to know the extent of the claims of Irish proprietary right.

It seems strange that a landlord who may clear a whole country-side of its inhabitants to the imminent peril of the peace, it may be of half a province, has the absolute right of commanding, if necessary, all the military in the county to aid him in the execution of his cruelty. Yet such is the law. The sheriff is bound to obey the Queen's writ, and if force be necessary to execute it ; he is entitled, and indeed bound to call to his aid, as part of the *posse comitatus*, all the military force that may be in the county. Soldiers are not exempt any more than civilians from the obligations which the law imposes on every one to aid the sheriff. The practical result is that a landlord has

And this is not done in the case in Ireland, just because we have the fiction of an identity with England. The owner of the soil is a "landlord," not a "zemindar"—the occupier is a "tenant," and not a "ryot." I believe in my conscience, that if we had Irish or Gaelic names to express the relation, if the owner were a "corbe" and the occupier a "kerne," an English Parliament would not for one session tolerate the continuance of the wrong. Our misfortune is, that English phrases are applied to relations that bear no resemblance to the things which the words describe in the English tongue. Ireland is denied the real benefit of English justice by the fiction that we are one country with England; and that "landed property is the same thing in Ireland as it is in England, or Scotland, or Wales." The fiction is as unreal as that by which Henry VIII. was declared king of all Ireland, when, in whole districts of the island, English authority was unrecognized and English law unknown; when "those who dwelt west of the Barrow dwelt west of the law." Our law books tell us that legal fictions never work wrong. Lord Clare has pointed out that the earlier fiction converted wars into rebellions, and confiscated estates that ought to

actually a right to order the military to drive out his tenants. And this right was in fact exercised at two of the evictions to which I have so frequently referred, those of Glenveagh and Rathcore.

This employment of the power of the executive to aid in the extermination of the people occurs, and has occurred frequently enough to identify, in the minds of the people, English power with their oppression. It has excited the indignation of many conservatives. Michael Thomas Sadler might be termed a bigot in his attachment to the principles of Toryism. Yet he thus wrote upon this subject, when Irish evictions were neither as frequent nor as cruel as they have been since. Writing in 1829 of "the notable scheme," even then propounded, "of thinning Ireland by emigration and monopoly, the object of which, however disguised, was to obtain for the proprietors a greater surplus produce." He continues:—

"In closing my remarks I would put one or two plain questions. Is a system which can only be supported by brute force, and is kept up by constant blood-shedding, to be perpetuated for ever? Are we still to garrison a defenceless country in behalf of those whose property was, generally speaking, originally conferred on the special condition of residence, but whose desertion occasions all the evils under which she has groaned for centuries?—*property so treated, that it would not be worth a day's purchase were the proprietors its sole protectors.* But they are aware that their absence is balanced by the presence of a body of military and police, which enables them to conduct themselves with as little apprehension as remorse. The possessions of the entire empire would be lost to their owners, were such conduct general; and are these so meritorious a class, that their utmost demands are to be extorted from a distant and suffering country, and themselves protected in the open neglect, or rather audacious outrage, of all those duties, on the due and reciprocal discharge of which the whole frame of the social system is founded? If they persist in this course, let them do so, but let it be at their proper peril! Let them urge their own claims, and defend their own outrages: the British soldier, who is ready to bleed in the battle in which his country's interest or honour is at stake, is too noble a being, methinks, to be degraded virtually into the exactor of the enormous rents of the absentee, which his desertion often incapacitates the wretched tenants from discharging, or to ' clear' his estates of human beings, when it may please him to utter the fiat from afar. I say I would leave them to settle this as they could, only that it would be practically difficult to sever their case from such as have fair claims upon public protection."—*Ireland and its Evils.* Pages 161, 162.

Michael Thomas Sadler believed that the only Irish landlords who were guilty of clearances were the absentees.

have been protected. The later fiction has been as mischievous as the earlier. Neither, indeed, was ever invoked except for the purposes of oppression and wrong. The native Irish were not given the protection of subjects, though they suffered the penalties of treason. We never hear of our identity with England when a difference is to be made to our loss. And on this land question the result of our incorporation with the freest and most liberal nation in Europe is this. A state of things exists in Ireland which would not be endured in England for one year. If Ireland were an independent country it would long since have been set right. If we were a dependent colony, or a mere subject dependence of the British Crown, justice would be done to us. If we were the subjects of any other civilized government protection would be given to the occupiers of the Irish soil. But just because we are advanced to the benefit and dignity of a partnership with the British nation a system of land tenure is maintained entirely unsuited to our condition, and which no other conceivable form of government would condemn us to endure.

And now, my Lord, I ask again, is it really to be expected that such a state of things can last for ever? Is it not very possible that British statesmen, in their duty to their Sovereign, in their duty to that "great and antient monarchy," in which they serve, may deem it the interest of England to enfranchise and conciliate the occupiers of the Irish soil? It is impossible for them not to turn wistful and serious thoughts upon this island, which ought to be, which might be, the pride and strength of that monarchy, but which is now its weakness and disgrace. Perhaps they think of those strange words of Spenser that seem like inspired prophecy—genius has its inspiration:—

"Marry there have been divers good plots devised and wise counsels cast about for the reformation of that realm ; but they say it is the fatal destiny of that land that no purposes whatever which are meant for her good, will prosper or take good effect, which—whether it proceed from the very genius of the soyle or influence of the starres, or that Almighty God hath not yet appointed the time of her reformation, or that he reserveth her in this unquiet state still, for some secret scourge which shall by her come unto England it is hard to be known, but yet more to be feared."*

May not the ministers of England think that the days are come in which the question is to be decided—which are either to be the time of Ireland's "reformation" or those in which if Ireland is any longer kept "in this unquiet state," some "secret scourge shall come by her to England." If ever English ministers feel that this is their choice—the claims of Irish landlords will not have much weight in the decision.

There are many to whom words like this will appear wild—but

* Edmund Spenser, 1596

surely the calm and thoughtful may foresee at least the possibility of events in which England could ill-afford to keep a discontented Irish nation by her side. May not English statesmen be wise enough to foresee this too? Surely, my Lord, these are matters for the serious consideration of your order. Secure as they think themselves in "the overwhelming power of England," the Irish landlords may refuse these concessions by which, if they had been left to themselves, they would long since have conciliated the good-will of the Irish people. They may contemptuously turn from proposals such as mine with a self-satisfied notion that the British Parliament will never sanction such a plan as this. Are you so sure of this? Has such a reliance been never disappointed before? In 1782 the whole policy of England to this country was absolutely reversed in the few hours which elapsed between the arrival of the Irish mail and the assembling of the House of Commons. We have seen events in Europe press on with startling rapidity to results which any man would have been deemed insane for predicting but one short year before. Who will guarantee us that British statesmen, even those who compose the present Cabinet, will always maintain the present treatment of the Irish occupiers at the expense of weakening the British power and disgracing the British name? What assurance have we that a crisis may not arise in which the most Conservative minister might feel it his duty to his Sovereign to purchase the loyalty of the Irish nation by concessions of which the most sanguine nationalist may not now dream? These things at least are just as possible as the humiliation of Austria in a week. Be assured, my Lord, Irish landlords have no exemption from vicissitudes which shake dynasties and thrones.

Might it not be prudent to contemplate the possibility of such things? the prospect of a time when the Irish land question might be settled by a hurried concession to popular demands, in which the safe-guards might be omitted which could protect all real proprietary right? Am I wrong in saying that one day or other this land question must be settled? If it must be so are there any persons more interested than the landowners in having it settled soon?

If we ourselves were free from the prejudices which a familiarity with this state of things has produced—if we could see it for the first time in some foreign country, would we say that it could be, or that it ought to be, upheld?

I have frequently been struck by perceiving the impressions made upon the minds of Irishmen when a consideration of what they see in other countries elevates their views of such questions to a point from which the mists and fogs of local prejudices are overlooked. Let me quote a passage supplying a striking instance of this from the writings of a gentleman whose authority your Lordship will not altogether despise. The writer is now in a position aloof from all political discussions, but I am sure he never will be in any position in which he will forget his love for his country, the character of which he has done so much to sustain. I quote the words of the present Lord Chief Justice of Ireland. They will, at least, tell us how an Irishman and a man of genius feels when he is compelled to contrast the condition of other countries with that of his own.

In Tuscany—Tuscany which Englishmen despised as submitting to the yoke of despotism—in Tuscany over the downfall of whose government Englishmen rejoiced—in oppressed and enslaved Tuscany the Irish traveller saw the homes of the peasant proprietors that spangle with comfort and industry the heights that overlook the valley of the Arno. He saw the terraced gardens to which earth has been borne up the steep by the toil of the peasant who knew that the fruits of his industry were his own. He saw what fixity of tenure had done there. He thought of the miserable Irish serfs at home—which of us have not thought of them when we saw comfort, and contentment, and happy cottages in other lands?—and emancipated from the poor prejudices that press upon us in Ireland, he wrote:—

"It is proved that the tenants holding by leases are prosperous; the occupiers of patches at a rent, miserable; while it must be carefully remembered that the small farmers referred to as successful and productive in their industry, are proprietors, not rack-rent tenants.

.   .   .   .

"It is not creditable to the collective wisdom of England to attempt nothing *on a bold and comprehensive scale* for the social improvement of Ireland. And as the evils under which she groans, or many of them, spring from the mode in which the land is held, and miserably or not at all cultivated, or suffered to lie waste, the attention of the legislature should be directed to the means calculated to remove and abate these deplorable evils.

.   .   .   .

"If the existence of what is called tenant right be productive of good in Ulster, *the principle should be fearlessly applied to the other provinces.*" *

Let me cite one testimony more. A similar effect is produced on the minds of Englishmen when the contrast is forced on them between Ireland and other countries in which there is a reformed land tenure. The quotation I am about to make will illustrate the statement I have made as to the opinion prevalent even in the venerable seats of English learning. In some of the colleges of Oxford and Cambridge, fellowships have been endowed for the express purpose of enabling their holders to travel, that they may bring back to their society whatever wisdom or experience they can gather in their observation of foreign countries. A gentleman filling this position, actually travelling and observing in discharge of a collegiate duty, has left on record his impression of this contrast:—

* Whiteside's *Italy.*

"The Irish, who make such good colonists when they emigrate, would, with a system of free-trade in land, make equally good citizens at home. The enormous tracts of waste lands would soon be brought into cultivation, as the mountain sides of Saxony and Switzerland, as the sunny plains of Prussia, and as the low lands of Holland have been under the same invigorating system. . . . If Stein and Hardenberg had been ministers of England, depend upon it they would have endeavoured long ago to introduce into Ireland, at least, that system which has raised the Prussian, Saxon, and Swiss peasantry from a social condition analogous to that of the Irish poor, to one which renders them worthy of being regarded as examples for the consideration of the world."

" Where the Irishman can make himself, by industry, a proprietor of land, and where he is not shackled by middle-age legislation, he becomes, immediately the most energetic and conservative of colonists. He there acquires faster than anyone else ; he effects more in a day than anyone else ; and he forces his rulers to write home to England—as the Governor of South Australia did some years ago—that the Irish are *the most enterprising, orderly, and successful of all the colonists* of those distant lands.* . . . Were we to enable the Irish tenant to make himself a proprietor, we should in twenty years alter the character of Ireland. The peasant would become conservative, orderly, and industrious ; the moor and waste land would disappear ; cultivation would spread its green carpet over the bogs and mountains; and the now unhappy island would become a powerful arm of Great Britain. . . . . The Irish farmers, who now send over their savings to the English Savings' Banks, or hide them among the rafters of their barns, would soon buy land ; and Ireland, so fertile, so admirably situated to carry on an immense trade with America, would soon become one of the most productive and prosperous islands of the sea. . This is no fanciful picture. No country has yet changed tenants-at-will for small proprietors, without being vastly benefited, and benefited, too, as surely Ireland would be."†

" Is there any country in Europe, either kingdom or republic, depending or independent, free or enslaved, which may not afford us a useful lesson?"‡

France has long since taught the world the terrible lesson of the ills to which feudal oppression of the occupiers of the soil may lead. She is teaching it now the noble lesson of the power that resides in a people who own and occupy their own soil. Belgium points out to us how a great population of small farmers who are owners in fee can live in comfort on a soil not blessed by nature as our own. No traveller can pass through its garden fields so rapidly as not to see what the ownership of the land, by the people, has done, even in inferior soil. In Germany we remember Prussia, and the great and noble measures which, more than 50 years ago, made those who had been serfs the owners of the soil. It was the emancipation of

---

* Is not more than verified by the testimonies I have cited from Bishop Keane and Arthur Young (*ante*, pages 194, 195, and 196).
† *Kay's Social Condition of the European People.*
‡ Bishop Berkeley's *Querist.*

her peasant occupiers that nerved the arm of Prussia to keep " the free, the German Rhine," when Blucher led the " landwehr" against the might of Napoleon's power. Had Prussian statesmen been slaves to the " right divine of landlords," the Prussian monarch would not now be the chief of the Fatherland. The edicts of Stein and Hardenberg, and not the needle-gun, won the battle of Sadowa. Even from Russia we hear, in the decree that has emancipated the serfs, the voice that tells us that the days are gone by when in any country the rights of property can mean the slavery of man. In the Alpine vallies, in every Swiss defile, we see in the bold and hardy freemen whom we meet, how happy may be the peasants who have won their land by the sword, and divided it among themselves. In Tuscany—enslaved, benighted Tuscany—as our presumption dares to call it—Irishmen look with surprise, and—when they think of home—with grief and shame, upon the luxuriant evidences of the wise legislation of Leopold the Reformer, and wish that some ruler as despotic and as enlightened had given to Ireland that fixity of tenure which has carried cultivation far out on the swamps of the Maremma, and has made cottages and gardens, and corn fields, and vineyards cover the hill side. There is not a country in Europe from which we may not learn. All forms of government reproach the miserable illiberality of our land legislation. All forms of religion join in the rebuke of our wretched bigotry. Every community in Europe, " either kingdom or republic, depending or independent, free or enslaved," Catholic, or Lutheran, or Protestant, or Greek, can point to the Irish Catholic peasant, kept as a serf in his own land, denied the right of tilling the soil for himself—to the Irish exiles, driven " sorrowing and reluctant" from their native land, and can upbraid us with these victims of that landlordism which in every other country in Christendom has given way to the claims of justice and civilization.

I will ask once more of your Lordship is it possible for any man to believe that this Irish land question must not be adjusted one day or other upon principles which will give to the occupier some property in the land? Is it possible for it so to be adjusted on terms more favourable to the proprietors than that which I have proposed ?

I pray you to observe the almost universal opinion in favour of peasant proprietors. Remember that the phrase " peasant proprietors," involves a system which means that we shall have no great landed estates—that the class of landed gentry, as we now understand it, shall no longer exist. A compulsory sale of the landed property of the country, in some form or other, is the only mode by which such a plan could be carried out. Do not despise the opinion which has grown and is growing in favour of such a plan. Do not believe anything impossible which shall be found essential to put an end to " Ireland's desolation." I am not now appealing

s

to any selfish interest. Some of the Irish landlords have said they are willing, on certain terms, to assent to a compulsory sale of their estates for the purposes of parcelling them among such proprietors. Full justice is not always done to the old proprietors in such transactions; and very probably if Irish landlords were unwise enough to allow the opinion against them to acquire the strength that would carry such a measure, they might find as little consideration shown to secure them the full value of the estates as was manifested in the act which public opinion sanctioned for the sale of incumbered properties. But, I say again, I am not appealing to considerations of self-interest. I am addressing my argument to those who, even though they might be willing to sell their own estates, might yet desire to see a landed gentry in Ireland retain their position in the country.

I propose to give to the occupier the most essential of the advantages of peasant proprietorship, without the slightest interference with the position of the landowners as they now are. In doing so I answer all the arguments, and they are powerful ones, of those who urge the necessity of making the occupier the actual owner of the soil. Give to every Irish tenant a lease for sixty-three years at a fair rent, and the arguments that are carrying conviction to many thoughtful minds of the necessity of a peasant proprietorship lose more than half their force.

Let me say, my Lord, that it is impossible to deny the great power of those arguments. If the advantages that are pointed out as following from a peasant proprietorship can only be obtained by parcelling out large properties into small fee simple estates, they are unanswerable. I believe I have suggested a mode by which we can obtain most of the advantages of "peasant proprietorship," without destroying the influence of the landed gentry of the country. If such a measure were passed that gentry would still exist, and would still exercise all the legitimate influence which station, and property, and education will always possess among the Irish people. The advantages of peasant proprietorship are, that you give to the occupier confidence, security, and the pride of ownership. But the mere payment of a rent is not necessarily inconsistent with all this. All that we must do is to give the occupier a tenure long enough to make him feel that he has a real and substantial property in the soil, and at a rent so moderate that he will feel sure of being able to pay it. If we accomplish this he really becomes a "peasant proprietor," although he has a landlord and pays a rent. I have already pointed out that there is reason to think such a proprietorship is the one most adapted to the habits, and even best suited to the wishes, of the Irish occupier of the soil.*

I propose, in truth, a compromise between that system of tenancy

---

* *Ante* note to page 257.

at will, which at present exists in Ireland—a system which all the intellect and thought of Ireland and of England, and of civilized Europe, has condemned, and that system of "peasant proprietorship" which has been advocated by the men best calculated to guide and influence public opinion, and which to many persons appears the only escape from the admitted and the intolerable evils of our present system.

This proposal of compromise the advocates of territorial rights in Ireland indignantly and scornfully reject. Might not their enemy exult and say—"Quos Deus vult perdere prius dementat."

I may, perhaps, with more chance of attention, submit these very same observations to those who urge the institution of a peasant proprietorship as the only remedy for the grievance which is destroying Ireland. I ask of them, to consider whether that grievance would not be substantially redressed by a measure which would give to the occupier a long and a secure interest in the soil; and whether it is wise to press any further proposal in the face of the difficulties that surround it.

I take up the words I have quoted from Mr. Mill.* There must be a "transformation" of the Irish tenants at will. Into what are they to be transformed? Mr. Mill answers—"they must be transformed into landed proprietors, as far as circumstances permit." I propose a species of proprietorship which can be created without any violent interference with the existing rights of property, and without removing the class of landed gentry from their place in the social system. This modified proprietorship would, I believe, secure most of the advantages which would result from giving to the occupier an absolute estate in fee simple, while it would avoid the difficulties and the objections by which the latter proposal is encountered. Perhaps I may even say that this is to effect the transformation "*as far as circumstances admit.*"

It is quite true that the value of "A PEASANT PROPERTY"—I use the word in distinction from "peasant proprietorship"—would depend upon the difference between the rent the occupier paid and the real value of his farm. At present I propose to make none. But the industrious tenant would soon make that difference a great one. In a few years the rent would bear a comparatively small proportion to the property which would have been created in his farm. I adopt the words of Lord Rosse. I propose to give him at once one of the "privileges" of proprietorship, that of creating a property in the soil. By giving the occupier that privilege I take nothing from the landlord except the power of prohibiting improvement on his land.

But I am now addressing your Lordship as representing the landlord interest in Ireland. I ask you to reflect on all that has been said, or all that can be said, in favour of a measure that would

---

* *Ante* page 260.

boldly establish peasant proprietorship in Ireland, and then I ask
you to remember that I have not proposed for the tenant an
interest beyond that which is commonly granted on many of the best
regulated properties. Long leases are universal both in England
and in Ireland, of all lands on which the tenant is expected to
improve. Even villa sites will be let on the most strictly entailed
estates for a lease at least of sixty-three years. I might say that
this very principle justifies the granting of such a lease to every
Irish farmer. We are one hundred millions behind England in the
improvement of the soil. The nation has a right to expect that sum
to be laid out upon the land. But I am not now arguing this, I
am calling your attention to this—I have proposed a term for the
tenant, by no means extravagant or unusual. There are many
proprietors living, whose sons would come into the reversion of the
leases which I propose to grant. Remember that the only suggestion
made for an arrangement like this, was one that contemplated a
perpetuity to the tenant with a fee-farm rent. Perhaps, my Lord,
if the question is ever to be adjusted, it was no desire to trench on
landlord privileges that made me fix on the number of sixty-three.

I know that there are those to whom all this will seem almost like
raving. There are landowners who will say, "no one will ever dare
meddle with my absolute rights; it is not a question of compromise."
Men in all ages and countries have talked so, and generally they
have "talked the loudest and the fiercest" at the very time when
changes were at hand. Believe me, we might as well think of
re-enacting the penal laws as of maintaining permanently our present
system of land tenure in Ireland, or of averting legislation which
will give to the Irish occupiers a property in the soil.

I will be told that such a measure is impracticable. So it may.
But nevertheless it will most assuredly be realized, as numbers of
impracticable things have been. With Grattan I recognize no real
"impracticability" in politics, especially in relation to the affairs of
the island in which we live.* The establishment of an actual

---

* " We are apt to conceive public cases impracticable—*everything bold and radical
in the shape of public redress is considered impracticable.*"
 " I remember when a declaration of right was thought impracticable ; when the
independence of the Irish Parliament was thought impracticable ; when the establishment of a free trade was thought impracticable ; when the restoration of the judicature
of our peers was thought impracticable ; when an exclusion of the legislative power of
the English Privy Council was thought impracticable ; when a limited mutiny bill, with
Irish articles of war in the body of it, and a declaration of rights in its front, was
thought impracticable ; when the formation of a tenantry bill, securing to the tenantry
of Ireland their leasehold interests, was thought impracticable ; and yet these things
have not only come to pass, but form the bases on which we stand. Never was there
a country to which the argument of impracticability was less applicable than Ireland."—
Speech in the Irish House of Commons, September 2nd, 1785.
   The measure of which Grattan thus vindicated the practicability was—the commuta-
tion of tithes ! !
   The personal recollection of many of us could supply a catalogue as long as Grattan's
of "impracticable measures which have not only come to pass, but which form the
basis upon which we now stand."

system of peasant proprietors in Ireland is not as impracticable as the obtaining of the elective franchise by Roman Catholics was the year before it was granted; as the abolition of close boroughs was in the eyes of the Duke of Wellington in 1830; free trade in corn in the eyes of Lord Melbourne in 1840; or even as household suffrage was in the eyes of most Conservative politicians last year.

I ask of landowners who will not rest on this blind and un-reasoning confidence that no change is possible—whether the change I propose be not the very least which could be proposed really to remove the evils which have made the condition of our Irish land tenure the scandal and disgrace of England throughout Europe. If we do not effectually remove these evils we are as far from settling the question as ever. Such a measure as I suggest would remove them. Your Lordship, indeed, appears to think that I give very little to the tenant when I do nothing more for him than to entitle him to a lease of 63 years at the fair value of his farm. It does, I admit, seem strange that a remedy so slight, an interference with the landlord so inconsiderable, should redress mischiefs so terrible, wrongs so mighty as those which I describe.

Yet such a measure would do all the occupier asks. It would give him security for his industry and his home. What a world of human misery and human happiness is compressed into the view suggested by these latter words!

There is a sense in which it would do nothing for him—it would take no portion of the property—of the landlord's property—to confer it upon him. He must still pay the landlord the full value of his fields. It would deprive the landlord of nothing from which he can honestly derive a pecuniary benefit—it would only take away that odious power of oppression

> " Which nought enriches him,
> But makes the tenant poor indeed."

It would give that tenant—I have adopted Lord Rosse's words—the great " privilege of proprietorship," that of improving the soil, with an assurance that the fruits of his industry would be his own. But this privilege would be in his hands but the means of creating a wealth which otherwise would not exist at all. If I may borrow Lord Dufferin's graceful imagery, it would be the fairy wand by which new wealth would spring into existence. The property which would enrich the tenant would not be taken from the owner. It would actually and literally be a new creation of wealth. The improvements effected by the tenant's industry would be an addition to the territorial resources of Ireland as completely and absolutely as if new acres had risen from the sea.

All that the Irish tenant asks is to be allowed to create that wealth—that you will place in his hand the " privilege," by the use of which he will at once enrich the country, the landlord, and himself. We would do much for the Irish occupier when we gave him an opportunity of creating and gaining a property in the soil of his native land—when we offered him at home that field for his industry which he is now driven to seek in far off lands, beyond the western main. We would call into existence a new Ireland for the industry of the Irish people. We would call into cheerful and industrious action those human energies which over the wide surface of Ireland are now fretting and wasting in idleness and discontent. It is by the exercise of such energies that God has willed that his earth should be made fit for the habitation of civilized man. All glories of human civilization, all grandeur of human greatness owe their origin to labour and to industry far humbler than that of the Irish peasant in his fields. And therefore it is that all history bears witness to the almost inconceivable results which have followed from social changes, apparently trivial, but which were in reality mighty movements because they emancipated the industry of man.

The knot that binds the arm of a giant may be a knot which the hand of a woman could untie. A pivot that a child may move may stop the machinery that lifts enormous weights. The statute that would give a lease to every Irish occupier may seem but a little one. Yet who can calculate the results that would follow from assuring the millions of the Irish people that when they worked in their fields the fruits of their industry should be their own.

I deny, then, my Lord, that even in its immediate and material effects the measure I suggest would do nothing. I ask you to turn back to the pages in which I have quoted the descriptions of what the industry of Irishmen, when encouraged, has done. Read the accounts of the reclaimation of the wild mountain given us by Bishop Keane*—read that of Sir William Osborne's Whiteboys, so vividly detailed in the pages of Arthur Young†—and then tell me what would be done in Ireland if industry like this were let loose upon her fields.

But above, far above, all these immediate material advantages I place the great moral, and social, and political good. Above all, the measure would elevate the Irish occupier to be a freeman from a serf. It would do so when it would give him security for his industry and his home.

> "The hour that makes a man a slave,
> Takes half his worth away."

Even this gives but a faint idea of all we could do for the Irish occupier when we would make him independent. I have written in vain if the thoughts of this do not suggest themselves to the mind of every reader.

---

* *Ante*, page 154.
† *Ante*, page 155.

I have no wish to repeat or dwell upon the proofs which incontestably establish that which indeed inevitably follows from the very statement—that the condition of the Irish tenant at will is one of serfdom. I have not cared to give more of the individual instances of oppression than were necessary to realize to the mind the actual life of those who are thus placed. To multiply instances is only to kindle passions which I would much rather allay. If there be any one who hesitates to believe in the abjectness of that slavery, I will ask him to read over once more the dismal story I have extracted from the records of a court of justice, of the death of Denis Shea, the poor homeless boy*—to read it as it is told in the calm and unimpassioned language of a judicial sentence—to remember the estate on which this occurred—and to form from this one example his own judgment of the extent to which the occupier of the soil is held in thraldom by his master.

But the fact of his serfdom is not denied. So far from being denied, it is avowed in all the publications in which the present state of proprietary rights has been defended as something so holy and inviolable, that not even for the most pressing national exigency must it be touched. It is written legibly and plainly in all our Irish statute law of landlord and tenant—in that ejectment code which as I have shown Irish landlords have framed specially for themselves.† This penal code was never fitted, it was never intended, to regulate any civilized relation of landlord and tenant. It is a series of ukases harshly enforcing the rights of the lord against the serf.

Let me say, my Lord, that which I ought, perhaps, to have said before, that you cannot measure the effects of this serfdom upon national wealth, even by its discouragement of permanent improvements upon the soil. His insecurity of tenure, in many instances, actually creates in the mind of the tenant a terror of appearing to be comfortable lest any indication of this nature should invite a raising of the rent. Where this feeling exists, it is needless to point out it discourages even the industry of which the tenant is permitted to enjoy the fruits, that which would realize its return within the year. Insecurity of tenure prohibits improvements, but it grievously discourages even the annual cultivation of the farm.

Is it possible, my Lord, to say that the mere security of tenure, the assurance that no matter what show of comfort, or even wealth he made, no one could ask him for an increased rent, would not do much directly to improve the physical condition of the Irish occupier of the soil?

This serfdom is one from which it is impossible to raise the occupier so long as his landlord has the uncontrolled and arbitrary power of driving him from his country and his home. No matter what rights or privileges you confer upon the tenant, so long as this

---

* *Ante,* page 176.
† *Ante,* page 187.

continues he is a slave. "A slave," to use the words of Arthur Young, "in the bosom of written liberty."* That slavery is not the result of any positive or written law. If it were it would be more endurable. It springs from insecurity of tenure; and under our present law insecurity of tenure must exist wherever the landlord pleases. Our law does not, like the old feudal laws, make the occupier a serf. But it gives the landlord the power of making him one at his will. The landlords boldly, and openly, and fairly tell us that they are determined to exercise the power.

Let us lay aside for a moment all consideration of direct material advantages, and calculate, if we can, the moral good that would result to the owner, the occupier, and to all classes of the community, from putting an end for ever to the serfdom in which the mass of the people are held. To how many heartburnings, and hatreds, and slowly-consuming enmities would we put an end. I believe it impossible to over-estimate the influence which such a measure would exercise upon the character of the whole nation. No country can escape the evil effects of holding the mass of the people in slavery. Ireland has felt in all ranks of her society, in all her social system, the mischief which inevitably results from the presence of slavery in the land. Rank exhalations rise and poison the moral atmosphere of the nation which has within its borders such a curse. Upon those more immediately concerned the effects are disastrous. We do our best by such a system to foster in the tenant all the vices of servility, of cunning, and of treachery and revenge— the servility in which even manly spirits are compelled by hard necessity to cringe to power—the cunning by which our nature teaches weakness to evade and cheat the oppression in which might tramples upon right—the treachery and violence by which outraged humanity often vindicates itself in "the wild justice," or, it may be, injustice, "of revenge." These are the lessons which we teach the occupier when we make slavery the condition of his occupation. Of the landowners I will only say that never yet have the masters of slaves been found fitted to discharge the duties which are imposed upon the higher classes of a free state. But the evil does not end here, great as it would be even if it did. The public opinion which has learned to tolerate the presence of serfdom, loses its purity, its energy, and its power. The opinion that defends it becomes demoralized. Familiarity with unresisted and unpunished oppression blunts those instincts in the breasts of nations which ought to be quick to detect, and sensitive to resent, the most minute approach to national or individual wrong. There can be no free nor honest public opinion in a country in which the great mass of the people are not free.

I forbear to pursue a subject which would admit of a far more

---

* Arthur Young, *ante*, page 66.

extended illustration. But even in a moral point of view the measure would do much not only for the Irish occupier but for the Irish nation—which would elevate the tenant from serfdom, and bring to his home at last the only EMANCIPATION which can make the slightest difference in his lot.

I cannot admit, therefore, that my proposal does little for the tenant, although it takes nothing from the landlord. It is just because it does so much for the tenant, and so much for the nation, at so little cost to the landlord that I believe it to be an adjustment of the land question which it would be the interest of the Irish landowners to make.

Let me say, my Lord, you offer me one compliment which truth forbids me to accept. You are pleased to say that when you read what I had to say against the landlords "you knew the worst." But surely, my Lord, you must feel that this is not so. How many topics of disquietude have I carefully avoided, or lightly touched? Do you expect that others will have the same forbearance? If the discussion of this question passes from the limits of calm enquiry within which I have endeavoured to confine it, do you think that others will not use the subjects of exasperation which I have avoided? Are there no opportunities for strong appeals to violent popular feeling in many of the scenes of the last twenty years? Can we expect that they will not be used? Or is there any rational ground for supposing that if popular agitation on this subject acquired intensity and strength, popular feeling would be satisfied by a measure such as I propose? Believe me, my Lord, if the landed proprietors are unwise enough to leave open for the next five years the question between them and the Irish people, the bill that will settle it will be drawn by very different hands from mine.

I have no mystery in these words. Any one who looks round on what is passing in the world can judge as well as I can. I believe it impossible, in the present condition of human affairs and human opinions, long to maintain a system of land tenure in defiance of the wishes of the Irish people for a change; and believing so, I am sure that the sooner that change is made the more likely is it to be a just and a careful one. Within the next few years—we know not how soon—events may happen which will force on English statesmen a settlement of this question, and a settlement which will be framed to satisfy the supposed wishes of the Irish people.

But if I am wrong in this—if no change is to be made in our land laws—if the old system of territorial ascendancy shall obtain a renewal of its lease of Ireland's " perennial desolation"—then, I am quite sure, we will have an emigration from Ireland, in the view of which all that has already been will seem trifling. Vague hopes of redress, they know not from what quarter, are now floating in the minds of the people. Undefined imaginings of a coming deliverance are agitating in secret the heart of many an Irish occupier of the soil. If these hopes be once more doomed to disappointment; if nothing is done to protect the right of the people to live at home—if there is no future for Ireland but a continuance of the same system of government which has now for two centuries kept our people serfs—the Irish race will desert their country with almost one consent, and there will be an outpouring of that people from their homes, so vast and so appalling, as to startle the most careless into the conviction that it is not safe to play or trifle with a subject which really involves a nation's life.

" What will be the end thereof" no mortal man can tell; but most assuredly he is a man more bold than wise who looks out upon the darkening clouds, and sees no cause of anxiety in the present state of the Irish land question.

Yet, I believe there never was a question of such magnitude that could be so easily adjusted. Many influences—of which the higher wisdom of statesmanship would make use—dispose the Irish people, if not to loyalty to peace. Assure them of justice on this land question and you will do more to crush disaffection than you can by all the troops you can pour into the country. But let no man persuade you that ever you will detach that people from any and every cause that is only hostile to British authority, until you can secure to them the means of living in comfort and freedom in their own land.

Would to God!—I say it, my Lord, earnestly and solemnly— Would to God! that I could see the rights of Irish property and the Irish people reconciled—the old feud for. ever at an end—and the gentry no longer feeling themselves, as too many feel, as aliens dwelling in an unfriendly land. Is it vain to hope that something may be done to effect this?

I have already said that " time is everything in the adjustment of this question, although it be one that has convulsed Ireland for 200 years. The concessions which this year would be grate- fully received as a measure of conciliation, in four years hence may be scornfully regarded as the offers of weakness and fear."[*] It may be that we have not even the four years to adjust this question with dignity and self-respect. I do not allude to any supposed danger from treasonable movements in Ireland—move- ments which, so long as we are isolated from the rest of the world, England is strong enough to crush[†]—I hope not unwise enough to

---

[*] *Land Tenure*, p. 104.

[†] I have already, on a former occasion, adverted, as far as I thought I ought to do, to that strange confederation which for two years so strangely agitated and alarmed the country (*Land Tenure*, pages 9, 10 ; preface to 3rd edition, pages 13-20). Even if the time were come when I could write upon this subject without reserve, this would not be the occasion for doing so. I am quite sure that a most instructive lesson could be drawn from a sketch which would fairly and impartially trace the progress— so far as it has been revealed—of that marvellous conspiracy, and the means, so far as we know them, by which, in spite of the most powerful counteracting influences, it made its way among the Irish people.

treat with contempt. It is useless for us to inquire whether the conspiracy against which the Government made such great preparations be really crushed. You do not destroy disaffection when you

Truth obliges me to say that such a sketch would give a very different impression both of the nature of that organization, and the motives and character of its leaders, from that supplied by the representations which have been coloured by the passions and the fears of the upper classes of this country.

It is of importance that those who are intrusted with the government of Ireland should form a correct estimate of this element which does unquestionably exist, and which is beyond all doubt a danger in the social state of Ireland. The most important lesson we can learn from it is the facility with which the hatred of the Irish exiles to British authority can be brought to aid and encourage the designs of those who plot against British authority at home. It was in the combination which was effected for the first time between the disaffected population in the United States and home discontent that both the power and the danger of Fenianism consisted. It was a combination that might easily have been foreseen. Nevertheless its actual realization is a fact of the full importance of which I fear a very inadequate conception is entertained. It is scarcely too much to say that at this moment the great mass of the Irish race, in whatever country they are scattered, or wherever chance has fixed their habitations, are united in one vast league against English power.

It is mere childishness to affect not to see this. It is the most monstrous of absurdities to despise it. Far wiser would be the statesmanship which would see in this something like the preparation of that "secret scourge" which Spencer prophesied that Ireland, if not "reformed," would one day inflict on England.

As to the strength of this confederacy in Ireland I have already pointed out that we have no means of forming any estimate of its numbers. But when the public are assured that it is contemptible, we must judge of the worth of such assurances by the preparations for resistance which Government thought it necessary to make. That there did exist in Ireland a formidable confederation it is impossible for any one who has observed the course of events for the last two years to doubt. It is, of course, a totally different thing to say that any confederation in Ireland could cope with the power that could instantly be brought to crush any attempt at open revolt. I only say that, whatever be their madness, or whatever be their secret plans, there is in Ireland a rebellious confederation strong enough to be formidable, or at least to give just cause for anxiety and alarm.

I am equally sure, that we will be entirely misled if we give credit to those statements which represent the conspiracy as entirely confined to the lowest class; as including no one even on a level with the substantial tenant farmers of the country. The confederation is, perhaps, only the more formidable because it is not headed by men taken, like Mr. Smith O'Brien and Lord Edward Fitzgerald, from the gentry and the aristocracy of the country. To a treasonable movement in Ireland such leaders give no real strength, they often were its weakness. But the confidence would be an utterly false one which would suppose that the Fenian confederacy has enrolled in its ranks none but the lower orders of society.

Still more false and dangerous would be the reliance on the assertion that there is no honesty or sincerity of purpose in those who have originated this movement. The stories which at first represented the Fenian organization as a mere banditti, bound together for pillage and massacre, now find credence with no sane man. Those who formed it incurred, no doubt, the guilt—it may be, the tremendous guilt—of planning an armed revolution. They contemplated the destruction, not merely of English Government, but also the destruction of all those territorial rights which English power has maintained. Wicked and wild as men may deem these projects, there have been those in all ages and in all countries who have engaged in similar designs with unselfish motives, and who have been formidable exactly as they have been sincere. Whatever is to be said or thought of those who in Ireland engage in such projects—let us not deceive ourselves. We have to deal with men thoroughly in earnest—men who have persuaded themselves that in entertaining such projects they are acting the part of true patriotism.

I know that it is regarded as "disloyalty" to suppose it possible that any but the base-minded can be drawn into an attempt to subvert the existing order of things. Yet in Ireland such an attempt has never yet been crushed without the discovery being soon

put down treason.   You do not destroy treason when you put
down an organization.   The conspirators remain even when the conspiracy is crushed.   You have still in Ireland members of the old

made that there were engaged in it self-sacrificing devotion and chivalry—which attract
even admiration and respect.   No man now speaks of Lord Edward Fitzgerald, of
Robert Emmett, or of Smith O'Brien, as the fierce passion of loyalty described
them at the time when they joined in treasonable designs.   The worst crime of misgovernment is that it drives into these guilty projects many, very many, of the high
and generous spirits who are the most ready to revolt at oppression.   "Curse on the
laws which deprived me of such subjects," was the bitter exclamation of an English
monarch who saw how Irish "traitors" fought against him.   Far deeper might be the
curse pronounced upon the system which has made "traitors" of many of those who
have suffered the inevitable doom with which every government visit those who plot in
vain against its power.   There are men now suffering the most degrading penalties of
convict prisons, gifted with all the qualities which, in a happier country, would have
made them valuable citizens and servants of the state ; and who, even in the course
that brought them to that doom, risked all that was dear to them in life for a cause
which they believed to be that of their country.   I watched the demeanour of these
men as they received the sentence which condemned them to a penalty almost as terrible as that of death.   It was not possible to observe it without the persuasion that
these men had confidence both in the justice and in the reality of the cause for which
they suffered.   I do not know that the annals of defeated treason can supply examples
of men submitting to their fate with more of the resolution of martyrs—sustained under
sentences which seemed to kill all hope in life by a stern and wild fanaticism, which
no one but themselves could understand.

I write these sentences with no reference to those who are now enduring those
sentences, but only because I am sure that it is of vital importance that we should
estimate fully all the strength that is arrayed against our present system of government.   We have to deal with a disaffection which has engaged in its cause self-
sacrifice and devotion, and political fanaticism which will induce men to risk and to
dare much.   We may denounce their projects as those of robbery and plunder—we
may brand that which they call patriotism as a sanguinary and heinous crime.   All this
will not alter the fact, or remove from the cause of disaffection those moral qualities
which our unfortunate misgovernment has allowed to be enlisted on its side.

I am sure that one of the elements which every one ought to consider in dealing
with Ireland is the existence of a treasonable organization, considerable even in its own
strength ; formidable in its alliance with the universal disaffection of the Irish race ;
attracting to its cause many of the sympathies which exist in the human heart for those
who are supposed to rebel against wrong ; and numbering in its ranks many, very
many men actuated by an earnest, a sincere, and a self-sacrificing devotion to the cause
which they believe to be the cause of their country's freedom.

I am quite sure also, that in writing these sentences, disclosing that which I believe
to be the real danger, I am far better and more truly discharging my duty to the
sovereign and the country, than if by denying the possibility of honesty, sincerity, or
love of country among those who have engaged in the cause of revolt—I were in
reality to contribute to deceiving those who guide our national affairs, and I am
perfectly persuaded that to disparage "Fenianism" as the mere scheme of pillage, or
denounce it as a mere device of swindlers, is to practise on those whose duty it is to
deal with the condition of Ireland a great and a mischievous deception.   The more you
condemn both the projects and the means by which they were to be effected, the
stronger is the argument against the system of government which engages in such
projects men with the qualities of earnestness and sincerity which fit them for higher
and better things.

It would be foreign to the subject of this note to allude to statements which have
been made of the treatment which these political prisoners are receiving in the carrying out of their sentence.   Yet every one who cares for the honour of the country
must hope that some authoritative contradiction will be given to statements which
have excited the indignation of many of the most resolute in their detestation of
treason.   The comments which have appeared, on this subject, in *Saunders's News*

organization, waiting anxiously for another and better opportunity—men easily collected whenever that opportunity comes. You have scattered throughout the country the disbanded militia of revolt. It is in "some moment of England's weakness and depression," in the words I have already quoted, that concessions may be extorted far more extensive than those which would now "be received with gratitude and exultation."* But when I point to changes that are possible, even within the next few years, I am not speaking of any rising of the Irish peasantry against the disciplined troops with which England now holds our country. I am speaking of world-wide complications, which may at any moment arise—complications which, when they do arise, will most assuredly place England in a different position to the Irish people and to the Irish land question from that in which she stands now.

It is vain to hope that in the present session of Parliment any real settlement of this great question can be attained. And yet, my Lord, I write with a deep conviction—I might almost add, with a dark foreboding—when I say that English statesmen of all politics will act unwisely if Parliament separate without some real honest attempt to reconcile the Irish people to the cause of England. Is it possible, even yet, to offer them a pledge of earnestness, of a sincere desire to redress those wrongs, which might be accepted by a generous and confiding people as a promise, on the fulfilment of which they were ready to depend?

Let a royal commission be issued, directed to men in whom all classes of the Irish nation may have confidence—let its proceedings be framed upon the precedent of that which inquired into the condition of the Irish poor in 1834. It should not confine itself to

Letter, the oldest, and certainly not the least influential, of the Irish Conservative journals, express feelings which are entertained by many whose opinions in politics that journal represents.

In *The Plea for the Celtic Race* I quoted the following passage from the *Spectator*:—
"We ask any decent Englishman who has carefully read Mr. Luby's speech, whether that is the sort of character that could not live under constitutional law? Whether that same man, born and bred in England, would not have been a respectable citizen? Whether in the United States he might not have been as loyal as Sheridan, or in Canada as D'Arcy McGhee? Then why not in Ireland? Simply because the English liberals, who day by day harmonize English legislation to the wants of English life, ... refuse, or rather neglect, to bring Irish legislation into accord with Irish wants."

I added—"This would, I venture to say, be realised by any generous man who would read the poems and ballads in which Charles Kickham, one of the prisoners now undergoing his sentence of penal servitude, has given expression to a sympathy with all that is beautiful in nature, and all that is gentle and true in humanity. The writer of these poems had qualities of heart and intellect which surely deserved another fate."—3rd edition, p. 100.

The writer of these ballads is now, if the statements made be true, undergoing unutterable degradation. Do all Englishmen forget the indignation which the narrative of Silvio Pellico kindled in the heart of the English nation? Well would it be for Charles Kickham and his associates if they could be transferred to the fortress of Spielberg, and suffer only what Silvio Pellico endured.

* *Edinburgh Review, ante* page 251.

collecting the opinions of landlords and agents in a room in Dublin Castle. Trusty delegates of that Commission should visit each locality in Ireland, and invite the poorest tenants to come and speak for themselves. It is only by enquiries from the people themselves that ever you will know the whole truth. Honest efforts ought to be made to ascertain what is really passing in the minds of the population—to collect all the facts connected with emigration and evictions, and the tenure of land. If such a commission were now issued. If it were placed in honest and efficient hands—before the next session of Parliament, a body of evidence and information would be collected, which would supply grounds for legislation, which no one could gainsay or resist.

In the mean time, let a short act be passed, staying all arbitrary evictions for one year. If such measures were adopted now, and adopted in such a manner as to convince the Irish people, that they came from the purpose of a good and honest heart to do them justice—all that enquiry might show to be justice—even after all the failures and all the disappointments they have endured—they might still trust and wait before they finally abandoned all hope of redress from the British Parliament and the British Crown.

Is not the occasion worthy of such an interference? Never could our Sovereign do an act more worthy of her own Majesty—never one more calculated to strengthen the foundations of her throne, and conciliate to her government the Irish people, than that of sending to Parliament a message, announcing the issuing of such a commission, and recommending the enactment I have described.

This would indeed be the message of peace to Ireland. Time and history may yet reckon and record the sum of all the mischiefs and miseries it might avert.

———————

With these sentences, my Lord, I might close this letter—at least with the addition of a few words acknowledging, as I do most cordially and sincerely, the kind (I must add, considering the view you take of my proposal), the generous manner in which you are good enough to speak of myself. That kindness would, in itself, almost encourage me to add a very few words upon a subject, the last to which I would wish to advert, that of my own motives in writing as I have done. A discussion in which my name was mentioned in an illustrious assembly, makes it, perhaps, fitting that

I should do so. I should certainly regret if I had marred even my imperfect advocacy of a great cause by indiscretions of language which would fairly expose me to rebuke.

There is a fiction which supposes that I can know nothing of what passes in the chamber in which your Lordship and your brother Peers deliberate upon national affairs This is one of the venerable fictions which injure no one, and in which I would, under any circumstances, be ready to believe. In the present instance I really know nothing, except certain comments attributed to a noble lord in the public newspapers, and on those publications in the newspapers I offer a very few remarks.

Sentences have been quoted from one of my tracts, as if they contained something peculiarly improper. I believe I cannot better reply to such criticism than by quoting the entire of the passage upon which, I cannot help saying, some "excellent indignation" has been thrown away. Surely what I have written has been strangely misunderstood. No one interested in the peace and tranquillity of Ireland ought to blame me for telling the people that they had the means in their own hands of obtaining redress from the British Parliament. In the few words of introduction, in which I offered to the consideration of the public the actual provisions of the measure which I suggested, I wrote:—

"I believe that if such a measure as I propose were once fairly and honestly adopted, by those who represent the landlord interest, it would be gladly accepted by the whole tenantry of Ireland as the final settlement of a question which has for generations torn and distracted Ireland— a question which, while it remains unsettled, makes the life of every Irishman less happy than it ought to be.

"But I do not hesitate also to avow my perfect and unfaltering belief that a measure such as this is within the reach of the Irish people themselves. I am not one of those who have much faith in the achievement of any great good for Ireland by that which is termed Parliamentary action. I have great faith in the power of truth and justice; and, when it has truth and justice on its side, in the ultimate triumph of the popular will. I cannot help entertaining a clear conviction, that if, throwing over all subterfuge and compromise, the Irish people were deliberately, distincly, and energetically to declare their resolute determination in favour of fixity of tenure for the occupiers of the soil, three years would not pass until, in the Imperial Parliament, a measure embodying the principles of that which I suggest would become law.

"If it could be carried by a mutual agreement among all classes interested in the land of Ireland, it would most assuredly be the great charter of Ireland's prosperity and peace."*

I prefaced these observations by a statement which I have already in this letter repeated and endeavoured to enforce. "If popular

---

* *Fixity of Tenure*, p. 11—Lord Dunsany's Speech.—*Times*, Feb. 5th, 1867.

feeling be thoroughly aroused on the subject, it may be that the landowners of Ireland will never again see a measure proposed for popular acceptance with such a jealous respect for their rights."

I repeat every word of this. I do not expect the great measure which will secure fixity of tenure to the Irish people to be carried or even advanced by any action in the English Parliament on the part of Irish representatives. Apart from all other reasons, it never can be carried by debates in a listless and a reluctant assembly—an assembly indisposed to all Irish discussions except those which affect the interests or engage the passions of English parties. Before " Fixity of Tenure" can do this it must become a power in the State. The influences which will compel the settlement of this question are influences far above the tactics of Parliamentary warfare—influences which neither ministers nor Parliaments can control. Thoughtful men who have watched over English history have seen that the days are gone by when Parliament controlled the opinion or the sentiment of the nation. Its function is every day becoming more and more that of registering national decisions already pronounced outside its walls.

But if I do not believe that parliamentary discussion can do much even to aid the advent of justice on the land question to the Irish people, I am quite sure that it is not possible for any number of vehement declarations on the part of any number of Irish landowners, who have seats in either House of Parliament, to do anything to prevent it. Surely, my Lord, he knows nothing of the elements that are involved in the struggle of a people for the right to live in their own land who can gravely express a hope that a few words from a Prime Minister, in reply to an appeal from an Irish Peer, will put an end to the demand for tenant right, or even extinguish my poor *Plea for the Celtic Race.*

" Hi motus animorum atque hæc certamina tanta,
    Pulveris exigui jactu, compressa quiescent."

I have, my Lord, a very sincere respect for both prime ministers and peers, but such language makes me wish that a scene for one of the frescoes of the new palace had been taken from the reign of the Danish conquerors of England. The illustration is an old one, but there may be, it seems, some new wisdom to be learned even from the lesson that Canute's courtiers had too much sense to wait, without changing their position, to be overwhelmed by the waves.

But, my Lord, I said more. I said:—

" I cannot help entertaining a clear conviction, that if, throwing over all subterfuge and compromise, the Irish people were deliberately, clearly, and energetically to declare their resolute determination in favour of fixity of tenure for the occupiers of the soil, three years would not pass until a measure embodying the principles of that which I suggest would become law."

I did not go on to fill up the details, because I did not wish to suggest or to offer advice when it was not my province to do either. But surely no one could misunderstand what I meant. The example of the English Corn Law League is before the Irish people. By earnestness and singleness of purpose that organization won the repeal of the corn laws from the proudest and most powerful aristocracy in the world. If the Irish people were to imitate that example. If those who have their confidence were to combine the tenant farmers of Ireland into one great " tenant league ;" if such an association were to use all rightful means of influencing public opinion, both in Ireland and England, to collect and authenticate all the instances which prove the need of protection for the occupier of the soil—to do, in a word, all that such an association might lawfully and honourably do to press on the British Parliament and nation the claim of the Celtic race to live in their own land—I do not believe that in the presence of the moral power of such an association our present system of land tenure could last three years.

I know that there is but little prospect of such a combination of popular power. The causes which would prevent it are many. Foremost, perhaps, among them is the persuasion that has taken hold largely of the popular mind that constitutional efforts to obtain redress are useless. I advert to the subject because I have been challenged to explain the sentences I have quoted. I will only say that I do not believe that it is a good or wholesome sign for the country when subjects that have a strong hold upon the popular heart yet seem to cause no visible excitement—when no voice gives utterance to feelings that are not the less deep because they are suppressed.*

I do not know that an allusion to the remote possibility of such a combination was a very serious offence.

Hard words against myself, in whatever assembly they are uttered, I can very cheerfully pass by. In angry criticism upon my proposal I only see the prejudices which, upon the subject, I expected everywhere to meet. I recognize, indeed, those which

---

* I see, with some surprise, the views I have expressed confirmed in a quarter from which I scarcely expected it. In a publication generally attributed to a very influential Conservative—one of the first selected for office by the present Government—I meet the following passage:—

" Nearly half a century has elapsed since the cry of 'Justice to Ireland' was a watchword through the land, and the voices of many who then uttered it are silent for ever, but still it ascends like a wail above their graves ! Then it was for equal rights and liberty, now the Irish nation only asks the bare permission to exist. Nothing indicates more plainly the miserable condition of Ireland than the utter apathy with which the recent attempt to get up a Reform agitation was received. Public spirit is dead, and those who are not looking for a revolution from beyond the Atlantic, sit down in hopeless apathy, despairing of any good result from attempting to reform or move that British Parliament which has so often disappointed the country's expectations, and turned a deaf ear to her reiterated appeals for justice."—*Ireland; Her Present Condition, its Causes and its Remedies.*

T

once I entertained myself. I am even content to have motives
imputed to me the most foreign from those which influence my
thoughts. I am not sure whether I am by one writer included
among those who, in meddling with this question, "seek political
capital, or profit, or notoriety;"* or by another among "clever and
briefless barristers, knowing and .probably caring nothing about
rural affairs, or the real relations of landlords and tenants, but seized
with a sudden zeal for tenant right and a seat in parliament;"†
but I do know that by the latter writer, one who assumes—and, I
doubt not, truly—the honours of the Irish Peerage, I have been told
that I have proposed a measure "of which I appreciate the ludicrous
and preposterous inequality in operation as well as in justice." I have
observed with some curiosity that scarcely any one. can write on
the side of our present system of land tenure without assuming that
every one who says a word against landlord dominion must be
influenced by some personal or unworthy motive. It is the old
story of our poor human nature. It has been truly said that
"tyranny contracts the mind." The same effect appears to attend its
advocacy, as if there were in the very fact of defending class injustice something that unconsciously warps even better natures towards
that which is rancorous and mean. Certain it is, that those who
undertake the task very generally fall into that peculiar style of
argument which has only one reasoning and one perception—that
of being positive that every opponent must be base—a singular
phase of human thought which has been well described as "the
offspring of a union, not uncommon, though unnatural, between
interest and spite."‡

No man worthy to approach this great question ought even to be
ruffled by criticisms like these. But I do not therefore the less
appreciate the generous testimony borne by your Lordship when
you say that much as you condemn what I have written, you firmly
believe that "I have written disinterestedly." You do me only
justice in this belief. I may have something to lose—I certainly
have nothing to gain by setting against me prejudices that are all-
powerful in the influential classes of Irish society; and if we cannot
pass through this discussion without these miserable imputations
of personal motives, I think I may appeal to those who will judge
me as you have, by that which I have written, whether anything
I have published on this question bears any of the marks by which
such motives are sure to be betrayed.

If I had not some confidence, not merely in the justice but in
the reality of my proposals, I would scarcely have devoted to the
subject the time and labour that I have did. No person, I think,
will charge me with having written to meet the views or suit the
convenience of any political party. I do not think I am open to the

---

* *Demurrer to Mr. Butt's Plea.* By a Land Agent.
† *The Irish Difficulty.* By an Irish Peer.   ‡ Lord Brougham.

accusation of having appealed to popular prejudice or passions. Patient and laborious investigation of documents and proofs— careful verification of statements, by a reference to the chronicles in which information is to be found—these are not the usual resources of those who write merely to win popular applause. This is the course of one who desires to make his appeal to reason and to thought. The task which aims at no higher end than that of stirring the passions or winning the favour of the multitude is surely a less labourious one than this. And those who will remember that I have been compelled to travel over exciting topics, will be, I think, the most ready to admit that I have endeavoured to temper and moderate the language in which I must, of necessity, express strong feeling, and state occasionally facts calculated to excite. I felt when I began to write, as well as I do now, that the subject is " one upon which there is litttle temptation to any one who entertains the views which I do to write." I was perfectly prepared to " be harshly judged by prejudices which are now all-powerful." " I knew that by many the suggestions I made would be denounced as invasions of the sacred rights of property." That by many more they would be branded as "impracticable and wild."[*] I would not have been willing to encounter all this if I had not a strong faith in my own convictions. Least of all would I have been willing to place myself in the position of standing alone as the advocate of " impracticable and visionary schemes. If there be any character from which any man of common sense would shrink, it is this. Believe me, my Lord, I was not insensible to the warning a great man has given those who " hazard schemes of government, except from the seat of authority." However mistaken or mischievous men may think the views I have expressed, no fair man who judges me by that which I have written will believe that anything but a deep conviction of their truth has prompted me to write as I have done.

Let me say once for all how I came to write. Two years ago I had formed views of the land question, as, I suppose, most persons in my position have. I was satisfied of that which lies on the very surface, that insecurity of tenure is a great evil. I was convinced that compensation for tenants' improvements was just and right ; but when I saw the people flying in masses from their homes I felt that really to understand the question we must go deeper than all this—that there must be some mischief deeply rooted in our social system, which in a country blessed with advantages like ours produced results so strangely contrary to everything which the laws which regulate the history of nations, or the conduct of classes or individuals might lead us to expect.

An accident turned my thoughts more intensely in this direction. Travelling on a southern railway I witnessed one of those scenes

* *Land Tenure,* p. 95.

too common in our country, but which, I believe, no familiarity
can make any person of feeling witness without emotion. The
station was crowded with emigrants, and their friends who came
to see them off. There was nothing unusual in the occurrence—
nothing that is not often to be seen. Old men walked slowly, and
almost hesitatingly, to the carriages that were to take them away
from the country to which they were never to return. Railway
porters placed in the train strange boxes and chests of every shape and
size, sometimes even small articles of furniture, which told that the
owners were taking with them their little all. In the midst of them
a brother and a sister bade each other their last farewell—a mother
clasped passionately to her breast the son whom she must never
see again. Women carried or led to their places in the carriages
little children, who looked round as if they knew not what all
this meant, but wept because they saw their mothers weeping.
Strong men turned aside to dash from their eye the not unmanly
tear. As the train began to move there was the uncontrollable
rush, the desperate clinging to the carriages of relatives crowding
down to give the last shake hands. The railway servants pushed
them back—we moved on more rapidly—and then rose from the
group we left behind a strange mingled cry of wild farewells, and
prayers, and blessings, and that melancholy wail of Irish sorrow
which no one who has heard will ever forget—and we rushed on
with our freight of sorrowing and reluctant exiles across a plain of
fertility, unsurpassed, perhaps, in any European soil. It was a
light matter, but still it was something in that picture—close to us
rose the picturesque ruins, which seemed to tell us from the past
that there were days when an Irish race had lived, and not lived
in poverty, upon that very plain.

The se are scenes which surely no Irishman should see without
emotion. The transient feeling they may excite is but of little use
except as it may be suggestive of thought. It was impossible not
to ask why were these people thus flying from their homes, desert-
ing that rich soil. I could not but feel that no satisfactory solution
of the question had yet been given. I asked myself if it was not
a reproach to those among us whom God had raised a little above
that people by the advantages of intellect and education if we gave no
real earnest thought to such an enquiry ; and I formed a purpose—I
almost made to myself a vow that I would employ, as far as I could,
whatever little power I had acquired in investigating facts in
endeavouring to trace the strange mystery to its origin.

The purpose may have been an unwise one, but I followed it
out. I endeavoured to recal to memory all that I had ever read, or
learned, or observed, that could throw light upon the subject. I
noted down all that I saw or heard that revealed what was really
passing in the various grades of Irish society. It is strange how
many little things that might pass unheeded, will, to a mind bent

upon one subject, suggest information. I carefully studied all the materials for forming a judgment which industry and observation could collect. I took many an hour from sleep to write down what I had thought or seen. While I was thus engaged, accident gave me an opportunity of becoming acquainted with some of the movements and the origin of that strange confederacy which—it is useless to deny it—has proved the depth and the intensity of Irish popular disaffection. I had the opportunity of reading the documents seized by the authorities, in which the confidential correspondence of the planners of that movement had been preserved. I was even obliged to study and understand the nature of the appeals which had such a wonderful effect upon the popular mind. I gained some further insight into the depths of Irish disaffection. I did believe that in reading the history of the past and observing the feelings of the present I had obtained, a view, even a clear view, of the causes which were driving the Irish people from Ireland. I even thought I could see a remedy. It is for others to judge how far I have been right in either; but, believing as I did, I think I would have been wrong if I had not given to the discussion of this great question, imperfectly as I was able to do it, a contribution which I had brought myself to think might be of use.

I had no temptation to modify my views to meet those of any party. I took counsel with no one. I represented and I represent no opinions but my own. No person is responsible for anything I have written but myself. I had, perhaps, a temptation to yield to some cherished prejudices in my own mind with which I was more and more forced to believe truth was inconsistent. I had a temptation to avoid or suppress conclusions by which I felt I must forfeit the good opinions of many whose good opinion and friendship I would have wished to keep. I wrote what I had thought out for myself. I did so with no intention of taking part in any political controversy, except so far as this might be involved in an essay on that which is, after all, a social more than a political purpose. I found that my proposal attracted the unfriendly criticism of many, whose even angry criticism I must respect. I could scarcely avoid explaining and defending it; and, as very often happens, I have been drawn into a discussion far beyond any limits of which I had ever thought.

I do not regret this. It is no loss to any Irishman to be compelled to go slowly and minutely over the history of the past. Even as a study in political or social science, there are few subjects better worth investigation than those connected with the condition of the Irish people for the last 200 years. Ireland in that period has but little history to those who know history only as the record of the events which affect dynasties, and sovereigns, and governments. There is much for those who place the real value of history in the tracing of the things which make up the every-day life of a people. In this sense I know of no stranger or more instructive passage in the life of mankind than the story of Ireland, from the day when strange proprietors were set over her confiscated soil. Her story—not in camps, or courts, or senates—but her story in her villages, her farms, her farm-houses, and her hovels, in all the changes of her peasant life—in the relations between those who owned and those who occupied her soil—in the serfdom, and misery, and the oppression of the old race—in the effects which all this produced upon national industry and prosperity—upon the character and condition of all classes. When we can bring all this in one view before our mind we have a great historic picture, in the scenes of which we see something very different from the mere images of beggary and crime—we see vividly pourtrayed before us the work-ings of all the elements and passions which create national happiness and misery—scenes which impress upon us the most striking illustra-tion of political and economic laws. May I stop to say, that surely we may perceive in that view those higher moral lessons which history teaches us, that sometimes, at least in national affairs, oppression and wrong are blunders as well as crimes. Who has profited by the grievous oppression of the Irish people? What cause has prospered which that oppression was designed to secure? The old people were crushed down to protect the English interest, the Pro-testant interest, and the new proprietors. Has the English interest been really upheld? If the most malignant and wily enemy of Enland had devised the policy by which Ireland was to be reserved to be her "secret scourge" in some future day, could his aim have been more effectually worked out than it has been by the result of the very system of government which was justified by the plea that the interests of England must be upheld?

Has the Protestant interest been strengthened? Ask the ques-tion in what sense we will, the answer is the same. In the higher sense it must be, that the religion of Protestants has now less hold upon the inhabitants of Ireland than it had upon the day when men professed to protect and advance it by surrounding it with the odious prerogative of oppression and wrong. Even in the lower sense, there is no thoughtful man who will say that the Protestants of Ireland, with all their advantages of property and education, and social position, occupy the place in their own country which they must do if no unjust ascendency had ever been attempted for them, and if no oppression had ever crushed down the people for their supposed benefit and in their name.

Have the Irish landowners profited? This is the strangest chapter of this strange history. No country on earth has had the same opportunity which Ireland had of acquiring agricultural wealth. For seventy years before the repeal of the corn laws she enjoyed almost a practical monoply of the richest market for agricultural produce in the world. The rapidity with which our exports of grain and animals increased within that period seems now almost incredible. A stranger who watched the progress of that trade would have said that the owners and cultivators of the soil in Ireland must be realizing enormous gains. The manufacturing population of England were actually paying the cultivators of Ireland a tribute each year of many millions for the food they sent them. Of that enormous tribute the landowners received an immense proportion. The export was of the raw produce of the farms; there was no deduction for the profits of the trader or the wages of the artizan. The Irish landowner, unlike the English, laid out nothing on the soil. His lands were improved and tilled entirely at the cost of the tenants, who gave him as rent the value of the entire produce over a miserable subsistence for themselves. He was exempt from the tax for the poor which fell so heavily upon his English fellow. All circumstances seemed to concur to place him in affluence. At the close of this, which should have been the golden period of Irish agriculture—when landowners at least might have been expected to have heaped up riches—we had a starving peasantry, ruined tenant farmers, and an incumbered proprietory. Ruin seemed to stare the Irish landowners in the face; a special tribunal was instituted to sell them out. Many, very many, of them were cruelly sold out. Many of the old territorial families were stripped of their estates. Many owners who manage to retain their ancestral properties are struggling with the difficulties which appear, we might almost say by some mysterious destiny, to depress the Irish landed interest below that of England.

Is it too late for all of us to lay these lessons to our hearts? For English statesmen to learn that there is but one way of maintaining an English interest in Ireland, and that is by letting all Irish affairs be managed with a single view to the interest of Ireland itself? For those who have a zeal for Protestantism to see that its cause can never be served by unjust ascendency, by unchristian intolerance and wrong? For us all to be assured that it is " vain to form schemes for the welfare of this nation which do not take in all the inhabitants, and a vain attempt to project the flourishing of our Protestant gentry exclusive of the bulk of the natives."* For our landowners to see that no class can have a real prosperity distinct from that of the nation—and that those who lay the foundation of their wealth or their power in the misery and discontent of the people are but building for a downfall, the ruin of which will be great in proportion to the massiveness and grandeur of the structure which they raise?

I do not regret that I have been compelled to go back upon the retrospect of Irish affairs which brings to us such lessons as these. For myself I have found in these enquiries an interest which far

* Bishop Berkeley, *ante* page 93.

more than repays me for all the labour they have cost. It may be that in the investigation of these details of our past history I have found something to convince a candid and impartial mind that when I pointed back to the policy of confiscation and conquest as the origin and source of our evils, I only spoke the words of soberness and truth. I know still " how hard it is to induce men to give to the social condition of Ireland the calm, the patient, the laborious, investigation by which alone the difficulies of that problem may be understood."* Nevertheless, my Lord, this vindication of my former treatise, which I have addressed to your Lordship, I offer to the consideration of all classes of my countrymen. The subject is one that deeply concerns us all. If I am right it is not possible to exaggerate its importance. In the earnest conviction that I have truth and reason on my side, I ask of those who are most strongly prejudiced against the slightest interference with proprietary rights, to weigh and judge of the reasons I have advanced. I know the strength of those prejudices. I know even the enmity which any one who encounters them provokes. I feel perfectly persuaded that there are men, good and honest men, who will regard with a personal resentment any man who has written as I have. Every man who attacks the prejudices that encircle wealth and power must be prepared for this. In one sense, therefore, I do not regard it. But I am far, very far, from being indifferent to the existence of such feelings. I feel pain at the thought that any of my countrymen should, however unjustly, regard me as the assailant of their property and their rights. But I would not, to escape ten thousand times that enmity, wish the "Plea" I have offered for the "Celtic Race" to be unwritten. The time had come when it was fitting that all the truth of our social condition should be unsparingly told That Plea may be ineffectual to avert the mischief which a perseverance in our present system must bring upon us all. I could only give the warning ; I have no power to assure that it shall be heeded. But whatever is to be the future of Ireland, I shall ever feel a pride in the recollection that if I have taken a part in the discussion, the issue of which may decide her destiny, I have not taken the side of the great, the wealthy, or the powerful. I have advocated the cause of the poor and oppressed, and raised an earnest, although, it may be, a feeble, voice for a people whom high-handed oppression is driving from their home.

May I add that I have now fulfilled every task and every duty which I set before myself. I almost feel as if I were unconsciously permitting myself to be drawn back into that thankless and, I fear, for Ireland, useless turmoil of political strife from which I had escaped. May I earnestly hope, that with this letter I may be permitted to close my share in the discussion. Deeply, vitally

* *Land Tenure*, p. 93.

important as I believe this question to be—convinced as I am
that there is no sacrifice from which any Irishman ought to shrink
who thinks he can aid in its settlement; yet, perhaps, I may safely
say that I have done my part. I cannot always withdraw myself
from those which are the ordinary engagements of my life, and none
but one who has tried it knows the harassing toil of writing on a
subject like this while the livelong day is devoted to occupations
sufficient in themselves to tax the energies of the mind—*Liberavi
animam meam.* I see nothing more than I can do; and I may
turn with a safe conscience to pursuits in which I will feel some
little satisfaction in the consciousness that I can follow them without
wounding the fierce prejudices that everywhere raise their hissing
crest in Irish society, and without incurring the enmity of those
from whom it may be my interest and certainly is my inclination to
conciliate good-will.

And yet most assuredly I have written in no spirit of hostility to
your Lordship's order. I must, of course, be judged by what I
have written ; but writing to your Lordship I cannot help thinking
that from the windows of your mansion you can look on scenes
which may tell you that all my early recollections are associated
with feelings not unfriendly to Protestantism or proprietary right.
I would not part with those recollections for a great deal. But the
more I cherish them, the more grieved I feel that in the mind of a
great, a generous, and noble people, both Protestantism and proprietary right are associated with oppression and wrong. But in
that which I have written, and that which I have proposed, I am
content to be judged by time. I still believe that "he is the truest
and best friend of proprietary rights in Ireland who aims at recon-
ciling them with the right of the people to live in their own land."
I have shown how by a very little concession a huge mischief may
be redressed, and a great feud reconciled. If the legislation I
framed was " cunningly devised," the whole device consisted in an
effort to retain nearly all of proprietary right, and yet make the
people free. I still think that when agitation on this question really
arises "no measure will ever be offered for popular acceptance which
will so scrupulously respect the rights of landowners" as does the
proposal I have made. And when the day of settlement—of the
settlement of this land question—does come, it may be that calm
and thoughtful men will look back upon these pages, and know
not whether to wonder most at the moderation of the proposal or
at the want of foresight of those who omitted to settle the quarrel
of centuries upon such terms.

That day of settlement, my Lord, must come. It were the
wildest dream of the arrogance of power to imagine it possible, in
the present state of the world and of the opinion of mankind, to
carry out to its completion the banishment of the Irish race. The
system of land tenure which is inconsistent with their remaining

in their country cannot be maintained. There are great principles which, by an irresistible influence, control the events which decide the fate of nations. There are, in all human transactions, elements of power, the precise action of which we cannot calculate, although we can with certainty foresee the result. All these elements forbid the exile of the old people. The great conscience of humanity would condemn that mighty wrong, no matter how many centuries had watched the progress of the injustice of which it would be the completion. And as surely as the thoughts, the feelings, the passions, and the conscience of multitudes have power over human affairs, so surely, some way or other, will the means be found by which the Irish people may dwell upon the Irish land.

I have the honour to be, my Lord,

Your Lordship's very faithful Servant,

ISAAC BUTT.

DUBLIN, *April 20th*, 1867.

DUBLIN: JOHN FALCONER PRINTER, 53, UPPER SACKVILLE-STREET.

www.ingramcontent.com/pod-product-compliance
Lightning Source LLC
Chambersburg PA
CBHW031410270326
41929CB00010BA/1399